IN A TIME OF TOTAL WAR

Justice, International Law and Global Security

Series Editor: Howard M. Hensel

As the global community enters the 21st century, it is confronted with a wide variety of both traditional and non-traditional challenges to its security and even survival, as well as unprecedented opportunities for global socio-economic development. International law will play a major role as the international community attempts to address these challenges and opportunities while, simultaneously attempting to create a just and secure global order capable of protecting and promoting the common good of the whole of mankind.

The Ashgate Series on *Justice, International Law and Global Security* is designed to encourage and highlight analytical, scholarly works that focus on the ways in which international law contributes to the management of a wide variety of contemporary challenges and opportunities, while, simultaneously, helping to promote global justice and security.

Also in the series

The Ashgate Research Companion to Military Ethics
Edited by James Turner Johnson and Eric D. Patterson
ISBN: 9781472416285

Shaping US Military Law
Governing a Constitutional Military
Joshua E. Kastenberg
ISBN: 978-1-4724-1910-1

Visions of Peace
Asia and The West
Edited by Takashi Shogimen and Vicki A. Spencer
ISBN: 978-1-4094-2870-1

The Law of War
Ingrid Detter
ISBN: 978-1-4094-6495-2

In a Time of Total War

The Federal Judiciary and the National Defense—1940–1954

JOSHUA E. KASTENBERG
USAF, US

ERIC MERRIAM
University of Central Florida and United States Air Force Reserve, USA

Routledge
Taylor & Francis Group
LONDON AND NEW YORK

First published 2016 by Routledge
2 Park Square, Milton Park, Abingdon, Oxon OX14 4RN
605 Third Avenue, New York, NY 10017

First issued in paperback 2021

Routledge is an imprint of the Taylor & Francis Group, an informa business

British Library Cataloguing in Publication Data
A catalogue record for this book is available from the British Library.

The Library of Congress has cataloged the printed edition as follows:
Kastenberg, Joshua E., 1967- author.
In a time of total war : the federal judiciary and the national defense - 1940-1954 / By Joshua E. Kastenberg and Eric Merriam.
pages cm. -- (Justice, international law and global security)
Includes bibliographical references and index.
ISBN 978-1-4724-5084-5 (hardback) -- ISBN 978-1-4724-5085-2 (ebook) -- ISBN 978-1-4724-5086-9 (epub) 1. Justice, Administration of--United States--History. 2. Courts--United States--History. 3. Military law--United States--History. 4. Civil-military relations--United States--History. 5. United States. Supreme Court--History. I. Merriam, Eric, author. II. Title.
KF8700.K35 2016
343.73'0109044--dc23

2015034824

ISBN 13: 978-1-03-209801-2 (pbk)
ISBN 13: 978-1-4724-5084-5 (hbk)

In a Time of Total War

The Federal Judiciary and the National Defense—1940–1954

JOSHUA E. KASTENBERG
USAF, US

ERIC MERRIAM
University of Central Florida and United States Air Force Reserve, USA

Routledge
Taylor & Francis Group
LONDON AND NEW YORK

First published 2016 by Routledge
2 Park Square, Milton Park, Abingdon, Oxon OX14 4RN
605 Third Avenue, New York, NY 10017

First issued in paperback 2021

Routledge is an imprint of the Taylor & Francis Group, an informa business

British Library Cataloguing in Publication Data
A catalogue record for this book is available from the British Library.

The Library of Congress has cataloged the printed edition as follows:
Kastenberg, Joshua E., 1967- author.
In a time of total war : the federal judiciary and the national defense - 1940-1954 / By Joshua E. Kastenberg and Eric Merriam.
pages cm. -- (Justice, international law and global security)
Includes bibliographical references and index.
ISBN 978-1-4724-5084-5 (hardback) -- ISBN 978-1-4724-5085-2 (ebook) -- ISBN 978-1-4724-5086-9 (epub) 1. Justice, Administration of--United States--History. 2. Courts--United States--History. 3. Military law--United States--History. 4. Civil-military relations--United States--History. 5. United States. Supreme Court--History. I. Merriam, Eric, author. II. Title.
KF8700.K35 2016
343.73'0109044--dc23

2015034824

ISBN 13: 978-1-03-209801-2 (pbk)
ISBN 13: 978-1-4724-5084-5 (hbk)

Contents

To our children:
Matthew and Elinor Kastenberg and Marissa Merriam

Preface

A modern democracy in which the government is constitutionally precluded from eroding the rights of its citizens is relatively new in human history. Western history from the time of ancient Sumer through the Protestant Reformation is replete with societal structures in which law favored the rights of monarchs or religious or ethnic majorities over that of the people. That is, people generally owed obligations to governing elites. When people asserted a right against monarchical, aristocratic, or religious authority, the results often proved disastrous to the people. One only need look at the peasants' rebellions of the fifteenth and sixteenth centuries, or the fate of religious dissenters in the late Middle Ages, to draw this simple conclusion.

However, during the Age of Enlightenment, certain rights began to be considered as inviolate from abridgement by the governing elites. The United States, and for that matter the modern system of government in Great Britain, embraced the idea that basic citizens' rights such as the right to a fair trial, freedom of conscience, and even an expanded voting franchise, required, in addition to other constraints, the absence of a standing army. In the early United States, opposition to a standing army was rooted in the fear that a force of professional soldiers, subject to the command of the president, could not only destroy the basic rights of male citizens, but could also be used to create a monarchy. Of course, the complete absence of a standing army would have spelled disaster for the United States, and so, after 1783, the nation possessed a small standing army.

From the formation of the Constitution onward, but particularly during crises, the intersection of national security, military policy, and governmental authority with individual rights and civil liberties was studied and debated, not only in the centers of government and in academia, but also by the citizenry. By 1940, the United States' population contained not only immigrants from countries in which rights such as freedom of speech and assembly, freedom of religion, and freedom of the press were non-existent, it also consisted of people who lived through three previous crises: the Civil War, World War I, and the global economic catastrophe known as "the Great Depression." During the Civil War, the federal judiciary issued two decisions upholding the President's vast authority to wage war and preserve the Union. In World War I, the federal judiciary largely upheld draconian prosecutions under laws such as the 1917 Espionage Act and Sedition Act of 1918, as well as under the first ever national conscription program. In these conflicts, the federal judiciary, and in particular, the United States Supreme Court, accepted the Executive Branch's claims of military and national security necessity. During the Depression and President Franklin Delano Roosevelt's response to it known as "the New Deal," the federal judiciary upheld vast grants of power from the federal Congress to the Executive Branch in areas the legal academy and government had traditionally considered to be the province of the states, or in areas federal courts had previously expressly determined were outside *any* government's authority.

In World War II, federal judges oversaw challenges to the government's assertions of authority, and in a number of instances, the courts sided with the rights of individuals over federal authorities. Yet, the judiciary also upheld a vast national conscription program, not only during the war, but after, and the judiciary upheld the constitutionality of interning a large number of citizens of Japanese ancestry. World War II remains alive in the United States memory, and a study of the nation's judicial elites is an important part of this memory. This is why this book continues through the presidency of Harry S. Truman and includes the early Cold War and the Korean Conflict. After all, the legal legacy of World War II defined how the United States "fought" the Cold War, including in Korea and Vietnam, but also in other lands and internally, and, how both President George W. Bush's and President Barak Obama's administrations have approached the use of military force overseas as well as in domestic national security measures. This book ends in 1954 because, as is later noted, that year marked the beginning of the decline of judicial deference to claims of military necessity, following its apogee in 1953. What follows is a study of how judicial elites shaped the intersection of national security, military policy, and governmental authority, on the one side, and individual rights and civil liberties on the other.

Both of us have been in the military since September 11, 2001, and both of us have been involved in national security policy. Our legal advice was not merely governed by statute, but also by an understanding of the intent of the Constitution's authors regarding the primacy of civil and individual rights, as well as the intent of judicial elites who shaped our nation's laws during crisis times. We hope this book provides a new insight into how the judiciary actively shaped military and national security policy, and what the intents of the various justices were in doing so. In that light, we hope this study is useful not only to legal practitioners and the legal academy, but also to military scholars, political historians, and national security analysts.

We are indebted to the archivists and librarians at the Manuscript Division of the Library of Congress, who often pointed us to other collections of interest we had not considered. We would also like to thank the University of Kentucky's Special Collections Library, and the University of Texas School of Law Library for their help in procuring the collections of Justices Stanley Reed, Fredrick Vinson, and Tom Clark.

-J.E.K. and E.M.

A hearty thank you to my former colleagues at the United States Air Force Academy for their willingness to spare me time for this project. Also, to Josh: I regard you as the finest military law historian in the nation. Your devotion to meaningful research and your capacity to record it astound me, and your ability to perform your military duties with honor and excellence while accomplishing exceptional academic projects inspires me. Your willingness to bring me along on this project has had a profound impact on my life, and I am forever in your debt. And finally, to Charlotte: I am eternally grateful for the many shared passages in each of our books of life, and for your support of my work on these chapters even as we began new chapters of our own.

-E.M.

Chapter 1
The Federal Judiciary in Total War, 1939–1945

At the United States of America's founding, the crafters of the Constitution determined that one of the cornerstones of a representative government was to have the federal military subordinate to civil authority. This subordination was explicitly placed in the Constitution, including in designating the civilian president as commander in chief and placing federal military funding in the hands of Congress every two years. But the subordination was also effected through the small size of the federal army, the creation of state controlled militias, and, during Jefferson's presidency, by the enactment of the Articles of War, which prohibited soldiers from not only disparaging the president, but also Congress. This basic construct remained intact through 1860, and after the end of Reconstruction, it returned until 1917. The United States' participation in the First World War was brief, and although historians have rightfully noted that civil and individual rights were barely protected between 1917 and 1920, with the election of President Warren G. Harding and a Republican-dominated Congress, the nation returned to its prewar construct of an army that was small and hardly intrusive in American society.[1]

This "normalcy," as Harding coined the term, was to change in the late 1930s with a burgeoning military establishment that affected American lives to a degree the nation had not seen since 1865, and unlike the Civil War, the military establishment's influence would remain through the end of the Cold War in 1990. Much of the cause of this change was external. The rise of Nazi Germany and an aggressive Japanese foreign and military policy required an expanded Army and Navy. By 1947, the Soviet Union replaced the Axis as the United States' paramount external threat. But it would be a mistake to consider that the causes of the change were solely external. The vast growth of the military establishment's influence occurred, in part, because of the United States' internal political, economic, and social forces. It also occurred because the federal judiciary—and particularly the Supreme Court—established a doctrine of limited jurisdiction in overseeing military matters since the beginning of the nation's existence, and also because after 1940 the judiciary had a discernable role in both enabling and limiting the alteration of civil and military relations. Between 1940 and 1953, the federal judiciary took a prominent role in reshaping civil and military relations, and, for

1 On World War I individual rights, *see, e.g.*, Geoffrey Stone, *Perilous Times: Free Speech in Wartime* (New York: W.W. Norton, 2005).

the first time in history, began to weave the broader aspects of civil and individual rights into military law.

On November 8, 1932, Franklin Delano Roosevelt, a Democrat, was elected to the presidency over his opponent, Republican Herbert Hoover with over 57 percent of the popular vote. Roosevelt's next election in 1936 would be even more sweeping. He defeated Republican Alf Landon with over 60 percent of the popular vote, and won 523 Electoral College votes to Landon's eight. The 1936 election results for the two houses of the Legislative Branch evidenced Roosevelt's mandate to govern. Of an available 435 seats, 334 Democrats were elected to the House of Representatives. The Republicans, already in a weakened state, were reduced from 103 seats to 88. In the Senate, the Democrats improved their supermajority, gaining five more seats for a total of 76, while the Republicans were reduced from 22 to 16. Moreover, a few Republican legislators such as Nebraska senator George Norris and California senator Hiram Johnson supported many of Roosevelt's New Deal programs. Never before had a single party so dominated Congress, and for a brief time the Democrats were almost unified in lockstep. Roosevelt and the Congressional Democrats had a clear mandate to pursue policies designed to ease the nation's suffering that had been wrought by the Great Depression in a manner that achieved a greater centralized federal authority than any peacetime president had ever sought to accomplish. Yet, the United States government, as it had been designed in 1787, was constructed on a system of checks and balances between *three* branches of government, and the Supreme Court stood as a barrier to Roosevelt's New Deal programs.[2]

By 1936, Roosevelt had appointed 49 federal judges, but he had not nominated any justices to the nation's highest court. Over the next six years, he was able to reshape the Court so that seven of nine justices were his selections and the Chief Justice, though originally appointed as an associate justice by Calvin Coolidge, was also his appointment. The federal courts of appeal and district courts also were filled in large numbers with Roosevelt's appointees. Between 1937 and Pearl Harbor, Roosevelt appointed a further 92 federal judges. By January 1, 1942, if a service-member or a civilian believed themselves aggrieved by the War or Naval Departments and appealed to the federal judiciary, there was a good chance that one of Roosevelt's judicial nominees would influence or decide the outcome of the appeal. However, there were constraints on what the judiciary could do with appeals against the military establishment. Traditionally, the judiciary did not grant service-members an open door to appeals, particularly those that arose from courts-martial. However, the federal judiciary could not jurisdictionally ignore the number of civilians who sued the War and Naval Departments, and the federal judiciary, for the first time in the nation's history, began to broaden the basis for reviewing service-

2 *See, e.g.*, Noah Feldman, *Scorpions: The Battles and Triumphs of FDR's Great Supreme Court Justices* (New York: Twelve Books, 2010).

members' appeals. Roosevelt's Court would preside over a fundamental shift in the jurisprudence of civil-military relations and military law.

The period between 1941 and 1953 was a watershed in judicial history, not only because federal judges were called upon to assess appeals from Executive Branch decisions arising during the total war known as World War II and the beginnings of the Cold War, but also because the federal judiciary—especially the Supreme Court—altered the traditional relationships between the military and civil society, and between service-members and the government. This alteration was not only part of an expansion of individual rights generally, it was also the beginning of the idea that a citizen might successfully assert a claim of a wrongful act against the government during a time of national crisis. However, while the judiciary was part of this expansion of individual liberties vis-à-vis the government, it also participated in developing the foundations of the United States' modern national security state.

During this time, courts wrestled with an apparent dichotomy between a security state and individual and civil rights. For instance, several justices who upheld the internment of American citizens of Japanese descent during the war—a decision essentially upholding governmental discrimination based on race—were later instrumental in enabling, as a means of redress in the federal courts, the constitutional principle of racial equality to enforce equal access to schools, government services, and businesses. During World War II, the lower federal courts upheld a vast expansion of the military's court-martial jurisdiction over citizens who worked or lived in the Hawaiian Islands and were employed on merchantmen, even though in 1866, the Supreme Court in *Ex parte Milligan* had determined that military trials of citizens were unconstitutional in areas of the United States where the civil courts functioned. On the other hand, the Court would overturn the convictions of persons prosecuted in federal court who published pro-Nazi propaganda based on a First Amendment right of freedom of speech.

I: The Judiciary and Military Governance, 1804–1941

The history of the Supreme Court's jurisprudential role in articulating and enforcing military law and civil-military relations is a complicated one. Through much of the nation's history, while the Court was involved in delineating presidential powers and the military's relationship to civilian society, it was especially deferential to internal military governance. While this book is a judicial history that examines the justices and their jurisprudence during World War II and the early years of the Cold War, understanding the context in which those justices wrote their opinions first requires a brief tour through pre-World War II precedent and experience.

The Jurisprudence

While the justices in World War II addressed unique issues arising out of a 12 million citizen conscripted military force, treason, espionage, war profiteering, and freedom of speech in wartime, there was a body of legal precedent to guide them. From 1804 to 1941, there were few Supreme Court cases specifically addressing military law, but of those few, several were significant.[3]

Among the earliest Supreme Court opinions addressing military law was *Little v. Barreme*, a case arising from a conflict between congressional enactment and a presidential order. Congress had authorized seizure of vessels sailing *to* French ports, but President John Adams subsequently authorized seizure of vessels *to* and *from* French ports. A United States Navy Captain, George Little, seized the *Flying Fish*, a Danish vessel sailing *from* a French port, and the owner of the seized ship sued. Though the case is primarily known for limiting presidential power in the face of contradictory congressional action, the Court's decision that Captain Little was personally liable for the unauthorized seizure served as an early notice to military officers that following unlawful orders could result in liability.[4]

Between the War of 1812 and the Civil War, the Court in three decisions upheld the concept of Executive Branch authority over the governance of soldiers. The three decisions require some explanation because of their importance to the doctrine of expansive wartime presidential powers.

Over a decade after the conclusion of the War of 1812, the Court unanimously decided *Martin v. Mott*, with an opinion authored by Associate Justice Joseph Story. Appointed by President James Madison, Story was one of the nation's premier constitutional law scholars. In addition to serving on the Court, he was a distinguished professor at Harvard's law school, and he authored the nineteenth century's foremost text on Constitutional Law. In his extra-judicial writings, Story conceded that a debate existed as to the need for standing armies in times of peace, but he sided with the proponents for a standing army, arguing, "the history of other countries, and our past experience, admonish us that a regular force, well-disciplined and well supplied, is the cheapest and the only effectual means of resisting the inroads of a well-disciplined foreign army."[5]

3 As will be discussed in detail below, the important principle of stare decisis—that is, not overturning prior decisions out of respect for precedent—did not mean that the judiciary would blindly defer to the military establishment's articulation of the needs of national defense.

4 *Little v. Barreme*, 6 U.S. 170 (1804).

5 Joseph Story, *Commentaries on the Constitution of the United States, Vol. II* [ed. Thomas Cooley], (Boston: Little Brown & Co, 1873), 92–6. On Story see, Roscoe Pound, *Joseph Story and the Making of American Law* (Cambridge: Cambridge University Press, 1915); and R. Kent Newmeyer, *Supreme Court Justice Joseph Story: Statesman of the Old Republic* (Chapel Hill, NC: University of North Carolina Press, 1985).

Mott involved the president's broad authority to determine when a national emergency existed and call forth the militia to meet the exigency. The War of 1812 was fought with little cohesion between the state militias and the nation's standing army. Anti-war dissension against Federalist governors in New England and a high rate of desertions plagued the nation's war efforts. *Mott* originated with a militia soldier's refusal to heed the New York governor's call to arms. The soldier was arrested, court-martialed, and sentenced to a fine and seizure of his private property. The soldier later argued that state militia soldiers were not required to comply with orders stemming from a presidential declaration of emergency, because it exceeded the president's authority and thus state governors were not required to heed it. The Court concluded that the president possessed the authority to determine when a national crisis existed, and which individual citizens were subject to the declaration. Although not a direct part of the decision, the justices understood that the president could only act subject to Congress' impeachment and appropriation powers.[6]

The Court could have rested its decision solely on the principle of Executive Branch powers, but Story emphasized the fundamental disciplinary aspect of courts-martial and characterized such trials as a unique instrument for instilling discipline. "A prompt and unhesitating obedience to orders is indispensable to the complete attainment of the object," Story wrote. "The service is a military service and the command of a military nature and in such cases every delay and every obstacle to an efficient and immediate compliance necessarily tend to jeopard the public interests." This was not all. Story finished the decision with an admonition to subordinate officers and soldiers questioning commands: "While subordinate officers or soldiers are pausing to consider whether they ought to obey or are scrupulously weighing the evidence of the facts upon which the commander in chief exercises the right to demand their services, the hostile enterprise may be accomplished without the means of resistance."

Two decisions issued during Chief Justice Roger Baldwin Taney's tenure further defined the nation's military law and provided the foundations for the great extent to which the military's jurisdiction could be expanded in an emergency. The first case, *Luther v. Borden*, originated in the Dorr Rebellion in Rhode Island. The Rebellion was not a national crisis, but it presented a microcosm of the nation's divisions, and it implicated the nature of American democratic government. In 1841, Rhode Island's large disenfranchised working class revolted against the state government. As it had prior to the Declaration of Independence, the state's antiquated charter of laws limited its voting franchise to its property owners. Led by Thomas Dorr, a popular revolutionary-type figure, the revolt became so widespread that the state governor implored President John

6 *Martin v. Mott*, 25 U.S. 19, 6 L.Ed. 537 12 (Wheat) 19 (1827); Kermit L. Hall, *The Oxford Guide to Supreme Court Decisions* (New York: Oxford, 2001) 176; also, Donald R. Hickey, *The War of 1812: A Forgotten Conflict* (Urbana: University of Illinois, 1995), 302; and John K. Mahon, *The War of 1812* (New York: Da Capo Reprint 1972), 227–8.

Tyler to either call the militia into federal service or use the Army to suppress the revolt.[7]

Tyler refused both requests, though as a Whig, he openly expressed sympathy with the governor and the landed gentry of the state. Ultimately, forces loyal to the governor suppressed the revolt, and in so doing made multiple arrests and damaged private property. The case of one aggrieved party reached the Court. Taney concentrated on the authority of a sovereign state to suppress rebellion through martial law. He determined that the political question (that is, who was in the right politically) was irrelevant to the decision. Instead, Taney concluded that the state governor possessed the authority to declare and enforce martial law until the threat of insurrection abated. The political question doctrine would later become a significant facet of military law, particularly during the Vietnam Conflict and Nixon's presidency. As a tangential, yet important matter, Taney upheld the efficacy of the 1806 Articles of War noting, "So, in this country, legislation as to the military is usually confined to the general government, where the great powers of war and peace reside. And hence, under those powers, Congress … has created the Articles of War, by which the armies of the United States shall be governed." While it is true Taney's opinion did not specifically address the acceptability of military *trials* of civilians, he likely would not have objected to such trials, given the broad reach of martial law over civilians permitted in his decision. However, Taney does not appear to have understood the extent to which his decision empowered President Lincoln and Judge Advocate General Joseph Holt to expand the military's reach.[8]

On the eve of the Civil War, the Taney Court decided *Dynes v. Hoover*, in which it determined that courts-martial were an exclusive instrument of the Executive Branch. *Dynes* arose from a challenge to the Naval Articles of War, but the Court ensured its ruling applied to both the sea and land branches of the armed forces. The decision set a precedent that the federal judiciary would only review whether a court-martial possessed jurisdiction over a person prosecuted in it, and not whether a court-martial was fairly conducted or whether military law permitted a conviction for a non-codified offense. More broadly, the decision signaled to the Executive Branch that it almost had free reign to conduct military operations and to hold its service-members to strict accountability as it saw fit.[9]

Dynes' continued recognition of Executive Branch prerogative to govern the military followed an earlier opinion that had reaffirmed the President's commander

---

7 For information on the Dorr Rebellion, *see* Marvin Gettleman, *The Dorr Rebellion, A Study in American Radicalism*: 1833–1849 (New York: Random House, 1973). *See also*, *Luther v. Borden*, 48 U.S. 1 (1849).

8 Brian McGinty, *Lincoln and the Court* (Boston: Harvard, 2008), 41–2.

9 *Dynes v. Hoover*, 61 U.S. 65 (1857); *see also*, Joshua E. Kastenberg, "A Sesquicentennial Historic Analysis of Dynes v. Hoover and the Supreme Court's Bow to Military Necessity: From its Relationship to *Dred Scott v. Sandford* to its Contemporary Influence," 39 University of Memphis Law Review (2009) 595.

in chief powers, even as it had limited his authority to unilaterally commit forces without a Legislative Branch authorization for war. In 1851 in *Fleming v. Page*, a decision arising from the war with Mexico, the Court recognized that the enlargement of United States territory by military conquest was not for the President to embark upon without the approval of the Senate. However, in terms of the President's authority over the federalized armed forces the Court held:

> His duty and his power are purely military. As commander-in-chief, he is authorized to direct the movements of the naval and military forces placed by law at his command, and to employ them in the manner he may deem most effectual to harass and conquer and subdue the enemy. He may invade the hostile country, and subject it to the sovereignty and authority of the United States.

In 1863, in what became captioned as the *Prize Cases*, the Court issued a companion decision arising from a challenge to the Union's seizure of southern commerce vessels. In that decision, the Court essentially held that President Abraham Lincoln had the authority to direct the nation's military forces in a conflict that had begun without a declaration of war.[10]

The Civil War provided the Court with occasion to opine on military trials to a degree it had not previously done. In 1864 the Court determined, in *Ex Parte Vallandigham*, that it did not have the jurisdiction to inquire into the military trial of a former congressman who had no military affiliation. Clement Vallandigham was an Ohio Democrat who both in and out of office advocated support for the Confederacy, and in rather vitriolic language, denounced Lincoln. Vallandigham, a civilian, was tried and convicted by military court for "publicly expressing … sympathy for those in arms against the Government of the United States." Though the Court's determination that it did not possess the authority to issue *habeas corpus* in military trials over civilians would later be overturned, *Vallandigham*'s general principle that the federal judiciary would not review the fairness of military trials influenced modern jurisprudence, particularly in the appeals of Japanese and German military officers and government officials convicted of war crimes in American military trials.[11]

Justice James Wayne's majority opinion in *Vallandigham* that the Court did not have authority to issue a writ of *habeas corpus* was, obliquely overturned shortly after the Civil War concluded. While the 1866 *Ex parte Milligan* decision is more known for the Court's holding that as long as the civil courts functioned, military trials could only be held against soldiers or enemy civilians, one of the aspects of *Milligan* that is rarely mentioned is that the Court reaffirmed the doctrine of the federal judiciary's limited jurisdiction over military trials where the Army, and by implication the Navy, *did* possess jurisdiction. Despite *Milligan*, after

10 Fleming v. Page, 50 U.S. (9 How) 603 (1851); The Prize Cases, 67 U.S. (2 Black.) 635 (1863).

11 *Ex Parte Vallandigham*, 68 U.S. 243 (1863).

the Civil War, the Court largely validated the expansive use of military forces to govern the Reconstructed South, to include military tribunals. For instance, in 1875 the Court upheld a commander's authority to establish military provost courts with jurisdiction over civil legal matters in an occupied southern state, with adjudicatory powers over that of the civil courts in the southern state.[12]

A judicially constructed barrier not found in any statute confronted court-martialed soldiers who tried to seek redress in the federal courts. Known as the *habeas* test, for an aggrieved court-martialed soldier to gain access to the federal courts, there had to be proof that a court-martial possessed no jurisdiction over the soldier. Thus, a civilian such as Lambdin Milligan could succeed in an appeal of a sentence assessed by a military trial, but only because the federal courts determined the military tribunal did not have jurisdiction. Similarly, a member of the state militia called into the federal service might also succeed in an appeal under certain conditions, such as if a court-martial panel was composed of regular officers instead of militia officers in violation of a statute. But gross injustices arising from evidentiary defects or other due process challenges were not a means for challenging courts-martial in the federal courts. As an example, in the appeal of Brigadier General David Swaim, a court-martialed officer sentenced to half pay in 1884, the Court decided that it would not examine the influence President Chester Arthur played in trying to direct a court-martial to a severe sentence. Today, such unlawful command influence might divest a court-martial of jurisdiction, but, in 1884, the justices did not find Arthur's conduct a basis for reviewing the merits of Swaim's appeal.[13]

In *Ex Parte Mason*, the Supreme Court in 1881 impliedly determined, in bypassing an issue decided by a lower court, that the Judge Advocate General's advice was not only not binding on the Executive Branch but also a privileged communication of which the federal courts could take no cognizance. This is an important point because at that time, the Army's Judge Advocate General not only served as the legal counsel to the Secretary of War, but in selected military matters, he also was counsel to the president. Private John A. Mason, a prison guard, had been court-martialed for attempting to kill Charles Guiteau after Guiteau was arrested for assassinating President James Garfield. Mason argued to the federal courts that that his court-martial should be overturned because President Arthur refused to follow the Judge Advocate General's advice to disapprove the conviction and sentence. The Judge Advocate General had advised Arthur that Mason's trial failed due process and that he was convicted of an offense which did not exist under the Articles of War, but the Attorney General disagreed. The Court

12 *Ex parte Milligan*, 71 U.S. 2 (1866). *Mechanics and Traders Bank v. Union Bank*, 89 U.S. 276 (1875).

13 *Swaim v. United States*, 165 U.S. 553 (1897).

rejected Mason's argument that the federal courts possessed jurisdiction to review his court-martial conviction.[14]

There were three notable exceptions to the judiciary's doctrine of limited review of military trials, but only one of these was based on the Constitution. In 1887, in *Runkle v. United States*, the Supreme Court restored a dismissed officer into retirement because neither the War Department nor Attorney General could prove that President Ulysses Grant had approved Major Runkle's dismissal, which had been adjudged by a court-martial almost a decade earlier. The Court did not rule on the fairness of the court-martial. Rather, it reminded the War Department that as long as it maintained the full record of a court-martial and possessed jurisdiction over the accused, the federal courts would not intervene in the military's discipline. In Runkle's case there were missing records, and the government could no longer prove that Runkle's dismissal comported with the procedural laws governing courts-martial. A second exception had to do with the difference between the state militias called into federal service and the "regular" or federal Army. At various intervals in the nation's legal history, but in particular between 1870 and 1903, when the militia forces were federalized, Congress had ensured through various statutes that courts-martial of militia soldiers were composed of militia officers. State governors also had the ability to pardon or annul the courts-martial convictions and sentences of militia soldiers. In 1902, the Supreme Court, in *McClaughery v. Deming* upheld this construct against a War Department argument that the statute was merely suggestive and conferred no individual rights. In 1907, in *Grafton v. United States*, the Court determined that the Constitution's prohibition against double jeopardy protected service-members from being prosecuted in the federal courts after an acquittal in a court-martial for the same offense, at least implying that a court-martial would similarly be precluded from proceeding if a federal court had prosecuted a service-member for the same offense.[15]

That said, the Court permitted Congress and the Executive Branch to enable an expansion of military influence in the law. In World War I, the Court recognized the authority of the government to create and operate a national conscription program and send conscripted soldiers into a foreign war. During the War, the Court upheld the convictions of citizens who counseled prospective registrants to evade conscription. Following the War, the Court upheld the concept that Congress and the President possessed the authority to determine that a national emergency continued even after the surrender of an enemy belligerent. The Court's decision that the First Amendment was not a defense against charges of "seditious" speech

---

14 *Ex Parte Mason*, 105 U.S. 696 (1881). The facts of Mason are found in *Ex parte Mason*, 256 F 2 (DC 1882).

15 *McClaughry v. Deming*, 186 U.S. 49 (1902). On the federalization of state militia forces *see*, Jerry Cooper, *The Rise of the National Guard: The Evolution of the American Militia* (Lincoln NE: University of Nebraska Press, 1997), 154–102; *Runkle v. United States*, 122 U.S. 543 (1887); *Grafton v. United States*, 206 U.S. 333 (1907).

designed to undermine conscription or the discipline of the nation's military forces continued not only through World War II, but still impacts military law. In 1918 Labor leader Eugene Debs was convicted and sentenced to incarceration in a military prison for violating the Espionage Act of 1917, even though he had no connection to the military. Debs was one of several citizens whose convictions for subversion were upheld. It is noteworthy that Oliver Wendell Holmes, Jr., and Louis Dembitz Brandeis, two justices with a profound influence in American jurisprudence and who later influenced justices Harlan Stone and Felix Frankfurter, architected some of these decisions.[16]

In the half-decade prior to the United States' entry into World War I, the Court signaled it would not intervene in the federal government's oversight over the state national guard. In 1914 a lieutenant colonel in the Ohio National Guard inspector general's office sued the state governor after the governor complied with a War Department order which limited the rank of state inspector generals to lieutenant colonel. Ostensibly Lieutenant Colonel Daniel Stearns, the aggrieved officer, believed that he should attain higher rank and the proper enforcement remedy was the federal courts. The Supreme Court decided that Stearns had failed to state a legal cause of action in the first place, with the understanding that even if he had a legitimate grievance, the federal courts would not provide him a remedy. Although at first glance the decision appeared to pit the officer against the state governor, the Court indirectly upheld the constitutionality of the 1903 "Dick Act," which created the National Guard and authorized the federal War Department to prescribe standards for training and the commissioning of officers in state militias. The "Dick Act" also did away with the requirement that militia soldiers could only be prosecuted in courts-martial composed of militia officers.[17]

The Court's unanimity in its 1914 decision was unsurprising. In 1911, in *Reaves v. Ainsworth*, the Court had upheld the forced retirement of an officer. Justice Joseph McKenna, a former congressman and attorney general, in authoring the opinion, attempted to show that the War Department had complied with the law governing promotions and officer fitness. In the end, however, in responding to Reaves' due process challenge that the War Department had failed to follow proper procedures, the Court held that federal courts did not have jurisdiction to review such actions, stating boldly "to those in the military or naval service of the United States the military law *is* due process." Thus, any argument for the judiciary's jurisdiction to determine the War or Naval Department's compliance

---

16 *Selective Draft Law Cases*, 245 U.S. 366 (1918); *Cox v. Wood*, 247 U.S. 3 (1918); *Ruthenberg v. United States*, 245 U.S. 480 (1918); *Hamilton v. Kentucky Distilleries*, 251 U.S. 146 (1919); *Debs v. United States*, 249 U.S. 211 (1919); *Berger v. United States*, 255 U.S. 22 (1921); and *Schenk v. United States*, 249 U.S. 47 (1919); *Hamilton v. Regents of the University of California*, 293 U.S. 245 (1934). *See also* Paul L. Murphy, *World War I and the Origin of Civil Liberties in the United States* (New York: W.W. Norton, 1979).

17 *Stearns v. Wood*, 236 U.S. 75 (1915).

with administrative procedures had no more of a basis than appeals arising from courts-martial.[18]

In 1922, the Court issued a similar decision to *Reaves* in *United States ex rel. French v. Weeks*. After the Armistice, Congress determined to downsize the Army from its unprecedented four million soldiers to a force of slightly more than 200,000, and it authorized President Woodrow Wilson to enact administrative procedures to accomplish the reduction in force. Wilson, in turn, directed Secretary of War Newton Baker to craft an administrative process to accomplish the reduction. Thousands of commissioned officers went before administrative boards to determine whether they would be permitted to retain a regular Army commission. In *Weeks*, the question of whether the War Department adhered to its own regulations was once more considered to be a tangential matter. When Colonel John W. French objected to the War Department's decision to retire him, the Court unanimously held that the judiciary did not have the jurisdiction to review the War Department's administrative actions.[19]

During World War I and in the decade after, not only did the lower federal judiciary—the courts of appeals and district courts—adhere to the principle that the military establishment's decisions were immune from judicial scrutiny unless the assertion of military jurisdiction over citizens occurred, the judges did so knowing that during the war, a significant realignment of civil-military relations had occurred. For example, military officers participated in the so-called Overman Senate sub-committee investigation of German wartime propaganda and Bolshevik inroads into the United States, and this sub-committee primarily targeted civilians. Major Edwin Lowry Humes, a judge advocate, served as the investigation's legal counsel advising on the loyalty of citizens employed in the banking and manufacturing industries as well as in university faculties. The War Department virtually controlled the issuance and enforcement of patents during wartime, and in one instance, a German patent for venereal disease was determined to be non-binding after the Judge Advocate General advised the Attorney General that the patent ceased to exist as a matter of military necessity. Congress empowered the War Department to regulate alcohol sales in areas outside of military installations that could only be considered state and municipal areas. The War Department went so far as to enforce anti-prostitution regulations in these same areas, and order municipalities to elevate bridges.[20]

---

18 *Reaves v. Ainsworth*, 219 U.S. 296, 304 (1910) (emphasis added).

19 *United States ex rel. French v. Weeks* 259 U.S. 326 (1922). The Army's reduction is well described in Army Reorganization Hearings Before the House Committee on Military Affairs, Sixty-Fifth Congress, 3d Sess., on H.R. 14560 "To Reorganize and Increase the Efficiency of the Regular Army" (DC: GPO, 1919).

20 *McKinley v. United States*, 249 U.S. 397 (1919); Max Thelen, Federal Control of the Railroads in War Time *Annals of the American Academy of Political and Social Science* Vol. 76, War Adjustments in Railroad Regulation (Mar., 1918), 14–24. Regin Schmidt,

Of greatest significance, citizens who had been ordered to be inducted into the Army under the Selective Service Act, but who refused to comply with the order were subject to both courts-martial and federal criminal trials. In 1917, a United States District Court determined that a soldier who was born in Austria and voluntarily enlisted into the Ohio National Guard in 1915 could be court-martialed for refusing to be federalized into the Army and that the federal courts were unavailable to him. The decision was perhaps unremarkable, except if one considers the basis for the appeal was that the soldier had never been naturalized and claimed Austrian citizenship. In essence, the soldier sought to be classified as an interned alien. The district court's decision not only provided a basis for the judiciary's approach to the treatment of enemy aliens in World War II, it also presaged a twenty-first-century neoconservative position that the Executive Branch had the sole and non-reviewable authority to determine whether a person was an unprivileged belligerent. The War Department—whose officers argued the case, rather than the Justice Department's attorneys—had only argued that in following nineteenth-century precedent, the Army always retained jurisdiction over its soldiers, even when a soldier fraudulently enlisted by lying about his age, but the district court's decision went further, and authored a decision supporting Executive Branch primacy.[21]

Another interesting aspect of that decision, captioned as *Ex Parte Dostol*, was that United States District Court Judge, David C. Westenhaver was not only appointed by President Wilson, but Secretary of War Baker had lobbied Wilson for Westenhaver's appointment. (Westenhaver and Baker had been law partners in Cleveland in the first decade of the twentieth century.) Westenhaver not only served as the trial judge on the trial of labor leader Eugene Debs, he also provided Baker advice on the use of the Army to contain "Bolshevism" in both Russia and the United States. The historic record contained in the various papers of presidents and military establishment officials indicates that several federal judges in the twentieth century advised the Executive Branch on national security matters. For example, in World War I, Judge Julian Mack, a United States District Court Judge in the Southern District of New York, served on a board that assessed the sincerity of conscientious objector applicants. Although there was no obvious prohibition against doing so, this type of conduct blurred the non-political nature of the judiciary.[22]

Red Scare: FBI and the Origins of Anticommunism in the United States, 1919–1943 (Copenhagen: Museum Tusculanum Press 2000).

21 *Ex Parte Dostol*, 243 F. 664 (D.D.C. 1917).

22 Fed. Rep. 664(ND OH, 1917); Westenhaver to Wilson, February 21, 1917; Wilson to Westenhaver, February 23, 1917 [NDB/3]; *Ex Parte Dostol on behalf of Hackenberg*, 243 Fed. Rep. 664(ND OH, 1917); and, Otto Schlobohm "The Constitutionality of the Selective Draft Law," 6 *Georgetown Law Journal* (1917), 11–18. Westenhaver maintained a close correspondence with Baker throughout the war, and encouraged Baker to consider using the Army to contain Bolsheivism both in Russia and in the United States,

In 1920, a district court decided in *United States ex rel. Wessels v. McDonald* that the judiciary did not possess the jurisdiction to determine whether a foreign citizen was subject to a court-martial under the Articles of War for the Navy. The appellant had been caught delivering the departure times of merchant ships leaving from eastern ports to German agents so that German submarines could more effectively attack wartime commerce to Britain and France. The appellant also lied to the Justice Department in claiming that he was a Swiss citizen, when, in reality, he was German. Again, although the decision is unsurprising, the judiciary recognized the constitutionality of a tremendous authority to determine the belligerent status of an alien vested in the commander in chief which could be delegated to the War and Naval Departments. The authority, moreover, was virtually non-reviewable by federal courts.[23]

Between *Wessels* and Adolf Hitler's ascension as Germany's Chancellor in January 1933, the United States became a signatory to several arms reductions treaties, and despite the Senate's determination to refuse to join the League of Nations and discussions of the Soviet threat, it initially appeared that the possibility of a new total war had diminished. In 1928 the United States signed the Kellogg-Briand Pact along with the major European powers and Japan outlawing aggressive war. German reparations payments were paid according to a set schedule throughout the 1920s, and in 1930, the United States entered into the London Naval Treaty. This agreement served to limit naval armaments in an effort to reduce the possibility of an arms race, such as had preceded World War I. But beginning the following year, Japanese forces invaded Northern China, the German government began a slow military buildup, and the Italian military invaded Abyssinia. These events are an important marker for two Supreme Court decisions.

In 1934, several California residents challenged the state's requirement, which mirrored the language of the Morrill Act of 1862, that all males entering into the University of California participate in a reserve officer training program. The state did not require, however, that male students accept a commission in the military or enlist in the military or National Guard. The appeal was based on a religious objection to military service, and the California Supreme Court

---

Westenhaver to Baker, August 23, 1920 [NDB/11]; On Mack *see* Harry Barnard, The Forging of an American Jew: The Life and Times of Julian W. Mack (New York: Herzl Press, 1974), 89–100.

23 *United States ex rel. Wessels v. McDonald*, 265 F. 754 (E.D.N.Y.). On the Baker and Westenhaver relationship *see*, Westenhaver to Wilson, February 21, 1917; Wilson to Westenhaver, February 23, 1917 [NDB/3]; Otto Schlobohm "The Constitutionality of the Selective Draft Law," 6 *Georgetown Law Journal* (1917), 11–18. Westenhaver maintained a close correspondence with Baker throughout the war, and encouraged Baker to consider using the Army to contain Bolshevism both in Russia and in the United States, Westenhaver to Baker, August 23, 1920 [NDB/11]; Baker to Westenhaver, January 22, 1918; Westenhaver to Baker, January 29, 1918 [NDB/6].

denied their challenge under state law. In *Hamilton v. Regents of the University California*, the United States Supreme Court also denied their challenge and determined that the Fourteenth Amendment did not prohibit a state requiring compulsory military training. The decision was rational in the sense that no citizen enjoys a right to a university education, and those citizens who religiously opposed military service were free to attend an institution of higher education elsewhere.[24]

The internal dynamics of the Court's decisional process in this decision have not been fully analyzed. The conservative justices—Pierce Butler, James McReynolds, Willis Van Devanter, George Sutherland, and Chief Justice Charles Evans Hughes—noted that in prior decisions, the Court had recognized that the individual states had the authority to mobilize citizenry to protect the nation as a whole. In the one decision cited for this proposition, *Gilbert v. Minnesota*, Justice Brandeis, the Court's leading liberal, had dissented from the majority's holding that the state could exert its own police powers to accomplish the national purpose of unobstructed enlistment efforts. Brandeis' *Gilbert* dissent, however, was premised on a First Amendment-based right to privacy that was not at issue in *Hamilton*. In any event, Brandeis was still on the Court at the time of *Hamilton* and this time he did not dissent. Perhaps, it was because the justices also informed the California state government that their initial argument—that is, there was no federal question involved and therefore the Court should deny the appeal on jurisdictional grounds—was baseless, Justices Brandeis, Benjamin Cardozo, and Harlan Fiske Stone did not dissent and instead concurred.[25]

In the published concurrence, Cardozo noted that the Court had not decided whether a peacetime draft was constitutional because there was no requirement in the California law that male students "bear arms for any hostile purpose." Cardozo also chastised the appealing citizens that if the Court were to side with their argument, conscientious objectors would be free to refuse to pay taxes to support the nation in wartime. However, the concurring justices disagreed with the majority's insistence on equating pacifism with disloyalty. Pierce Butler, in authoring the majority decision, cited *United States v. Macintosh* and *United States v. Schwimmer* to this effect. Both of those decisions, however, arose from denials of naturalization by aliens seeking citizenship. The appellants in *Hamilton* were already citizens, and because Brandeis dissented in *Macintosh* and *Schwimmer*, he and Stone were offended by the majority's use of the two decisions. Stone went so far as to inform Butler that the use of the two decisions "unnecessarily rub salt into the wounds of a great many very worthy people who, I am convinced, dwell on a higher ethical spiritual plane than I do."[26]

---

24 *Hamilton v. Regents of the University of California*, 293 U.S. 245 (1934).

25 *Gilbert v. Minnesota*, 254 U.S. 325 (1920).

26 Stone to Butler, November 28, 1934 [HFS/61]; Cardozo to Stone, November 20, 1934 [HFS/61].

Another significant aspect absent from the final published decision is the extent to which the justices believed the individual states possessed the authority to train potential officers, or more broadly, prepare for war. Stone, who would become Chief Justice, appears to have considered that the decision was important in light of Germany's early remilitarization, Japan's militarism, and the Soviet Union's activities.[27]

The Court of the 1930s showed deference to the military establishment in another decision, though in a less direct manner. Before he sat as chief justice, Charles Evans Hughes penned in the American Bar Association Journal, "the war power of the national government is the power to wage war successfully." In 1936 in *United States v. Curtiss-Wright Export Corporation*, the conservative Hughes-led Court, which had opposed Roosevelt in so many other cases, determined that the Executive Branch was constitutionally the supreme authority and "sole organ" of the United States government in foreign affairs, and that the president's authority was not dependent upon congressional delegation. With this precedent, Roosevelt did not have to worry about the Court becoming an obstacle in his plans to support Britain and France, including his "Lend Lease" program which clearly antagonized the Nazi German government and brought United States neutrality into question.[28]

Between 1936 and 1940, Germany reoccupied the Saar, annexed Austria and Czechoslovakia, invaded Poland, and found itself at war with the Britain and France. Japanese encroachments into China had become increasingly pronounced, and in 1938 the Japanese Air Force bombed and sunk a United States gunboat on the Yangtze River. Although the United States would not enter into the war until after December 7, 1941, there was, among the United States population, a small vocal minority population that adhered to a pro-German fascist front, as well as the Communist Party of the United States that opposed intervention, until the German invasion of the Soviet Union in 1941. The possibility of a United States entry into world war was increasingly in the consciousness of the nation and its judiciary.

In 1940, the Court in *Minersville School District v. Gobitis*, with only Stone dissenting, determined that public school students could be compelled to salute

27 Stone to Butler, November 28, 1934; Butler to Stone, November 30, 1934 [HFS/61].

28 42 A.B.A. Rep. 232, 238. *Curtiss-Wright*, 299 U.S. 304 (1936). Congress had authorized the President embargo on arms shipments to South American countries engaged in the Chaco War based on the President's sole discretion. President Roosevelt had done so, and an arms dealer who violated the embargo and was prosecuted defended itself by alleging Congress had improperly delegated legislative power. Only McReynolds dissented in the decision. The Court also upheld federal preemption in internal security matters over state government. *See, e.g.*, *DeJonge v. Oregon* 299 U.S. 353 (1937); and *Hines v. Davidowitz*, 312 U.S. 52 (1941). Stone dissented in this latter decision in which he argued that a state could augment the federal government with its own internal security laws.

the United States flag. At issue was a Pennsylvania law directed at all students, but that affronted the beliefs of Jehovah's Witnesses, who at the time were victims of rampant discrimination, and whose tenets disavowed military service in wartime. In authoring the decision, Justice Felix Frankfurter claimed not to pass judgment on the "wisdom of training children in patriotic impulses," but he also admonished that "national unity is the basis for national security." Stone's answer to Frankfurter was that "history teaches us that there have been but few infringements of personal liberty by the state which have not been justified, as they are here, in the name of righteousness and the public good, and few which have not been directed, as they are now, at politically helpless minorities." A sizeable percentage of conscientious objector challenges in World War II arose from Jehovah's Witnesses, making *Gobitis* important precedent. However, to Frankfurter's anger, the Court would overrule *Gobitis* three years later in *West Virginia State Board of Education v. Barnette*.[29]

Neither *Gobitis*, which has come to be called "the flag salute case," nor the decision on presidential authority to prohibit arms shipments in *Curtiss-Wright* directly addressed the Executive Branch's ability to command in wartime. However, the decisions provide insight into the Court's willingness to permit the commander in chief to be a commander with the attendant powers to fully command in wartime and suggested a governmental authority to compel national unity and allegiance.

Whether these Executive Branch authorities were over economic regulation, conscription, internal security, or war crimes, by 1941, the Court had signaled that it would with limited exception defer to the stated national necessities in wartime. On the other hand, the Court would not necessarily enable civil liberties to be trammeled in the name of military necessity or national emergency. Notably absent, however, from the Court's decisions during the war were any decisions involving the military's justice system.

The Justices

From the beginning of the United States, federal judges have, in the main, been attuned to the needs of national defense. By the late 1800s, several of the justices' personal concerns with the national defense—and even involvement in setting defense policy—was explicitly apparent. Moreover it was not unusual for the military establishment to seek the guidance of justices. For instance, in 1889 General Nelson A. Miles, one of the Army's ranking commanders sought Associate Justice Stephen J. Field's advice on whether the Army should be used

29 *Minersville School District v. Gobitis*, 310 U.S. 586 (1940); *West Virginia State Board of Education v. Barnette*, 319 U.S. 624(1943). On Jehovah's Witnesses and conscientious objection, *see* Charles Moskos and John W. Chambers, *The New Conscientious Objection: From Sacred to Secular Resistance* (New York: Oxford University Press, 1993), 11.

to maintain control over a mine during a labor strike. Appointed by Lincoln in 1863, Field had adopted a distrust of both a standing army and Executive Branch supremacy into his jurisprudence and advised against using the military for what was essentially a law enforcement action. On another occasion, Field insisted that it was inappropriate for the Army to safeguard a Supreme Court justice. He had survived an assassination attempt from a personal enemy and Miles had simply offered the service of a cavalry company to protect him. Field made it clear to Miles that the Army had to be subordinate to the civil government in both fact and appearance and the use of soldiers to guard a justice imperiled the appearance of a subordinate military. During the Pullman Strike in 1894, Miles and Secretary of War Daniel Lamont concluded that only a minimal use of the regular Army was "lawfully acceptable." In their discussion, Miles alluded to the earlier guidance Field had given.[30]

In 1914 Justice William Rufus Day informed Senator Philander Knox, a Pennsylvania Republican, that he believed the Japanese Navy would attack American military installations in Panama or Hawaii. Day's reasoning to Knox is noteworthy not only for his prescience, but also because he would shortly be called upon to determine unique appeals arising from the nation's entry into the first "total war" of the twentieth century. "Racially the Japanese are a war-like people," Day began. "Their awakening and development during the last sixty years have been marvelous. Their success in the wars with China and Russia aligned Japan with the Great powers and aroused their national ambitions and fed the desire, common to the victorious, to strive for further conquest."[31]

Prior to the United States' declaration of war on the German Empire in April 1917, Chief Justice Edward Douglass White informed Vice President Thomas Marshall that German violations of American sovereignty and international law made it impossible not to go to war with Germany. During the war, the Army's Judge Advocate General consulted with Justice Louis Brandeis over the constitutionality of national conscription to ensure unanimity on the Court. Associate Justice James Clarke McReynolds contemporaneously informed Secretary of War Newton Baker that conscription was constitutional. It was unsurprising that the Selective Service Act was unanimously upheld to be constitutional in its application.[32]

---

30 Stephen J. Field to Nelson A. Miles, October 18, 1889; Field's advice to Miles was conveyed to the Judge Advocate General's Department. *See*, Miles to Judge Advocate General n.d. [NAM/1]; Nelson A. Miles to Daniel Lamont, July 14, 1894 [NAM/2]. On Miles, *see* Robert A. Wooster, *Nelson A Miles and the Twilight of the Frontier Army* (Lincoln NE: University of Nebraska Press, 1992), 201–50.

31 William Rufus Day to Knox, August 20, 1914 [PKP/21].

32 *Selective Draft Law Cases*, 245 U.S. 366 (1918).; Thomas R. Marshall, *Recollections of Thomas Marshall: Vice President and Hoosier Philosopher* (Indianapolis: Bobbs-Merrill, 1925), 337.

Finally, several justices served not only in the military, but also in Executive Branch positions that determined military and national security policy. Chief Justice William Howard Taft is the most obvious example of a justice who influenced the shaping of the nation's military establishment. He had, after all, served as Secretary of War before becoming president. And between the time he left the presidency and became chief justice, he inserted himself into a congressional debate on courts-martial reform. From 1902 until 1904, William Henry Moody also served as Secretary of the Navy under Theodore Roosevelt and took part in ensuring that the United States built a modern navy second only to Great Britain. He would later serve on the Court for a brief four years between 1906 and 1910 and left due to failing health. Levi Woodbury likewise served as Secretary of the Navy during Andrew Jackson's presidency. Nathan Clifford, Joseph McKenna, William Moody, Charles Evans Hughes, James Clarke McReynolds, Edward Terry Sanford, and Harlan Fiske Stone served as Attorney General or other prominent positions in the Justice Department in which they advised several presidents on military policy

II: The Justices and the Nature of Total War

The United States entered World War II on December 8, 1941, one day after Japanese naval forces attacked American naval and air bases in Hawaii and in the Philippine Islands. Even prior to the Japanese surprise attack, the government had become involved in the war. American military equipment had been transferred to the United Kingdom under the "Lend-Lease program." American naval vessels guarded against German submarines in the Atlantic, and naval officers shared intelligence with their British counterparts between 1939 and the end of 1941. Roosevelt warned Spanish dictator Francisco Franco, that any attack against the British naval base on Gibraltar would result in the freezing of Spanish assets in United States banks. When Japanese forces invaded Chinese territory prior to the German attack on Poland in 1939, Roosevelt protested in strong language and eventually placed an embargo on trade with Japan. By 1940, the United States military was being enlarged and slowly coming into what could be only described as a "war footing."

The nature of warfare had changed since the Civil War. In 1865, war was mainly fought on the ground and on the surface of rivers, bays, and oceans. In World War I, both sides harnessed the industrial revolution to arm millions of conscripted soldiers, and the death count exceeded any prior conflict. New weapons such as poison gas, aircraft, submarines, and machine guns contributed to the scope of that conflict. Yet, for the most part, with the exception of naval blockades and attacks on ocean-going commerce, the primary focus of the belligerent nations was on the traditional land forces and ocean-going commerce.

By contrast, in World War II, civilian populations were directly targeted for destruction. Airpower theorists after World War I concluded that an opposing nation's "center of gravity" was its industrial capacity. The German Luftwaffe bombed civilian populations in Poland, in the Netherlands, and eventually in the United Kingdom and Soviet Russia. The British Royal Air Force and eventually the United States' Army Air Forces retaliated with larger and larger air raids on German industrial centers. American aircraft not only firebombed Japanese cities, the use of two atomic weapons resulted in the tens of thousands of Japanese civilian deaths. Existing international law was supposed to contain warfare to the battlefield, but in World War II, the battlefield included non-combatant populations. During the Japanese invasion of China, Japanese forces besieged Chinese cities and millions of civilians were intentionally diseased and starved to death. The German, Italian, and Japanese militaries also employed spies, propaganda, and espionage efforts across the world. Not only did the Nazi government infiltrate saboteurs into the United States during the war, prior to the war small spy rings were formed in the hopes of establishing links to the Deutsch American Bund and other pro-Nazi groups in case the United States entered into the war. Germany also supported the isolationist America-First organization's leadership in the hopes of pushing anti-British and anti-Semitic propaganda to keep the United States neutral. Thus, not only did civilian populations play a support role for military efforts, they became participants and targets. The distinction between military and civilian became blurred, and this aspect influenced military-related jurisprudence.[33]

In comparison to the size and strength of the German military, in 1941 the United States land and air forces were woefully unprepared and under-strength. Only the United States' naval power and geography presented a formidable deterrent to Germany or Japan. Within the government, there was a reasonable worry as to whether nation would unify if war occurred. On the other hand, the United States' economy and industrial potential greatly overshadowed German and Japanese capacity. Roosevelt had successfully campaigned for a historic third term with the promise not to become directly involved in the war. Within his Democratic Party, as well as in the Republican Party, several prominent men were outspoken isolationists. No less than Henry Ford and Charles Lindbergh accused the Jewish population in America of pushing the nation into war, and there were an unknown number of residents and citizens who supported Nazi Germany. Very few of these people sought to militarily align the nation with Hitler, but their anti-Semitism, coupled with accusations that Roosevelt had "unconstitutional" socialistic goals or ties to communism, and their distrust of the United Kingdom, concerned Roosevelt and senior War Department officials who worried that if the nation went to war, a "fifth column" could undermine

33 *See, e.g.*, Herman Knell, *To Destroy a City: Strategic Bombing and its Consequences in World War II* (New York: Da Capo, 2003); Iris Chang, *The Rape of Nanking: The Forgotten Holocaust of World War* II (New York: Basic Books, 1997); Francis MacDonnell, *Insidious Foes: The Axis Fifth Column and the American Home Front* (New York: Oxford, University Press, 1995), 128–9.

national cohesiveness. Less than a month before the attack on Pearl Harbor, J. Edgar Hoover, the Federal Bureau of Investigation Director, warned Attorney General Francis Biddle that Army General Albert C. Wedermeyer had pro-Nazi sympathies after being assigned in Germany from 1936 to 1938 as a military observer.[34]

There were also questions as to the constitutional permissibility of Executive Branch authority over the population in war. During the Civil War, the federal government did not commandeer northern industries, nor did it create a universal draft. In World War I, Congress, in what became known as "the Lever Act," enabled an expanded executive branch authority to oversee the production and shipment of foodstuffs. The Lever Act was also used to enforce prohibition as well as to investigate "Bolshevik" influences in American industry and universities. Congress and the Court during the New Deal had not only empowered the Executive Branch to regulate interstate commerce by overseeing labor management relations in large industries, the Court also considered a single farmer harvesting and using grain for his own consumption to be "interstate commerce," thereby allowing the Executive Branch to penalize him for violating a federal regulation. While that decision, *Wickard v. Filburn*, issued in 1942, was controversial for a number of reasons, it not only later enabled the Court to uphold the constitutionality of civil rights laws through the Constitution's Commerce Clause, it also indirectly enabled the judiciary to assume that the Executive Branch possessed unrivalled authority over the citizenry in wartime, including the seizure of any industry deemed important to the nation's war efforts. World War II would be a "total war" like none the nation had experienced under the Constitution.[35]

III: Conclusion

In 1945, after the United States led an allied coalition to defeat Germany and Japan, there was, at best, a brief respite from the nation's war footing. But, the Soviet Union embarked on an aggressive foreign policy to not only create a system of buffer states to protect against an invasion, its military subjugated Eastern and Central Europe and the Soviet government assisted nascent communist revolutionary movements across the globe. For this fact alone, it is unsurprising that within three years of the Japanese surrender, Congress enabled the first

34 J. Edgar Hoover to Biddle, December 1, 1941 [FBP-GL/2–23]. Hoover's concern about Wedermeyer was misplaced and Wedermeyer was instrumental in planning operations such as the Normandy invasion. *See, e.g.*, Sean J. Savage, *Roosevelt: The Party Leader, 1932–1945* (Lexington KY: University of Kentucky Press, 1991), 167; Robert Dallek, *Franklin D. Roosevelt and American Foreign Policy, 1932–1945* (New York: Oxford, 1995), 248–50.

35 *Wickard v. Filburn*, 317 U.S. 111 (1942).

peacetime conscription program. The judiciary would be confronted by several challenges to this program to include determining the extent to which religious rights would be accorded a status in the national security determinations.

In the decade after the war, the Court would also be confronted with appeals arising from wartime courts-martial as well as claims made against the government. Appeals challenging the Executive Branch's decision to exclude "war brides," and the extension of military jurisdiction over civilians employed overseas would also come before the Court. And, most critically, the extent of government secrecy would come as a challenge before the Court. Many of the justices and judges who determined these issues were progressive in their approach to the rights of organized labor as well as civil and individual rights, in comparison to their predecessors. What follows is an analysis of how the justices and judges attempted to shape the military legal construct of the nation.

Chapter 2
The "Stone Court," Military Governance, and World War II

From his inauguration in 1933 until one of the most important labor cases in history four years later, *National Labor Relations Board v. Jones and Laughlin Steel Corporation*, President Roosevelt concluded that the Supreme Court was the primary barrier to his plan for the nation's recovery from high unemployment and a flagging economy. Until *Jones and Laughlin*, a majority of the Court's justices opposed Roosevelt's New Deal programs, often overriding the other two branches of government. The Court voided expansive federal regulations over farm prices, bankruptcies, railroads, coal mining, and labor conditions. Six of its justices—Charles Evans Hughes, Willis Van Devanter, James McReynolds, Pierce Butler, George Sutherland, and Owen Roberts—were hostile to organized labor, a key Roosevelt constituency. Roosevelt, in response, unsuccessfully tried to enlarge the Court so that the New Deal would remain intact. The so-called Court packing plan proved widely unpopular, even among Congressmen in Roosevelt's own party, and it provided Roosevelt's opponents with political fodder to liken him to a despot. But Roosevelt's threat to expand the number of justices also prodded Hughes and Roberts to shift from opposing the New Deal to upholding it. While their shift did not equate to embracing Roosevelt's policies, it did change the tone of the Court from actively intruding into Congressional legislation to deferring to Congress and the Executive Branch.[1]

From 1937 to the end of his presidency on April 12, 1945, Roosevelt successfully nominated nine men to the Court, each of whom supported key aspects of the New Deal. Federal government programs took on an expanded federal oversight into areas traditionally reserved to the states, counties, and cities, and the Court's decisions enabled the federal government's growth. The "Roosevelt Court" also ushered in an era where the Court took a role in the increased protection of civil rights and liberties. In 1938, in *United States v. Caroline Products*, the decision's author, Justice Harlan Fiske Stone, placed a footnote in the majority opinion in which he commented that legislation restricting civil rights such as freedom of speech might encounter heightened judicial scrutiny. "Footnote 4," as it has come to be known, has been cited in hundreds of federal judicial decisions involving individual rights. While

---

1 *See, e.g.*, William E. Leutchenberg, *The FDR Years: On Roosevelt and His Legacy* (New York: Columbia University Press, 1995), 221; Melvin Urofsky, *A March of Liberty: A Constitutional History of the United States*, Vol. II, 1877-Present, 693–8.

Carolene Products has seldom been cited in appeals arising from courts-martial, its progeny of opinions have been used in myriad opinions ranging from whether the Department of Defense could consider homosexuality in denying security clearances, to the extent of military jurisdiction.[2]

Even after the Japanese Attack on Pearl Harbor on December 7, 1941 and the United States' subsequent declaration of war on Japan, Germany, and Italy, the Court did not fade into a political backwater. Issues involving the military trials of German saboteurs captured on American soil, the extent to which speech could be charged as treason, and whether Executive Branch regulations could replace Congressional legislation in criminalizing conduct were at the time unique to the nation, and the nation took a great interest in the Court's decisions. The Court's upholding the forced relocation of citizens of Japanese descent into military controlled internment camps was also widely reported on, as was the imposition of martial law in the Hawaiian territory. The judiciary's Civil War and World War I experiences had only provided some answers to the unique questions of government power which arose during the world war.

Although Roosevelt called for national unity during the war, such unity was often absent from the Court. There is a consensus amongst judicial historians that at least four, if not five, of Roosevelt's appointees were brilliant men that were considered to be leading jurisprudential thinkers. Eight of the nine justices Roosevelt appointed served long enough to influence the development of the nation's military law. (One, James Byrnes, served only for one year before leaving at Roosevelt's request to lead the Office of Economic Stabilization.) Their pre-Court experiences, particularly their military experiences (for those who served in the military as well as those who did not) visibly influenced their jurisprudence. The relationship between personalities and jurisprudential philosophy are part of this study, because in some of the more important decisions, the lack of cohesive majorities, or even dissents, occurred as a result of differing views of military necessity.[3]

During the war, the Court issued significant decisions on the Executive Branch's authority, to include the long term-detention of a sizeable minority citizen population, the use of military trials over enemy combatants captured on United States soil, conscription laws, the demarcation between free speech and

---

2 Louis Lusky, "Footnote Redux: A Carolene Product Reminiscence," 82 *Columbia Law Review* (1982) 1093–105. Lusky, later a Columbia University law professor, was Stone's clerk at the time the decision was authored; Lara Kalman, *The Strange Career of Legal Realism* (New Haven: Yale, 1996), 20–21. *See, e.g.*, *High Tech Gays v. Defense Industrial Security Office*, 668 F. Supp. 1361 (N.D. Cal 1987).

3 *See, e.g.*, American National Biography, John A. Garraty and Mark C. Carnes, eds., (New York: Oxford University Press, 1999), 139–41; Noah Feldman, *Scorpions: The Battles and Triumphs of FDR's Great Supreme Court Justices* (New York: Twelve, 2010); and James F. Simon, *The Antagonists: Hugo Black, Felix Frankfurter and Civil Liberties in Modern America* (New York: Simon and Schuster, 1990).

treason, conscientious objection, and martial law. Symbolic of the cases involving Executive Branch authority is *Yakus v. United States.* This decision arose under the Emergency Price Control Act, an anti-inflationary measure which vested an executive agency with the authority to enforce pricing on goods and services. The Price Control Act also enabled the Attorney General to prosecute individuals who violated price control regulations. But the regulations were created by the Executive Branch, rather than legislated through Congress. The Court determined that a 60 day period allowing a citizen to challenge the legality of the regulations sufficed to ensure due process, though this scheme required a citizen to proactively challenge a regulation in court before violating it. *Yakus* was a unique departure from traditional federal criminal law, because, with the exception of certain criminal offenses unique to the military establishment, it was Congress who ordinarily created criminal offenses, without delegation to the Executive Branch.[4]

One area of appeals that the Court did not address in World War II was challenges arising from the military's internal disciplinary structure. Although the opportunity arose for the Court to hear courts-martial appeals, the justices only peripherally did so. It was not until after Stone's death in 1946 that courts-martial challenges came directly before the Court. Nonetheless, there is a significant relationship between the appeals the Court determined during the war—that is, the question of what the military may be used for—and the military's internal disciplinary construct.

Harlan Stone

On June 12, 1941 Roosevelt appointed Harlan Stone to replace Charles Evans Hughes as chief justice. Stone was not truly a Roosevelt appointee because he had already served on the Court for 16 years. In the estimation of Alpheus Thomas Mason, Stone's biographer, while Stone was not a scholar like Oliver Wendell Holmes or a social architect like Louis Brandeis, he possessed a brilliant intellect nonetheless. His talents included drafting concise opinions and establishing consistency in his jurisprudence in placing individual rights at least co-equal to property rights. There is a consensus that while Stone was a professorial judge with a deep sense of how the law had to serve democracy, he was a better associate justice than chief justice, because he did not possess the ability to corral the New Deal justices, particularly his friend Felix Frankfurter.[5]

4 *Yakus v. United States*, 321 U.S. 414 (1944). Arguably, *Yakus* was not the first decision of its type. The Court, in 1911 upheld the law of criminal trespass as it applied to sheep-grazing on federal lands in violation of regulations set by the Secretary of Agriculture. *See United States v. Grimoud* 220 U.S. 506 (1911).

5 Alpheus Thomas Mason, *Harlan F. Stone: Pillar of the Law* (New York: Viking, 1953), 5.

Stone was born in 1872, in rural New Hampshire, attended Amherst University and then Columbia's law school. At Amherst he befriended fellow student Calvin Coolidge. On graduation from law school he joined a private practice, but soon found himself as an adjunct professor on Columbia's law faculty. In 1910, the university appointed him dean of the law school, a position he held until 1923, when he resigned and joined the nation's largest law firm, Sullivan and Cromwell.[6]

Stone might have remained a well-respected and highly paid attorney, but for the fact that Coolidge was elected Vice President in 1920, and when President Warren G. Harding died on August 2, 1923, Coolidge became president. Coolidge inherited a corrupt administration from Harding that was enmeshed in scandals such as Teapot Dome, and while Harding tolerated corruption, and perhaps benefited from it, Coolidge determined to rid the Executive Branch of it. To accomplish this, he nominated Stone as Attorney General, and on April 7, 1924, the Senate confirmed him by a vote of 71 to six. As Attorney General he appointed J. Edgar Hoover to head the Bureau of Investigation, the predecessor to the Federal Bureau of Investigation.[7]

Although Stone was conservative in the economic property rights sense, he was also an internationalist and opposed government intrusions into individual rights. In 1920, he protested Attorney General Mitchell A. Palmer's "Red Raids," which resulted in questionable deportations, and he accused the Justice Department of violating civil liberties under the guise of security. He also stressed that he did not approve of state anti-syndicalism laws that were designed to criminalize "radical" labor organizations. Stone's frequent correspondents included Charles Beard, one of the leading American historians in the early twentieth century, the eminent legal historian Charles Warren, the nation's leading international law scholar John Bassett Moore who later served on The Hague Tribunal and International Court of Justice, and Justice Oliver Wendell Holmes.

After a year as attorney general, Stone was nominated to the Supreme Court by President Coolidge. Because Congressional Democrats considered Stone to be too cozy with business interests, he volunteered to personally appear before the Senate Judiciary Committee, a now-commonplace procedure that was unusual at the time. The Senate easily confirmed Stone as an associate justice and did so again when Roosevelt nominated him to be elevated to Chief Justice. Although he owed his chief justice position to Roosevelt, he did not consider himself a New Dealer and scoffed at the suggestion that he had become one. To his friend Judge George Moore he wrote, "Whatever the rest of the world may think, Washington is under no illusion that I am a new dealer." Roosevelt's economic policies were

---

6 Melvin Urofsky, *Division and Discord: The Supreme Court Under Stone and Vinson* (Columbia, SC: University of South Carolina, 1997), 10–11.

7 Arthur Schlesinger, *Robert Kennedy and His Times* (New York: Houghton Mifflin, 1978), 245; Urofsky, *Division and Discord*, 11–12.

not what Stone would have chosen. But he was consistent in his jurisprudence in that he deferred to Congress and the Executive Branch.[8]

Prior to Pearl Harbor, Stone's judicial view of military service was most evident in his approach to conscientious objector cases. In 1919, while still law school dean, he authored a *Columbia University Law Review* article titled "The Conscientious Objector," defending the exemption of conscientious objectors from military service, if their particular Judeo-Christian faith required it. "Both morals and sound policy require that the state should not violate the conscience of the individual," he concluded. Stone's reasons for writing the article stemmed from his World War I service on a presidentially-directed War Department Board of Inquiry that adjudicated roughly 2,300 conscientious objector claims.[9]

In the 1930s dozens of citizens petitioned Stone, claiming that as a result of rulings his draft board issued, they had been convicted in courts-martial or civil courts. The courts-martial convictions were problematic because these sometimes resulted in a loss of citizenship. Stone's response to these petitions is instructive for analyzing not only his judicial approach to conscientious objection, but also in his view of the limits of Executive Branch authority over individuals in wartime. Two examples of his responses to aggrieved petitioners show that where national loyalty and the national defense were concerned, he embraced a jurisprudential deference to the military establishment.

In late 1934, a Mr. Brent Allison lobbied Stone for assistance in overturning a 1918 court-martial conviction for desertion after failing to serve in uniform. In World War I, a citizen called for service also became immediately subject to military jurisdiction even though the individual had not as yet received pay, donned a uniform, or taken an oath of service. In World War II, amenability to military jurisdiction did not occur until an individual was lawfully inducted through taking an oath of allegiance. Brought before a court-martial, Allison was convicted of desertion and, as a result of his conviction, lost his citizenship. This fact troubled Stone because had Allison been convicted in civilian criminal court, as many conscientious objectors had, he would not have lost his citizenship. The loss of citizenship as a result of desertion dated to the Civil War when the Legislative and Executive Branches were convinced that many desertions were the product of anti-

8 Stone to George Moore, June 24, 1941 [HFS/22].

9 *See*, Statement Concerning the Treatment of Conscientious Objectors in the Army (Washington, DC: War Department, 1919), 20; *See also*, Keppel to Walsh, April 8, 1919; Attorney General Gregory to Walsh, March 21, 1919 [Thomas Walsh Papers hereafter TWP/162]; also *see*, John Whiteclay Chambers II, "Conscientious Objectors and the American State from Colonial Times to the Present," in Charles C. Moskos, *The New Conscientious Objection: From Sacred to Secular Resistance* (New York: Oxford, 1993), 35. Moskos, a pioneer of military sociology concluded that Stone's view became the liberal consensus for conscientious objection. However, Stone's role in interrogating conscientious objectors has not always been portrayed in a flattering light. *See, e.g.*, Christopher Capozolla, *Uncle Same Wants You: World War I and the Making of the Modern American Citizen* (New York: Oxford, 2008), 57–61.

war and pro-slavery elements within the Union. Frustrated with an unresponsive War Department, Stone turned to President Roosevelt for help. "Other similar objectors, sentenced in the civil courts for violations of the Espionage Act who served their sentences, were restored to citizenship," Stoned urged. "Mr. Allison's case would seem to be identical to theirs, except that he was sentenced in a military tribunal."[10] Roosevelt promised Stone he would investigate Allison's claims and ultimately the President, too, found them meritorious. However, Allison refused to sign a loyalty oath "before God," and this became a sticking point that precluded restoration of his citizenship. Stone would not assist Allison further on this matter, concluding that Allison's refusal to swear loyalty to the United States—an oath which those convicted in civil courts had to make for citizenship restoration—was a personal and not a moral or legal issue.[11]

While Stone showed a sense of humanity and fairness toward Allison, another petitioner's claims met with a different response. In 1936, a Mr. Walter Briehl sought Stone's assistance in expunging his conviction for refusing to serve. In early 1918, Stone's committee determined that Briehl did not meet the criteria for conscientious objector status as his refusal to serve was not rooted in a religious conviction, but instead under the belief that the war was fought for "profiteers and bankers." Briehl's request was laced with intemperate language, and Stone's reply provided a clear picture of his views of a democracy in arms. "Organized society is as much a reality as ice and snow in the Arctic," he began. "It must function by majorities, it contemplates that minorities who are against all war or a particular war may vote or speak against it, but it cannot admit of the right of minorities to resist and still remain organized society."[12]

Stone was not forgiving of aliens seeking citizenship who claimed they would refuse to bear arms in the defense of the nation. In *United States v. Schwimmer*, he agreed with a majority of justices that a female Hungarian national who, as a pacifist, expressed admiration for the United States, but refused to bear arms in the defense of the nation, could be denied citizenship. Justice Pierce Butler, in writing for the majority, conceded that pacifism was a noble ideal, but "the duty of citizens by force of arms to defend our government against all enemies whenever necessity arises is a fundamental principle of the Constitution." The majority concluded that a refusal to do so detracted from the strength and safety of the government. Stone did not join with Holmes' dissent

---

10 Allison to Stone, November 2 [HFS/45]; Stone to Roosevelt, November 28, 1934 [HFS/45].

11 Roosevelt to Stone, December 1, 1934 [HFS/45].

12 Stone to Walter Briehl, March 4, 1936 [HFS/45]. Apparently Stone's reply resonated with Briehl. In 1973, Briehl wrote to Justice William Douglas commending his decision to sustain a stay against a district court's injunction to stop the military from bombing Cambodia. "To me and many others your act of the highest level of humanitarianism and statesmanship stands from the sorditness [sic] of the whole Indo-southeast Asian political madness." Briehl to Douglas, August 13, 1973 [WOD/1639].

which pointed out the obvious fact that the nation did not conscript women, let alone women approaching their fifth decade of life. Two years later In *United States v. MacIntosh,* Stone concurred with the majority in determining that a male Canadian national who would only bear arms in defense of the United States if he believed the conflict was morally justified could be excluded from citizenship. In this case, the majority conceded that although Christians might object to war and the nation itself was "a Christian nation" it is also "a nation with the duty to survive." Later, in the aftermath of World War II, but while Stone remained on the bench, the Court would significantly marginalize both *Schwimmer* and *MacIntosh* despite Stone's and Frankfurter's opposition.[13]

Stone corresponded with prominent men in the legal academy, historians, the military, and government. His reliance on historian Charles Beard for research assistance provides insight into his view on judicial activism. On the eve of *Jones Laughlin* Stone asked Beard for his opinion as to the framer's intent on the extent of federal authority, particularly where the authority encroached into areas generally reserved for the states. Beard advised Stone that "the majority of the Constitution's framers intended to put all general interests under the Federal Government and to restrict to the states matters of local interest." Stone adopted Beard's interpretation of the framers' intent into several decisions.[14]

Hugo Black

Senator Hugo Black of Alabama, Roosevelt's first nomination to the Court, appears to have occurred as more of a "test-case" in the aftermath of the failed packing scheme. He was not Roosevelt's first choice to become a justice. Senate Majority Leader Joseph Robinson was, but he died prior to an opening on the Court. However, Black had supported Roosevelt's court-packing plan, and Roosevelt believed the Senate was likely to confirm Black with little opposition. Indeed, the Senate would have difficulty opposing him as a matter of senatorial courtesy even though Black had supported Roosevelt's court-packing plan. As a justice he

---

13 *United States v. Schwimmer*, 279 U.S. 644 (1929) and *United States v. Mackintosh*, 283 U.S. 605 (1931). Both decisions were overruled by *Girouard v. United States*, 328 U.S. 61 (1946).

14 Stone to Beard, March 14, 1936 [HFS/6]; Beard to Stone, April 19, 1936 [HFS/6]; Stone to Mary Beard, June 4, 1936 [HFS/6]. In this last letter, Stone explained the virtues of dissenting and concurring opinions to Beard writing, "the business of writing dissenting opinions *see*ms to be a form of self-expression and, like others of the type, is chiefly valuable for its subjective effect. I find that I rest better after writing them, which is perhaps sufficient justification."

remained loyal to Roosevelt, giving speeches on the importance of standing up to Adolf Hitler and supporting Lend-Lease to Britain.[15]

Born in impoverished rural Alabama in 1886, Black dropped out of high school to attend medical school. He did not find the practice of medicine fulfilling and enrolled in the University of Alabama's law school, graduating with highest honors. He successfully defended an African-American inmate who was forced to work in a prison labor gang after the expiration of his jail sentence, winning $150.00 from an all-white jury. Black served as a police court judge in 1910, but resigned the next year. In 1914, he was elected as a county prosecutor. Although he had supported William Jennings Bryan's anti-imperial pacifism platform in 1908, he joined the Army on August 1, 1917, believing Wilson's declaration of war against Germany justified. In turn, the Army commissioned him as a captain and assigned him to an artillery regiment. Before the regiment was shipped to France, the war ended. As he entered deeper into politics Black joined the Ku Klux Klan, in all likelihood because he believed that affiliation with this supremacist organization was essential for political advancement. In 1926, he successfully ran for the United States Senate, and was reelected in 1932.[16]

In Congress, Black fought against moneyed interests and was generally pro-labor. His more notable positions included supporting New Deal programs such as the Works Progress Administration and the Tennessee Valley Authority. In 1932, he criticized President Herbert Hoover's handling of the Bonus Army and developed a lifetime distrust of General Douglas MacArthur as a result of MacArthur's conduct in suppressing the Bonus Army demonstrators. Black also was intimately involved with the widely reported court-martial of Brigadier General William "Billy" Mitchell, and Black introduced legislation to restore Mitchell's retirement in 1935. Moreover, Black knew that MacArthur's role in Mitchell's court-martial had contributed to the conviction.[17]

Despite rumors of his Klan membership that might have kept Roosevelt from nominating him in the first place had Black been open about his past prior to the confirmation vote, on August 17, 1937, the Senate confirmed Black by a vote of 63–16. After Black's confirmation, the *Pittsburgh Post-Gazette* headlined his

---

15 *See, e.g.*, Black, Speech to the Colorado Bar Association, September 12, 1941 [WOD/309].

16 Howard Ball, *Hugo L. Black: Cold Steel Warrior* (New York: Oxford, 1996), 52–60; Roger K. Newman, *Hugo Black: a Biography* (New York: Fordham, 1994), 16–124.

17 Senator Lynn Joseph Frazier to Black, May 3, 1935 [HLB/117]; Black to Frazier, May 11, 1935. Frazier, a North Dakota Republican drafted legislation to restore Mitchell to rank, but believed Black, a New Deal Democrat would be more likely to push the legislation. For Black's senate record, *see* Newman, 123–267; also, Gerald T. Dunne, *Hugo Black and the Judicial Revolution* (New York: Simon & Schuster, 1977), 48–50. On the Mitchell—Black relationship, *see* Arthur M. Schlesinger, *The Coming of the New Deal, Vol. II, 1933–1935* (New York: First Mariner, 1958), 455–6; On MacArthur's role in Mitchell's court-martial, *see* William Manchester, *American Caesar: Douglas MacArthur, 1880–1964* (New York: Little Brown and Co., 1978), 218.

Klan past. In a radio broadcast, he admitted to briefly being a member, but then dropping his membership in the racist organization after becoming a senator. Because Black's allies included the executive director of the National Association for the Advancement of Colored People and other minority leaders, he was able to hold onto his position. His fellow eventual justice, Frankfurter was not concerned with Black's Klan membership, understanding that it was "a politically designed affiliation," which accompanied southern politics. Regardless of his role in the Klan, it has been aptly observed that Black was one of the foremost proponents of civil rights to ever sit on the Court. Indeed, in 1953 Black would dissent from decision involving two death sentences for African-American airmen arising from Air Force courts-martial on the basis that he believed racism had tainted the proceedings.[18]

Throughout his judicial tenure Black believed the Court was morally required to provide heightened protection for veterans. With fellow justice William O. Douglas, he urged that ambiguities in statutes had to be resolved in favor of the individual veteran because of their military service. This included entitling a World War I veteran who served less than a week to an honorable discharge with full benefits, as well as judicially intervening in an Army discharge of an officer accused of homosexuality on flimsy evidence. In a 1959 case, *Tak Shan Fong v. United States*, he unsuccessfully argued that honorable Army service in the Korean War entitled a Chinese immigrant who entered the nation unlawfully to full citizenship. For unknown reasons Black did not publish his draft dissent in which he criticized the Immigration and Naturalization Service for terminating a deportation hearing in 1953 with the sole purpose of permitting the man to be conscripted into the Army, and then restarting the deportation process after the man received an honorable discharge. The gist of his unpublished dissent was centered on what he believed the United States owed to veterans: citizenship, with its full rights.[19]

One of Black's more important contributions to the shaping of military law arose early in his judicial tenure. In 1938, the Court decided *Johnson v. Zerbst*,

18 Frankfurter to Irving Brant, September 28, 1937 [Brant/7]. One commentator described that southerners believed Black "went from wearing white robes to scare Blacks to wearing black robes to scare whites."

19 *Tak Shan Fong v. United States*, 359 U.S. 102 (1959). Douglas and Warren also dissented, but without publishing. Black's draft dissent began: "He did serve honorably, not merely for ninety days, but for two years. In it an obvious inference that Immigration Authorities held up the proceedings to have Petitioner serve two years in the Army during the war in Korea." Black concluded the two page dissent by stating he would reverse the conviction for illegal entry into the country and order the government to naturalize (provide citizenship) to Tak Shan Fong. Black, draft dissent, undated, 1959 [HLB/338]. Black's coupling of citizenship to military service would earlier be seen in *Trop v. Dulles*, a more contentious decision then *Tak Shan Fong*. In *Trop*, Black's arguments linking military service to citizenship prevailed. 356 U.S. 86 (1958). While these two decisions fall outside of the time frame of this book, both evidence Black's view of veterans' rights.

a decision which reversed a federal conviction of two Marines, after the United States Attorney and then the federal judge denied them counsel. This decision did not arise from a court-martial, but rather it extended federal *habeas* jurisdiction to include review errors which "amounted to a deprivation of constitutional right." During World War II, and in the following Cold War period, *Johnson v. Zerbst* would provide an avenue to soldiers collaterally attacking courts-martial convictions. In authoring the decision, Black did, in fact, consider its implications in courts-martial, though his belief that the decision would open the door to greater judicial review is not readily apparent in the published decision.[20]

Stanley Reed

Like Chief Justice Stone, Roosevelt's second appointment, Stanley Reed had served in both Republican and Democrat administrations. Reed earned bachelor of arts degrees from both Kentucky Wesleyan University and Yale University, but was not a law school graduate. He did attend the University of Virginia's law school for one year as well as the Columbia University Law School, and he also studied law in Paris at France's preeminent university, the Sorbonne. In 1910, he set up a legal practice in Maysville, Kentucky and two years later was elected to the state legislature. In 1918, the Army commissioned him a lieutenant and assigned him to military intelligence. After the war he joined a law firm in which he represented tobacco growers as well as the Chesapeake and Ohio Railroad. In 1929, President Hoover appointed Reed as general counsel to the Federal Farm Board and in 1932, to the Reconstruction Finance Corporation. He remained in this position after Roosevelt's inauguration and argued the constitutionality of various New Deal programs before the Court. In 1935, Roosevelt appointed Reed solicitor general. When, in 1938, Roosevelt nominated Reed to the Court, the Senate readily confirmed the nomination.[21]

A conservative in the sense of being deferential to Congress and the Executive Branch, Reed's judicial colleagues considered him a genial man, but not one of the Court's more scholarly justices. Reed seems to have thought this about himself too, describing himself as such to Frankfurter. He often sided with Frankfurter, except in military cases, where never sided with aggrieved soldiers.

20 Black, Conference Memorandum, undated [HLB/254]; *Johnson v. Zerbst*, 304 U.S. 458 (1938).

21 There is a consensus amongst legal historians that Reed was well liked and remained outside of the personal conflicts of the other justices. Nonetheless, he did so as a follower rather than a leader. *See, e.g.*, Melvin Urofsky, *The Warren Court: Justices, Rulings, and Legacy* (Santa Barbara, CA: ABC-CLIO, 2001), 40; Timothy Hall, *Supreme Court Justices: A Biographical Directory* (New York: Facts on File, 2001), 307–8; also Peter Renstrom, *The Stone Court: Justices Rulings, and Legacy* (Santa Barbara, CA: ABC-CLIO 2011), 54–6.

Reed intended to dissent in *Brown v. Board of Education*, but in late 1953, Chief Justice Earl Warren and Frankfurter impressed on him the importance of unanimity in the decision. Contemporaneous with the Court's discussions in *Brown*, was a case involving racism in a court-martial. When Black, Douglas, and Frankfurter railed against due process shortcomings in the court-martial which sentenced two African-American airmen to death, Reed quietly sided with the majority in not interfering with the military. Reed sought to protect the maximum extension of military jurisdiction as a Cold War necessity. More than any of Roosevelt's appointees, Reed's record on the Court evidences that he believed in almost absolute deference to the military.

Reed also tended to defer to law enforcement and government generally, just as he deferred to the military establishment. In 1943, he dissented in a decision where federal agents had violated a statute by not bringing civilian defendants before a federal magistrate before their confessions. He criticized the majority opinion as "relying on a technicality." In 1947, he convinced the Court to uphold a state conviction where a prosecutor and judge encouraged the jury to consider the defendants' failure to testify in their own defense as evidence of their guilt. This conduct was already prohibited in federal courts, but as a matter of deference to state sovereignty, Reed was unwilling to force the state courts to apply the Fifth Amendment to criminal proceedings.[22]

Felix Frankfurter

Born in Vienna, Austria in 1882, Felix Frankfurter was the last justice who was a naturalized citizen. He did not learn English until age 12, when his parents immigrated to New York. A product of New York City's public schools, including the City College of New York, he was an excellent student with academic interests ranging from science to philosophy. He attended Harvard University's law school, graduating in 1906, and joined a large firm. Although Frankfurter experienced anti-Semitism, it did not stifle his meteoric rise in academia or government service, and both conservative and progressive leaders recognized his brilliance. Frankfurter was a progressive in the same sense as Louis Brandeis or Theodore Roosevelt. As an advisor to both Roosevelts, he believed that the government could cure social ills if its programs were based on sound data. He also argued for due process rights such as a trial free from external coercion on juries and the right to an impartial judge. Theodore Roosevelt eventually accused him of sympathizing with anarchists and communists to the detriment of the United States. As a justice, he advocated for judicial restraint, and in

22 *See, e.g.*, *The Supreme Court in Conference (1940–1985), The Private Discussions Behind Nearly 300 Supreme Court Decisions*, Dickson ed. (New York: Oxford, 2001), 649–62. The two cases are *McNabb v. United States*, 318 U.S. 332 (1943), and *Adamson v. California*, 332 U.S. 46 (1947).

doing so frequently deferred to Congress and the Executive Branch, avoiding constitutionally based results where possible.

His adherence to judicial restraint may, at first blush, present a picture of contradictions. For instance, in 1945 he explained to Irving Brant, a *de facto* advisor on Court nominations to Roosevelt, his jurisprudential philosophy: "When an undesirable statute survives judicial scrutiny the popular democratic process has an immediate means for correction, and if American popular opinion is behind a socially undesirable statute it greatly promotes democratic processes to try to educate opinion to undoing what is unwise. But if the oligarchichal process of the Supreme Court strikes down the statute, only the action of five oligarchs can undo the deed."[23] Frankfurter, however, also believed that a statute that denied civil rights to people, or prosecutorial misconduct that denied individuals a fair trial, was unconstitutional. To future Justice Sherman Minton he defended his efforts to reverse a conviction against a well-known offender, "it is a fair summary of history to say that the great safeguards of human liberty have most frequently been forged in controversies involving not very nice people."[24]

Arguably, no twentieth century justice surpassed Frankfurter's wide-ranging mastery of law, social sciences, the humanities, and science. When Roosevelt nominated him, he had expected Frankfurter to become the Court's intellectual leader, but this did not occur. He was overbearing, professorial, arrogant, and pedantic in his approach to the other justices, and he alienated Black and Douglas. Although he acknowledged the intelligence of fellow justices Stone, Jackson, Black, and Douglas, he derided the latter two, calling them "the axis of evil," a phrase used to describe Germany, Italy, and Japan in World War II. Black stalked out of one judicial conference after Frankfurter deigned to lecture him. On another occasion, Douglas left the judicial conference with instructions to inform him when Frankfurter finished speaking. Douglas took to nettling Frankfurter, and what resulted was a failure between the three justices to effectively dissent in a cohesive manner in several military law decisions where a close alignment might have strengthened their position.[25]

Early in his career Frankfurter showed that he distrusted the integrity of prosecutions of notorious figures. He denounced the trial and death sentences of Fernando Nicola Sacco and Bartolomeo Vanzetti as a farce. Despite lobbying from Albert Einstein, members of the British Royal Family, labor leaders, the Italian Government, and the Vatican, the two men were executed. In 1916, Thomas Mooney and William Billings, two radical labor leaders were accused of bombing a building during a "Preparedness Day parade" in San Francisco. Like the Sacco and Vanzetti trial, a state court found the two men guilty and sentenced them to death. Frankfurter's position on this trial was similar to the Sacco and Vanzetti trial. Though Mooney's and Billings' sentences were commuted to life in

---

23 Frankfurter to Irving Brant, January 16, 1945 [Brant papers, Box 7].

24 Frankfurter to Minton, January 25, 1950 [RHJ/163].

25 Ball, *Hugo L. Black*, 139.

prison, Frankfurter lobbied for their release nonetheless. In 1936, the Court heard Mooney's appeal, but Frankfurter's appointment was over two years away.[26]

In 1929, President Herbert Hoover created the National Commission on Law Observance and Enforcement to study the problems of rising crime, prohibition enforcement, and police and judicial practices. Known as the Wickersham Commission after its leader, former Attorney General George Wickersham, in a one year period of time, it produced a 14 volume study. Hoover appointed several leaders of the bar in addition to Frankfurter, including Newton D. Baker and Roscoe Pound, to the Commission. This was not Frankfurter's first association with Baker or Pound. In World War I, Frankfurter served as a judge advocate and reported on labor conditions in the mining industries in Arizona and Colorado to then Secretary of War Baker. In 1922, Pound enlisted Frankfurter to study criminal justice in Cleveland. Frankfurter concluded that public fears of crime were often manipulated into accepting harsh police practices.[27]

In the Wickersham Commission investigation, Frankfurter studied what had become known as "Third Degree" interrogation practices, as well as the prosecution of the Mooney-Billing's case. (The report concluded that the Mooney trial was shamefully conducted.) The report's impact was significant in influencing the judiciary to take a closer look at both state and federal criminal trials. In 1932, for the first time in history, the Court overturned an Alabama state court conviction and death sentence of eight African Americans. Led by Chief Justice Hughes, the Court concluded the threat of mob violence and the last minute appointment of defense counsel created a grossly unfair trial in violation of the Sixth Amendment. Until 1932, the Court would not have granted review of this type of appeal because the justices had historically not applied Bill of Rights protections to state criminal trials. In 1936, the Court overturned a federal conviction based on prosecutorial misconduct, also for the first time in history.[28]

Frankfurter's position on civil liberties and individual rights, his support for Mooney, Billings, Sacco, Vanzetti and others, to include the Bisbee deportations, and victims of the Palmer Raids gave liberals reason to expect he would champion minority causes and individual rights. This did not occur nearly to the degree New Deal liberals hoped for, although his role in *Brown v. Board of Education* cannot be understated. He too pushed for a unanimous Court to declare that separate was

---

26 Bernard Schwartz, *A History of the Supreme Court* (New York: Oxford University Press, 1993), 240.

27 Sheldon Glueck, *Roscoe Pound and Criminal Justice* (New York: Oceana Press for the National Council on Crime and Delinquency, 1965); also, *see, e.g.*, John Henry Schlegel, *American Legal Realism and Empirical Social Science* (Chapel Hill: University of North Carolina Press, 1995), 296; and, Feldman, *Scorpions*, 11–12.

28 Bennet L. Gershman, "Hard Strikes and Foul Blows: Berger v. United States 75 Years After," 42 *Loyola University of Chicago Law Journal* (2010), 177–205.

inherently unequal, claiming that when Chief Justice Vinson, who was likely to have voted to uphold *Plessy v. Ferguson* died, it was proof of the existence of God.[29]

Of all of the justices serving on the Court since 1945, Frankfurter possessed the greatest familiarity with the broader aspects of military law. Once on the Court he would influence the military establishment more than any justice in twentieth century history. From 1910 to 1913, he served as the War Department's Insular Affairs solicitor during Henry Stimson's first tenure as Secretary of War, and he was commissioned as a judge advocate during World War I, in a capacity that placed him as an advisor to the War Industries Board. Frankfurter's service in World War I requires an added comment. On the eve of the United States' entry into World War I, the Army's Judge Advocate General, Major General Enoch Crowder, recruited several of the nation's foremost legal scholars to the Judge Advocate General's Department, including Harvard professors Edmund Morgan, Eugene Wambaugh, the dean of the Northwestern University Law School John Henry Wigmore, James Brown Scott, one of the leading international law experts, and Frankfurter. In March 1916, Crowder sought Frankfurter's advice on the Army's authority over state militia. Crowder was particularly concerned with a bill that Congressman George Chamberlain of Oregon had proposed, which would enable the state militias to set their own training standards. Frankfurter's advice impressed Crowder and the two men began to regularly correspond.[30]

When, in June 1916, Congress authorized an expanded reserves, Crowder penned Frankfurter, "I am going to assume that you have the desire to serve your country in a real emergency and that you may wish to avail yourself of this opportunity to place yourself in the position to do so." After Frankfurter obtained a commission, he effectuated a meeting between Crowder and Justice Louis Brandeis to discuss how to create a "constitutionally sound conscription program." In the Civil War, disgust with the Union's conscription program, which enabled wealthy citizens a means for avoiding military service contributed to riots across the north. This did not occur in World War I, in part, because both Crowder and Frankfurter helped design the draft law to limit exemptions, and

---

29 Samuel Walker, *Popular Justice: A History of American Criminal Justice*, 2d ed., rev. (New York: Oxford University Press, 1997), 132; for Frankfurter's role in the Cleveland Commission *see* his preface in Raymond Blaine Fosdick, Reginald Heber Smith, *Criminal Justice in Cleveland* (Cleveland: The Cleveland Foundation, 1922), V. For information on Frankfurter's role in studying the effect of the Third Degree in prosecutions, *see* Wickersham Commission Reports (Microfilm Publications of America) Reel 12, RG 10, Entry 48; on Frankfurter's claim of "God's existence" *see*, Schwartz, *A History of the Supreme Court*, 286.

30 Crowder to Frankfurter, March 18, 1916 [FF-Harv/Reel 30]; Crowder appears to have become impatient with Frankfurter over coming on duty in late 1916, six months prior to the declaration of war against Germany. On October 19, 1916 Crowder wrote Frankfurter, "why have I not received a report of your physical examination. I have Wambaugh's and expect to have Wigmore's shortly. I am very anxious to include you with these two." Crowder to Frankfurter, October 19, 1916 [FF-Harv/30].

together, they administered conscription. Shortly after Congress's declaration of war on the Imperial German Government, Frankfurter impressed on Crowder the importance of not placing American soldiers under British or French command, fearing that constitutional challenges to conscription would be entertained by the federal judiciary.[31]

Frankfurter never served as a military prosecutor during the war. He was instrumental in keeping the War Department relatively neutral in labor disputes and although today this is all but required, in 1916–1918, it was not so. He also opposed Assistant Attorney General Charles Warren's draft legislation to empower the Executive Branch to create military commissions trials for citizens accused of hampering the war effort. Although such military trials occurred during the Civil War, Frankfurter believed it unconstitutional in light of *Ex Parte Milligan*, and even if lawful, a poor reflection on the nation's democratic ideals as stated by President Wilson. Ultimately Wilson, Attorney General Thomas Watt Gregory, and the War Department's leadership denounced Warren's suggested legislation, and it never came before a congressional vote. Warren left public office and became an influential legal scholar, but remained close friends with Frankfurter, despite their earlier public disagreement regarding military commissions for civilians.[32]

In 1919, General Crowder became involved in a bitter dispute with his Deputy Judge Advocate General, Samuel T. Ansell. Without notifying Crowder, Ansell had argued to Secretary of War Baker that greater civilian and judge advocate oversight of the military justice system was necessary to curb abuses. When Crowder and Baker disagreed, Ansell lobbied Senator George Chamberlain of Oregon, who ordered a subcommittee to study the need for reform. Chamberlain also worked with Ansell to reform the Articles of War so that Army courts-martial mirrored federal criminal trials. The subcommittee, headed by Senator Francis E. Warren, a Civil War veteran and General John J. Pershing's father in law, did not adopt Ansell's and Chamberlain's positions. Its hearings were accompanied by a bitter debate involving congressmen and academicians. Frankfurter publicly took a neutral position in the dispute, though he quietly assisted Crowder counter Ansell's charges. Ultimately, the Articles of War and the military justice processes remained in place, with little modification, until after World War II.[33]

31 Crowder to Frankfurter, August 14, 1916 [FF-Harv/30]; Frankfurter to Crowder, October 16, 1916 [Frankfurter, Reel 30]; Frankfurter to Crowder, February 8, 1917 [FF-Harv/30]; Samuel Ansell to General John M. Palmer, September 14, 1939 [John McCauley Palmer Papers/3].

32 Daniel R. Beaver, *Newton D. Baker and the American War Effort*, 1917–1919 (Lincoln, NE: University of Nebraska Press, 1966), 52.

33 William R. Roalfe, *John Henry Wigmore: Scholar and Reformer* (Evanston, IL: Northwestern University Press, 1977), 124–35. The Ansell-Crowder debate is ably covered in Jonathan Lurie, *Arming Military Justice: The Origins of the Court of Military Appeals, 1775–1950*, Vol. I (Princeton, NJ: Princeton University, 1992), 113–36; and, David

Frankfurter cultivated relationships with dozens of prominent men and women. His list of correspondents, ranged from the nation's foremost legal scholars such as Charles Fairman, Charles Warren, and Roscoe Pound to distinguished jurists such as Holmes, Brandeis, Benjamin Cardozo, and Learned Hand. He regularly spoke with scientists such as Albert Einstein, Niels Bohr, and Enrico Fermi and historians such as Daniel Boorstin, Charles Beard, Catherine Drinker Bowen, and Henry Steele Commager. Most significantly he served as an informal, but frequent advisor to Franklin Roosevelt, even before Roosevelt's election in 1932 to the presidency.[34]

Frankfurter's role in staffing the War and Naval Departments was without parallel among jurists. In 1940, he convinced Roosevelt to nominate Henry Stimson as Secretary of War and Frank Knox as Secretary of the Navy. Frankfurter was convinced that Stimson, a progressive Republican, could assure that conscription would be acceptable to congressional Republicans. The two men had a long-standing relationship. When Stimson was appointed United States Attorney for the Southern District of New York in 1906, he hired Frankfurter as an assistant prosecutor. The two men developed a life-long friendship from that point onwards. Frankfurter would provide specific advice to Stimson on key stages of the nation's preparation, participation, and conclusion of the war. Frankfurter advised Stimson on Lend-Lease, agreed Roosevelt should seek a declaration of war from Congress as early as the Fall of 1941, and advised Stimson on the legality of the decision to use the atomic bomb.[35] Thus, Frankfurter provided not only policy advice to the War Department and Roosevelt, he provided legal advice from the bench.

Shortly after Stimson's confirmation, Frankfurter lobbied Roosevelt to appoint federal judge Robert P. Patterson as Undersecretary of War. In 1912, Patterson entered Harvard's law school where he studied under Frankfurter. A veteran of World War I, Patterson fought at Chateau Thierry and in the Meuse-Argonne, and

---

Lockmiller, *Enoch Crowder: Soldier, Lawyer, and Statesman* (Columbia, MO: University of Missouri Press, 1955), 204–14.

34 *See, e.g.*, Frankfurter to Bowen, June 13, 1960 [CDB/2]; Bowen to Frankfurter, July 6, 1963 [CDB/2] Frankfurter conveyed to Bowen that while he found John Adams to be "difficult," he admired the nation's second president as much as he did Washington, and he believed that he decided cases as Adams would have. He also helped Bowen research and edit biographies of Sir Edward Coke and Francis Bacon. Frankfurter corresponded with Einstein and Bohr on the threat of nuclear war and the fate of Robert Oppenheimer.

35 Richard N. Current, *Secretary Stimson: A Study in Statecraft* (New York: Archon, 1970), 137; Godfrey Hodgson, *The Colonel: The Life and Wars of Henry Stimson, 1867–1950* (New York: Knopf, 1990), 61; Sean L. Mallory, *Henry L. Stimson and the Decision to Use the Bomb Against Japan* (New York: Cornell University, 2008), 159; When Grenville Clark proposed to Stimson a detailed political plan for Roosevelt to bring the nation into the war, he first obtained Frankfurter's concurrence. Grenville Clark to Henry Stimson, September 29, 1941 [Henry Lewis Stimson Papers, Manuscripts and Archives, Yale University Library (microfilm reel 104 at Library of Congress)].

the Army awarded him the Silver Star. In 1930, President Hoover appointed him to the United States District Court for the Southern District of New York. Patterson's appointment was enormously gratifying to Frankfurter who penned to him, "you will always be my prize baby-student—favorite editor in chief of the law review. I add to the source of your good wishes your membership on the Court for which I have the oldest affection and the most continuous interest."[36]

Nine years later, at Frankfurter's urging, Roosevelt appointed Patterson to the Court of Appeals for the Second Circuit. Later, while in the War Department, Patterson was responsible for the recruitment and training of all soldiers. At the time of his appointment, the Army numbered 280,000 soldiers, and by the end of that year it was enlarged to 375,000. By war's end in August 1945 it numbered over 8 million.[37] Noted in greater detail later, Frankfurter was instrumental in crafting a 1942 decision which upheld the legality of prosecuting German saboteurs by military commission. He convened a meeting between Patterson and Stone to discuss the status of the German saboteurs before the Court reviewed their appeals. In 1945, Patterson sought Frankfurter's assurance that a similar result would occur in an appeal of a military commission trying a German spy and an American turncoat named Colepaugh and Gimpel at Governor's Island, New York. Frankfurter not only urged Patterson to pursue the military commission, he reviewed the charges against the two men to ensure their trials comported with military procedure.[38]

When, in 1945 the military justice system came under intense criticism, Frankfurter advised Patterson to convene a "board of study" and appoint General James Doolittle to chair the board to recommend appropriate reforms. On Frankfurter's suggestion Patterson appointed two federal judges, Morris A. Soper a judge on the Court of Appeals for the Fourth Circuit, and Alexander Holtzoff, a judge on the United States District Court for the District of Columbia to the committee. Holtzoff, a World War I veteran whose parents emigrated from Russia, attended Columbia Law School, studied under Stone, and often called

---

36 Frankfurter to Patterson, July 5, 1932 [Patterson/10] . Frankfurter's participation in identifying persons to fill key positions in the Roosevelt Administration was not limited to the War and Naval Departments. He also participated in discussions regarding the Attorney General and Secretary of Labor. *See* Grenville Clark to Henry Stimson, August 11, 1941 [Henry Lewis Stimson Papers, Manuscripts and Archives, Yale University Library, (microfilm reel 104 at Library of Congress)].

37 Keith E. Eiler, *Mobilizing America: Robert P. Patterson and the War Effort, 1940–1945* (New York: Cornell, 1997), 11–43; Keith D. McFarland and David Roll, *Louis Johnson and the Arming of America: The Roosevelt and Truman Years* (Bloomington, IN: Indiana University Press, 2005), 97.

38 Myron C. Cramer to Patterson, July 12, 1945 [Patterson/132]. Frankfurter's correspondence contains no evidence that he actually reviewed the charges, but the Judge Advocate General, Major General Cramer, believed this to be the case. On Colepaugh and Gimpel *see*, Francis Biddle to Henry Stimson (cc to Hugo Black), June 1, 1945 [FBP/5/f-21].

on the chief justice for advice. In 1946, Holtzoff served on a committee that was instrumental in shaping the Uniform Code of Military Justice, and would later author several military law decisions, appeals of which were granted *certiorari* by the Court.[39]

In order to quell criticism against the military justice system, in the closing days of World War II, the Army developed a clemency review process to release hundreds of incarcerated soldiers, and in the case of many deserters, to provide a means for reentering the Army and extinguishing their convictions. Owing to a large number of inmates in Britain and France, the European Theatre of Operations (ETO) command administered its own clemency program. At Frankfurter's suggestion, having experienced the 1919 battles over military justice, Patterson advised General Dwight Eisenhower to liberalize the grants of clemency. "Failure to reduce promptly excessive sentences imposed by courts-martial during the last war caused widespread public criticism in the administration of military justice and serious injury to the Army," Patterson conveyed.[40]

In 1919, Frankfurter, along with Roscoe Pound, defended Professor Samuel Elliot Morrison's right to freedom of speech after Harvard's conservative trustees accused Morrison of anti-American sentiments. Frankfurter went so far as to enlist Holmes and Brandeis to come to Morrison's aide. Later, following the attack on Pearl Harbor, Frankfurter convinced Roosevelt to name Morrison as the Navy's chief historian with the commissioned rank of commander so that he might become, "the historian of this war." Roosevelt responded to Frankfurter that he personally directed "Sam Morrison to be taken into the Navy with a commission, in order that he might write the story." Morrison went on to become an admiral and a first rate naval historian, who influenced naval policy in the Cold War. Had Frankfurter not come to Morrison's aid, Morrison would likely not have contributed to shaping the United States' post-war naval policies.[41]

Among Frankfurter's other War Department relationships were three of his former students, John J. McCloy, Kenneth Royall, and Frederick Bernays Wiener. McCloy, a controversial assistant secretary of war during World War II, became president of the World Bank after the conflict, and then was appointed United

39 On Holtzoff's service on military reform committees, *see* Robert Patterson to Holtzoff, March 5, 1946 [AH-AHC/6]; On Holtzoff seeking Stone's advice, *see* Leventhal to Burger, November 17, 1972 [Leventhal/157]; also *see* Keith E. Eiler, *Mobilizing America*, 401.

40 On Frankfurter's role *see* Patterson "Notes" [Patterson/42]; for Soper's biography *see* Anon., "Remembering the Fourth Circuit Judges: A History from 1941 to 1998," *Washington and Lee Law Review* 55 (Spring 1998): 471, 514–19; on Frankfurter's role in Patterson's letter to Eisenhower *see* undated, 1945 [Patterson/132].

41 Frankfurter to FDR, April 15, 1942; FDR to Frankfurter, April 18, 1942 in Max Freedman, *Roosevelt and Franklin: Their Correspondence*, 1928–1945 (Boston: Little Brown & Co., 1967), 655–6.

States High Commissioner in Germany overseeing de-Nazification. He also enabled pardons and early releases for German industrialists whose businesses utilized slave labor and he lobbied against reparations payments to American citizens of Japanese descent for their internment during World War II.[42]

Frankfurter's relationship with Royall dated to 1917, when Royall studied under Frankfurter at Harvard. In World War I, Royall served in the American Expeditionary Forces in France as an artillery officer. By 1937, he was a prominent North Carolina attorney and state senator representing Raleigh and he suspected that Roosevelt considered Frankfurter for the Court. Royall wrote to his former professor that he would lobby Congressional Democrats in his state to back the appointment. Frankfurter responded to Royall that rumors of his nomination were unfounded, but he "appreciated the friendship that lies behind the inquiry."[43] In 1942, Frankfurter lobbied the War Department to commission Royall into the Judge Advocate General's Corps with the rank of colonel. Shortly after, Frankfurter pressured Undersecretary of War Robert Patterson, to convince Royall to defend German saboteurs who landed in the United States. Royall's career was not hurt by his defense, despite offending Roosevelt, and by January 1945, he had been promoted to brigadier general. Two years later, Royall replaced Stimson and Patterson as Secretary of War and then, when that position was abolished, he became the Secretary of the Army. Royall believed that Frankfurter was the individual most responsible for his rise in the Department. When, in 1949, Truman removed Royall because of his opposition to quickly integrating the Army, Frankfurter came to Royall's defense. And, in 1960, Frankfurter helped ensure Royall was part of the Democratic Party convention which resulted in John Fitzgerald Kennedy's nomination.[44]

Frederick Wiener, another former student of Frankfurter's at Harvard, was also an important influence in the post-war evolution of military law. Like Royall, he maintained a lifelong friendship with Frankfurter. In 1967, William O. Douglas recommended Wiener head a commission to examine courts-martial during the Vietnam conflict even though Wiener and Douglas had divergent beliefs on the extent of military jurisdiction. At no time would Wiener advocate, as Douglas would, to narrow the scope of military jurisdiction to what would become termed

---

42 *See* Roger K. Newman ed., The Yale Biographical Dictionary of American Law (New Haven: Yale, 2009), 369–70.

43 Royall to Frankfurter, May 20, 1937 [FF]; Frankfurter to Royall, May 22, 1937 [FF]. There is no biography on Royall, but for a general outline *see* William S. Powell, *Dictionary of North Carolina Biography, Vol. V* (Chapel Hill: University of North Carolina Press, 1994), 260. For Frankfurter's view of Royall as "a close relation," *see* Joseph P. Lash, From the Diaries of Felix Frankfurter (New York: Norton, 1974), 171.

44 Frankfurter to Royall, April 20, 1942; Royall to Frankfurter, January 16, 1945; Royall to Frankfurter, July 28, 1947. For Royall's opposition to integrating the Army, *see* Dale R. Herspring, *The Pentagon and the Presidency: Civil-Military Relations from FDR to George Bush* (Lawrence, KS: Kansas University Press, 2005), 70–71.

as "service-connected offenses." That is, Wiener consistently argued that the military should be able to maximize its jurisdiction over servicemen.

Born in New York in 1906 to German immigrant parents and related to Sigmund Freud, Wiener attended Brown University. After he graduated in 1927, he went to Harvard Law School and graduated in 1930. In 1933, after three years in private practice, he became the Public Works Administration's legal counsel. One year later he was hired as the Interior Department's solicitor. A committed New Dealer, he corresponded with Frankfurter, who in turn used his influence to place Wiener into the Judge Advocate General's Department as a reserve officer. From 1937 until shortly after Pearl Harbor, Wiener was a special assistant to Attorney General Homer Cummings. He was activated to duty on December 12, 1941, with the rank of captain and by the end of World War II, he was a colonel.

Wiener not only argued a significant number of cases at the War Department's behest before the federal courts, he also served in the Pacific theatre of operations and he came under fire in Okinawa. In 1940, he authored a manual on martial law, which was later used in Hawaii and in the nation's other overseas territories. At the end of the war, he authored a treatise on the Articles of War, and in the 1949 Congressional hearings on military justice, he was influential in the creation of the Uniform Code of Military Justice. In his private capacity, he also argued against expanding military jurisdiction over civilian dependents and contractors residing with the military overseas. In 1957, he succeeded in convincing the Court of the need to eliminate military jurisdiction over dependent civilians on overseas military bases.[45]

Frankfurter might have been expected to blindly have an allegiance to the military establishment, given his associations in the War and Naval Departments. But his judicial deference jurisprudence and views on individual rights led to inconsistent results. During his tenure on the Court, he was uniquely influential in shaping the legal parameters of the nation's military law. Further, he affected the policy decisions of several departmental and service secretaries and under-secretaries who were his former clerks or students

William O. Douglas

Roosevelt's fourth appointee, William O. Douglas, began his judicial tenure fully supporting the New Deal and its commensurate expanded Executive Branch authority in the realm of economic regulation. Douglas exemplified the difficult balance the Court's justices faced between deference to the military establishment, which he clearly favored during the war, and protecting civil liberties, for which he would become known after the war. Toward the end of Truman's presidency, he began to intertwine his foreign affairs and social beliefs with his jurisprudence. In doing so, he led a majority of justices to restrict the Legislative Branch's traditional

45 *Reid v. Covert*, 354 US 1 (1957).

authorities over the governance of the military. Conservatives targeted him for impeachment and accused him of intentionally undermining national security. Married four times, Republicans later claimed he was not only irrational in his jurisprudence, but also immoral. President Richard Nixon would try to convince Congress to impeach Douglas in 1969, but his efforts failed.

Born in Minnesota in 1898, at the age of three, Douglas' family migrated to Yakima, Washington. In 1904 his father died, leaving his family in poverty. He also suffered from polio, but made a full recovery by the time he graduated high school. Despite the poverty of his youth, he excelled academically, graduated as valedictorian from his high school, and received a scholarship to attend Whitman College. He served briefly in the military during World War I. Like Black and Frankfurter, Douglas did not go overseas. On Douglas' discharge papers, a Captain Chris Jensen noted Douglas possessed "excellent character," and labeled him, "a trustworthy soldier in every respect." Moreover, the discharge certificate indicated that the Army intended Douglas to attend officers training camp, and only the November 11, 1918 Armistice precluded this advancement.[46]

In 1925, Douglas enrolled in Columbia University's Law School. Following graduation, he briefly worked at the Cravath firm in New York, and then returned to Washington State. Shortly after, he accepted faculty positions at Columbia Law School and then Yale's Law School.[47] After Roosevelt was elected president in 1932, Douglas left academia and served a stint as a member of the newly formed Securities and Exchange Commission under Joseph Kennedy. Because Roosevelt respected Douglas' abilities, he nominated him to the chairmanship of Securities and Exchange Commission in 1937. Two years later, Roosevelt nominated him to the Supreme Court. Douglas had many influential supporters including congressmen, jurists, and notably Frankfurter, and Ambassador Joseph Kennedy.

Douglas was only 39 years old when he joined the Court, and when he retired in 1975, he served longer than any justice in American history. He was to have a profound influence in the shaping of the nation's military laws, even though his 1969 capstone decision, *O'Callahan*, was ultimately reversed. By the mid-1960s, Douglas would subscribe to Arthur Schlesinger's warnings that an Imperial Presidency undermined democracy and he sought to weaken the Executive Branch and defense establishment as a means of preventing the United States entering into armed conflict. However, through 1952 he largely supported the Executive Branch.[48]

Douglas' relationship with the military was inconsistent. He supported the war against Germany, Japan, and Italy so strongly he considered resigning from the

46 For Douglas' military experience *see*, Military Discharge Certificate, William O. Douglas, dated December 20, 1918. [WOD/1771].

47 James F. Simon, *Independent Journey: The Life of William O. Douglas* (New York: Harper & Row, 1980).

48 *See* Philip J. Cooper, "William O. Douglas: the Conscience of the Court," in Charles M. Lamb, ed., *The Burger Court: Judicial and Political Profiles*, 163–5 (2000).

bench to take a more direct role in the war. A prolific writer, most of Douglas' wartime efforts came in the form of speeches and statements later published in his book *Being an American*.[49] These speeches were a form of propaganda designed to create support for the American war effort, demonstrating his support for Roosevelt and the military efforts However, these speeches also highlighted civil rights and the American ideals of freedom and liberty he believed would prevail in the face of totalitarianism, and that would later serve as a bedrock of Douglas' jurisprudence. Despite his claims later in life that he despised the military's conformist requirements, in World War II he wrote over two dozen endorsements for citizens trying to join the Army's Judge Advocate General's Corps. In all of his endorsement letters Douglas emphasized the criticality of military discipline. Ultimately, Douglas would be viewed as "anti-military" because of his unrelenting criticism of the United States' activity in Vietnam, including his unsuccessful efforts to get the constitutionality of the President's military activity decided by the Court.[50]

Frank Murphy

Between 1940 and 1949, no justice sided more with service-members or against the extension of military authority than Roosevelt's fifth nomination to the Court, William Francis "Frank" Murphy. During World War II, when even Black and Douglas sided with the Executive Branch in upholding the forced relocation of United States citizens of Japanese ancestry, Murphy dissented, decrying the legalization of racism.[51]

Murphy was born in 1890, graduated from the University of Michigan in 1912, and then earned a law degree at that university's law school in 1914. Commissioned into the Army in 1917, he experienced the military's justice system as a judge advocate. While in training at Fort Sheridan he defended a lieutenant charged with manslaughter after the lieutenant accidentally killed a sergeant at a rifle range. Before heading to France in August 1917, his first officer efficiency report read "fine mind, thorough, will make an excellent officer." Although he trained to be an infantry officer, his commanders recognized his legal talents and appointed him brigade judge advocate. In this capacity, Murphy assisted the United States Attorney in prosecuting a civilian quartermaster in a

49 William O. Douglas, *Being an American* (New York: John Day, 1948).

50 James C. Duram, *Justice William O. Douglas*, 38 (Boston, MA: Twayne, 1981), 30–39; Bernard Schwartz, *The Ascent of Pragmatism* (Boston: Addison Wesley, 1989), 19; Howard Ball, "Loyalty, Treason, and the State, An Examination of Justice William O. Douglas's Style, Substance, and Anguish" in *He Shall Not Pass This Way Again: The Legacy of William O. Douglas*, Steven Wasby ed. (Pittsburgh: University of Pittsburgh Press, 1997), 7; Douglas to The Judge Advocate General, October 1, 1944 [WOD/669].

51 *Korematsu v. United States*, 323 U.S. 214 (1944).

United States District Court for theft, and he prosecuted the civilian's co-actor, a captain, in a court-martial. Both men were found guilty and the court-martial sentenced the captain to 20 years at hard labor. The *New York Times* reported the trials bringing Murphy briefly into a national spotlight. While defending another soldier in a court-martial, Murphy offended several senior officers with his closing argument: "this case is brought to trial only as a result of the gross and wanton negligence on the part of those who investigated the case." After this trial, Murphy was prevented from serving as a judge advocate again, but, as his biographer Sidney Fine noted, Murphy's wartime experience shaped his future career.[52]

Following his Army service, Murphy was appointed as the assistant United States Attorney for the Eastern District of Michigan in 1919, and taught law at the University of Detroit. He later served as a criminal court judge, and in 1930, he was elected mayor of Detroit. He was a Democrat and an avid New Deal supporter. Three years later, as a reward for supporting the New Deal, Roosevelt appointed Murphy Governor General of the Philippines. The position was officially abolished in 1935 as the islands moved toward independence, but Murphy stayed as high commissioner through 1936. Dating to his time as governor general, Murphy clashed with General Douglas MacArthur, and when, in 1946 Murphy dissented from a decision upholding the military commission and death sentence of two Japanese generals, MacArthur's allies wrongly argued that his animus toward the general was the reason for the dissent.[53]

On his return from the Philippines, Murphy was elected Michigan's governor, Democrat leaders considered him as a potential successor to Roosevelt. He only served one two-year term and was defeated for reelection after ignoring a judge's order during a labor strike involving the United Auto Workers, and he sided with the striking union. In 1939, Roosevelt nominated Murphy Attorney General where he created the Department of Justice's first civil rights section. As Attorney General, Murphy concentrated on prosecuting organized crime, political corruption, and wealthy tax evaders. Senator Harry Truman clashed with Murphy for his prosecution of Thomas J. Pendergast who had run the Kansas

52 "Captain and Civilian Arraigned on Graft Charge at Battle Creek," *New York Times*, March 20, 1918, p. 2; "Captain Pillenger to Serve Four Years," New York Times, August 2, 1918, p. 2. The Secretary of War reduced Pillenger's sentence to four years, and the civilian was sentenced to two years imprisonment by the District Court; Sidney A. Fine, *Frank Murphy in World War One* (Ann Arbor, MI: Michigan Historical Collections, 1969), 22–41.

53 Brigadier General Bonner Fellers to Murphy, May 24, 1943 [Fellers-Hoover/2]. Murphy to Fellers, August 11, 1943 [Fellers-Hoover/23]; Brigadier General Fellers was an intelligence officer who had served as a liaison officer to the British Army in North Africa prior to being transferred to the Pacific theatre of operations. He apparently shared a similar view of MacArthur. Sidney A. Fine, *Frank Murphy, The Washington Years* (Ann Arbor: University of Michigan, 1984), 1–2; Melvin I. Urofsky "The Roosevelt Court," in William Henry Chafe, *The Achievement of American Liberalism: The New Deal and Its Legacies* (New York: Columbia University Press, 2003), 70–72.

City Democrat machine that Truman had relied on for political support. Of note, Murphy supported anti-lynching measures, but he also oversaw the indictments of pro-German, anti-Franco, and Communist Party members for failing to register with the Government as required by the Smith Act. Officially titled as the Alien Registration Act of 1940, the Smith Act criminalized attempts to overthrow the government, as well as advocacy to do so, and required foreigners to register with the government, and enabled deportation of aliens who joined political organizations such as the Communist Party of the United States.[54]

On January 4, 1940, Roosevelt nominated Murphy to replace Pierce Butler, a justice who opposed the New Deal. Although Murphy was qualified to serve on the Court, he was considered lazy in his jurisprudence and he was nowhere near the scholar that Black, Frankfurter, and Douglas were. Nor did he possess their work ethic. He believed he had a duty to protect minorities from discriminating laws and government action, and he shaped his decisions to this end. He also remained steadfastly loyal to the New Deal. Not all pro-New Deal scholars supported Roosevelt's selection of Murphy. Frankfurter frequently disparaged him and opposed his selection to the Court, preferring Learned Hand or someone else of a like mind. Indeed, Frankfurter frequently disparaged Murphy as "Saint Frank" or simply "the stooge." Edward S. Corwin, who, along with Charles Warren, was one of the nation's leading constitutional historians and a frequent correspondent with Stone and Frankfurter, wrote to Stone in reference to Murphy, "quite confidentially, I am not throwing up my hat over the latest appointment to the Court." Nonetheless, the Senate easily confirmed Murphy. Though he only served on the Court until his death in 1949, he was able to begin a trend toward lessening deference to the Executive Branch in military matters. Along with Roosevelt's seventh selection Wiley Rutledge, Murphy provided in his dissents in military law cases the basis upon which Black, Douglas, Warren, Brennan, Marshall would later shape the nation's military law.[55]

The context of Murphy's military law jurisprudence is note-worthy. Shortly after the Japanese attack on Pearl Harbor, he attempted to rejoin the Army in a reserve capacity, while remaining on the Court. Murphy's conduct, including directly petitioning Army Chief of Staff, George C. Marshall, angered Stone, who found out about Murphy's efforts from Congressman Emmanuel Celler. Celler inquired to the chief justice whether "Murphy could legally enjoy the dual role of a Judge and a commissioned officer in the Army." Stone sought Black's advice on how to answer Celler, who in turn suggested against providing an answer, and instead encourage Murphy to cease his efforts.[56]

54 Fine, *Frank Murphy, The Washington Years*, 59–117.

55 Corwin to Stone, January 10, 1940 [HFS/10]. In this same letter, Corwin extolled Samuel Freeman Miller, a Lincoln appointee to the bench. *See also* Howard Ball, *Hugo Black: Cold Steel Warrior*, 125.

56 Stone to Black, August 25, 1942 [HFS/67].

Robert Jackson

In 2003, Pulitzer Prize winning historian, William E. Leuchtenburg referred to Robert Houghwout Jackson as "the most important figure of the twentieth century no one has heard of." Jackson did not have the formal college and legal training of Frankfurter, Black, or Douglas, but in several respects he was their equal. Frankfurter called him the Court's most literarily gifted justice. When, in September, 2005, John Roberts was questioned during his confirmation hearings by the Senate Judiciary Committee to name a justice he most admired, he responded by naming Robert Jackson.[57]

Born in Pennsylvania and raised in Western New York, Jackson did not go to college and only briefly attended Albany Law School. He had, in fact, intended to spend his life as a country lawyer. A fourth-generation Democrat, he served as an advisor to Roosevelt when Roosevelt was state governor. In 1933, Jackson was appointed general counsel to the Internal Revenue Service, then assistant Attorney General where he worked under Murphy and Francis Biddle, and he eventually replaced Stanley Reed as Solicitor General. On January 18, 1940 Jackson was sworn in as Attorney General. While in that position, he advised Roosevelt on implementing the selective service laws which would eventually govern conscription during World War II. On December 10, 1940, he wrote to Frankfurter, calling conscientious objectors "blockheads." Additionally, Jackson worked closely with Federal Bureau of Investigation Director, J. Edgar Hoover in investigating conscientious objection claims. It was in this context that a year before the Japanese attack on Pearl Harbor, Hoover warned Jackson that communist groups planned to disrupt conscription.[58]

In March 1941, Jackson informed Undersecretary of the Navy James Forrestal that Roosevelt had the authority as commander in chief to seize the Allis-Chalmers Corporation. The Milwaukee based corporation had failed, in the National Labor Relations Board's estimation, to negotiate in good faith with their union workers, who in turn threatened to strike. Jackson advised Forrestal that since the success of Lend-Lease to Great Britain relied on industrial output, the government could consider their corporation's labor policy as "a refusal to manufacture." Prior to Jackson's advice, J. Edgar Hoover conveyed to Jackson that communists were fomenting a strike at Allis-Chalmers as well. Jackson did not state he believed that the government could, after taking over the plant, force a permanent wage hike, and he was also not convinced of the veracity of Hoover's advice on this occasion. Moreover, Hoover conceded that the corporation's

---

57 William E. Leuchtenburg, forward in Robert H. Jackson, *That Man: An Insider's Portrait of Franklin D. Roosevelt* (New York: Oxford University Press, 2004), vii; Schwartz, *A History of the Supreme Court*, 248; Urofsky, *The Warren Court*, 248.

58 Melvin Urofsky, *The Warren Court*, 49–50; Jackson to Frankfurter, December 10, 1940 [RHJ/93]; J. Edgar Hoover to Jackson, October 14, 1940 [RHJ/93]; Hoover to Jackson, March 27, 1941 [RHJ/93].

president had been a leading contributor to the America First movement, a group with anti-Semitic members who sought to make the nation wholly neutral. Ultimately, the government did not seize the corporation, but this would not be the only time that Jackson stated he believed the government possessed the authority to seize a corporation. On the other hand, as a justice under a later presidential administration, he would be instrumental in curbing the Executive Branch's authority to take over private corporations in similar circumstances.[59]

In 1941 when Charles Evans Hughes announced his retirement, Roosevelt nominated Stone as Chief Justice, and nominated Jackson to replace Stone as associate justice. Had Roosevelt not decided to seek a third term, Jackson was on the president's "short list" for his succession. From almost the start of his judicial tenure, Jackson clashed with Black. Jackson quipped that to disagree with Black meant to go to war with him. The two men were usually opposed to each other on national security and military law matters, but their differences became personal and in a labor law appeal, Jackson accused Black of unethical conduct for accepting an award at a dinner where a number of sponsors were litigants in cases pending before the Court.[60] The feud between Jackson and Black may have been primarily fueled by each man's desire to replace Stone as Chief Justice. In fact, when Truman appointed Frederick Vinson to replace Stone, rumors abounded that he did so to mollify Black, who had purportedly threatened resignation if Jackson was appointed.[61] By the war's end, Jackson and Frankfurter allied with Stone, while they referred to Douglas and Black as "the axis."[62]

Jackson profoundly influenced the shaping of a number of laws, particularly in Executive Branch authority, but his influence in other aspects of military law would prove short-lived. This was not a result of a lack of effort on his part, but he died before the significant issues involving jurisdiction arose in the second half of the 1950s and into the 1960s. While serving as an associate justice, he uniquely served as the United States' lead counsel in the Nuremberg trials which prosecuted Herman Goering, Albert Speer, and a number of other Nazi leaders. This conflict precluded him from deciding whether the Court would assume jurisdiction of the American trials of Japanese war criminals.

Wiley Rutledge

When Roosevelt's last judicial vacancy on the Court opened in 1943, he nominated Wiley Rutledge, whom he had appointed to the Court of Appeals

59 Jackson to Forrestal, March 17, 1941 [RHJ/93].

60 Dennis J. Hutchison, *The Black-Jackson Feud*, 1988 Sup. Ct. Rev. 203, 236–7 (1988).

61 *Ibid.* at 220.

62 *See, e.g.*, Jeffrey Rosen, *The Supreme Court: The Personalities and Rivalries that Defined America* (New York: MacMillan, 2007), 147.

for the District of Columbia in 1939. Like Stone, Frankfurter and Douglas, Rutledge's legal background included a tenured law faculty position. Rutledge had risen to become dean of the Washington University, Saint Louis Law School, and then later dean of the University of Iowa Law School. Prior to Roosevelt's presidency Rutledge publicly advocated for government programs that ultimately became a part of the New Deal. He believed the government had to curb odious child labor practices and he championed minority rights. Along with Murphy, Rutledge dissented from several military law and national security decisions, arguing that expanded Executive Branch authority undermined civil rights.

While on the court of appeals, Rutledge urged that a constitutional right to counsel become the law of the land for all felony cases, to include state criminal trials. He also expanded tort suits to enable injured parties to sue hospitals, third-party defendants, and upheld several administrative decisions concerning New Deal legislation. His biographer, John Ferren notes that Rutledge adopted Roscoe Pound's judicial philosophy that fixed rules were antithetical to fair justice. Although he would only serve on the Court for six years, Rutledge began a trend of advocating for greater judicial review in overseeing the nation's military laws which Black, Douglas and later Earl Warren, William Brennan, and Thurgood Marshall adopted and honed. Had Rutledge not served on the Court, Black, Douglas, Warren, Brennan and Marshall might have still liberalized the military's legal construct, but Rutledge first defined the direction the five would later take.[63]

Given the largely New Deal orientation of the Supreme Court during World War II, which had in the years prior to the war focused on the rights of organized labor and, to a lesser extent, expanding the Bill of Rights into the federal law, it might appear that the justices would be reticent to uphold the vast expansion of the Executive Branch's authority, and particularly the growth of the military establishment's influence into the nation's political and legal construct. During the war, several justices, and in particular Frankfurter, would play a role in Roosevelt's wartime domestic and foreign policies, well before challenges to these policies would come before the judiciary on appeal. However, the justices would not abandon the principle of civil and individual rights and they would not *always* side with the Executive Branch. To be sure, there were instances where vast numbers of citizens were confined on the basis of race without due regard for their constitutional rights, and a majority of the justices would side against these citizens in their appeals. But, in other appeals the justices upheld free speech protections to a degree that would have been unthinkable in the Civil War and World War I.

---

63 John Ferren, *Salt of the Earth, Conscience of the Court*, (Chapel Hill: University of North Carolina Press, 2004), 87.

Chapter 3
The Court, Total War, and the Citizen, 1941–1945

By 1940 the War and Naval Departments envisioned a mass conscription program which would bring millions of citizens into uniform. Following the nation's declaration of war on Japan, Germany, and Italy, a Selective Service program was initiated that would enable an armed force of 12 million men. In World War I, the armed forces numbered roughly four million men, and the refusal to submit to conscription was prosecutable in court-martial. In World War II, a citizen could only be court-martialed once actually in the armed forces. A person was legally considered to be in the military after taking an oath and receiving pay. That said, with 12 million men in uniform, there were thousands of courts-martial likely to occur. In fact, during World War II the Army conducted 1,700,000 courts-martial. By the end of the war in 1945, 45,000 soldiers and airmen were in prison serving sentences in excess of five years, and more than 100 executions had been carried out. Yet, not until 1946 would the Court grant an appeal from a court-martial, or a military trial of an American citizen. Hundreds of soldiers and civilians appealed court-martial convictions through the federal courts based on claims that, if true in a civilian criminal trial would likely result in a reversal. With the exception of Justice Murphy, none of the justices would regularly grant *certiorari* in court-martial appeals.[1]

While the nation remained at war, the Court also proved unwilling to favor the rights of veterans from prior wars, or interfere in the prosecution of foreign espionage agents. However, the justices were willing to restrain the government in its prosecution of Americans alleged to have aided an enemy nation or caused subversion. Infamously, the Court's willingness to restrain the government did not extend to the military's prospective treatment of United States citizens of Japanese descent.

At times, the Court appeared apathetic to how the war might have affected the sensibilities of prosecutors, judges, and juries in non-military cases. For instance, in 1943 William Reid, a formerly convicted "dope peddler," was convicted "of making an oral threat to take the life of the President of the United States." Apparently, during a dinner table discussion Reid informed his peers that he hated Roosevelt, "believed Hitler a wonderful man," and claimed that if he "had the money, he would go to Washington D.C., and kill the president."

1 Jonathan Lurie, *Arming Military Justice: The Origins of the United States Court of Military Appeals*, Vol. I (New Jersey: Princeton University Press, 1992).

Reid's comments were made in March, 1941. While in confinement and awaiting trial, the government discovered that three other convicts were willing to testify that Reid had expressed pro-Nazi sympathies. Reid unsuccessfully appealed to the Court of Appeals for the Fifth Circuit and Supreme Court for an injunction against his prosecution, and following his conviction and sentence of four years, he unsuccessfully appealed to have his conviction overturned. Only Justice Murphy expressed an interest in granting the appeal, arguing, "the government burdened the record with inflammatory remarks," thereby making it impossible for Reid to receive a fair trial.[2]

The denial of Reid's appeal is a largely forgotten episode in the Court's history, and Murphy's arguments to his fellow justices, with the exception of his own collection, are not recorded in the justices' collections. In August 1942 a federal court sentenced a naturalized citizen named Max Stephan to death after he was convicted of treason. Stephan was born in Germany but had lived in the United States for over 20 years. He helped an escaped German prisoner of war by providing him shelter and money. Stephan appealed against his sentence, but only Murphy voted to grant certiorari. The Court's denial of Stephan's and Reid's appeals does, however, place into context the justices' approach to not only civil liberties in wartime, but also provides insight into why the Court did not grant a single appeal from a wartime court-martial. After all, as Murphy pointed out in a memorandum to his fellow justices, the evidence used to convict Reid was based on his pro-Nazi statements, but there was no evidence to indicate that Reid could actually carry out his prewar threat against the president.[3]

I: The Court's Avoidance of Court-Martial Appeals

During World War II, a number of appeals originating in courts-martial percolated through the federal courts. Many of these challenges encompassed issues later deemed worthy of judicial review, but, as noted, during the war, the Court did not grant *certiorari* from any of the appellate or district court decisions.

The first of these cases, *Romero v. Squier*, originated before the war. In 1940, Army officials, including the semi-retired General Douglas MacArthur, accused Captain Rufo Romero, a West Point commissioned officer stationed in the Philippines, of reproducing classified maps of military installations and attempting to provide them to the Imperial Japanese Government. There was sound evidence to this accusation since the maps, which were supposed to be guarded in a protected location, were found in Romero's home, and he had been seen with known Japanese agents. Moreover, initially Romero's legal counsel did

2 Murphy, draft argument to dissent from denial of certiorari, n.d.; [FM-UM/129].

3 *Ibid. United States v. Stephan*, 50 F.Supp. 738 (ED MI 1943); *Stephan v. United States*, 319 U.S. 783 (1943). Roosevelt ultimately commuted Stephan's sentence to life in prison.

not enter a plea of guilty or not guilty, but instead pursued a not guilty by reason of insanity defense. In other words, Romero admitted that he provided Japan classified material, but denied mental responsibility for his actions.[4]

Romero was defended by a fellow officer who was not a licensed attorney, and a civilian attorney who he retained at his own expense. Romero did not have the opportunity to choose a judge advocate as his defense counsel. During portions of the trial involving the presentation of classified evidence, the court-martial excluded his civilian counsel. As a result, Romero was represented by a licensed attorney for only part of his trial. The court-martial found Romero guilty and sentenced him to a dismissal and 15 years imprisonment.

Both at his court-martial and in seeking relief to the federal judiciary in his subsequent *habeas* action, Romero raised two primary objections. He claimed to be a victim of a wrongful search and seizure. The Court of Appeals for the Ninth Circuit considered this issue meritless. Romero also argued that he was denied counsel within the meaning of the Sixth Amendment. The appellate court took the interesting step of disregarding *Dynes v. Hoover* and concluded that the Sixth Amendment applied to courts-martial, entitling Romero to a qualified counsel equivalent to the right to counsel in a civilian court, and that the federal judiciary had jurisdiction to review this issue. But the court then held that when "defended by a brother officer of his choice," an accused did not enjoy "a constitutional right to have also a civilian associate lawyer for the portion of the trial in which military secrets are revealed."[5]

Romero raised two other issues: First, that he was denied counsel during the pretrial investigation (the military's rough equivalent of a grand jury), and second, that the prosecuting judge advocate had failed to forward a complete record of trial to the Secretary of War and President. In response, the appellate court held that a military accused did not have a right to counsel during the pretrial investigation, and it determined that an incomplete record did not result in a jurisdictional defect.

When Romero petitioned for a writ of *certiorari*, only Justice Murphy took an interest in the case. There was a reason why the Court could have granted *certiorari*. In 1932, in *Powell v. Alabama*, the Court had extended for the first time, the Sixth Amendment right to counsel to state criminal prosecutions. Among the factors the Court noted in *Powell* for the need for counsel was public hostility to the defendants. This factor was also present in Romero's court-martial. Romero's court-martial had been well covered in newspapers, and there existed a significant anti-Japanese bias in both the Philippines and the military, even prior to Pearl

4 *Romero v. Squire*, 133 F.2d 528 (CA 9, 1943). There is little on the Romero trial, but *see* Ricardo Trota Jose, *The Philippine Army, 1935–1942* (Manila: Ateneo De Manila University Press, 1992), 174–5. Professor Jose notes that Squire suffered from alcoholism and a shortage of money, leading him to provide the Japanese military intelligence for greed rather than ideological reasons.

5 *Romero v. Squire*, 318 U.S. 735 (1943).

Harbor. Romero clearly aided Japan prior to Pearl Harbor and likely contributed to the United States and Filipino defeat in 1942. *Time Magazine* and the *New York Times* covered Romero's court-martial as did several foreign newspapers including the *Canberra Times*. Later in *Hartsel v. United States*, *Cramer v. United States*, and *Viereck v. United States*, the Court determined that wartime fears had no place in the logic of the nation's court-rooms. But none of those cases arisen from a military court, and this made Romero a different petitioner than civilian petitioners.[6]

In 1940, the Court of Appeals for the Fifth Circuit in *Sanford v. Robbins* determined that traditional double jeopardy prohibitions did not apply to courts-martial, even though the Articles of War expressly protected soldiers from multiple trials on this basis. In 1918, 16 African-American soldiers were accused of rape and court-martialed. Two defense counsels represented all 16 soldiers, and the court-martial tried all 16 at the same time, even though the soldiers advanced different defenses. All 16 men were convicted and sentenced to life in confinement. In 1919, President Woodrow Wilson declared the court-martial invalid and ordered the soldiers retried. Once more the soldiers were court-martialed and found guilty. In 1939, one of the soldiers appealed on the basis of double jeopardy. The district court did not issue a published decision, but it hesitantly indicated it would uphold the second court-martial, if it believed it had jurisdiction.[7]

The Fifth Circuit upheld the lower court, though it authored a tortuous decision. It first held that the original court-martial had proper jurisdiction and President Wilson had merely exercised his discretion in ordering a new trial. Further, the Fifth Circuit rejected the defendants' claim to conflict-free defense counsel because it had previously determined that the right to counsel was not absolute. The court found the first trial was incomplete because the President had not confirmed the death sentence, and, as a result, double jeopardy did not attach to the first court-martial, thereby enabling a retrial. "We conclude that the second court-martial correctly overruled the defense of former conviction; but whether right or wrong, its judgment, not having been revised or reversed, must stand."[8]

In *Schita v. King*, the Court of Appeals for the Eighth Circuit determined that a court-martial record could be so fundamentally defective that its jurisdiction was void to begin with. Even though the military did not possess a judicial appeals process, in following the Court's nineteenth-century decision in *Runkle*, an incomplete record of trial could still prejudice a soldier trying to seek relief through the War Department, or through a *habeas* appeal. In 1917, the Army court-martialed Sergeant Valdo B. Schita, a "colored soldier" at Governor's Island, New York, and convicted him of murdering another soldier and sentenced him to

6 "The Philippines Spy Trial," *Time Magazine*, December 2, 1940; *New York Times*, November 25, 1940, pp. 1. *Canberra Times*, November 27, 1940, pp. 1.

7 *Sanford v. Robbins*, 115 F.2d 435 (CA 5, 1940), *cert. denied*, 312 U.S. 697 (1941).

8 *Ibid.* at 439.

confinement for life. The appellate court provided a more descriptive character of Schita as "born a Zulu, became successively a member of the Native Constabulary of South Africa, the Canadian Army and finally the United States Army." In reality, Schita was a British Army veteran of the 1898 Sudan campaign against Islamist tribal forces, the Boer War in South Africa, and the battles of Mons and Loos on the western front in 1914 and 1915. How Schita came to the United States Army remains a mystery. He was likely a disturbed veteran, suffering from battle fatigue, at a minimum. However, in his prison records there is medical evidence he survived a poison gas attack and neurologically suffered from it.[9]

Although over two decades had passed, Schita appealed his court-martial conviction in the U.S. District Court for the Western District of Missouri, alleging that 20 years earlier the Army denied him the right to a defense counsel of his own choosing, and that his civilian counsel was unprepared to defend him. He also claimed that the court-martial did not permit him to call witnesses on his own behalf, witness testimony occurred outside of his presence, and defense witnesses were bullied by the government. Equally troubling, he argued that he was convicted of felonious assault, an offense he was never charged with, (though he was investigated for it), and the murder of a second enlisted man. By the time Schita appealed, he was confined in a federal hospital for "defective delinquents." Apparently, the move from a military prison to the hospital triggered the appeal.

The Eighth Circuit noted that Schita had proceeded in his appeal without counsel. The court also recognized that the district court ruled against each of Schita's allegations of denial of due process without any evidence to dispute the allegations. The Army's record keeping in this instance was appallingly poor, and its representatives simply could not rebut Schita's claims. The appellate court conceded that Schita's allegations "taxed credulity," but in the absence of a complete trial record, it would not protect the court-martial from collateral attack. Rather than free Schita, however, the appellate court remanded the case to the lower court. In a second review by the district court in 1944, the Army produced the entire court-martial transcript after officers in the Judge Advocate General's Department claimed to have found it. Not surprisingly the district court ruled once more that the court-martial had proper jurisdiction and had fairly prosecuted Schita. This time the appellate court concurred with the lower court's dismissal and denied Schita relief. The appellate court discovered that Schita had, in fact, been represented by Martin Littleton, a former congressman from New York and one-time district attorney, who died in 1934. On June 5, 1944, one day before allied forces landed in Normandy, the Court denied Schita's motion for *certiorari*. Solicitor General Fahy and Assistant Attorney General Tom C. Clark opposed Schita's appeal for *certiorari*, but two justices, Murphy and Rutledge did

9 *Schita v. King*, 133 F.2d 283 (CA 8, 1943).

not. Despite his efforts Murphy could not convince Douglas, Black, or any other justice to vote for *certiorari*.[10]

Other cases had similar possibilities for *certiorari*. In early 1943, the Court of Appeals for the Second Circuit Court issued *United States ex rel. Innes v. Crystal*, an appeal originating in the Army's transfer of a defense counsel during a court-martial. Innes also alleged the prosecution presented testimony to the court-martial outside of the presence of himself and his counsel. If true, the court-martial had clearly denied him his Sixth Amendment right to confront witnesses, as well as denied him the right to defense counsel. The court-martial convicted Innes of assault with intent to commit sodomy, and sentenced him to a dishonorable discharge and 15 years imprisonment.[11]

Two of the nation's leading constitutional scholars, Augustus N. Hand and Jerome N. Frank, and a third judge named Charles Clark, determined that the transfer of defense counsel did not constitute a jurisdictional defect. However, Hand, Frank, and Clark concluded that the taking of testimony in the accused's absence could constitute a jurisdictional defect, but that the record of trial did not support Innes on this point. Interestingly, in 1865, the Judge Advocate General's Department stated in its *Digest of Opinions*, that absent extraordinary circumstances, the presence of accused and counsel during testimony was required and there were several instances during the Civil War in which Secretary of War Stanton and President Lincoln voided courts-martial on the advice of the Judge Advocate General because of a failure to allow accused soldiers to be present during all testimony. However, the *Digest* was advisory rather than binding on the Secretary of War and President, and there were also instances where the term "extraordinary circumstances," was stretched to include "military convenience."[12]

With only Murphy urging appellate review, the Court denied *certiorari* on the basis that Innes had been transferred out of the Second Circuit's jurisdiction and would have to appeal again in another district court, a decision echoed decades later when the Supreme Court ruled the Second Circuit did not have jurisdiction over a *habeas* appeal from suspected terrorist Jose Padilla, and then denied his subsequent petition for *certiorari* because after he filed in the correct court, the government transferred him from military to civilian custody on the eve of the

10 *Schita v. Cox*, 139 F.2d 971 (CA 8 1944). Schita died in the federal penitentiary in 1945 at the age of 80. According to his penitentiary medical records, Schita was a veteran of the Sudan Campaign of 1898, the Boer War, and trench warfare on the western front in 1915. There is no record as to how Schita came into the United States. Schita's information is found in the Missouri State Archives. On Murphy's attempts to convince a vote for certiorari *see* Murphy's notes in [FM-U.M/ R-131] for, *Schita v. Pescor*, 322 U.S. 761 (1944), rehearing denied, 323 U.S. 380 (1944).

11 *United States ex rel. Innes v. Crystal*, 131 F.2d 576 (CA 2, 1943).

12 Joshua Kastenberg, Law in War, Law as War, Brigadier General Joseph Holt and the Judge Advocate General's Department in the Civil War and Reconstruction, 46.

Court's decision to grant *certiorari.* The Court had a second opportunity to hear the *Innes* appeal after he later appealed to the United States District Court for the Middle District of Pennsylvania. He renewed his collateral attack on the basis that the judge advocate presented evidence outside of his and his counsel's presence. The district court conceded that the record of the court-martial had been changed and new evidence highlighting Innes' claims might exist. However, that court decided that the proper avenue to dispute the record of trial existed in the War Department and not in the federal judiciary. Thus, while Innes might have a claim, the district court embraced the traditional narrow view of jurisdiction and decided, "nevertheless, where a court-martial had jurisdiction of the offense charged, had jurisdiction to try the offender for the offense, had acted within the scope of its lawful powers, and the sentence is one which the court could under the law pronounce, its decision and sentence cannot be reviewed and set aside by the civil courts by writ of *habeas* corpus." Innes next appealed to the Court of Appeals for the Third Circuit, which shortly after issued *United States ex rel. Innes v. Hiatt*. This time Judge Albert Maris, another highly respected scholar, authored a decision which upheld the lower court, although the judges conceded that the Fifth Amendment applied to courts-martial. Again, Innes failed to get to the Supreme Court, because only Murphy favored granting *certiorari.*[13]

In *Mosher v. Hudspeth*, decided in 1941, and *Mosher v. Hunter*, decided in 1944, the Court of Appeals for the Tenth Circuit determined that a soldier court-martialed twice, albeit for separate offenses, was not entitled to the presumption that his sentences ran concurrently. A court-martial sentenced Mosher to life imprisonment for murder in 1920, but a clemency review board, internal to the War Department, recommended commutation of the sentence to 30 years and the Secretary of War followed this recommendation. While awaiting final review of his court-martial, Mosher escaped and was court-martialed for desertion and larceny. The second court-martial sentenced him to 15 years. After serving his full 30 years, he appealed to the federal courts, arguing that it was a violation of his constitutional rights to have to serve an additional 15 years from the second court-martial.[14]

Mosher appealed to a federal judge near Fort Leavenworth, Kansas, but the district court denied him relief. On December 15, 1941, the Court of Appeals for the Tenth Circuit upheld the lower court on the basis of deference to the traditional jurisdictional test for courts-martial (federal civilian courts did not have authority to issue a discharge from the military under *habeas* if the court-martial "had jurisdiction to try the offender for the offense and the sentence was

13 *Innes v. United States, certiorari denied*, 319 U.S. 755; and, *United States ex rel. Innes v. Hiatt*,141 F.2 664 (CA 3, 1944); Appointed by Franklin Roosevelt to the District Court in 1936, and Third Circuit in 1938, Maris had authored and edited the Restatements of Law. *Rumsfeld v. Padilla*, 542 U.S. 426 (2004); *Padilla v. Hanft*, 547 U.S. 1062 (2006).

14 *Mosher v. Hudspeth*, 123 F.2d 401 (CA 10, 1941); 316 U.S. 670 (1942); *Mosher v. Hunter*, 143 F.2d 745 (CA 10 1944).

one which the court under the law could pronounce"). Mosher appealed to the Court, but was denied *certiorari*. Only Murphy and Frankfurter were interested in reviewing the case, but for different reasons. Murphy wanted to ensure that the law was clear regarding concurrent sentences and wanted to settle any ambiguity adverse to the military, while Frankfurter argued that the law was already clear. As a result of the denial of *certiorari*, Frankfurter's position prevailed for the next two decades because the military was free to liberally ignore a requirement for concurrent sentences. Mosher appealed a second time, but on the basis that since the Army had dishonorably discharged him, he was no longer subject to military jurisdiction, and therefore the second court-martial should be voided. The Tenth Circuit quickly dismissed this claim in 1944.

Altmayer v. Sanford, decided by the Court of Appeals for the Fifth Circuit in 1945, raised several issues similar to those in *Romero*. The accused soldier was represented by civilian counsel as well as an officer who was not a lawyer. However, the night before trial, the accused soldier was not permitted to meet with his civilian counsel. A commanding officer who was not assigned as a judge advocate to the trial was permitted to cross examine a female officer who came under his command, even though the Articles of War did not permit this very conduct. The Fifth Circuit concluded that even if error occurred, it did not void the jurisdiction of the court-martial.[15]

In addition to the cases decided by the courts of appeal discussed above, a number of district court decisions that could have risen to the Court did not. In 1943, the District Court for the District of Virginia heard arguments in *McCune v. Kilpatrick*, a case originating from a prospective Army court-martial of a civilian cook assigned to a naval vessel. McCune, the civilian cook, was a World War I Army veteran who belonged to a union and believed that providing food to soldiers on board the vessel violated the terms of his contract which had only required service to sailors and merchant marines. On being ordered by an Army officer to serve meals, McCune left the vessel, which sailed without him. The Army charged McCune for deserting from the vessel after refusing to take orders from Army officers. While awaiting trial, McCune filed a *habeas* writ in federal court. This innocuous court hearing might seem trivial, but the War Department certainly did not view it as such. Judge Advocate General Myron Cramer personally argued to the District Court, with Assistant Attorney General and future justice Tom Clark assisting him.[16]

Judge Charles Wyche, a World War I veteran and Roosevelt nominee recognized that a civilian is not normally amenable to military jurisdiction, although he stated he believed Congress could statutorily authorize such jurisdiction. The Articles of War conferred jurisdiction over civilians in several instances, but McCune argued the Navy possessed jurisdiction rather than the Army, and then only under the merchant seamen statutes and not the Naval

15 *Altmayer v. Sanford*, 148 F.2 161 (CA 5, 1945).

16 *McCune v. Kilpatrick*, 53 F.Supp. 80 (D. Va. 1943).

Articles of War. The War Department's rationale for exercising jurisdiction was that McCune had deserted "the armies in the field." (The Articles of War might permit the Army to exercise court-martial jurisdiction if this term were to be liberally construed to extend to a naval vessel.) Finally, McCune urged that he did not know that he was amenable to the Articles of War when he deserted. Wyche not only found that the Articles of War's jurisdiction included naval vessels, he also determined McCune's insistence that he did not know he was amenable to the Army's jurisdiction meritless. Perhaps to a civilian judge who remembered a basic tenet of law that ignorance does not constitute an offense, McCune's argument would seem frivolous. Yet, commanders were required to read the Articles of War to their soldiers twice a year, and Wyche ignored this point in ruling for the Army. There simply was no evidence that McCune was put on notice of the military's jurisdiction.

Wyche was not alone in upholding Army jurisdiction over civilians in maritime employment, or civilians accompanying the forces. In 1944, the United States District Court for the Eastern District of Ohio decided an issue almost identical to *McCune*. That court found that the "high seas" were not a jurisdictional barrier to the Articles of War. The civilian, Jacob M. Berue, had assaulted an Army officer on board a merchant vessel which carried Army cargo. The Army court-martialed Berue in Casablanca, and after his conviction, transferred him to a military prison in Ohio. Like McCune, Berue unsuccessfully argued that the Army did not possess jurisdiction over him, and his lack of knowledge of the Army's jurisdiction should have prevented a court-martial. He also argued that if the Articles of War extended to him, it also extended to over 200,000 merchantmen without their knowledge. The district court answered this statement on the basis of military necessity: "If that be the result, this court cannot assume the responsibility of attempting to reform the law as it is written. It may be said, however, that since the Congress has by a single act subjected several million men of military age to military law, without their consent, and at $50 per month, it is not unconscionable to subject two hundred thousand more men engaged in the war effort at a much higher wage, to the same law."[17]

There were over 50 federal judicial determinations involving military jurisdiction over civilians, or the fairness of courts-martial and none of these decisions made it to the Court. Of note, future justice Thurgood Marshall unsuccessfully argued two cases before the federal courts, challenging the fairness of the courts-martial of two men assigned to the Tuskegee Airmen. This was not to be his only experience with military law, and in 1953 he would be involved in a critical decision, *Burns v. Wilson*, discussed in Chapter 6. Even in 1946, what the Court was interested in, in terms of military law, only was the extension of military jurisdiction over civilians in territories, as well as war crimes.[18]

17 *In re Berue*, 54 F.Supp. 252 (D. Oh. 1944). Roosevelt appointed Melvin Underwood, a former congressman, to the Ohio District Court.

18 *See Adams v. Ryan*, 136 F.2d 988 (CA 5, 1943).

II: Conscientious Objector and Selective Service Cases

In both world wars the nation relied on conscription or "selective service" to field mass military forces. Although the Constitution is silent on both conscription and conscientious objection to military service, the fact that freedom of religion is a fundamental right meant that some percentage of society would resist compulsory military service for reasons of faith. In World War I, Congress initially only determined that persons belonging to an organized faith whose tenets explicitly included an opposition to all war could be exempted from military service. However, as a result of Frankfurter's lobbying, Baker directed the War Department to expand exemptions for people who interpreted their faith to oppose war.[19]

The nation's experience with conscription in World War I was an important barometer for the judicial approach to conscription in World War II. By November 11, 1918, there were over 450 citizens imprisoned in the military prisons at Fort Leavenworth, Governor's Island, and Alcatraz who were denied conscientious objector exemption from military service, but who also refused to follow conscription orders. This was a small number in comparison to the numbers of citizens that failed or refused to comply with the Selective Service Act of 1917. Of the 24 million citizens who were required to register, three million did not do so. The Selective Service Act created three categories of men who refused to comply with it. Men who failed to register for conscription came to be identified as "slackers." Registering for conscription and being conscripted were two different matters, because it was possible to register and never be ordered to serve. Men who refused to appear before a local induction board became classified as "delinquents." Again, this class of person was not yet necessarily compelled to be inducted into the Army, because they could apply for exemption or conscientious objector status, or be determined as medically or morally unfit. Finally, men who the local boards had ordered to be inducted into the Army, but refused to comply with the order were classified as "deserters" and subject to the Articles of War. The Justice Department prosecuted thousands of "slackers" in federal court and together the Justice and War Departments, along with state and local law enforcement, conducted mass arrests known as "slacker raids."[20]

In the 1918 *Arver v. United States* decision, also known as the *Selective Draft Law Cases*, the Court did not consider the extension of military jurisdiction over civilians. It was, however, the only time where the Court ruled that a national

---

19 Jeremy K. Kessler, "The Administrative Origins of Modern Civil Liberties Law," *Columbia Law Review* (June 2010) 1083.

20 General Enoch Crowder, *Second Report of the Provost Marshal of the United States to the Secretary of War On the Operation of the Selective Service System to December 20, 1918* (DC: GPO, 1919), 199; John Whiteclay Chambers, *The Tyranny of Change* (New Brunswick, NJ: Rutgers University Press, 1992), 240; Thomas J. Knock, *To End All Wars*, 132.

wartime conscription was constitutional. There are three critical aspects to the decision beyond its broad reach. The petitioners in *Arver* had argued that the Constitution's militia clause restricted the federal government from conscripting citizens into the Army, and instead, left to the individual states the responsibility to do so. Such an enlistment scheme had, after all, been in existence in the War of 1812, and more importantly, during the Civil War. The justices dismissed this contention with the simple answer that the Constitution expressly provided to Congress the authority "to raise and support armies." The Court concluded this part of its decision by noting that if only the states had the power to conscript, the Constitution would be nullified. As to the broader constitutionality of drafting individuals into the military, the Court recognized that only one state appellate court had ever decided a challenge to conscription, and this occurred in Pennsylvania in 1863. The justices also pointed to several Confederate state supreme court decisions that enabled conscription. However, those decisions were of limited precedence since they rested on state, rather than federal authority, the fact that decisions from the Confederate states possessed no precedential value, and the Confederacy did not possess an operative supreme court as a court of final review. The second argument advanced by the appellants was that because Congress had exempted theological students, ordained ministers, and religious sects that advocated total aversion to war, the government had created a law favoring particular religious beliefs, thereby violating the Constitution's Establishment Clause. The justices, dispensed with this argument with a short discussion and a notable lack of case law. The oddest aspect of the decision was the Court's holding that the Selective Service Act was constitutionally sound by relying on the fact that other democratic Western nations had conscription. Legal conservatives have historically disfavored the use of foreign or international law in American courts, but the justices made an exception with the challenge to conscription. The inclusion of the conscription practices of other nations were partly Frankfurter's contribution to the decision. He, along with, Major General Enoch Crowder, the Judge Advocate General, and John Henry Wigmore, the dean of Northwestern University's law school, advised Solicitor General John W. Davis to argue that the conscription programs of other nations with representative governments evidenced the constitutionality of conscription.[21]

There are religions which have, as an absolute rule, a prohibition against killing. For example, the Quaker Society of Friends, opposed the taking of another's life under any circumstances. Although religious conscientious objectors were subjected to public scorn, the judiciary and Congress tolerated such movements in part, because of the First Amendment, but also because the leadership of these movements did

21 General Enoch Crowder, *Second Report of the Provost Marshal of the United States to the Secretary of War On the Operation of the Selective Service System to December 20, 1918* (DC: GPO, 1919); Wigmore to Crowder, n.d. October 1917 [JHW-NW/32]; and, Jeremy K. Kessler, "The Administrative Origins of Modern Civil Liberties Law," *Columbia Law Review* (June 2010) 1083.

not attempt to hinder the nation's war efforts. For instance, the Society of Friends' leadership made it clear on December 8, 1941 that it would not obstruct the war. To religious societies opposed to mandatory military service, the judiciary's avoidance of a constitutionally-based determination regarding conscientious objection was the driving reason to continue to raise appeals throughout the World War II and the Cold War. Nonetheless, the Court would adhere to statutory bases for determining conscientious objector appeals, rather than conduct a constitutional analysis.[22]

Most of the conscientious objector decisions that came before the courts were issued after the conclusion of the war, but two important decisions were decided during the conflict. In *Falbo v. United States*, the Court decided that a citizen who claimed conscientious objector status was amenable to the federal criminal laws for a failure to "report for assignment to national service." Falbo argued that because the classification determination of local selective service boards was not subject to judicial review, the Selective Service Act was unconstitutional. The Court's majority countered that the local board classification was only an intermediate step in the induction process into armed service, non-combatant duty, or national service, and that judicial review was possible after final determination of status. Relying on *Martin v. Mott*, the Court found there was no constitutional requirement that individuals be able to challenge their local selective service board determinations in federal court. This decision upheld the Selective Service Act's construct which only permitted a challenge to an induction order after an individual was already in the military or convicted in a civilian court. In his dissent, Murphy argued that "no person should languish in prison," under this construct. It would not be until the height of the Vietnam conflict that the Court would determine that a citizen who was denied conscientious objector status by a board had the right to appeal to the judiciary for a remedy.[23]

Falbo was published on January 3, 1944. On March 27 of the same year, the Court decided *Billings v. Truesdell*. Douglas authored a majority opinion that blocked the military's jurisdictional reach from citizens who were lawfully conscripted, but not fully inducted. As a matter of law, in World War II, induction occurred when an individual swore an oath to serve and received some pay from the military. In this appeal, a civilian named Arthur G. Billings disagreed with his local board's determination of his amenability to military service. He considered himself a conscientious objector, but not wanting to incur criminal liability, he protested administrative determinations of his fitness while meeting all legal requirements of mustering for duty. When, while at Fort Leavenworth, he refused

22 *See*, Diary of Frederick J. Libby, entry for December 8, 1941 [FLP/6].

23 *Falbo v. United States*, 320 U.S. 549 (1944) holding, "a board order to report is no more than a necessary intermediate step in a united and continuous process designed to raise an army speedily and efficiently." Falbo was convicted of knowingly failing to perform a duty required of him under the Selective Training and Service Act of 1940 (the Act), 50 U.S.C.S. app. §§ 301–18. *Martin v. Mott* is found at 12 Wheat 19 (1824).

to take an oath of military service or be fingerprinted, Army officials notified him that he was already inducted into the military. Billings disagreed with the local commander's statement that he was already within military jurisdiction and continued to refuse to take the induction oath. The Army charged him under the Articles of War with refusing to obey lawful orders. After filing a *habeas writ*, both the district and appellate courts determined that despite his refusal to undertake an oath, Billings was lawfully within the military's jurisdiction.[24]

Although the lower courts agreed that Billings had not taken the oath, and recognized the oath was a legal requirement to be amenable to military jurisdiction, they sided with the Army's argument that since the refusal to take the oath took place on a military installation, the Army possessed *de facto* jurisdiction over him. The Court disagreed, but on a statutory rather than Constitutional basis. Indeed, Douglas conceded that originally, the Articles of War would have conferred jurisdiction to the Army over persons such as Billings. But, since Congress had vested "in the civil courts exclusive jurisdiction over all violations of the World War II conscription act prior to actual induction," Douglas determined the lower courts and the War Department were wrong and that Billings' trial should only have occurred in a United States District Court. Frankfurter was not satisfied with the majority opinion and insisted that it clarify that Congress could have clearly statutorily extended the military's jurisdiction to the time a selective service board notified a citizen that he was to report to an induction center. "I take it, however, that we are really concerned in defining legal bounds in the recruiting of an army in what is still a crucial period in the conduct of the war," he urged. In essence, Frankfurter did not want the Court to prevent Congress from expanding the military's jurisdiction if another national emergency arose.[25]

Initially Rutledge drafted a dissent which would have permitted the military to decide when an individual was subject to its jurisdiction, but Frankfurter talked him out of it. "I tell you my difficulty as to your line. I am a little troubled by the conclusion that the military, to wit, the Commander in Chief has the authority to decide when civil jurisdiction ends and when military jurisdiction ends," Frankfurter admonished Rutledge. "A line of such far reaching importance should, if possible, be attributed to Congressional definition and not to the military, even by the Commander in Chief's discretion."[26]

Ironically, Billings' socialist party political affiliations, if known at the time of his induction, would have kept him from military service. In 1944, he ran for the United States Senate as a Socialist Party candidate in Kansas, and he also

24 *Billings v. Truesdell*, 321 U.S. 542 (1944). For a fuller recitation of the facts in Billings' case *see*, *Ex Parte Billings*, 46 F. Supp. 663, 664 (D. Kan, 1943).

25 Frankfurter, Conference Memorandum, February 28 [WR/96].

26 Frankfurter to Rutledge, February 29, 1944 [WR/96]. Rutledge's biographer John M. Ferren, does not mention Rutledge's intended dissent in Billings. Coupled with Rutledge's opinion in Galloway, as discussed below, it appears that until war's end, Rutledge took a conservative view towards the Executive Branch's war power.

taught law at the University of Texas, but espoused a socialist doctrine. In his court hearing, he testified that he believed Japanese and German atrocities were grossly exaggerated and the war was fought at the "behest of bankers, Jews, and the British." After the war, he was removed from his faculty position at the University of Texas Law School, and disappeared into obscurity.[27]

In the midst of the war, the Court of Appeals for the Second Circuit issued *United States v. Kauten* in which that court determined that in order for an individual to be eligible for exemption, the individual had to be opposed to all wars, and not simply the war in which the conscription was undertaken. *Kauten* arose from a conviction for failing to report for duty after a citizen had adopted Gandhi's philosophy of non-violence. The citizen claimed that the war in Europe was being waged by nationalities with historic animosities, and therefore was not a compelling reason to shed American blood. Kauten, interestingly, did not oppose the war against Japan, but the War Department would not promise him which theatre of war he would be sent to. Nonetheless, the appellate court determined, "In the early days of the draft, many thousands of the American people distrusted our foreign policy. If men holding such views had been *ipso facto* classed as conscientious objectors, the military effort might well have been seriously hampered." Kauten appealed to the Supreme Court, but none of the justices voted to grant *certiorari*. Until the Vietnam Conflict, the Second Circuit's reasoning would be embedded in jurisprudence, even if the decision was only occasionally cited.[28]

III: Treason, Espionage, and the Civilian

In World War II there was no effort by the Executive Branch to have the military prosecute United States citizens accused of subverting the nation's war-making abilities. This was a departure from the Civil War practice of prosecuting civilians in military trials who were accused of treason, or in some cases even black-marketing. In World War I, Congress expanded the nation's criminal laws to include a failure to register as an agent of a foreign government and limitations on free speech, but it did not contemplate prosecuting civilians in military trials. World War II was different from World War I in three relevant respects. Prior to the United States entry into the war there were visible pro-German, anti-British, and anti-Jewish political organizations in the United States that embraced Nazi ideals. And, some of the nation's leading citizens such as Henry Ford, Charles Lindbergh and Senators Gerald Nye, Burton K. Wheeler, and Hiram Johnson had espoused isolationism, often with verbal attacks against

27 Frankfurter to Stone, March 11, 1944; on Billings, *see*, e.g. Susan R. Richardson, "Reds, Race, and Research: Homer P. Rainey and the Grand Texas Tradition of Political Interference," in, Roger L. Geiger, *Perspectives on the History of Higher Education* (New Brunswick: NJ, Transaction Publishers, 2005), 145.

28 *United States v. Kauten*, 133 F.2d 703 (CA 2, 1943).

Jews or Great Britain, as well as statements admiring Germany. Their followers had the potential to hamper the nation's war efforts, and a small number of them aided Nazi Germany.

The second difference is that while in World War I the German military killed American citizens prior to the United States entry into the war, the deaths occurred incident to naval operations on the high seas directed against belligerent forces. And while German agents conducted espionage activities in the United States, these were directed at undermining British and French war-making abilities. The United States entry into the war was not caused by an attack on American territory that was intended to bring the United States into the war. Indeed, the Imperial German Government did not want the United States to join Britain, France, Belgium, and Italy. In World War II the United States' entry into the war occurred in response to the Japanese attack on Pearl Harbor, even though American aid to Britain and France predated the attack.

A third difference between the two world wars was the level of German efforts to sabotage United States industries and citizenry's enthusiasm for war. In World War I German agents committed acts of sabotage, even before the United States entry into the war, and their diplomatic corps' role in attempting to stoke an anti-American alliance with Mexico became a national scandal leading to a declaration of war. In World War II, the Germans operated a larger and more sophisticated spy and sabotage network, albeit one which was not ultimately effective.

How the Court approached civil liberties in wartime must be reviewed in the context of how likely the threat from Germany or Japan seemed. This is true regarding decisions involving the use of the military to detain civilians or prosecute belligerents, or simply the criminal prosecution of civilians in United States District Court. Both categories provide a barometer for gauging the federal judiciary's deference to military needs not only during the war, but throughout the following six and a half decades. Some decisions, such as the internment of United States citizens of Japanese descent, remain inexplicable as the Court acquiesced to a racist agenda, while other decisions indicate that the justices did not believe civil and individual rights disappeared in wartime altogether.

In *Viereck v. United States*, Stone authored a decision which reversed a citizen's conviction for failing "to register as in the employ of a foreign agent." Prior to the attack on Pearl Harbor, George Sylvester Viereck had registered with the State Department that he was an American correspondent for a German newspaper, the *Munchner Neueste Nachrichten*, and he had published articles criticizing Great Britain. Viereck was born in Germany, immigrated to the United States as a youth and became a naturalized citizen. During World War I, he edited a German language newspaper and aligned with Senator Robert La Follette to campaign against the United States entering the war. Unlike several other anti-war leaders, including former Congressman Victor Berger, a Socialist Party leader, and labor leader Eugene Debs, the Justice Department did not prosecute Viereck in World War I. But he maintained an affinity for Germany, and even interviewed Adolf Hitler in 1923. In 1938, Congress passed a law requiring registration for this type of activity, and it amended the statute in 1939, and again in 1942.[29]

In addition to his newspaper writing, Viereck formed two public committees which were not merely isolationist, but also anti-French and anti-British. He also authored two speeches for the isolationist senator, Gerald Nye. Although Viereck had registered as an "author and journalist," he did not register as being a foreign agent, and he did not disclose all of his activities in forming the two committees. The Justice Department, rather than the military prosecuted Viereck for his failure to disclose his activities and a federal jury convicted him.[30]

Viereck unsuccessfully challenged his conviction in the Court of Appeals for the District of Columbia. In response to his claim that the law did not put him on notice that he was required to report in specific detail his activities to the government, the appellate court responded, "It is considered a healthy aspect of our legal system that no person who sees a sign, 'Danger, Thin Ice,' is supposed to skate around until he finds the exact breaking point." Future Chief Justice Frederick Vinson authored this line. Viereck also claimed that the federal prosecutor had acted unethically during the case, and while the appellate court agreed the prosecutor had made inflammatory statements, it determined that the prosecution's conduct did not rise to the level of a due process violation.[31]

With the exception of Douglas and Black (and Rutledge and Jackson who did not participate), the Court disagreed with the lower court and overturned Viereck's conviction. There were two aspects of Viereck's trial which troubled the majority. The first was that one of the criminal statutes used to convict Viereck had been applied *ex post facto*. Secondly, and more important, was the conduct of the prosecutor in the trial. Stone cited to *Berger v. United States*, a decision that held that prosecutorial misconduct could be a basis for reversing a conviction, to reinforce the principle that a prosecutor had the duty to refrain from inflaming the passion of the jury. *Berger* arose from a federal prosecution in United States District Court. Stone also added: "At a time when passion and prejudice are heightened by emotions stirred by our participation in a great war, we do not doubt that these remarks addressed to the jury were highly prejudicial, and that they were offensive to the dignity and good order with which all proceedings in court should be conducted." Ironically, in the ensuing decade, the judiciary would not always accord servicemen the same high standards in courts-martial.[32]

29 *See*, "LaFollette Favors repeal of Draft Law," Viereck's American Weekly, Vol. VII, No 1, August 8, 1918, pp. 11; Viereck to LaFollette, August 2, 1917 and other letters are found in Robert Marion LaFollette's papers [RML/I:B-82].

30 *Viereck v. United States*, 318 U.S. 236 (1943).

31 *Viereck v. United States*, 130 F.2d 945 (CA DC 1942).

32 Douglas and Black did not disagree with the majority on the prosecutor's conduct, but believed that it had not risen to the level warranting reversal and a remand. Initially Stone did not cite *Berger*. Instead he cited to a case he authored. But Frankfurter urged him

Viereck was argued on February 1 and 2, 1943, and decided one month later. Almost contemporaneous with that decision was an appeal involving William Schneiderman, a Communist Party of the United States of America (CPUSA) member who immigrated as a three year old to the United States in 1908, and gained citizenship in 1927. In 1932, he ran for the Minnesota governorship as a CPUSA member, at least evidencing his belief that communism could become a dominant political force through the electoral process. But in 1939, the Justice Department determined to strip Schneiderman of his citizenship, despite his having no criminal record or any evidence of seditious activity. The Justice Department's reasoning had to do with Schneiderman's communist activities which predated his naturalization, though this was a specious basis because he had never hidden his activities from the government. Wendell Willkie who had run as the Republican presidential candidate in 1940, against a presidency accused of socialist sympathies, represented Schneiderman.[33]

Murphy, Douglas, Black and Rutledge believed that the government had overreached in its zeal to contain subversive ideologies, though both Douglas and Rutledge concurred instead of joining with majority. Murphy, who wrote the majority decision, noted there was a difference between advocating abstract principles and a call to violent action. Douglas countered that Congress could legislate that a communist affiliation was a basis for denying citizenship but had not done so, and therefore Schneiderman had not broken any laws. Rutledge took a harder line on the rights of citizenship than the other three justices in concluding that denaturalization should only occur if an individual receives citizenship by fraud.[34]

Frankfurter dissented and accused the majority of not wanting to offend the Soviet Union because of a wartime alliance. To Stone he wrote that "political considerations" were "the driving force behind the result of this case," and that if Schneiderman were a "Bundist" the opposite result would have been reached. "For me, the essence of this case is the very simple vindication of the old truth that one cannot serve, in thought or in feeling and action, two independent masters at the same time," he concluded.[35]

In his dissent, Stone recited Karl Marx's admonition that an evolution to communism could only be achieved by violent ends. "The fountain head of

---

to cite to *Berger* and Stone agreed to do so. Frankfurter to Stone, undated [HFS/69]. Stone to the conference, undated [HFS/69].

33 *Schneiderman v. United States*, 320 U.S. 118 (1943).

34 Robert Jackson disqualified himself from the case because he acted as Attorney General during the District Court and Circuit Court of Appeals stages. He wrote to Frank Murphy, "I take no part in this decision. This case was instituted in June of 1939 and tried in December of the year. In January 1940 I became Attorney General of the United States and succeeded to official responsibility for it. That is the sole cause of my disqualification. I desire the reason to be made a matter of record." Jackson to Murphy, undated [RHJ/125].

35 Frankfurter to Stone, May 31, 1943 [HFS/69].

Communist principles, the Communist Manifesto, published by Marx and Engels in 1848, had openly proclaimed that Communist ends could be attained 'only by the forcible overthrow of all existing social conditions," Stone wrote in his draft dissent. "After 1920 these teachings were revived and restated in Party publications which, in the period we are now considering, were used in the Communist educational program that petitioner was directing." While Frankfurter agreed with Stone, he urged him to moderate the dissent with the statement that absent acts and public statements, membership in the CPUSA alone "does not disprove attachment to the Constitution." But Stone did not include this line.[36]

Frankfurter's conduct in this opinion is troubling. He abused Murphy by suggesting that Murphy place into his decision that Stalin deserved to be ranked alongside Thomas Jefferson as a protector of religious freedom. Moreover, Frankfurter's views on denaturalization as well as those on expatriation (the loss of citizenship from persons born in the United States) were hardly consistent in the 1950s, including in four military law cases as to whether military service shielded a person from the denial or loss of citizenship. When, in the 1950s he claimed that the government unfairly treated his friend, the eminent scientist Robert Oppenheimer, by tarring him with communist sympathies, he easily could have taken some of the blame because he urged his fellow justices, and by implication the government, to lower the bar for proving that an individual's alleged ties to communism posed a threat to government's survival.[37]

On June 24, 1944, the Court issued *Hartzel v. United States*, another appeal involving a citizen who distributed anti-war literature. This time the prosecuted citizen was born in the United States and had served honorably in the Army during World War I in France. Unlike in *Viereck*, the United States prosecuted Hartzel under the 1917 Espionage Act for distributing anti-war literature. During his trial, Hartzel admitted that he authored and distributed hundreds of the pamphlets through the United States mails. One of his pamphlets read "[Roosevelt] reproduces within his body our internal breakdown; he is in fact a degenerate who now seeks ways of having us cure him of his ailment … For we now follow, not a little child, but a man with a child's disease." Hartzel had mailed his pamphlets to the United States Army Air Forces chief of staff, as well as a number of other military organizations, which ought to have raised a question as to whether he suffered from delusion.

Joined by Stone, Black, and Rutledge, Murphy authored the majority decision reversing the conviction. Owen Roberts concurred, arguing that there was not enough evidence to sustain the conviction. Douglas sided with Frankfurter, Jackson, and Reed in dissenting. Given Douglas' stated affinity for Roosevelt, it is difficult to not conclude that Hartzel's attack on the president offended him.[38]

---

36 Frankfurter to Stone, June 13, 1943 [HFS/69].

37 Frankfurter to Murphy, June 2, 1943 [RHJ/125].

38 *Hartzel v. United States*, 322 U.S. 680 (1944).

In *Cramer v. United States*, the Court overturned a treason conviction of a naturalized citizen. Treason is a different offense than any crime found in United States law because it is the only offense specifically enumerated in the Constitution. The decision was related to *Ex parte Quirin* in which several German saboteurs were prosecuted in a military trial and executed by the War Department. In 1942, Federal Bureau of Investigations agents observed Anthony Cramer meeting with Walter Thiel, a German national living in the United States, and discovered Cramer had safeguarded Thiel's money. Cramer was convicted in a trial and sentenced to 45 years imprisonment and a $10,000 fine. He was born in Germany in 1900 and he and Thiel had worked together in Detroit in 1929 and remained friends. In 1936, the two men became business partners in a Florida restaurant, but in early 1941, Thiel returned to Germany while Cramer remained in the United States. Both men were also members of a pro-German organization. When Thiel returned, he asked Cramer to safeguard a large amount of money, which Cramer willingly did. Cramer admitted to an FBI agent that he believed Thiel had returned to the United States by submarine to spread pro-German propaganda. The Court of Appeals for the Second Circuit found that Cramer's acceptance of money and his knowledge of Thiel was enough to sustain a conviction for treason. The majority of the justices, however, disagreed.[39]

The basis of the reversal had to do with the quantum of evidence required to prove treason. Cramer had knowingly met with two German saboteurs and provided them money, but it was unclear as to why he did so or what the money would be used for. To the majority, treason had to be proven based on an overt act and the act itself had to be done with the intent of being treasonous. This standard eliminated the possibility of a citizen being convicted after being unknowingly duped by a foreign agent or another treasonous citizen. But it would also bar a conviction for knowingly aiding a foreign agent or treasonous citizen without knowing what the intentions of the agent or treasonous citizen were. Implicit in this reasoning was that Congress could pass a law that made it a criminal offense to aid a foreign agent, so long as the criminal offense was not called treason with its attendant possibility of capital punishment. For instance, in a later contentious case involving two citizens accused of transferring classified nuclear information to Soviet agents, the citizens were prosecuted under the Atomic Energy Act and not under the Constitution. They were convicted and sentenced to death nonetheless, though not for treason.[40]

Frankfurter did not conclude that the majority had set too high a standard to prove treason, although he initially was reluctant to decide the case on Constitutional grounds. "I myself am not troubled by the fear that a traitor could not be convicted of treason in a case like Cramer," he argued to Jackson. "In

39 *Cramer v. United States*, 137 F.2d 888 (CA 2, 1943). The appellate court held "Two elements are essential to a conviction for treason: a treasonable intent and an overt act in manifestation of that intent."

40 *Cramer v. United States*, 325 U.S. 1 (1945).

the first place that assumes he is a traitor, and in the second place it disregards the readiness of the Constitution to let some traitors escape in order to make it more difficult to manufacture evidence against people who are not traitors." While Cramer was not *per se* a military law case, Frankfurter worried that if Cramer's conviction was sustained, servicemen could be prosecuted for treason after criticizing military leaders.[41]

Somewhat surprisingly, Douglas and Black dissented. Black believed that Cramer had received a fair trial. When Stone approached him to write for the majority, Black answered, "if a conviction is not be sustained on the evidence produced here, I doubt if there could be many convictions for treason unless American citizens were actually found in the Army of the enemy." Douglas closed his dissent with a caustic comment: "Such a result makes the way easy for the traitor, does violence to the Constitution and makes justice truly blind." Ironically, it was arguably the restrictive holding in *Cramer* that prevented a large volume of treason trials during the anti-communist movement's heyday in the 1950s, a position Douglas would favor. In his *Almanac of Liberty*, published in 1954, Douglas wrote *Cramer* established that there must be more than evidence of "an intent to betray; he must translate the intent into action. Each act must have two witnesses. And the act must confer some actual tangible benefit on the enemy. So ruled the Court in 1944 ... The construction given was so restrictive that some thought no prosecutor would thereafter chance an indictment under the head of treason." However, Douglas did not highlight his earlier dissent.[42]

IV: The Treatment of Captured "Unprivileged" Combatants *Ex parte Quirin*

Perhaps the most important military law decision during the war involved a military trial that took place six months after the attack on Pearl Harbor. The decision is significant, partly because the Court suggested, without directly holding, that enemy combatants might be entitled to some Constitutional protections in wartime. The Court did not, in its unanimous opinion, delineate what those protections were, and left this question open. The Court issued a short *per curiam* decision on July 31, 1942, two days after oral arguments, but then supplemented the *per curiam* with a lengthier decision on October 29, 1942.

During the six months following December 7, 1941, the Japanese military had driven the United States forces from the Philippine Islands, Guam, Wake and several other islands held by the United States. The territories had been under American control since 1898. Japan's military forces also landed in the Aleutian Islands, and across the Pacific had pushed the Chinese military under Chiang Kai-shek and Mao Tse Tung into a long retreat and, British military and colonial

41 Frankfurter to Jackson, March 24, 1944 [RJ/131].

42 Black to Stone, March 25, 1944, [HLB/272], also [HFS/73]; William O. Douglas, Almanac of Liberty, 347. Douglas did not note that he was a dissenting justice in the case.

governments from Burma, Malaya, Thailand, and Singapore had surrendered. The Japanese occupied French Vietnam and Dutch Indonesia, and stood ready to invade Australia and India. Fears that the Japanese Navy would return to invade Hawaii and continue an offensive in Alaska were also reasonable, since their military occupied the outer Aleutian Islands. The Japanese military operated with efficiency and barbarity. The only apparent glimmer of hope that the Japanese advance might be stemmed occurred on June 7, 1942 when an outnumbered United States Navy inflicted the loss of four aircraft carriers on the Japanese Navy at a Battle of Midway.[43]

The situation for the allies against Germany and Italy was little better. By July, 1942, no sizeable American forces had yet to engage the Axis powers in the Atlantic theatre. Commanded by Erwin Rommel, the German *Afrika Korps* and their Italian allies had forced the British across North Africa almost to the Suez Canal, an essential lifeline for the British Empire. German submarines sank allied shipping at alarming rates. And, in the Soviet Union, Axis forces renewed their offensive during the spring of 1942, conquering most of the European geography in that country. Soviet losses of life numbered in the millions, though that country ultimately proved enormously resilient.[44]

In addition to the bleak outlook for the United States' fielded military forces, fears of espionage, sabotage, and "an enemy from within" surfaced. By the time of Pearl Harbor, the German High Command had, in fact, developed extensive plans to destroy American industrial capacity including aluminum milling operations essential to aircraft production, hydro-electric facilities and railway lines. Although just coming out of the economic depression which began in 1929, the United States still possessed the greatest industrial capability in the world, and this was the aspect German military leaders feared most about the United States' entry into the war. An American-supplied Soviet military, coupled with millions of Americans in uniform could be devastating to Nazi Germany. In the spring of 1942, two American citizens who returned to Germany prior to the war and six German nationals were conveyed across the Atlantic in German submarines to New York and Florida with plans to destroy war industries as part of High Command's strategy.[45]

After George Dasch, one of the saboteurs who had once served in the United States Army, turned himself in to the Federal Bureau of Investigation, federal agents captured the remaining seven men before they could destroy anything. Not since the Civil War had the question of what to do with spies and saboteurs

43 On Midway, *see, e.g.*, Ronald Spector, *Eagle Against the Sun: The American War With Japan* (New York: Vintage Press, 1985), 167–78.

44 Richard T. Lee and Richard F. Starr, *Soviet Military Policy Since World War II*, (San Francisco: Stanford University Press, 1983) 24–5.

45 Louis Fisher, *Nazi Saboteurs on Trial* (Lawrence, KS: Kansas University Press, 2003), 1–9; Pierce O'Donnell, *In Time of War: Hitler's Terrorist Attack on America* (New York: The New Press, 2009), 1–10.

come before the Supreme Court. In World War I, the Army captured and court-martialed a German officer named Lothar Witzke who had travelled under a false name and conducted espionage operations. However, Witzke did not appeal to the judiciary and President Wilson commuted his death sentence to life. In 1921 President Harding released Witzke to return to Germany. There was, and is, a fundamental difference between prisoners of war who are accorded specific international law rights, and unprivileged combatants such as spies and saboteurs. Roosevelt, Attorney General Biddle, and Stimson wanted the men prosecuted in a military trial, although many of the ranking officials in government concluded that the captured Germans could be summarily executed without a trial.[46]

In an unusual meeting which likely would not be considered judicially ethical today, Frankfurter advised Stimson to convene a military tribunal staffed with military officers sitting in judgment of the accused German saboteurs. This meeting occurred shortly after the saboteurs were taken into custody. Frankfurter wanted the War Department to conduct a trial akin to the military commission trials of the Lincoln assassin conspirators or Captain Henry Wirz, the Confederate commandant of Andersonville Prison in 1865. Even more unusual was a meeting between Hugo Black and Owen Roberts, Attorney General Biddle, Major General Myron Cramer, the Army's Judge Advocate General, and the saboteurs' two defense counsel which occurred after the military commission began.[47]

Frankfurter initiated this meeting as well. The Army had appointed Colonel Kenneth Royall and Colonel Cassius M. Dowell, a career Army officer, to defend the captured Germans. There should, in hindsight, be little question that Royall and Dowell defended their clients to the best of their abilities, but whether they sincerely hoped for the Court to provide a reversal based on jurisdiction is another matter. Stone initially sought to recuse himself because his son, a judge advocate, had assisted the defense during the military commission, but Frankfurter talked him out of doing so after the attorney general represented that all parties to the case urged Stone to participate. Murphy recused himself because his son was also involved in the proceedings.[48]

At first glance, *Quirin* shows that the justices were unified in their approach to Roosevelt's decision to have the War Department, rather than the Justice Department, prosecute the case. In part the unity appears because the Court issued a *per curiam* decision the day after oral argument, holding the military commission was lawfully constituted and had jurisdiction over the defendants. Three months later, after the saboteurs had been executed, the Court issued a unanimous full opinion. Though Stone authored *Quirin*, Frankfurter was its primary architect. By the time of the unusual meeting, Frankfurter's mind had already been made up that the Executive Branch had the authority to prosecute foreign spies in military

46 Urofsky, *Division and Discord*, 60; Fisher, *Nazi Saboteurs on Trial*, 1–9.

47 Urofsky, *Division and Discord*, 61.

48 Sidney Fine, *Frank Murphy*, The Washington Years, 404.

courts, even when caught on United States soil, and the other justices willingly went along with him, though Douglas and Black tempered his zeal.[49]

The rapidity with which the Court issued its decision belied the fact that Frankfurter wanted the decision to clearly state that summary execution (execution without trial) was permissible under the law of war but a beneficent president permitted a trial. Black and Douglas opposed the inclusion of this statement. In a lengthy memorandum titled "Frankfurter's' soliloquy" that Black and Douglas found obnoxious, Frankfurter used phrases towards the German saboteurs such as "curs," who "should be hung." The "soliloquy," in retrospect, was reminiscent of the very language of the prosecutor in *Viereck* that troubled Stone.[50]

While Frankfurter was instrumental in the ultimate wording of the decision, Black took a prominent role in ensuring *Quirin* would not narrow *Milligan*. He accepted that Congress could "doubtless declare all violations of the laws of war to be crimes against the United States," but insisted that *Milligan* remain untouched by declaring that the saboteurs were alien combatants, and therefore subject to military tribunals, unlike in *Milligan* where the defendants were United States citizens. To fail to do so would, "subject every person in the United States to trial by military tribunals for every violation of every rule of war which has been or may hereafter be adopted between nations among themselves, might go far to destroy the protections declared by the *Milligan* case." Though one of the *Quirin* saboteurs, Herbert Hans Haupt, was a naturalized United States citizen, the Court held that status was irrelevant because of his actions as an enemy belligerent, thus distinguishing him from *Milligan*.[51]

Douglas, who would later assert that it was unfortunate the Court took the case, nevertheless agreed with the Court's consensus that the President possessed the constitutional authority to prosecute foreign saboteurs captured on American soil in a military trial. When Attorney General Biddle told the Court the Army was going to execute the saboteurs regardless of the justices' decision, Douglas, Black, Murphy and Frankfurter took it as a blatant affront to the Court. Douglas went further and later used the episode to argue that the Pentagon's leaders did not believe the military was required to conform to the nation's law. On the other hand, Biddle retracted his comment.[52]

Douglas vehemently disagreed with Frankfurter on summary execution, insisting that no reference to it be made in the published decision, and that the published decision stress the rule of law. He hinted to Stone that he would author

49 *Ibid.*

50 [the "Soliloquy" is found in [WOD/77]; *See*, David G. Glazier, *The Laws of War: Past, Present, and Future: Article: Precedents Lost: The Neglected History of the Military Commission*, 46 *Virginia Journal of International Law*, 5, 79–80 (2005); also Sidney Fine, Frank Murphy: The Washington Years, 404.

51 Black to Stone, October 2, 1942 [HFS/269].

52 William O. Douglas, *The Court Years* (New York: Random House, 1980), 138–9.

a concurring opinion, and the chief justice who wanted to show unanimity, took Douglas' threat to heart.[53]

As a result of Douglas' insistence, the opinion contains the sentence, "Unlawful combatants are likewise subject to capture and detention, but in addition they are subject to trial and punishment by military tribunals for acts which render their belligerency unlawful" without any reference to summary execution. In influencing the published decision, Douglas upheld Roosevelt's policy toward captured unlawful combatants without expanding the president's authority beyond what was challenged, or creating an unnecessary controversy with the inclusion of language on the right to summarily execute saboteurs.

Quirin has come under intense criticism, particularly in the legal academy after the September 11, 2001. But even before George W. Bush's presidency, Justice Antonin Scalia called *Quirin*, "not the Court's finest hour," and believed the decision undermined *Milligan*. Yale Professor Bruce Ackerman argued that the decision provides "the slam dunk argument for apologists of presidential power." Ackerman's characterization of empowering Executive Branch proponents is fair. On the other hand, his contention that the justices feared that Roosevelt would disregard their decision if they failed to uphold the Executive Branch's authority is not supported by the available historic record. *Quirin* does not stretch to United States citizens, and after September 11, 2001, scholars and Bush Administration lawyers who argued that it does missed the fundamental limitation of the decision.[54]

V: The Rights of Veterans during Wartime

Sandwiched between *Quirin* and the end of the war is a now mostly forgotten decision, *Galloway v. United States*, in which the Court determined that the Seventh Amendment's right to a full jury trial did not apply to suits against the federal government, and existed only at the government's discretion. Although the constitutional dimension of the decision alone marks the case as a bulwark against private citizen suits in jury trials against government agencies, that the

---

53 Douglas' memorandum to Stone is as follows:

> I would like to *see* the sentence which I have underlined on pg. 6 omitted. That sentence is susceptible of the interpretation that it would have been lawful for the Executive to have disposed of the petitioners summarily without a trial by a tribunal. That may be true, although if I had to vote today, I would be inclined to vote the other way. The proposition however, is not before us and I think that the omission of that sentence would not detract from the force and substance or the paragraph at the bottom of pg 6.

WOD to Chief Justice Stone, October 17, 1942 [WOD/77].

54 Bruce Ackerman, *Before the Next Attack: Preserving Civil Liberties in an Age of Terrorism* (New Haven: Yale University Press, 2006), 23; 111–12; James Staab, *The Political Thought of Justice Antonin Scalia: A Hamiltonian on the Supreme Court* (Lanham, MD: Rowman and Littlefield, 2006).

decision involved a veteran is of added importance. *Galloway* had both symbolic and philosophical significance for the Court's future approach to the rights of service-members and the nation's broader military law.

Galloway arose as a result of a federal judge directing a verdict before the jury could decide on the ultimate contested issue in a suit involving a World War I veteran seeking payment through the government's war risk insurance program. In the terms of the day, Galloway was "a moron" suffering from psychosis. His guardian's contention was that his mental state occurred as a result of his frontline service in a horrific war, and in truth, Galloway was only one of thousands who suffered from post-war psychological infirmities.[55]

The Seventh Amendment guarantees the right to a jury trial in federal civil trials where the issue in dispute exceeds 20 dollars. All of the justices agreed that Congress could deny jury trials in lawsuits against the federal government based on sovereign immunity, but as in the case of many of the Court's decisions, *Galloway* was met by a divided Court on the question of whether directed verdicts were acceptable once Congress granted a statutory right to a jury trial when suing the federal government. Although the constitutionality of directed verdicts in civil suits where the government was a party had been decided affirmatively in 1850, Black believed that when Congress granted a citizen an avenue to sue the United States in a jury trial, it had to follow the Bill of Rights, and a directed verdict was antithetical to the right to a jury trial. More so, he argued that veterans as a class of citizen should receive extra protection from the government. (Interestingly, the veteran did not raise this issue on appeal.) The majority of the Court disagreed with Black on this point. In conference, Frankfurter, in speaking for the majority, reasoned that a directed verdict negated the potential for repeated trials. In turn, Black argued that while repeated trials are an evil, "the basic premise of the Seventh Amendment is that usurpation of a jury's function by a judge is a far greater evil." Stone assigned Rutledge, the Court's newest justice, to write the majority decision on the day following Black's memorandum, but Stone did not consider the case as significant as Black did, until he saw Rutledge's draft opinion.[56]

Rutledge posited that in order to prevent injustices, the federal judiciary's authority to direct verdicts and issue summary judgments was little different than ruling on the admissibility of evidence or instructing juries on a host of matters. Rutledge also initially opined that not only did the Seventh Amendment not apply to veterans seeking compensation from the government even in jury trials, but Congress did not, in "permitting suits on War Risk Insurance policies, explicitly make disputes triable by jury." In other words, Rutledge was willing to have the nation's veterans, soon to number almost 20 million citizens, excluded from the Seventh Amendment in suits against the government. Of the justices in the majority, only Jackson agreed with this point. On March 29, 1943 he

55 *Galloway v. United States*, 319 U.S. 372 (1943).

56 Black to Rutledge, April13, 1943 [WR/92].

complimented Rutledge for writing "in grand style without sacrifice of accuracy and precision without being dull."[57]

On April 28, Stone let Rutledge know his disagreement with Rutledge's position on the Seventh Amendment's application to citizens. "It is quite true that Congress can dispense with a jury trial in suits brought against the United States, but when it authorizes a suit with a jury trial, I cannot say that it does not require the kind of trial of which the Constitution speaks," Stone admonished. The Chief Justice added that he was convinced Galloway had received a fair jury trial within the meaning of the Seventh Amendment, but unless Rutledge removed the offending contention, he would concur. Frankfurter, though he endorsed Rutledge's position on the authority of judges, called Rutledge's Seventh Amendment commentary a "fiction without warrant," and threatened to dissent as well. But, it was Reed who brought the point home to Rutledge on the broader issue of whether the Bill of Rights applied to veterans. "Like some of your other brethren, I am disturbed by the Section III of your opinion," Reed began, "I think that Congress intended for veterans to have the kind of jury trial that was given other litigants with all the protections of the Seventh Amendment." Based on the three justices' criticisms, Rutledge removed his position on veterans from the opinion, which brought Frankfurter to compliment him on "killing [Black's dissent] dead."[58]

Black countered the majority opinion by highlighting the stressors of combat, then commonly known as "shell shock," and bringing attention to the fact that some servicemen never recovered. He assigned his clerk, John Paul Frank, later a Yale professor and lifetime friend, to delve into the issue of insanity in World War I veterans. Frank informed Black that "persons suffering from the shock of actual conflict on the battlefront may suffer from an incurable affliction, such as [Galloway's]." Moreover, Frank pointed out that many veterans in a similar state were unable to engage in continuous employment. Black incorporated these facts into his second draft dissent. As for Black's final draft dissent, Murphy called it "a magnificent opinion. It preaches the gospel as I know and understand it." Douglas joined Black with the simple, "I agree."[59]

Although the drafts were in final form by May 19, Black had another matter for Rutledge to consider. Rutledge's opinion suggested that Galloway's attorney had acted unethically. This troubled Black who wrote to Rutledge, "I know nothing whatever about this soldier's lawyer. Your opinion, however, seems to me to be a plain charge that he has willfully suppressed testimony—action which is universally considered reprehensible … my own belief is that if anyone

57 Wiley Rutledge, Draft Opinion, March 29, 1943 [WR/42]; Jackson to Rutledge, March 29, 1943 [WR/42].

58 Stone to Rutledge, April 28, 1943; Frankfurter to Rutledge, April 27, 1943; Reed to Rutledge April 28, 1943; Frankfurter to Rutledge n.d.

59 Black to John P. Frank, undated, 1942 [Frank Papers (JPFP) 1]; Murphy to Black, April 27, 1943; Douglas to Black, April 29, 1943 [HLB/269].

did this, it was the government." In a short time, Rutledge would come over to Black's position that all too often the government was in error in its treatment of service members.[60]

VII: Internment of Citizens

The most troubling legacy of the Stone Court is its three decisions upholding the detention of United States citizens of Japanese descent. Although the fundamental issue in each of the Court's three decisions went to the heart of Due Process, the two secondary issues of judicial deference to claims of military necessity and as to how whether the military could be used to sequester citizens for any reason were implicated as well.

On February 19, 1942, Roosevelt issued Executive Order 9066 which empowered the Secretary of War and the commanding general of the western defenses to declare "military areas" from "which any or all persons may be excluded." Although the order did not mention any specific race or ethnicity, it was directed at persons of Japanese descent. Long discriminated against, Japanese Americans residing in the United States were forced into relocation camps in the western United States. Lieutenant General John DeWitt, the commanding general of the western defenses and a friend of Hugo Black's testified to Congress that the Japanese American population posed a threat to the nation's security. He was not alone in urging the existence of an internal threat. However, the information the War and Naval Departments provided to Roosevelt before issuing the Executive Order was simply not based on any real widespread threat. Future Chief Justice Earl Warren, then California's attorney general, supported the detention program, as did a large number of other politicians and government officers with one exception. J. Edgar Hoover, the Federal Bureau of Investigation director opposed what he considered to be a violation of civil liberties. With over 100,000 wholly innocent citizens taken from their property and sent into one of 10 concentration camps, it was likely inevitable that the federal judiciary would consider the order's constitutionality.

In *Hirabayashi v. United States*, the Court upheld the military's authority to impose a curfew, although it recognized that the curfew targeted only one race of individuals. Gordon Hirabayashi had been arrested for failing to report to the relocation center and violating the curfew. The Court determined that however "odious to a free people" racism was, the curfew was relevant to the nation's safety. Murphy, Douglas, and Rutledge concurred, but their concurrences read more like dissents. Douglas insisted that a citizen should at least have the opportunity to prove their loyalty. He worried that unbridled judicial deference to the military would permit a military commander who "knows there are only 10% of the group who are disloyal [to] nevertheless may hold the entire group in confinement for

60 Black to Rutledge, May 19, 1943 [WR/92].

the duration without any opportunity on the part of the 90% to prove their loyalty." This infuriated Frankfurter who complained to Stone the justices as acting "as though they were engaged in a rivalry grocery business," rather than collaborators and that Douglas would invite "a thousand habeas corpus suits in the district courts." According to Murphy's biographer, Murphy acquiesced to Frankfurter in writing a concurrence instead of a dissent because Frankfurter pushed for unity in wartime. Murphy was clearly worried about the Court's acceptance of military necessity. In his draft dissent, he penned that the majority required the government to only "prove reasonable grounds" for the exclusion and internment of citizens. He believed that the United States' treatment of Japanese Americans was too similar to the Nazi's treatment of European Jews to ignore. In response, Reed argued to Murphy, "you cannot wait for an invasion to see if loyalty triumphs."[61]

In *Korematsu v. United States*, the Court upheld the arrest of an individual for violating the exclusion order, but sidestepped the issue of detention. This time Roberts, Jackson, and Murphy dissented. Roberts argued that the refusal to go to a concentration camp could hardly constitute a crime, and Murphy called the relocation a legalization of racism. Murphy explained his dissent to Judge Jerome Frank on the Court of Appeals for the Second Circuit with the comment that he "want[ed] to work and write in defense of human liberty and decency," with the implication that military necessity could not be a strong enough reason to use race as a basis for denying citizens constitutional rights. Douglas wrote a concurring opinion, which initially was captioned as a dissent, allowing that the exclusion, and even the evacuation were lawful, but then opining the concentration camps were unconstitutional. At Frankfurter's and Black's forceful request, Douglas elected not to publish his concurrence.[62]

Finally, in *Ex Parte Endo*, decided the same day as *Korematsu*, the Court unanimously held the military could not detain a citizen who was not suspected of a crime and who the government conceded was loyal, but the justices left untouched the military's ability to exclude and detain citizens when a loyalty determination had not been made.

While not directly related to "military law" if the term "military law" is narrowly defined, the three cases had an impact nonetheless for several reasons. Although the relocation program was an essentially civilian run program, it utilized service members and it occurred at the behest of the War and Naval

61 Douglas to Stone, May 31, 1953 [HFS/68]; Frankfurter to Stone, June 4, 1943 [HFS/68]. In this same letter, Frankfurter claimed that Black had made the comment: "if he were the commanding general, he would not allow these men [the citizens of Japanese descent] to go back even if the Court should establish their loyalty"; Murphy, draft dissent in *Hirabayashi v. United States*, first circulation [FM-UMI/127]; Sidney Fine, *Frank Murphy: The Washington Years*, 442–3; John D. Fasset, *New Deal Justice: The Life of Stanley Reed of Kentucky* (New York: Vantage, 1980), 337.

62 William O. Douglas, *The Court Years* (New York: Random House, 1980), 280; Murphy to Frank, January 12, 1945 [FM-UMI/129].

Departments. As a result, civil-military relations were implicated in the decision. While Douglas later expressed regret and shame for his decisions to uphold the programs, he was almost alone in this. Solicitor General Charles Fahy, who argued the cases and later became a judge on the Court of Appeals for the District of Columbia, admitted error in 1962 to Francis Biddle, Roosevelt's Attorney General: "I thought the evacuation unnecessary and unwise but did think it would be upheld as constitutional if the military decided it was necessary." These cases raise another concern, discovered only later, about the Court's reliance on the military's representations. Fahy's later feigned deference to military necessity belied his role in the case, as he had deliberately suppressed military and FBI reports concluding Japanese-Americans were not a security risk and hid them from the Court.[63]

Fahy's private admission typifies light to how far the Court would defer to military necessity during wartime. The question of judicial review of military authority and actions was a central part of Frankfurter's concurrence and Jackson's dissent. Harkening to President Lincoln's rhetorical question of decades earlier "[a]re all the laws, but one, to go unexecuted, and the government itself go to pieces," Jackson averred that the *success* of military actions might be more important than their *legality*, and that the armed services, which "must protect a society, not merely its Constitution," might engage in measures that would not be within the limits of the law that controls civil authority during peace. Jackson believed military actions could be "permissible" without being constitutional, but that the Supreme Court should not sanction the military's action. Frankfurter was troubled by this proposition, accusing Jackson of "dialectic subtleties" inconsistent with the understanding of the Framers, and retorting in his concurrence that "the provisions of the Constitution which confer on the Congress and the President powers to enable this country to wage war are as much part of the Constitution as provisions looking to a nation at peace." This dispute thus raised the critical question of whether the military was required to act within the boundaries of the Constitution and whether the Court should opine on military action or simply defer.[64]

Jackson was fundamentally concerned that the majority's "construction of the due process clause" that allowed the *Korematsu* exclusion order was a "far more subtle blow to liberty than the promulgation of the order itself," because "a military order, however unconstitutional, is not apt to last longer than the military emergency," while judicial sanction would last indefinitely. In the context of due process, this concern was somewhat allayed after the

63 Fahy to Biddle, December 12, 1962 [Fahy/3]; David G. Savage, *U.S. Official Cites Misconduct in Japanese American Internment Cases*, Los Angeles Times, May 24, 2011 (citing statements by then Acting Solicitor General Neal Katyal that Fahy failed in his duty of candor to the Court).

64 *Korematsu v. United States*, 323 U.S. 214, 243–6 (1944) (Jackson, J., dissenting); *Ibid.* at 224 (Frankfurter, J., concurring).

war's end, when the Court looked through the lens of hindsight and a majority of justices determined that martial law, even in the territorial areas controlled by the military, should not go so far as to deny citizens an avenue for redress in federal court. On the other hand, the Court would uphold the military's authority to prosecute foreigners in American military war crimes trials.[65]

Also, the decision brought the American Civil Liberties Union into military law jurisprudence. Customarily, the ACLU had been aloof to courts-martial, and had only taken a minor role in conscientious objector cases. However, Osmond K. Fraenkel and Whitney North Seymour, two of the ACLU's leading attorneys, represented Koremastu and Endo. The ACLU approached both appeals, not only as a matter of civil rights, but also as an opportunity to argue to the judiciary that the Executive Branch's assertion of authority had to be curbed.[66]

VIII: Conclusion

The Court's wartime decisions were to have a lasting impact on the nation's military law through the end of the twentieth century and into the current military campaigns in Iraq, Afghanistan and the "War on Terrorism." Indeed, the legal watershed of World War II will likely last far into the future in several respects. As long as the military is given responsibility for detaining and prosecuting foreign persons accused of war crimes, *Quirin*, along with *In re Yamashita*, analyzed in the next chapter, will provide some parameters as to future military trials, particularly regarding how far the judiciary may review the Executive Branch's conduct, absent legislation. It is unlikely that the internment of whole classes of citizens will ever be repeated. The "Civil Rights Revolution" that occurred during Earl Warren's tenure in Court, should relegate calls to strip persons of their freedom because of their religion or ethnicity to pundits on the airwaves.

The Court's conscription and conscientious objection jurisprudence established a common denominator for later decisions, but throughout the history of twentieth-century conscription, that denominator informed the lower courts to avoid constitutional questions and rest decisions on statutory interpretation. This is remarkable since freedom of religion is a First Amendment matter, and deference to legislation regarding religion is mostly unique to the military law. On the other hand, the Stone Court's protection of free speech in wartime was an important departure from what had occurred during the Civil War. Arguably, decisions such as *Viereck*, *Schneiderman*, *Hartzel*, and *Cramer*,

65 *Ibid.* at 245–6 (Jackson, J., dissenting).

66 Fraenkel, diary entries for May 11, 1942 and June 20, 1942 respectively in which he notes the ACLU's concern with the Executive Branch's assertion of power [OF-SGM/1]. *See also* John R. Vile, *Great American Lawyers* (Santa Barbara CA: ABC-CLIO, 2001), 295–6.

enabled citizens to more freely protest the government's actions in wartime, including challenging the legality of the nation's military involvement in foreign wars. Both the Executive Branch and Congress would soon after the war create "loyalty programs" and enact laws to curb what the Court enabled, in an effort to prevent communist infiltration into the government and defense industries. Ultimately, the judiciary would force a balance between government action and the rights of citizens, but this would take more than two decades to occur.

The Court's wartime jurisprudence did not end with the surrender of Japan and Germany. The justices would soon expand on the Court's wartime jurisprudence during Stone's last term as chief justice, and its decisions issued during that term would prove enormously influential in American military and national defense policies to the present.

Chapter 4

1946 the Last Year of the Stone Court: The Aftermath of a Total War and the Eve of the Cold War

Shortly after Germany's surrender, President Harry S. Truman nominated Ohio Republican Senator Harold Hitz Burton to replace Owen Roberts on the Court. Neither the Army's enforcement of military justice, nor the needs of a disciplined fighting force, was alien to Burton. He served in the front-lines during World War I, and fought in the battles of Ypres-Lys and St. Mihiel. By the war's conclusion, Burton had earned the Belgian Croix de Guerre and the Army's Silver Star. At Ypres-Lys, while training with the French Army, he led an isolated and leaderless French company against a German position. At St. Mihiel, he was assigned as a forward artillery observer and held his position under intense German machine-gun fire and chlorine gas clouds. Like Frank Murphy, Burton also witnessed courts-martial proceedings during that conflict, from which he concluded the military's criminal justice system did not adhere to the same due process standards as federal criminal courts.[1]

Before the war, Burton attended Harvard's law school and then joined an Ohio law firm. Following the declaration of war on Germany, he enlisted in the National Guard. In August 1917, he was commissioned second lieutenant, and in December of that year, after arriving in France, he was promoted to captain and placed in charge of an infantry company under French instruction. When the war ended, he returned to Ohio to pursue a political career. He was elected to the state legislature in 1929, as mayor of Cleveland in 1935, and senator in 1941.[2]

1 For Burton's wartime service, *see*, Harold Hitz Burton, *600 Days Service: A History of the 361st Infantry Regiment of the United States Army* (Portland OR: James Kearns & Abbot Co., 1921), 58–91. While Burton was an editor-author of the book, there is little about him in it. He ensured that the book was sent free of charge to the soldiers who served in the regiment as well as the surviving parents or spouses of soldiers killed during the war.

2 Documents relating to the General Court Martial of 1st Lt. James Thompson of Toronto Ohio, in Papers of Harold Hitz Burton [HHB/27]. Burton wrote to Lt. Col Fletcher Andrews, the presiding officer of a reviewing panel, "Lt Thompson holds the Air Medal with five clusters, the Distinguished Flying Cross with one cluster, and a Presidential Unit Citation with one cluster. He did twenty-eight missions over enemy territory considered among the toughest in the entire campaign and he has one German fighter to his credit."

During World War II, Burton was actively involved in military affairs, serving on Senator Truman's committee investigating war profiteering and waste in government contracting. Burton also inspected air bases in North Africa and Italy. Although Burton was a Republican, Truman respected his abilities and ultimately nominated him to the Court in late 1945 to replace Roberts.[3]

In the closing days of the Second World War, Senator Burton assisted James Thompson, an Army Air Forces first lieutenant to overturn a court-martial conviction. Lieutenant Thompson's court-martial was commonplace during World War II. He was accused of an offense, charged, and tried, all within a one month period. But he was also a highly decorated bombardier in the European Theatre. He had flown in 28 missions in the Eighth Air Force during the early air war over Germany, including three missions in a lead formation over Berlin, meaning he had accomplished the nearly impossible task of completing a 25-mission tour in an exceedingly dangerous air campaign. His aircraft crash-landed in Britain four times, but this did not sway him from seeking further service and he volunteered to serve a second tour of duty. Although not permitted to do so because he had been reassigned as a forward instructor, he nevertheless flew several "special missions." During the period Thompson flew, bomber crews traversed European airspace with little fighter protection, and the loss rate of air crews per mission was 1 in 16. In short, he had outlived the odds against his survival, but refused a safer position when offered.[4]

While on leave in the United States, Thompson married a young woman from his hometown of Toronto, Ohio. He also forged six checks and went absent without leave. A civilian psychiatrist diagnosed Thompson as suffering under the stresses of war resulting in "uncontrolled outbursts of psychopathic behavior." Despite this, his court-martial convicted him and sentenced to five years confinement and a dismissal.

The court-martial sparked a public outrage in Toronto, culminating with a large number of its citizens appealing to Burton and other elected officials for help. Along with Congressman Earl Lewis and Senator Robert Taft, Burton lobbied the Judge Advocate General to reconsider the case. "Under the above circumstances ... it seems to me that the sentence imposed is unjust and greatly contrary to the public interest," Burton argued to Major General Myron Cramer, the Army's Judge Advocate General. "It seems to me not only cruel, but entirely

3 Mary Francis Berry, *Stability, Security, and Continuity: Mr. Justice Burton and Decision Making on the Supreme Court* (Westport, CT: Greenwood, 1978), 11–23; *see also* Burton, *Military Installations in North Africa and the Middle East. Remarks of Senator James M. Tunnell in the Senate of the United States, February 15, 1945, and remarks of Senator Harold H. Burton, February 19, 1945, relative to their investigation of military installations in North Africa and the Middle East* (Washington, DC: Government Printing Office, 1945).

4 Documents relating to the General Court Martial of 1st Lt. James Thompson of Toronto Ohio, [HHB/ 27].

out of proportion to the offenses committed and such a sentence is destructive of the very spirit of America for which we fight." In turn, Cramer recommended to Secretary of War Stimson that Thompson's case be overturned and he be permitted to reenter the Army Air Forces in his old rank. Stimson followed Cramer's advice and Thompson returned to the Army.

As it would turn out, Burton as a senator was more inclined to point out deficiencies in the nation's military law than Burton as a justice would. Once on the Court he was cautious, deferential to Congress, and respectful of *stare decisis*. Truman nominated Burton to the Court for a number of reasons. The Republicans were resurgent, and it was unlikely that a New Deal nominee such as Black or Douglas would be confirmed. Unlike fellow Ohioan Robert Taft, Burton was a liberal Republican and an internationalist, and the Taft wing of the Republican Party welcomed having Burton on the Court, thereby opening another senate seat. Burton also approved of expanded executive authority in wartime, though he had criticized Roosevelt prior to the war, particularly on the constitutionality of "Lend Lease." In the field of military law, Burton was a staunch conservative among his brethren. Ultimately, all four of Truman's appointments to the Court were made on the basis of his personal relationships, and Burton was a known quantity.[5]

Burton's confirmation occurred quickly and with little opposition. He resigned from the Senate on October 30, 1945 and quickly took his place on the Court where he immediately became steeped in two pending cases, *In re Yamashita*, in which he played a passive role but voted with the majority, and *Duncan v. Kahanomoku*, where he aligned with Frankfurter in opposing the majority's view of essentially upholding *Ex Parte Milligan*. Both decisions were significant to national security and, more narrowly, military law. Burton maintained a diary that, like his correspondences, provides insight into the justices' intents and perceptions of how pending military law appeals might affect national security. His diary evidences the degree to which some of the justices communicated with the military establishment, including several justices' reliance on Frederick Wiener. While in the Senate, one of the committees on which he served was involved with the future of Philippine independence and as a result, he was interested in Japanese atrocities during the war. On several occasions, War Department personnel, including Wiener, briefed him on the Japanese military's destruction of Manila as well as the impact of Philippine guerilla operations on the Japanese ability to continue to fight.[6]

5 For analysis of Burton's jurisprudence, *see* Melvin Urofsky, *The Supreme Court Justices: A Biographical Dictionary*, 77–84 (New York: Routledge, 1994). The standard, and *see*mingly sole, biography of Burton is Mary Francis Berry, *Stability, Security, and Continuity: Mr. Justice Burton and Decision Making on the Supreme Court* (Westport, CT: Greenwood Press, 1978); *see also*, Jan Palmer, *The Vinson Court Era* (New York: AMS Press, 1990), 12.

6 Burton, diary entry, June 7, 1945 [HHB/R-1].

I: Acrimony on the Court

The Court Burton joined was hardly collegial. By the cessation of hostilities with Japan, in-fighting amongst the nine justices had resulted in a fractured Court. Chief Justice Stone did not approve of much of the other justices' extra-curricular activities. He was angry with Owen Roberts' chairing an investigation into the Pearl Harbor attack, even though Roberts' service on the commission arguably strengthened unity in the nation's war efforts. He was also upset with Murphy's attempts to rejoin the Army without leaving the Court. When, in 1945, Jackson accepted Truman's offer to serve as the chief prosecutor in the Nuremburg Tribunals against leading Nazi officials, Stone denigrated the trials as a "high grade lynching," which applied *ex post facto* laws contrary to American notions of fair play.[7]

On March 20, 1945, Roosevelt sent General William Donovan, the commander of the Office of Strategic Services—the predecessor of the Central Intelligence Agency—to see if Douglas could advise the president on the asylum rights of political refugees in non-belligerent countries. Roosevelt worried that Switzerland, Sweden, Ireland, Portugal, the Vatican, Turkey, and Argentina would offer Nazi war criminals asylum, such as that had enabled Kaiser Wilhelm II to escape prosecution in the Netherlands after World War I. Douglas' memoirs are silent on this request; what remains is a cryptic note to Donovan that he did not consider non-belligerent governments as possessing the right to offer asylum to persons charged with an international tribunal. Cognizant of Stone's anger with Murphy, Roberts, and Jackson, Douglas did not formally offer Donovan any assistance.[8]

Although much of the scholarship on the Court's internal antagonisms center on Black and Douglas in one camp and Frankfurter and Jackson in another, Frankfurter was angry with Murphy and Rutledge as well. In 1944 Frankfurter passed a note to Murphy accusing him of having as clients, "reds, whores, crooks, Indians, and all other colored people, longshoremen, M't-gors and other debtors, R.R. employees, Japs, Women and Most Children." The note ended with a question "must I become a Negro rapist before you give me due process?" By this time Murphy referred to Frankfurter as "a shit" rather than by his name.[9]

Acrimony on the Court even affected cases. On June 18, 1945, the Court denied a rehearing in *Jewell Ridge Coal Corporation v. Local No 6167, United Mine Workers of America*, a case it had decided a month earlier. The discrete issue in *Jewell Ridge*—whether coal miners' transit time to and from the mines

7 John Ferren, *Salt of the Earth, Conscience of the Court*, 280–81; also, Richard Lael, *The Yamashita Precedent: War Crimes and Command Responsibility* (Wilmington, DE: Scholarly Resources, 1982), 55.

8 Donovan to Edith Waters and Douglas, March 20, 1945 [WOD/667].

9 William Wiecek, *The Birth of the Modern Constitution: The United States Supreme Court, 1941–1953* (New York: Cambridge, 2006), 104.

constituted "work time" under the Fair Labor Standards Act—could hardly be considered as directly impacting national security. But mass strikes in the coal and steel industries were a different matter, and for the most part, the justices considered industrial peace a national security matter. The Court, in a five to four decision, ruled in favor of the union. Jackson was convinced, however, that there was another problem with the decision. He had, along with Frankfurter, Stone, and Roberts, dissented, and he accused Black of unethical conduct in failing to recuse himself because the attorney representing the union had been Black's law partner 18 years earlier. For his part, Black determined to derail Jackson's efforts to become chief justice, though Jackson was soon to do himself more harm than Black could accomplish. Jackson provided a journalist with information on this feud, an act Truman found intolerable. Rutledge, Murphy, and Douglas sided with Black.[10]

Black and Roberts also did not see "eye-to-eye." When Roberts announced his retirement, Black refused to sign a standard farewell letter that acknowledged Roberts' "fidelity to principle." The Chief Justice then had Black write a new draft letter, but Frankfurter circulated both. In the end, Roberts received no letter from his fellow justices.

A number of distinguished scholars including Carl Swisher, Charles Warren, and Charles Beard, publicly asked whether the Court had become unstable. Worried about the efficacy of the Court, Truman later sought former Chief Justice Charles Evans Hughes' help to nominate a new chief justice to replace Stone after Stone's death at the conclusion of the 1945 term.[11]

Dissension amongst justices was nothing new to the Court, but in Stone's last term it had the potential to impact two critical military law decisions, as well as a number of labor issues that could directly affect national security. Moreover, as communism emerged as a leading political concern, the Court would have to take cognizance of new laws designed to limit the spread of that ideology, but which collided with the First and Fifth Amendments. Although the internal conflict among the justices was not the primary reason for the Court's unwillingness to review challenges arising from courts-martial, it was a factor nonetheless. Between 1941 and 1946 the Court never once granted *certiorari* to a Navy or Army court-martial, and only Murphy, Rutledge, and Black ever voted for a grant of review. On the other hand, the justices almost unanimously agreed that appellate review of unresolved conscientious objector challenges, the exercise of martial law in Hawaii, and two military trials of Japanese generals, were critical to undertake.

---

10 *Jewell Ridge Coal Corp. v. Local No. 6167, United Mine Workers*, 325 U.S. 897 (1945). *See also* Dennis J. Hutchinson, "The Black-Jackson Feud," *The Supreme Court Review* 1988: (1988), 203–43.

11 William Wiecek, *The Birth of the Modern Constitution*, 420.

II: The Court, the Debt to Veterans and the Post-War Status of Conscientious Objectors

From the end of the war, the Court played a role in protecting veterans preferences in employment and privileges while deciding cases detrimentally to those who had opposed military service. In 1944, Congress enacted the Servicemen's Readjustment Act, which became more commonly referred to as the "G.I. Bill." This law was a significant expansion of the benefits normally accorded veterans and later enabled hundreds of thousands of veterans to obtain college educations and purchase homes. According to one study, the G.I. Bill resulted in the United States maintaining its economic expansion, but the law's critics contended that it cemented veterans into a position of political prominence never before seen. Conscientious objectors, including citizens who performed alternative duties, were denied the G.I. Bill's benefits. Almost from the start, the Court would provide evidence to critics that veterans were accorded a special status to the detriment of those who opposed military service. For instance, in 1951, the Court in *Robertson v. Chambers* unanimously held that the definition of "service records" was to be broadly construed beyond the norm of statutory interpretation when veterans benefits were at stake.[12]

In 1945, the Court issued *In re Summers*, a decision that arose from a state exclusion of conscientious objectors from the practice of law. In 1943, the Illinois Supreme Court required a bar applicant to affirm his willingness to serve in the state militia or federal military in times of emergency. On its face, the requirement would have excluded Jehovah's Witnesses, Mennonites, and Quakers from the practice of law. In the closing days of World War II, Clyde Wilson Summers, a devout Methodist, appealed to the Court from the Illinois state supreme court's decision denying his bar admission. Owing to his sincere religious convictions, he had obtained conscientious objector status. In ruling adversely to Summers, the Illinois Supreme Court did not publish an opinion. In his brief, Summers argued that he was denied admission to the bar based on his religious beliefs in violation of the Fourteenth Amendment.[13]

As part of the unique judicial function in the state, the state supreme court ordered the Illinois Attorney General to argue the state's position to the United States Supreme Court. The Illinois attorney general's response was three-fold. First, the Court did not have jurisdiction to review the case, since the decision of the state supreme court did not consist of "a case or controversy." Second, the state urged that there was no right to become a member of the bar and that admission to practice is a privilege outside of the Fourteenth Amendment's protections. Third, the state had an interest in ensuring that its judicial officers

---

12 *See* Glenn C. Altschuler and Stuart M. Blumin, *The GI Bill: A New Deal for Veterans* (New York: Oxford, 2009), 1–11; *Robertson v. Chambers*, 341 U.S. 347 (1951). Douglas authored *Chambers* but there were no dissents or concurrences.

13 Brief of Petitioner, Appellate brief, at 7–8.

would uphold the entirety of the state constitution and its laws, and a citizen who could not do so could also be excluded from becoming an officer of the court.[14]

The Court determined that "a case or controversy" did exist to confer jurisdiction. However, in an opinion authored by Reed, the majority concluded that the state supreme court had not trammeled on Summers' First and Fourteenth Amendment right to freedom of religion. The majority concluded that since the United States could exclude aliens from citizenship who refused to take up arms in the defense of the nation, as had been decided in 1929, a state could deny a citizen admission to the practice of law for the same reason. Thus, as a consequence of Summers' Christian beliefs, he was prevented from becoming an Illinois-licensed attorney. During oral arguments Jackson appeared to sympathize with Summers, stating, "I suppose that a few literal Christians would not be a bad thing for the bar." Nonetheless, Jackson ultimately voted with the majority.[15]

Black disagreed and wrote a forceful dissent, which Douglas, Murphy, and Rutledge joined. He argued that Illinois had discriminated against Summers on the basis of his religious beliefs and reasoned that since Summers had satisfied every other requirement for admission to the bar, the only logical conclusion was that the state used Summers' faith to prevent his becoming a lawyer. Black pointed out two absurdities in Illinois rules. First, he stated that "a lawyer is no more subject to the call for military duty than a plumber, a highway worker, a Secretary of State, or a prison chaplain." He also noted that Illinois had not drafted any citizen since 1864 and its constitution prohibited the conscription of conscientious objectors except in time of war.

Black received considerable assistance from Rutledge in formulating the dissent. Initially, Black was satisfied with a dissent that only accused the state judiciary of trammeling religious liberty. Rutledge encouraged him to add that the punishment of conscientious objections, which in World War II were almost wholly based on religious grounds, constituted a bill of attainder that excluded a class of persons as a punishment without trial, much as had been the case after the Civil War in *Ex parte Garland.* In *Garland*, issued in 1866, the Court had determined that the admission of lawyers could not be predicated on past political affiliation, including a prior loyalty to the doctrine of secession, because such a prohibition constituted a bill of attainder. "I think those strengthen your position," Rutledge urged Black. Black also received editing assistance from Harold Evans,

---

14 *In re Summers*, 325 U.S. 561 (1945). Although *Summers* was not designed to uphold limiting CPUSA members or sympathizers from the bar or other employment, and thereby limit such persons from military law and national security litigation, it nonetheless provided a means for doing so.

15 The two decisions referenced by the majority for the proposition that because the exclusion of aliens based on a refusal to bear arms in the nation's defense are lawful, so too would the exclusion of a citizen from the practice of law are, *United States v. Schwimmer*, 279 U.S. 644 (1929), and *United States v. Mackintosh*, 283 U.S. 604 (1931).

an attorney who drafted an *amicus* brief on behalf of the Religious Society of Friends, a Quaker organization. The original draft dissent appeared to state that under the Illinois scheme, a Quaker had a choice of serving in the military to retain bar membership, or be thrown out of the Society. Evans pointed out that this was not the case, and Black deleted the language. Notably, a number of religious and international organizations supported Black's dissent including the Women's International League for Peace and Freedom, the post-War World Council, the United Methodist Church, and the Congregational Church.[16]

In two respects, *Summers* characterized the Court's military law and national security jurisprudence even though Summers was neither a serviceman nor a threat to national security. First, the exclusion of a class of persons from the legal profession was rare in American jurisprudence. Former Confederate officers were initially precluded from practicing law before the federal courts, but, as noted, the Court found this to be a bill of attainder. And in 1874, the Court also upheld an Illinois' exclusion of women from the practice of law.

Summers was the first in a line of decisions that enabled exclusion from public employment or professional licensing based on political affiliation or beliefs. At first glance, it is strange that the Court would weaken *Ex parte Garland,* but in the aftermath of World War II and in the midst of the Cold War, there was an underlying reason for the majority's approach. For the next 15 years the federal judiciary operated in an environment where attorneys with ties to the CPUSA argued military law issues before it. Secondly, in an oblique manner, *Summers* influenced the more than two dozen conscientious objector decisions that arose after World War II by the simple fact that many of the justices began to consider the lifetime ramifications of conscientious objection and the possibility of religious discrimination.

Unlike courts-martial, conscientious objector cases that arose during World War II continued to keep the Court's interest. Two Jehovah's Witnesses, William Murray Estep and Louis Dabney Smith were convicted of refusing to submit

---

16 *Ex Parte Garland,* 71 U.S. 333 (1866); Rutledge to Black, June 1, 1945 [HLB/227]; Harold Evans to Black, June 13, 1945 [HLB/227]. Evans wrote,

> There are a considerable number of members who do not carry out the testimony of the Society against all war as inconsistent with their interpretation of Christianity. This is borne out by the fact that a number of Quakers are serving in the Armed Forces. It is not the general practice of the Religious Society of Friends to disown those who violate its peace testimony, though that testimony remains unchanged.

Ibid. Black sought "clarifying language from Evans and Evans provided an alternate statement on the Quakers which is contained in the published dissent. *See* Black to Evans, July 10, 1945 [HLB/227] and Evans to Black, July 18, 1945 [HLB/227]. Women's International League for Peace and Freedom to Black, July 24, 1945 [HLB/227]. The United Methodist Church's leadership council informed Black they "rejoiced in your judgment on the matter." UMC to Black, June 13, 1945 [HLB/227]; and, as to the Congregational Church, *see* Merrill F. Clark to Black, June 15, 1945 [HLB/227].

to induction into the Army. On September 30, 1943, Smith refused to report to an induction center, and his own father had him arrested. Smith claimed to be a minister and refused to take an oath or go through an induction ceremony. Despite Smith's refusal, the Army notified him that he was lawfully in the military and ordered him to report to training, which he partially complied with. However, he refused to wear a uniform. In response, a local commander court-martialed him, but following *Billings*, which had blocked the military's jurisdictional reach from citizens who were lawfully conscripted, but not fully inducted, the Judge Advocate General ordered Smith's release for trial before the federal court. A federal court then convicted him of refusing to report. On appeal, Smith claimed that because he was physically brought to the induction center, he had not refused to report for induction. The Court of Appeals for the Fourth Circuit found this argument meritless. Smith also argued that the trial court had excluded evidence that he was a minister and therefore exempt from conscription. Because both the induction and the appeals boards had already ruled against Smith, the Fourth Circuit agreed with the trial court's exclusion of the evidence. The Court would reverse.[17]

Estep, the named party, came to the Court through a similar route as Smith. In 1942, Estep registered for the draft, but claimed that as a minister he was exempt from induction. The local draft board refused to acknowledge his ministerial status and he appealed. During his appeal, he attempted to provide three affidavits attesting to his ministerial status, but the appeals board refused to consider the affidavits. After being ordered to report for duty in the Navy, Estep discovered that his file was missing documents and he provided 11 new affidavits. When the board once more ordered him to be inducted into the Navy, Estep refused. He was prosecuted in United States District Court for Pennsylvania, and that court refused to permit him to argue that he was exempt from induction in the first place. The Court of Appeals for the Third Circuit twice decided the case adversely to Estep, once before a three judge panel and then *en banc*. However, there were two dissenting opinions that made Estep's case more likely for a grant of *certiorari*.[18]

One of the unresolved issues from *Falbo* and *Billings* was whether Congress, in not legislating a judicial appeal process to review the decisions of local induction boards, meant to exclude judicial review altogether. Because Stone was in the minority, Black, as the sitting senior justice in the majority, assigned Douglas to author the decision. In a memorandum prior to circulating his draft opinion, Douglas argued that because religious rights were the central issue for the Court to consider, it could not be the case that the exclusion of judicial review was intended. Douglas also urged that a conviction based on an arbitrary decision by a selective service board was not warranted in such instances as

17 *Smith v. United States*, 148 F.2d 288 (CA 4, 1945).

18 *United States v. Estep*, 150 F.2d 769 (CA 3, 1945).

in Estep's appeal. Douglas did not want Estep to lose the right to vote simply because as a Jehovah's Witness, he sided with his faith against military service.[19]

Only Burton and Stone disagreed with Douglas on this point. The Court's published decision rested on a broad principle that when individual rights conflicted with the Executive Branch, judicial review was appropriate. The majority recognized that the Selective Service Act did not expressly grant individuals access to the courts, and Congress had called the decisions of appeals boards, "final." But, the majority refused to accept Congressional silence as a blanket approval for the selective service boards to make unchecked determinations on individual cases, particularly since some of the boards' decisions exceeded their lawful authority. As a result, the majority overturned the lower courts insofar as they excluded evidence that the boards failed to consider evidence of religious exemption. The majority believed that to hold otherwise would ignore the Sixth Amendment's guarantee of a right for a person on trial to present a relevant defense. This ruling did not, however, mean that the courts would substitute their judgment for that of the local boards.[20]

Murphy, Rutledge, and Frankfurter agreed with this approach yet authored concurrences. Murphy recognized that modern war required a mass conscription effort. But he disagreed that the judiciary could only intercede once an individual was lawfully inducted, and therefore subject to military jurisdiction. He called any remedy from that point "illusory," and his conclusion would later integrate into his concurrence in a martial law case, as well as his dissent from the Court's judgment in the war crimes trial of two Japanese generals. "All of the mobilization and all of the war effort will have been in vain if, when all is finished, we discover that in the process we have destroyed the very freedoms for which we fought," he noted. Rutledge's concurrence was briefer. He had earlier dissented in *Yakus*, a decision upholding the constitutionality a congressional delegation of authority to an executive agency, the authority to essentially create a criminal offense. He reinforced his opposition to permitting administrative agencies the authority to operate without judicial review. Frankfurter's lengthy concurrence is almost a dissent, as he chastised the majority for finding all eight circuit courts in error. In the end, a result of *Estep* was the Court ensured that defendants in selective service cases who claimed they were wrongly denied conscientious objector status could attack the local and state selective service boards' denials as a defense in criminal trials.

Estep was not the only conscientious objector decision to come before the Court in 1946. In *Eagles v. United States ex rel. Samuels*, the Court, in a unanimous

---

19 Douglas memorandum to the Court (undated) [WOD/130]. *Estep v. United States*, 327 U.S. 114 (1946).

20 *Ibid.* The Court held, "We cannot readily infer that Congress departed so far from the traditional concepts of a fair trial when it made the actions of the local boards 'final' as to provide that a citizen of this country should go to jail for not obeying an unlawful order of an administrative agency."

decision authored by Douglas, determined that the use of "theological advisory panels" composed of individuals belonging to a specific faith to provide local selective service boards advice on the practices of specific religions did not give rise to an unlawful abdication of authority by the selective service boards. In theory, an advisory panel comprised of members from the same religious faith of a conscientious objector applicant could aid a diverse selective service board in their determination to grant or deny an exemption. An advisory panel would also be helpful in thwarting allegations of a board's prejudices. Samuels, a student at an Orthodox Jewish seminary, challenged the role of a Jewish advisory panel that had informed the selective service board that the seminary did not only train future rabbis, but also laymen preparing to enter into business professions. The Court unanimously held such panels were lawful, but the Court enabled a defendant to assert as a defense in a criminal trial that an advisory panel's advice was flawed. This aspect satisfied Murphy, who had earlier expressed concerns that the Court not foreclose all *habeas* appeals.[21]

A companion decision to *Samuels*, captioned as *Eagles v. United States ex rel. Horowitz*, presented a slightly different issue. Horowitz had sought a deferment on the ground that he attended a religious school. In 1941, Horowitz notified the local board that he was pursuing a degree in social work and sought a deferment until the completion of his studies in 1943. In 1943, he notified the board of his intention to become a rabbi. The theological advisory panel doubted the sincerity of Horowitz's claims and advised the local board to classify him eligible for induction. However, the advisory board's report was marked confidential and unlike in *Samuels*, its members were not rabbis, but Jewish laymen. Douglas, in authoring the unanimous decision, opined that since the laymen were Jewish, Horowitz could hardly claim prejudice. Frankfurter appears to have been the only justice to provide commentary on this point, agreeing with Douglas. Reed was concerned that Douglas' initial draft would have required the theological advisory board's report to be open as a confrontation right. Both Frankfurter and Reed opposed a decision that required mandatory disclosure of all reports and Douglas agreed to omit any allusion to the propriety of confidential reports from the decision.[22]

Finally, in a less contentious decision than *Estep*, the Court in *Gibson v. United States* determined that a citizen charged with violating the Selective Service Act could not be denied the opportunity to present a defense that the local and appeals boards denied a full and fair hearing on a citizen's claim to a ministerial exemption. Conscientious objectors could still be assigned to labor camps of "national importance." The Court found Congress did not intend for congregations to be deprived of their religious leaders and afforded this narrow class a complete exemption from military service. As a result of *Gibson*, a

---

21 *Eagles v. United States ex rel. Samuels*, 329 U.S. 304 (1946); Murphy to Douglas, December 20, 1946 [WOD/146].

22 *Eagles v. United States ex rel. Horowitz*, 329 U.S. 317 (1946); Frankfurter to Douglas, December 4, 1946 [WOD/146]; Reed to Douglas, December 6, 1946 [WOD/146].

conscientious objector who was charged with failing to report for camp could argue as a defense at trial that the local and appeals boards had wrongly denied him the ministerial exemption.[23]

III: Survival of *Ex parte Milligan*: Martial Law and Jurisdiction over Civilians

Almost immediately after the Japanese attack on Pearl Harbor on December 7, 1941, the federal territorial government of Hawaii declared martial law in a manner not seen since the Civil War. This declaration occurred in the unique context of Hawaii's territorial status and relationship to the United States. In 1898, the United States government formally annexed the islands into a territory. Two years later the territory was granted self-government, though the independence of the government was limited to domestic matters. By 1941 the Hawaiian government resembled most state governments, but federal oversight in internal matters existed to a higher degree than in any state. The territorial governor was responsible to the President, and unlike in the 48 contiguous states, the federal military presence in Hawaii was everywhere. When Japanese forces attacked on December 7, 1941, they struck sovereign United States soil. Shortly after the attack, Joseph Poindexter, the territorial governor, declared martial law and, with the President's approval, suspended the civil courts. To enforce and adjudicate the law, the governor turned to General Walter Short, the commanding general over all Army forces in Hawaii. By December 9, 1941, Hawaii was under a military government, albeit with the governor still the executive of the islands.[24]

This could not have occurred in one of the 48 states unless either *Milligan* was ignored or the civil government had ceased to function. Neither of these two conditions existed. Instead, what occurred in the Hawaiian Islands was a conflict between the federal judiciary and General Robert Richardson, who replaced Short as commanding general of the islands. Richardson supplanted the civil judiciary with a system of military provost courts. Some of the civil judges were employed in the provost courts, but the design of the system, overseen by Colonel Thomas Green, a future Judge Advocate General of the Army, was reminiscent of what had been set up in the southern states after the Civil War during Union Army occupation. There was judicial precedent for provost courts, but only when civil courts were unable to function.[25]

In a post-war report, Green claimed that of the two federal judges available on the island, Delbert Metzger, the senior judge, refused to participate in any military operations and Ingram Stainback was an eager volunteer who repeatedly asked

23 *Gibson v. United States*, 329 U.S. 338 (1946).

24 William H. Rehnquist, *All Laws But One* (New York: Knopf, 1998), 109.

25 *See, e.g.*, *Mechanics and Traders Bank v. Union Bank*, 89 U.S. 276 (1875).

Green and Richardson to serve as a military judge. Green conceded that Stainback was "a brilliant lawyer, but possessed a violent temper." Stainback also was a political foe of Governor Poindexter and, in Green's estimation, tried to accrue power to oust the governor. Green also lauded Metzger, acknowledging that he had attempted to remain neutral in challenges to the extension of military law over the citizenry. Yet, Green also defended the martial law order by claiming that military courts were more likely than the civil courts to give citizens and other residents of Japanese ancestry a fair trial.[26]

The first six months following the Pearl Harbor attack were undoubtedly a time of extreme fear for both the residents of Hawaii and the military establishment. The Japanese Navy operated unopposed across the Pacific, and it was not lost on the local Hawaiian population that the Japanese Army occupied Attu and Kiska, two Aleutian Islands with similar territorial status. Moreover, the Japanese military had defeated American forces in the Philippines, on Guam, Saipan, and Wake Island. Geographically, after the fall of Wake Island, Hawaii was the next logical area for Japan to launch an offensive.[27]

When, on December 8, General Short issued an order closing the civil courts, he intended the closure to be of short duration. However, Short was removed from command following the investigation into the Pearl Harbor attack and Richardson kept martial law in place through 1944. After Richardson assumed command, Green concluded that the provost courts were not able to adjudicate civil matters such as divorces, and contract enforcement between civilians, and he advised Richardson to minimize the military's involvement in such matters. As a result, Richardson reopened the civil courts for all non-criminal matters.

In August 1943, the Army detained two naturalized citizens of German descent and held them without trial. Neither of the two men was charged with a crime, and they appealed via *habeas* writ to federal judge Metzger. By this time, the Japanese military was in a slow, arduous, and apparently irreversible retreat. Nevertheless, the military government motioned the court to quash the appeal. Although their motion failed, the government retained the petitioners in custody, and Metzger ordered Richardson to appear and explain why the two men were still detained. Richardson evaded federal process and fled a United States marshal attempting to serve Metzger's order. On Green's advice, the general further refused to produce the two men. An enraged Metzger then held Richardson in contempt and fined him $5,000. Richardson responded by suspending *habeas*, and ordered the federal court to discontinue all pending *habeas* proceedings. Additionally, Richardson issued an order punishing anyone who disobeyed his decision with a $5,000 fine or five years imprisonment. Ultimately, the Court of Appeals for the Ninth Circuit

---

26 Major General Thomas H. Green, *Martial Law in Hawaii, December 7, 1941—April 4, 1943* (Washington, DC: Judge Advocate General's Department, 1947), 126; on Green's opinion of Metzger, *see* 526.

27 J.F.C. Fuller, *The Second World War: A Strategical and Tactical History* (New York: DaCapo Reprint, 1992), 132–4.

upheld the detention of the two citizens, but the Army released them on Secretary of War Stimson's orders. California attorney general Earl Warren joined Green and Richardson on the appeal.[28]

Richardson's actions were reminiscent of events that occurred in the Civil War. In 1863, General Ambrose Burnside ordered the arrest and trial of Clement Vallandigham, a former congressman and virulent anti-Lincoln copperhead. Vallandigham had publicly criticized the war and like many copperheads, he encouraged soldiers to desert the Army. Burnside acted without Lincoln or Secretary of War Stanton's knowledge. In a reprise of the Vallandigham incident 80 years earlier, Richardson's actions caught Stimson, Attorney General Biddle, and Roosevelt by surprise. Roosevelt had Biddle and Stimson travel to Hawaii and negotiate an end to the impasse between Metzger and the general. Roosevelt's cabinet officers and most of the justices believed Richardson's conduct outright unconstitutional. Yet, the issue of martial law was hardly settled.[29]

Green later characterized the fight between Metzger and Richardson as an unfortunate incident that detracted from policing the island, but he did not criticize Metzger. "These incidents were not lost on local politicians who took full advantage of each one to polish their political image," Green lamented. "Nevertheless, martial law rocked along in reduced form until October 24, 1944, when, after nearly three years of operation, it was terminated by a Presidential Proclamation on that date." Neither Metzger nor the majority of Supreme Court justices would agree with Green's concluding comment that martial law had "served its purpose admirably well."[30]

With the criminal courts closed since the end of 1941, civilians in Hawaii were prosecuted in military trials for offenses which the military courts had no traditional competency. In 1942, a military court convicted a civilian named Harry E. White for stock embezzlement and sentenced him to five years in prison. White had preserved an objection to the military's jurisdiction, raising it before the provost court, as well as before Judge Metzger. Additionally, in 1944 Lloyd Duncan, a ship worker who assaulted two Marines, was arrested and prosecuted in a provost court. He too objected to trial by the provost court, which overruled him and sentenced him to six months in prison. Like White, Duncan appealed to Metzger.

In Duncan's case, decided on April 19, 1944, Metzger determined that the issue was not whether the provost court had afforded a fair trial, or even whether the assault on two marines gave rise to a military offense, but rather whether the

---

28 *See Ex Parte Zimmerman*, 132 F.2d 442 (CA 9, 1942). Problematic to the arrest of Hans Zimmerman, one of the naturalized citizens, was that he was a licensed naturopath (a holistic doctor of alternative medicine) and treated Judge Delbert Metzger. However, even Green believed the evidence against Zimmerman was inconclusive. *See* Thomas H. Green, *Martial Law in Hawaii*, 569.

29 Brian McGinty, *Lincoln and the Court* (Boston: Harvard, 2008), 187.

30 Thomas H. Green, *Martial Law in Hawaii*, 568.

military had jurisdiction over a civilian at all. Ingram Stainback, the former judge and new territorial governor, had fought against General Richardson to limit the military's jurisdiction, but had succeeded only in convincing the War, Justice, and Interior Department leadership to agree to a restoration of civil courts for non-criminal matters such as contract disputes and divorces. Before Metzger, Stainback testified that he believed martial law should be fully rescinded. The military produced an exceptional witness. Admiral Chester Nimitz, commander of the Pacific Fleet, testified that the continuance of military courts over all criminal matters remained essential.[31]

Whatever Metzger's animus towards Richardson, Metzger did not belittle Nimitz's position. Nimitz's reputation as a humble, yet extraordinarily successful naval commander, was, to Metzger, an important consideration. Yet, Metzger was mindful that in the aftermath of the Pearl Harbor attack, the government was altogether too willing to extend military jurisdiction over civilians at the expense of individual liberties. To Metzger, what made martial law more egregious in Hawaii was that Congress had never granted the War Department the authority to enact it in the first place. To this end, he ordered Duncan's release.

One week later, Metzger issued a similar ruling in White's case. This time Metzger opined that following the naval victory at Midway, six months after Pearl Harbor, the justification for martial law no longer existed. After weighing the government's arguments, Metzger concluded that the best the government could do was to prove that at some time its leaders believed in the necessity of martial law. These beliefs did not, in Metzger's opinion, affect the reality that White had been prosecuted for fraud, a common law offense for which military courts had no competence to adjudicate. This issue would arise again in the 1950s and 1960s as the military's jurisdiction over civilians in overseas installations was challenged. Metzger's ruling against military jurisdiction prevailed in the long-run, but not initially in the Court of Appeals for the Ninth Circuit.[32]

As in the federal district court cases involving the Army's jurisdictional extension over merchant seaman, the War Department's leadership viewed *Duncan* as a critical case. Once more Major General Myron C. Cramer, the Army's Judge Advocate General, joined the Justice Department in arguments, and he brought with him two judge advocates assigned to the war crimes division, William J. Hughes and Eugene Slattery. Opposing the War Department were J. Garner Anthony, who had served as the territorial attorney general and opposed martial law, and two lawyers employed by the American Civil Liberties Union. Duncan had retained Anthony from the time he was charged in the military tribunal and Anthony remained on the case through the Supreme Court decision.[33]

31 *Ex Parte Duncan*, 66 F.Supp. 976 (1944).

32 *Ex Parte White*, 66 F.Supp. 982 (1944).

33 Anon. *The Judge Advocate General Journal*, Vol. II, No 1 (1945): 1–66, 6.

The Ninth Circuit combined and then unanimously reversed Metzger's two decisions in a single decision. William Healy, an Idaho state politician appointed to the court by Roosevelt, authored the majority opinion. Healy was joined by two Roosevelt appointees: Clifton Matthews, a former United States Attorney for the Arizona territory, and Francis Arthur Garrecht, another Roosevelt appointee who had read law in Washington and was active in that state's politics. Healy, like Metzger, sidestepped the issue of whether the military courts had provided fair trials. Instead, he focused on the applicability of *Quirin*, *Hirabayashi*, and *Milligan* to the legality of martial law. But he interpreted *Milligan* too broadly, claiming that the *Milligan* Court had recognized that "a military substitute in the administration of ordinary criminal justice for the duration of the emergency" could occur. He did not acknowledge that the *Milligan* majority noted the existence of functioning civil courts negated military courts, and it was unlikely that the government had the authority to remove the jurisdiction of functioning civil courts, simply because of a potential danger. Curtis Wilbur, a former Secretary of the Navy and chief justice of the California Supreme Court concurred with the majority but felt compelled to add that contrary to Metzger's interpretation, the *Milligan* Court never addressed whether a change in wartime status from an immediate emergency to nearby (but increasingly distant) war automatically terminated martial law. Wilbur also missed the majority's intent in *Milligan*, all the more so because the *Milligan* majority clearly did not concern itself with how dire an emergency had to become before the military could supplant the civil courts, but rather the existence of functioning civil courts negated the possibility of a military takeover of the judicial system at all. Likewise William Denman concurred in reversing Metzger, but urged that neither Duncan nor White had standing to petition the court via *habeas* in the first place.[34]

The Court's decision to grant *certiorari* on February 12, 1945, occurred one week before the campaign for the island of Iwo Jima began. This campaign resulted in over 6,000 United States Marine combat deaths in a one month period. The War Department viewed Iwo Jima as a critical base for launching further air attacks against Japan. Over 22,000 Japanese soldiers and sailors there were under orders to fight to the death, orders most followed. Though fighting still raged in the Philippines and other areas in the Pacific, and Germany had yet to be beaten, it appeared the Axis powers were going to be defeated. Nevertheless, the War Department predicted a full scale invasion of Japan would be costly and not occur until 1946.

Thus, the Court was set to decide a crucial military jurisdiction case with the war ongoing, indications that the Soviet Union would become a dangerous adversary in the post-war environment, and the War Department urging the Ninth Circuit's decision be upheld. Garner continued to defend Lloyd Duncan, but he was joined by Osmond Fraenkel of the American Civil Liberties Union who represented Harry White. Fraenkel argued that the expansion of military

34 *Duncan v. Kahanamoku*, 146 F.2d 576 (CA 9 1944).

jurisdiction beyond the narrow confines of military offenses would result in an Executive Branch more powerful than the system of checks and balances could tolerate. Black and Douglas later adopted this argument into their jurisprudence.[35]

The Court reversed the Ninth Circuit. Black authored a plurality opinion, with Murphy and Stone authoring separate concurrences and Burton issuing a dissent that Frankfurter joined. Except Burton and Frankfurter (and Jackson, who did not participate), the justices believed that the two consolidated cases should have been tried in a civil court and that the military had no constitutional authority to oversee a civil judicial system on American soil when the civil courts were fully functioning. Black noted that the military authorities had considered *Vallandigham* as controlling on the issue of jurisdiction. Now, in arguing before the Court, the solicitor general abandoned the Executive Branch's earlier argument to the Ninth Circuit that the local military commander possessed an inherent authority to declare martial law. Instead, the Solicitor General urged the Court to infer from the Organic Act—the law governing the territories—a congressional grant of authority enabling the declaration of martial law. To dispute the Solicitor General's position, Black had to sidestep his earlier positions in *Hirabayashi* and *Korematsu*, but he clearly articulated that nowhere in the Organic Act had Congress specified that the governor general could suspend the civil courts.[36]

To reinforce his decision, Black turned to the long-standing precedent that military courts were an anathema to Anglo-American law, and the Constitution specifically subordinated the military to the civil authority. He noted that George Washington used the military to suppress the so-called Whiskey Rebellion, but the rebels were tried in civil courts. Moreover, he also reminded the country that in 1899 in Idaho the military assisted in stopping a violent strike, but the ring-leaders were prosecuted in the civil courts. Turning to *Quirin* and *Milligan*, Black concluded: "Courts and their procedural safeguards are indispensable to our system of government. They were set up by our founders to protect the liberties they valued." Black accepted Congress might have enabled martial law in the territory, but not the supplanting of the federal courts, as long as those courts functioned.

Murphy's concurrence did not substantively differ from the majority opinion, though he strongly criticized the use of the military to supplant civil government as a move toward despotism. More than Black, Murphy articulated that if the Executive Branch's position were to prevail, it would overturn *Milligan*. This was not quite true because Milligan had been tried in Indiana for violating a military order restricting speech, and Duncan and White were prosecuted in a military run tribunal for violating civil laws. Nonetheless, Murphy was correct in writing that the military trials "lacked constitutional sanction," and that the military's desire for more expedient courts and the requirement of recognizing civil liberties were inherently "irreconcilable."

35 Fraenkel, diary entry for October 15, 1945 [Fraenkel Papers-JSM-P].

36 *Duncan v. Kahanamoku*, 327 U.S. 324 (1946).

The differences between Stone's concurrence and Black's majority opinion are illustrative in how the World War II-era justices viewed the expanse of *Milligan*. Stone seems to have adopted Chief Justice Chase's *Milligan* concurrence into his legal reasoning, while Black maintained Davis' *Milligan* majority opinion in his. Chase, it may be remembered, did not argue that the majority had erred in the result in *Milligan*, but rather, was wrong in presuming that Congress could not legislate the military trials of civilians. Black's and Stone's discussions, more than their published opinions, provide insight into their beliefs on whether an expansive martial law could exist at all in the United States or its sovereign territories. Stone had wanted Black to concede that "if the civil courts were unable to function for two or three years," the Executive Branch could create military courts. Black responded to Stone "the views that you express in your note concerning these cases are correct only in the event that the majority opinion in the *Milligan* case was incorrect. The *Milligan* majority in my judgment expressed Constitutional views that were sound then and sound now." This did not end the matter, and Stone argued that David Davis' majority opinion had only pointed out that the military's jurisdiction was more extensive in 1865 than it needed to be. To Stone, had the pro-Confederate insurgents in *Milligan* committed their offenses in a border state or in the south, a military trial would surely have been upheld, even though the men were United States citizens and not part of the Confederate rebellion. Black refused to concede this point. Stone's concurrence reflected that had Congress legislated military tribunals in the Hawaiian Islands and a wartime emergency necessitated the creation of such tribunals, he would not have voted to reverse.[37]

Burton authored the dissent, but it was as much Frankfurter's opinion as it was Burton's. Frankfurter was upset with the decision, and viewed it as a direct attack on Roosevelt's administration of the war effort. "What the Court is really doing in this case whether it does so patently or not, is to express an historic judgment," he complained to Burton. "And the majority opinion commits the fatal error of trying to be wise after the event and I am doubtful whether even in the light of hindsight it is fair to condemn what the military contemporaneously did in Hawaii." However, for all his disgust with the majority, Frankfurter did not write a dissent himself, relying instead on Burton to do so. It is not difficult to guess that Frankfurter hoped to make a new ally in Burton and lock him into a decision that would shape national security in the post-war environment.[38]

Burton's correspondence with Frankfurter, and for that matter Black, evidenced how conservative he would be on national security matters. On February 9, 1946, Frankfurter took the opportunity to offer his advice to the Court's newest justice. "Expansive rhetoric about the dreadful brass hats after they have safeguarded our liberty stirs such a responsive cord in people that you may agree with me in thinking it worthwhile to indulge in a little puncturing

---

37 Stone to Black, January 17, 1946 [HLB/280]; Black to Stone, January 18, 1946 [HLB/280]; Stone to Black, January 19, 1946 [HLB/280].

38 Frankfurter to Burton, February 16, 1946 [HHB/129].

rhetoric such as furnished by Justice Field in *Dow v. Johnson*, 100 U.S. 158, 169–70," Frankfurter suggested. Burton did not include verbatim the language Frankfurter urged him to place into the dissent: "But, the real question here is, what were the requirements of the Constitution and the laws which controlled the commander in chief, and the other military authorities during the period here in question in Hawaii?"[39]

Three days later, Frankfurter encouraged Burton to include an additional paragraph into the dissent and this time Burton did so. "Under our system, the legality of the actions of military authorities may happily be challenged in the courts even though they involve military decision under circumstances such as those that existed in Hawaii after December 7," Frankfurter's suggested paragraph began. "In passing on such an issue, the courts must view the circumstances, as a matter of legal requirement, by putting themselves in the place of those who had no choice but to act one way or another when the exigency was upon them." Frankfurter then commented that it "was psychologically impossible" to do so, and as a result, tremendous care must be taken by judges not to judge wartime military actions by "the inapplicable standard of hindsight." Burton edited Frankfurter's suggestion, but the tenor and substance were clearly included in the dissent.[40]

After Burton passed the draft dissent to Frankfurter, Frankfurter lobbied Burton to add that at any time during the war a federal judge could have been petitioned to issue an injunction, but none of the petitioners had attempted this avenue of redress. "It makes concrete and vivid that we are now deciding in the comfort of peace that what the military did under the hazards of war illegal," Frankfurter suggested. Burton again adopted Frankfurter's reasoning into his dissent.[41]

Burton's correspondence with President Truman about *Duncan* explains why he dissented, and indicates what Truman expected from his first Court appointee. Burton informed Truman that he considered Hawaii a battlefield during the war's duration, a position that separated him from the rest of the Court. "In emphasizing the zones of discretion which the Constitution allots to the executive and legislative branches of the Government as well as to the judiciary, you will recognize this point of view is drawn from my experience in France as an infantry officer," the justice assured the president before concluding his opinion was also based on his political experience. The following day, Truman thanked Burton for his dissent, penning "I think your approach to the situation is much more in line with what is necessary than in the majority opinion, although I am no lawyer as you know."[42]

---

39 Frankfurter to Burton, February 9, 1946 [HHB/129].

40 Frankfurter to Burton, February 12, 1946 [HHB/129].

41 Frankfurter to Burton, February 14, 1946 [HHB/129].

42 Burton to Truman, 25 February 1946 [HST, R/3]; Truman to Burton, 26 February 1946, [HST, R/3].

Green—the Army lawyer who had overseen the military courts system in Hawaii—later recounted erroneously that Murphy authored the majority decision. Green criticized Murphy's reasoning as rooted in "fear and opposition to the kind of subordination of executive legislative and judicial authorities to complete military rule." Green criticized Murphy as being under the mistaken belief that the military had arbitrarily seized power in Hawaii. Although Green found Stone's concurrence more reasoned then "Murphy's" majority opinion, he urged that Burton (and by implication Frankfurter) were correct in their recitation of the facts underlying the declaration of martial law and the need for the military supersession of the courts.[43]

Duncan received immediate attention from the nation's leading scholars and participants. For instance, Charles Fairman, who served as judge advocate in World War II and then returned to Stanford University as a law professor (and who as a Frankfurter acolyte would later battle Black over the meaning of the Fourteenth Amendment), authored, "The Supreme Court on Military Jurisdiction: Martial Rule in Hawaii and the Yamashita Case," in the *Harvard Law Review*, in which he agreed with Black. Fairman stated the obvious point that *Duncan* was consistent with *Milligan*, though he took issue with some of Black's historic examples. Noteworthy to Fairman's analysis was a brief discussion on the lack of mechanisms for appeals from courts-martial and other military tribunals. In 1947, J. Garner Anthony, authored an article titled "Hawaiian Martial Law in the Supreme Court," in the *Yale Law Review*, which similarly concluded that Black was right and Burton wrong. To Professor John Frank, *Duncan*, like *Milligan*, was a victory for civil rights. He congratulated Black for "safeguarding the necessary military power and fully meeting the criticism of the dissent that this is a peacetime evaluation of a wartime situation." Frank's congratulatory letter mirrored Black's intent of ensuring the efficacy of *Milligan*.[44]

IV: Continuum of Deference: *In re Yamashita*

In contrast to the Court's rebuke of military jurisdiction in Hawaii, it exhibited significant deference to military tribunals in the trials of two captured Japanese generals. Over a two day period beginning January 7, 1946, the Court heard arguments arising from the United States' military's prosecution of Tomoyuki Yamashita and Masaharu Homma. Most of the Court's discussion, and the lengthier decision, focused on Yamashita; the Court would simply apply its reasoning in Yamashita's case to Homma's and deny *habeas* and *certiorari*, even though General Douglas MacArthur believed Homma's crimes worse than

43 Thomas H. Green, *Martial Law in Hawaii*, 580–88.

44 Charles Fairman, "The Supreme Court on Military Jurisdiction: Martial Rule in Hawaii and the Yamashita Case," 59 *Harvard Law Review* 833–60 (1946); J. Garner Anthony, "Hawaiian Martial Law in the Supreme Court," 57 *Yale Law Journal* 27–54 (1947); Frank to Black, undated, [JPFP/1].

Yamashita's. Murphy and Rutledge dissented from the lack of review in Homma's challenge for largely the same reasons the two justices would ultimately dissent in Yamashita's case.[45]

Both trials were unique, because unlike the prosecution of senior German officers and government officials, and the majority of prosecutions of high ranking Japanese officers and government officials, these two trials were not conducted in an international tribunal that was subject to other nations' interpretations of legal obligations arising from international law. Rather, they were solely *American* military tribunals. Authored by Stone, the Court's majority determined that American military trials of captured enemy prisoners were part of a military commander's authority, and thus, as an exclusive instrumentality of the Executive Branch, the trials were not subject to judicial review. In this vein, the Court's decision rested on *Dynes v. Hoover* as well as its wartime *Quirin* decision. However, in what became captioned as *In re Yamashita*, the Court retreated from *Quirin's* suggestion that due process applied to the trials of enemy combatants.[46]

Ultimately, Black, Reed, Frankfurter, Douglas, and Burton sided with Stone. Stone had hoped for a unanimous decision, but at one point he almost lost Black to the dissent. Black's contribution to the decision would prove significant to the later conduct of judicial review of courts-martial. Stone and Frankfurter insisted that Yamashita and Homma's trials comported with due process, though, as discussed below, Black threatened to dissent if they persisted in placing any language to this effect in the decision. To Murphy, Yamashita's trial was another instance of racism infecting due process such as what had occurred in the Japanese internment, and to Rutledge, the trial was simply an anathema to a constitutional democracy.[47]

Under the law of war, Yamashita's conduct was as prosecutable as that of Henry Wirz, the notorious commandant of the Andersonville Prison during the Civil War. There was a similarity in the status of the two men, despite the differences in rank. (Wirz was a mere captain, while Yamashita led an army.) Both men commanded soldiers who were cruel in their treatment of non-combatants and both men were foreigners. Wirz was a Swiss national who was never naturalized as a citizen. It is an irony of the military justice system that Wirz was prosecuted and sentenced to death while other Confederate leaders, some of whom, such as General George Pickett who had caused Union prisoners of war to be murdered, were eventually permitted to return to prosperous life. Nonetheless, Wirz's malfeasance and long-term neglect of the welfare of prisoners of war contributed to the deaths of thousands of prisoners of war.[48]

---

45 *Application of Homma*, 327 U.S. 759 (1945).

46 Douglas MacArthur, *Reminiscences* (New York: McGraw, 1964), 297.

47 Sidney Fine, *The Washington Years*, 452.

48 On Wirz and Pickett, *see* Joshua Kastenberg, *Law in War, Law as War, Brigadier General Joseph Holt and the Judge Advocate General's Department in the Civil War and*

Yamashita was a successful field commander in the aftermath of December 7, 1941. He was held in high regard in Japan and the Emperor appointed him to head a Japanese military mission to Germany in 1940, where he reviewed the German Army preparing to invade the Soviet Union. General Tojo assigned him to command the Japanese Twenty-Fifth Army for the invasion of British-held Malaya. Yamashita's soldiers speedily outfought their British and Australian opponents whose garrison outnumbered the Japanese by a margin of over two to one. To compensate for a lack of numbers, Yamashita's soldiers infiltrated behind British lines dressed in native clothing. On February 15, the British commander, Lieutenant General Arthur Percival surrendered his 70,000 soldiers into Japanese captivity. The conditions of the captivity were as poor as those suffered by American soldiers captured in the Philippines.[49]

Yamashita's early 1942 Malayan victory was strategically at least as important as the Japanese seizure of the Philippines. Malaya contained over a quarter of the world's tin and over 40-percent of its rubber. The Philippines did not have these essential war-making industrial materials, though the loss of these islands was symbolically a horrific defeat for the United States, and more personally for MacArthur. Although Yamashita was not prosecuted for war-crimes that occurred in the Philippines in 1942, his soldiers in Malaya committed two notable offenses, killing non-combatants in the Alexandra Hospital, and massacring thousands of Chinese citizens believed to be anti-Japanese. Yamashita ordered several of his own soldiers responsible for the hospital killings executed, indicating he did not tolerate this extreme level of abuse, but he did not stop the killings of ethnic Chinese in Singapore.[50]

In one fundamental respect, Yamashita was set up for failure. After his stunning victory, Tojo had him transferred to a remote area in Manchuria. He only arrived in the Philippines on the eve of MacArthur's 1944 invasion to find an effective guerilla network fighting his soldiers. When he took command in

---

Early Reconstruction, 1861–1865 (Durham, NC: Carolina Academic Press), 262. Pickett was in command during an event called the New Berne Massacre in which captured Union soldiers who were North Carolina natives were tried and executed for treason.

49 T. Dodson Stamps ed., *A Military History of World War II, Vol. II: Operations in the Mediterranean and Pacific Theatres* (New York: USMA, 1953); Keith Simpson, "Lieutenant General Arthur Percival," in John Keegan ed., *Churchill's Generals* (New York: Quill, 1991), 256–73.

50 Edwin Hoyt, *Three Military Leaders: Heihachiro, Isoroku Yamamoto, Tomoyuki Yamashita* (Tokyo: Kadansha International, 1993).

T. Dodson Stamps ed., *A Military History of World War II, Vol. II: Operations in the Mediterranean and Pacific Theatres* (New York: USMA, 1953); Keith Simpson, "Lieutenant General Arthur Percival," in John Keegan ed., *Churchill's Generals* (New York: Quill, 1991), 256–73.

Hoyt, *Three Military Leaders*, 143–51; Martin Blumenson, *The Duel for France, 1944: The Men and Battles that Changed the Fate of Europe* (New York: DaCapo reprint, 2000), 350–58.

the Philippines, he had 230,000 soldiers under his command, but many of his soldiers were dispersed throughout the islands. Although he determined that he did not want to hold onto Manila when the United States invaded, he was ordered to defend the one million resident capital city at all costs. Yamashita had little control over 10,000 sailors under the command of Admiral Iwabuchi Sanji, who also insisted on holding Manila. On February 4, 1945, allied forces under MacArthur's command attacked Manila. By the time the area was liberated two weeks later, over 100,000 civilians had been killed, many by the deliberate actions of the Japanese forces. By 1945, the War Department was flooded with intelligence on the gravity of Japanese atrocities, which included the murder of children and medical personnel. In comparison, when Allied United States and Free French Forces liberated Paris, the German commanding general, Dietrich von Choltitz evacuated the city and only a few civilians were killed. Hitler had ordered Choltitz to destroy Paris, but the general refused to do so.[51]

Yamashita surrendered on September 2, 1945. On September 24, MacArthur ordered his subordinate, Lieutenant General Wilhelm Styer, to prosecute Yamashita in a military trial. Truman, Stimson, and the Chief of Staff of the Army, George C. Marshall supported MacArthur. His order for the trial provided Yamashita with the right to counsel, to cross-examine witnesses, and to have all of the testimony translated into Japanese. Moreover, the order permitted Yamashita the right to refuse to testify without any adverse consequences. This latter right did not exist in the Nuremberg trials, and in this respect, Yamashita's trial had some similarities to contemporary courts-martial. On October 8, the military prosecutors read 65 charges against Yamashita to the tribunal, which consisted of five American general officers. One of the charges was comprehensive, alleging that "between 9 October 1944 and 2 September 1945, at Manila and at other places in Philippine Islands ... [Yamashita] unlawfully disregarded and failed to discharge his duty as commander to control the operations of the members of his command, permitting them to commit brutal atrocities and other high crimes against the people of the United States and of its allies and dependencies." The other charges listed specific acts such as the torture and murder of over 32,000 Philippine citizens, murder of American prisoners of war, hundreds of rapes, and destruction of property.[52]

The defense team, which consisted of United States military attorneys as well as two Japanese officers who had been attached to Yamashita's staff, unsuccessfully sought additional time to prepare for trial and objected to the broad charge on the basis that it failed to allege any specific violation of the law of war. When, on October 8, 1945, the prosecution charged Yamashita with

51 Hoyt, *Three Military Leaders*, 151; also, Robert Ross Smith, *Triumph in the Philippines* (Washington, DC: Office of the Chief of Military History, Department of the Army, 1963), 239–41.

52 Richard Lael, *Yamashita Precedent*, 75–80; Phillip Piccigallo, *The Japanese on Trial: Allied War Crimes in the East, 1945–195* (Austin: University of Texas Press, 1979), 51.

an additional 57 offenses, his defense counsel also unsuccessfully sought more time to prepare for trial. Yamashita's trial began on October 29 and concluded on November 20. Only one witness tied Yamashita directly to the atrocities, but the atrocities were so widespread that he clearly knew that soldiers under his command had committed them. Although Yamashita was convicted and sentenced to death, he was zealously defended by his defense counsel. During the trial they affronted MacArthur by first appealing to the Philippine Supreme Court. Moreover, the defense counsel prepared all along to petition the United States Supreme Court for *habeas*.[53]

The Executive Branch's determination to prosecute Japanese war criminals was little different than their desire for establishing the International Military Tribunals for German war criminals. Stimson and the War Department's lawyers assumed that because of the Japanese conduct in China, the Philippines, and the Dutch, British, and French colonies, as well as the Japanese treatment of captured prisoners of war, the international community would agree to a scheme of trials similar to those that had occurred in Germany. Moreover, there was little if any domestic opposition to the claim that the attack on Pearl Harbor was an unjustified aggressive act of war to which the planners could be held accountable. Finally, the decision to take Yamashita to trial before an American military commission rather than an international tribunal was partly because the international apparatus for the trial of higher ranking officers was just being constructed and MacArthur desired quick trials.[54]

Although Frankfurter took no direct part in the decision to implement a military tribunal such as had been the case in the trial of the German saboteurs, his mark was on Yamashita's and Homma's trials nonetheless. In late 1944, following Frankfurter's advice, the War Department established a War Crimes Office under the command of General Myron Cramer. This office assisted MacArthur in drafting charges against Yamashita and other Japanese military leaders. Kenneth Royall, John J. McCloy, and Frederick Wiener participated in ensuring that Stimson's design for a military tribunal for lesser Japanese civil officials and military officers could apply to higher ranking officers such as the two generals. In so doing, they placed officers such as Yamashita subject to both international and national trials. Wiener not only advised the War Department, he ultimately drafted the government's written argument on the issue of jurisdiction to the Court. Years after the trial, he reminisced that he shared his work with Frankfurter prior to Yamashita's argument before the Court.[55]

---

53 George F. Guy to T. Harvey Reid, February 26, 1946 [Guy papers-AHC/1]; Adolph Frank Reel, *The Case of General Yamashita* (Chicago: University of Chicago Press, 1949), 197–200.

54 *See, e.g.*, Richard Lael, *The Yamashita Precedent*, 59–60.

55 Wiener to the Army Judge Advocate General, September 19, 1977 [FBWP]; Wiener, Personal Notes [FBWP].

Wiener's role in preparing the solicitor general to argue is noteworthy for another reason. He had been injured during the invasion of Okinawa and in December, 1945, medically transported to Walter Reed Army Hospital. While there, the Army returned him to the reserves, and he rejoined the Justice Department. By this time, Solicitor General Fahy and Atorney General Biddle had left the Justice Department. Fahy entered private practice, and Truman appointed Biddle to serve as a judge on the Nuremberg trials of Nazi leaders. They were temporarily replaced by Howard McGrath and Harold Judson, "neither of whom, unhappily had any familiarity with military law," in Wiener's words. Wiener wanted to de-emphasize that the military commission had been prosecuted in a fair manner, because he believed it had not been. However, he also believed that because Yamashita had failed to take any steps to investigate the conduct of his subordinates to ensure compliance with his orders, he was guilty. To Wiener's anger, McGrath attempted to argue that the trials of accorded both Yamashita and Homma due process. This same disagreement would ultimately divide the justices.[56]

Yamashita's counsel determined to follow the same path that the German saboteurs' counsel had, by applying directly to the Court, hoping that the end of hostilities would result in a different decision. One of Yamashita's defense counsel would later explain that the defense hoped to distinguish Yamashita's case from *Quirin* on the basis that in 1942, the war was raging, but in October 1945, the war was over. There was historic precedent for this appeal strategy. During the Civil War, the Court, in 1863, in *Vallandigham*, ruled that it did not have the jurisdiction to review the trial and imprisonment of the former congressman. After that war, five of the same justices determined in *Milligan* that the Constitution prohibited the military from prosecuting civilians in the United States where the civil courts were functioning. The conduct of the petitioners in *Milligan*, which included plotting an armed insurgency in Indiana, was far more egregious than that of Clement Vallandigham. The difference between the two cases, as William O. Douglas would later write, may have been that *Milligan* was decided when the passions of the conflict had subsided. Douglas likewise retrospectively claimed that *Korematsu* would have been decided differently in 1946 than it was two years earlier. Eight of the nine justices deciding the extent of Yamashita's rights to the jurisdiction of federal courts had also decided the military jurisdiction over the German saboteurs.[57]

Historic precedents such as those hoped for by Yamashita's counsel can be far more illusory than case precedents, and this was true in 1946. On December 15, 1945, Stone, Reed, Frankfurter, Rutledge, and Burton, attended the annual "Gridiron Dinner," in Washington D.C., they were seated with Dwight Eisenhower, and Admiral Ernest J. King, Admiral Marc Mitscher, and Nimitz. Mitscher and Nimitz openly discussed the impending trials of Japanese War criminals, while

56 Wiener to the Army Judge Advocate General, September 19, 1977 [FBWP].

57 General Kenneth Hodson to George F. Guy, June 29, 1967 [Guy Papers-AHC/2]; William O. Douglas, *The Court Years*, 38; Reel, *The Case of General Yamashita*.

Burton did not record if any of the justices participated in these discussions.[58] The justices at least obtained a first-hand account of the military's interest in the case.

Surprisingly, on December 20, 1945, Douglas railed against granting *certiorari* in the first place, without giving any reason. In fact, he initially wanted to publish a dissent from the order scheduling oral argument, but Stone, Frankfurter, and Burton convinced him against this. Howard Ball, in his study on Douglas' and Black's role in the "American Constitutional Revolution" stated that Douglas was "strangely silent" in Yamashita's case. Given Douglas' later disdain for military trials and his political ambitions, more than one scholar concluded that he feared any decision in Yamashita would affect his electoral chances, and so he consciously decided to place greater importance on his political ambition. On the other hand, he also may have worried that the decision would be acrimonious from the start and create a venue for foreign litigants being tried in war crimes tribunals in the Pacific and in Europe. What is clear about Douglas' actions is that he did not join in the dissent.[59]

Shortly after the conclusion of arguments, to Frankfurter's relief, Stone assigned himself to write the majority decision. Both men hoped the unanimity in *Quirin* would be repeated and Frankfurter threw himself into researching for Stone. For the second time in three months, Frankfurter encouraged a fellow justice to cite to Stephen Field's majority opinion in *Dow v. Johnson*. In that decision, Field, who had earlier retreated from supporting the Executive Branch's assertion of primacy over civil rights in wartime, articulated an exception to the subordination rule in wartime when the acts of commanders occurred in hostile enemy held territory. But the question in *Dow* was whether a federal or state court possessed jurisdiction to rule on the alleged military taking of civilian private property for personal gain, or put in another way, the jurisdiction to decide whether a commander acted within his authority or exceeded it. The Court, in *Dow*, determined that the federal and state courts did not possess such authority during the time of war when the acts occurred in hostile territory. Frankfurter was a scholar of history, and it cannot be missed that he encouraged Stone to cite Field, a nineteenth-century justice who was unfriendly to the expansion of military jurisdiction.[60]

Frankfurter was also concerned about the applicability of the 1929 Geneva Convention and the Articles of War to the decision. The 1929 Convention required that accused persons were placed on notice of the criminality of their actions at the time of their actions. Notice is, after all, a fundamental tenet of constitutional due process. Also, he worried that Article 25 of the Articles of War, which would have prevented the use of affidavits in lieu of testimony, did not govern war

58 Burton, diary entry for December 15, 1945 [HHB/1].

59 Douglas, Memorandum, December 20, 1945 [WOD/137]; Sidney Fine, *Frank Murphy: The Washington Years*, 453; Howard Ball, *Of Power and Right: Hugo Black, William O. Douglas and America's Constitutional Revolution* (New York: Oxford, 1992), 124.

60 Frankfurter to Stone, January 15, 1946 [HFS/72].

crimes tribunals held in times of war, and thus would be challenged to the Court. A question arose whether the trial of Yamashita occurred in time of war, since the Japanese Government had already surrendered by the time of the trial. In a second letter to Stone, Frankfurter argued that the Geneva Convention's articles applied only to prisoners of war on trial for offenses that occurred during their imprisonment and not for war crimes that occurred prior. Between Frankfurter's two letters, Stone had circulated his first draft opinion.[61]

Reed initially approved of Stone's draft opinion without much comment other than calling it "satisfactory." However, as time passed Reed reread the draft and sent a second letter to Stone, and although this time he called it "a fine piece of work," he lobbied for additional statements as to the fairness of the trial. Reed urged Stone to write into the opinion a paragraph on the irrelevancy of placing Yamashita on notice. Moreover, to prove the trial fair, he argued that the procedures of the trial should be painted with a veneer of universal application. "I think that American soldiers could have been tried by a military commission for the acts for which Yamashita is convicted," he added. This argument enraged Black, who believed that the trial was not fair by American standards, but also believed the fairness of the trial was irrelevant to the issue before the Court.[62]

On January 28, 1946, Black informed Stone that he would not join in the majority's decision so long as it incorporated Reed's views. Black was particularly appalled at Reed's suggestion that the time allotted to the defense to prepare for the monumental case was adequate, or that under the "Federal Constitution," the trial, if conducted against a citizen, would have been upheld. "[These] additions place us in the attitude of defending the Commission's action rather than saying that it is beyond our powers of review."[63]

As if to reinforce to Stone that he was certain of his position, Black began to draft a concurrence, which could easily have been read as a dissent. "I am constrained to express my complete disagreement with that part of the Court's opinion which decides that the Fifth Amendment Due Process Clause applies to these military proceedings and then proceeds to hold that the condemnation of Yamashita conformed to the Constitutional standard of Due Process," Black began his draft. Equally telling, Black added that the Commission had, in fact, violated the principle of notice as required by the 1899 and 1907 Hague Conventions, but that the violation of this fundamental tenet of Anglo-American law did not negate the Commission's jurisdiction. The draft concurrence concluded with the statement that it "is not to be taken as approval of what has been done, but only as a representation of [his] belief that the Constitution leaves to the military power to make a final judgment in this narrow field which [he] outlined." Black shared his draft with Stone and in a cover letter added that he

61 Frankfurter to Stone, January 22, 1946 [HFS/72].

62 Reed to Stone, January 22, 1946 [HFS/72]; Reed to Stone, January 22, 1946 [HFS/72].

63 Black to Stone, January 28, 1946 [HFS/72].

had "serious doubt" that the charges against Yamashita stated an offense under the laws of war, adding that the United States had failed to notify the foreign neutral nations of the intent to charge Yamashita such as Switzerland which, in turn, violated international law. These issues were why, Black reminded Stone, he voted for argument in the first place.[64]

The day after Black informed Stone that he was likely to concur, rather than join the majority, Stone reassured Black that he would shortly re-circulate his opinion which would, he promised, "show the narrow effect of the rulings on the evidence question." Stone understood that this might not be enough to sway Black, but he asked Black to make "concrete suggestions of alterations" or to circulate his own concurrence.[65]

When Stone re-circulated his opinion, Reed weighed in on the issue of depositions. The Articles of War expressly permitted depositions in lieu of live testimony in non-capital cases, but was silent as to their use in capital cases. In federal criminal trials and capital courts-martial, depositions introduced over the objection of the defendant or accused soldier violated the Sixth Amendment Confrontation Clause. Reed modified his earlier stridency and now claimed he did not approve of Stone's statement that the evidentiary rulings in Yamashita's case complied with the Articles of War. On the other hand, Reed claimed that the use of depositions in Yamashita's trial was justified, and would concur on this basis. Black maintained his determination to concur as well. Stone ultimately compromised, and in his final draft decision articulated that both Article 25 and Article 38 (the article governing hearsay and opinion evidence) did not specifically apply to the trials of enemy combatants. Stone's attempt to convince Reed was convoluted in the sense that he argued that military commissions were free to ignore evidentiary rules when the accused was an enemy combatant, but not when the accused was a United States serviceman. Reed agreed, but this made little sense, because the limited purpose of utilizing a military commission to try a United States soldier, something which had not occurred since the Civil War, could only occur when witness presence or court-martial empanelment were infeasible due to wartime exigencies.[66]

Frankfurter found his patience at an end with Black, Reed, Rutledge, and Murphy, telling Stone that he supported the revised decision "without a change of a comma." He then added a quote from Holmes, something he would repeatedly do throughout his judicial tenure: "please remember Holmes' remarks to his brethren when they asked him to take out some of the choicest things in one of his opinions: I bring you a fine steaming plum pudding and one of you asks me to take out this luscious plum and another that one until finally you leave nothing but a

---

64 Black, Draft Concurrence, January 28, 1946 [HLB/283]; Black to Stone, undated [HLB/283].

65 Stone to Black, January 29, 1946 [HLB/283] [HFS/72].

66 Reed to Stone, January 30, 1946 [HFS/72]. For the trial of military personnel in military commissions, *see* Joshua Kastenberg, *Law in War, Law as War*, 64.

piece of dough and call it a plum pudding." For a justice who prided his service on the Wickersham Commission and publicly proclaimed the injustice of the Mooney and Sacco and Vanzetti trials, his statements that Yamashita's trial was not only fair for a captured war criminal, but also fair under American military standards, is perplexing.[67]

On January 31, Reed informed Stone that he would join the majority opinion in its entirety. Shortly after, Black did as well. Douglas, who had been silent on the debate, agreed at the same time as Black joined with Stone. Jackson probably would have joined, but could not do so because of his presence in Nuremberg. Burton, who had likewise taken a quiet role in the deliberations, also agreed with Stone.[68]

Both Rutledge and Murphy made it clear they would dissent from the beginning. The two justices believed that the entire proceeding had been bereft of due process and this fact alone vitiated any jurisdiction the military trial had in the first place. Perhaps stemming from his arguments in *Korematsu*, Murphy also believed that Yamashita's trial was infected with racism. Rutledge was not as convinced as Murphy on this point, but like Murphy, he believed that Yamashita was prosecuted *ex post facto* and that the trial lacked in due process safeguards. However, Rutledge would not join with Murphy because Murphy was willing to concede that the military commission was lawfully established, and Rutledge insisted it was not.[69]

Murphy's draft dissent did not trouble Stone or Frankfurter, and both justices expected Murphy's arguments. When Rutledge circulated his draft dissent in early January, however, it caught Stone by surprise that Rutledge had articulately argued that the trial was deficient in conventional fair trial standards. Rutledge centered his arguments that Yamashita was convicted of failing to control his troops, a charge unknown to military law at the time, while the Germans on trial in the international tribunals were prosecuted for actually ordering the criminal activity for which they were charged. Stone reacted by arguing that the trial was fair in its entire application until Black threatened to rebel and file a concurrence. Rutledge had powerful allies for his dissent both in the lower courts and in academia, including Charles Fairman who Stone had successfully lobbied to become the Clerk of the Court.[70]

When the final decision was ready for publication, the majority was emphatic from the start that the justices were "not concerned with the guilt or innocence" of Yamashita and would confine the decision to the issue of jurisdiction, much as the Court had done in *Vallandigham* some 80 years earlier. Moreover, the

---

67 Frankfurter to Stone, January 30, 1946 [HFS/72].

68 Reed to Stone, January 30, 1946 [HFS/72].

69 Sidney Fine, Frank Murphy: The Washington Years, 453; John Ferren, *Salt of the Earth, Conscience of the Court*, 305.

70 John Ferren, *Salt of the Earth, Conscience of the Court*, 310–12. On Fairman, *see* Stone to Fairman, July 8, 1944 [HFS/12].

majority distinguished *Milligan* from Yamashita's trial because the trial in question was held with an enemy military officer as the accused, and not a group of civilians. As to the question of whether the jurisdiction of military commissions terminated with the end of a formal state of war, the majority rightly noted that the overwhelming bulk of credible legal scholarship available concluded that the military's jurisdiction continued after the surrender of an enemy. Following this holding, the majority then analyzed the more difficult substantive issues. Yamashita was never prosecuted for ordering atrocities, but rather, for failing to prevent them. There were no clear treaty obligations to this point, though certainly, the 1899 and 1907 Hague Conventions could be read to extend to the obligation of a commander to exert control over forces under their command, where the commander had the authority to prevent it. During the Civil War and the Philippine Insurrection, United States officers were court-martialed under the Articles of War for direct involvement in atrocities, though with mixed results.

As noted, a fundamental difference between courts-martial and the military commission that tried Yamashita was the use of deposition testimony. The 1916 Articles of War prohibited the use of depositions in courts-martial where the accused soldier faced a capital offense. Deposition testimony in such instances could eviscerate the right to confront one's accusers as guaranteed in the Constitution's Sixth Amendment. The majority agreed that Yamashita would not be entitled under the Articles of War to similar protections, because that law specifically exempted military commissions from the protections afforded accused soldiers in courts-martial.

Less clear was whether the nation's obligations under the 1929 Geneva Convention required a different result. The convention clearly stated that enemy prisoners of war were entitled to be tried for offenses under the same laws and procedures that the prosecuting nation used over their own military forces. Stone, with Frankfurter's urging, was able to muster the majority to decide that this requirement existed for prisoners of war whose offenses occurred while in captivity, and not for war crimes such as Yamashita's. In the end, the majority believed none of the alleged deficiencies vitiated the military trial's jurisdiction.

Murphy's dissent attacked the majority for determining that due process, in its full form, did not protect some accused persons prosecuted in United States courts. Murphy acknowledged that Yamashita's soldiers committed widespread atrocities, "while under the heavy and destructive attack of our forces." Nonetheless, because the War Department did not charge Yamashita with taking direct part in the atrocities, his charge of failing to control his forces was an *ex post facto* violation of due process. Murphy had a point. During the Civil War, for instance, the military commissions over captured Confederate raiders, privateers, the assassination conspiracy, and the Andersonville Prison commandant all were charged with violations that were already codified as offenses. Murphy also commended the Court's majority for disregarding the government's contention that the military tribunal in its entirety existed outside of the scope of judicial review. Nonetheless, he chastised the majority for failing to recognize the greater implications of the due process violation, namely that it hampered the establishment of an international order based on a respect for law. Borrowing from Abraham Lincoln, Murphy concluded, "an uncurbed spirit of revenge and retribution, masked in formal legal procedure for purposes of dealing with a fallen enemy commander, can do more lasting harm than all of the atrocities giving rise to that spirit ... leaving forlorn and impoverished the noble ideal of malice toward none and charity to all."

Rutledge also dissented, first attacking the principle charge of Yamashita's failure to act. He and Murphy agreed that Murphy would limit his dissent to the charge, and Rutledge "to the balance," meaning the other procedural defects. To Rutledge, the charge was "unprecedented" in American history. On May 7, 1945, the Court decided *Screws v. United States* in which it reversed a conviction of a Georgia sheriff and other policemen who murdered an African-American prisoner. The sheriff and policemen were prosecuted in federal court for conspiring to deny the prisoner of his civil rights under the Fourteenth Amendment. Perhaps surprisingly in retrospect, an all-white jury convicted the white defendants. The Court found that the statute was vague in its wording and therefore the conviction had to be reversed. Rutledge then attacked the constraints on the defense's opportunity to prepare for trial, the use of hearsay evidence to secure a death sentence, and the majority's interpretation of the obligations under both the Articles of War and Geneva Convention. Privately, to Professor John Frank, a former Black clerk, Rutledge would compare the Court's opinion to one as bad as *Dred Scott*.[71]

Interestingly, John Frank's correspondence with Black is not only instructive as to the role Black took in modifying Stone's and Frankfurter's position on due process, it also provides insight into how some prominent legal scholars evolved from supporting the nation's military justice system to eventually viewing it as lacking fairness. By the time *Yamashita* was argued, Frank had left his position as Black's clerk and taught law at University of Iowa. Frank conceded that the military had jurisdiction over Yamashita and the offenses under which the Army charged him were also law of war violations. But he called the trial an outrage nonetheless because of the abundant use of double and triple hearsay, as well as the accused's right to a complete defense. "The provisions of the Sixth Amendment had been particularly so flagrantly violated that the commission could not know whether the accused was guilty or innocent and the case should have been reversed for a new trial," he urged

71 *Screws v. United States*, 325 U.S. 91(1945). Rutledge penned Frank, "a dissenter is apt to exaggerate in his view of what the majority do. Maybe I do so here. Nevertheless, in my honest and I hope sober judgment, this case will outrank *Dred Scott* in the annals of the Court." Rutledge to John Frank (undated, 1946) [WR/137].

Black. Frank was not a merely a bystander on this case either. Captain Adolf Reel, one of Yamashita's defense counsels, was his cousin.[72]

Black did not take offense to Frank's characterization of the government's conduct in the case, and since the Court's opinion had not been published, Frank was unaware of Black's position on the issue of due process. Nor did Black's reply directly address the issue as to whether the fairness of the trial was an issue for the Court to consider. Instead, Black responded by urging Frank to consider an issue which Frank had not raised, but was at the center of Black's reasoning nonetheless. "In the absence of an Act of Congress or a treaty, what is the extent of the power of courts to control the action of the military in the enforcement of battle rules designed to regulate the battle conduct of the enemy?" Black asked. "Which Constitutional Amendments apply to the regulation of enemy conduct in fighting American troops?" Frank, like Rutledge, worried that the avoidance of addressing the trial's fairness would later preclude the judiciary from deciding on the fairness of all military trials including courts-martial. Indeed, he compared Stone's opinion to "a magician in the Vaudeville show," which hid the important issue. Later, Black would ensure that *Yamashita* did not apply to citizens, including soldiers, but he also concluded that the charges in *Yamashita* could apply to soldiers, if the military alleged that Yamashita's defense of not ordering his soldiers to commit atrocities was not tenable in courts-martial.[73]

As in much of the Court's wartime work, *Yamashita* appeared externally to be a harmonious decision for six of the eight justices participating, but this was not the case. However, Frankfurter passed Murphy a note after he read his dissent stating that while he disagreed with the dissent, he "wholly respected the utterance of [Murphy's] conscience taking a contrary view," adding, "This applies to Wiley." But, then in Frankfurter's derogatory fashion, he added that he could "not say as much all around." It was clear at this point that Frankfurter had marked Black and, to a lesser extent, Douglas, as watering down the majority into what he believed to be a hardly usable decision. Again, for a justice who championed Sacco, Vanzetti, Mooney, and the Bisbee defendants, and served on the Wickersham Commission, his acceptance of the fairness of Yamashita's trial is a mystery.[74]

Douglas, for his part, agreed that officers who failed to stop servicemen from committing atrocities could find themselves convicted for that failure. But this was nothing new to military law because in the Civil War and during the Filipino insurrection, there were courts-martial of service members for this very conduct. Moreover, Wiener stressed this point to the War Department when drafting the Solicitor General's brief, urging that the same standards of responsibility would

72 Frank to Black, February 5, 1946 [JPFP/1].

73 Black to Frank, February 16, 1946 [JFPF/1]. Still unbeknownst to Frank, Black did in fact force Stone and Frankfurter to abandon their arguments that Yamashita's trial comported with due process standards. When informed of this on March 9, 1946 Frank responded by calling Stone's opinion, "downright dishonest" [JFPF/1].

74 Sidney Fine, *Frank Murphy, The Washington Years*, 458.

ultimately apply to United States service members. In 1972, Douglas informed journalist Irving Brant that Nixon's attorney general "should bone up on the Yamashita decision," and prosecute senior officers for the My Lai massacre as well as other law of war violations for failing to stop their occurrence. Brant argued to Douglas that the Burger Court would be "caught in a bind, because of its zeal for law and order." Two of Yamashita's defense counsel, George Guy and Reel, argued that neither General Westmoreland nor the Secretary of Defense or President should be denied due process such as Yamashita had been.[75]

In 1949, Adolf Reel published his memoirs of the *Yamashita* trial and appeal with the prestigious University of Chicago Press. Titled *The Case of General Yamashita*, the book was largely a narrative that humanized Yamashita and criticized MacArthur's role in overseeing the case. Although Reel criticized the governance of the commission throughout the book, he was not as forceful as Murphy's dissent. Reel also undermined the value of his memoirs to his contemporaries by arguing that the Nuremburg trials lacked the same due process guarantees as Yamashita's trial, namely that the charges against the defendants at Nuremberg had no basis in law and therefore violated the due process principle of notice.[76]

By its very nature, *The Case of General Yamashita*, was bound to draw criticism. In response to Reel, MacArthur argued that "there were no new principles of law, either national or international." About Homma, the general emphatically stated that if he "didn't deserve his judicial fate, no one in jurisdictional history ever did." By the time of the publication, Reel had become a prominent lawyer representing labor unions. MacArthur's former aide, General Courtney Whitney, himself a trained lawyer and in 1949 the Chief of the Army Government Section, accused Reel of stoking anti-American sentiment in Japan at the behest of pro-Communist subversive elements. Whitney's alleged evidence for this claim was the fact that Reel's book had been translated into Japanese and Reel's ties to organized labor. Following the publication of the book, J. Edgar Hoover likewise considered Reel a communist and moved to deny Reel access to a security clearance. Neither Wiener nor Frankfurter joined in Whitney's attempts to tar Reel as pro-communist, but Whitney might have succeeded nonetheless. In light of the Taft–Hartley Act, which removed suspected communists from positions of union leadership, Whitney conducted a smear that was simply not cemented in any reality. Tellingly, *Yamashita* was the last military case in which Reel engaged as a lead counsel.[77]

---

75 Brant to Douglas, June 17, 1972 [Brant 13]; Wiener to the Army Judge Advocate General, September 19, 1977 [FBW]; Joan Whelan, "Guy Sees Little Comparison in Yamashita, Calley Cases," Casper Star Tribune, June 3, 1971 [George Guy Papers-AHC/2]; A Frank Reel, "Playing Pontius Pilate: War Crimes Procedure Hypocritical," Montreal Star, April 1, 1971 [George Guy Papers-AHC/2].

76 Reel, *The Case of General Yamashita.*

77 Douglas MacArthur, *Reminiscences*, 295–7; Courtney Whitney, "*The Case of General Yamashita:* Memorandum" (US Army, 1949), 19–22; Herbert Philbrick to J. Edgar

Although Frankfurter did not openly criticize or secretly try to defame Reel, the book was not well received by a number of prominent jurists, particularly in Reel's characterization of the justices. "Justice Frankfurter led in posing questions that seemed to be designed to aid the government's case," Reel argued. "His questions indicated to me that he believed that the Court must uphold Yamashita's conviction and that he was concerned with finding logical basis for that decision which might provide common ground on which the greatest possible number of his colleagues would agree." Wiener told Frankfurter he "forced himself" to read Reel's book and found it "superficial." Likewise Frankfurter called the book "flapdoodle," and unsuccessfully sought Harvard University professor Charles Curtis to write a criticism of it.[78]

V: Fears of Communism in the Ranks and in War Industries

Contemporaneously to the Court's deliberations in *Duncan* and *Yamashita*, Federal Bureau of Investigations Director, J. Edgar Hoover warned Truman that approximately 12,000 servicemen had active ties to the communist party. Fear of communists in the nation's defense industries was nothing new to the New Deal justices. In March 1941, when Nazi Germany appeared the most likely and dangerous enemy, Undersecretary of War Robert Patterson noted to Robert Jackson, then serving as attorney general, that both he and General Henry "Hap" Arnold believed "communistic elements" caused a labor slowdown at Boeing's aircraft manufacturing plant in Seattle. "The Boeing Co, as you doubtless know, makes our B-17 heavy bombers and is one of our most important aircraft plants," Patterson warned. "Reports have come to us from Air Corps officers at the plant that there is a definite slowdown because of communistic elements among the employees." Patterson also wondered whether Jackson would permit Hoover to place agents in the facility.[79]

Communists in the military ranks were another matter. By 1945 Paul Crouch had departed the CPUSA and he convinced J. Edgar Hoover that other men, including a World War I veteran named Dwight James Freeman, spread subversion into military installations in Hawaii and California. Freeman, a leader in the Church of Latter Day Saints appeared to be innocent of any wrongdoing. He obtained an honorable discharge following wartime service in France and became influential in his church in California and then Hawaii. However, in 1955

Hoover, April 20, 1959 [Philbrick Papers/168]; "Republicans Uncover the Real Reel," The GOP Minuteman, February 3, 1959 [Philbrick Papers/168].

78 Reel, *The Case of General Yamashita*, 215. Reel noted his familiarity with Frankfurter as: "I had studied under Frankfurter at Harvard law School and had become somewhat acquainted with his particular mode of logical thinking and his extremely practical judicial philosophy."

79 Robert P. Patterson to Robert Jackson, March 5, 1941 [RHJ/ 87].

Freeman was convicted under the Smith Act along with six others in a trial known as the "Hawaiian Seven." During the post-war demobilization, Crouch conveyed to Hoover and Attorney General Clark that there were over 100 communists in classified positions in Hawaii. Although Crouch likely exaggerated these numbers, his own past, which included a stint in Army intelligence while clandestinely being a communist, did provide some credence to his claims.[80]

During World War II, the Federal Bureau of Investigation discovered that the Soviet Union directed espionage activities aimed at the United States military. For instance, William Ullman, a commissioned Army Air Force officer provided the Soviet Union information on the B-29 bomber as well as plans for the Normandy invasion. Another officer named Ilya Wolston was accused of conveying similar information, though the allegations were never substantiated. The Articles of War prohibited espionage and, just as in the case of Rufo Romero, these individuals could have been prosecuted. But the military proved unable to ferret out Soviet agents. Additionally, while there were criminal laws that prohibited spying that applied to all persons regardless of amenability to military jurisdiction, these laws had a checkered history. During the war, the War Department's leadership appeared to desire that the attorney general prosecute these cases, yet this seldom happened.[81]

When Congress enacted the Smith Act in 1940, which prohibited individuals or organizations from acting to overthrow the government (or encouraging others to do so), and required aliens to register with the government, it did not do so with the needs of military discipline in mind. But in 1941 after the Federal Bureau of Investigation raided the Minneapolis offices of the Socialist Workers Party, an organization influenced by Leon Trotsky whose members had been influential in labor unrest prior to the Japanese attack on Pearl Harbor, the implications of the Smith Act in enforcing military discipline became evident. The Socialist Workers Party was not part of the CPUSA (which had promised a no-strike policy during the war), but rather it was an organization at odds with the CPUSA. In all, 29 individuals belonging to the Socialist Workers Party were prosecuted in federal court, alleged by the Justice Department to have fostered "insubordination in the armed forces," in violation of both the Smith Act and a Civil War-era statute. The jury acquitted all Party members of violating the Civil War-era statute, but convicted 23 of the civilians of violating the Smith Act.

In *Dunne v. United States*, the Court of Appeals for the Eighth Circuit, upheld the convictions and sentences of the 23 men, in the process finding

---

80 United States Army Surveillance of Dissidents, Report on Resistance Inside the Military, April 18, 1968 [UPA/17]. On Crouch, *see* Attorney General Herbert Brownell to Crouch, June 8, 1954 [Paul Crouch/15]; also, *Crouch v. United States*, 13 F.2d 348 (CA 9, 1926). *See also*, Joseph Alsop, "The Powerful Imaginer," Washington Post, April 19, 1954. On Dwight Freeman, *see Fujimoto v. United States*, 251 F.2d 342 (CA 9, 1958).

81 On Soviet espionage in the United States in World War II, *see* John E. Haynes and Harvey Klehr, *Early Cold War Spies* (New York: Cambridge, 2006), 23–66.

the Smith Act constitutional. The three judge panel, consisting of one Wilson and two Roosevelt appointees, reasoned, "an armed force which lacks loyalty, morale or discipline or wherein is insubordination, disloyalty, mutiny or refusals to do their duty is far worse than no armed force at all and is positively an active menace to constituted government and to the liberties of the people." The judges did not arrive at this conclusion simply because of a personal dislike of communism. One of the organization's stated goals was to place men into the Army, and then encourage demonstrations against poor food, housing, lack of leave, and assignments to missions. Although the CPUSA did not support this Leninist organization, its promise of no strikes during wartime ended with Japan's surrender on September 2, 1945.[82]

On January 9, 1946, J. Edgar Hoover informed Truman's military aide, Brigadier General Harry Vaughan, that Irving Goff, a former OSS officer, urged his fellow New York-based communists to demand the speedy return of soldiers from the Pacific theatre. This activity was to be done in concert with communist servicemen in the Pacific. Two days later, Hoover warned Vaughan that the CPUSA duped the Veterans of Foreign Wars, the American Legion, and Jewish War Veterans to stage a rally in New York to further demand demobilization. At the same time, servicemen in Hawaii and in the Philippines held public demonstrations numbering in the thousands, also demanding demobilization.[83]

On January 18, Hoover advised Vaughan that Eugene Dennis, a CPUSA leader soon to become part of named Court decision, was leading a "four-man secretariat [that] is advocating a work stoppage demonstration to protest demobilization and threatening to cause agitation and trouble among members of the armed forces." Hoover also warned that Dennis would spearhead a strike at the Western Union Corporation. Because the military relied on Western Union to transmit orders, the processing of individual demobilization orders would grind to a halt. To Hoover, the communist activity was a two-front operation. In eastern cities, citizens would demand demobilization and the military, due to a slowdown in processing orders, would look incompetent in returning veterans to civilian life. This would lower morale and readiness amongst the remaining servicemen. A minority of servicemen did, in fact, protest the slowness in demobilization, but their efforts resulted in little gain.[84]

In February, Hoover provided Vaughan a report detailing how effectively the CPUSA had infiltrated the military. The report named less than 50 persons, although it included four officers. Hoover implicitly cautioned that "Negro

---

82 *Dunne v. United States*, 138 F.2d 137 (CA 8, 1942).

83 Hoover to Truman, January 9, 1946; January 11, 1946, [HST R/21]; Robert Ferrell, *Harry S. Truman: A Life* (Columbia, MO: University of Missouri Press, 1994), 227–8. R. Alton Lee, "The Army Mutiny of 1946," *The Journal of American History*, Vol. 53, No. 3 (Dec., 1966), 555–71.

84 Hoover to Truman, January 18, 1946; January 29, 1946, [HST R/21].

soldiers" were susceptible to communist recruiting, a bias that he would later express against civil rights leaders through the post-war period. Although he claimed as many as 15,000 soldiers had communist sympathies and the party wanted to place communists in uniform, he did not articulate any activities beyond the previous demobilization protests and slowdown from the prior month. Importantly however, Hoover shared this information with both Army and Navy intelligence, Attorney General Tom Clark, and Chief Justice Stone. Frankfurter, Jackson, Reed and Burton independently believed that communist infiltration in the defense establishment, no matter how small or ineffective, posed a significant risk to national security and foreign policy. Later, when Tom Clark joined the Court, he too added to the consensus that communism had found its way into the defense establishment.[85]

Even though the American military that emerged from the victory of World War II was a highly disciplined force, the smallest demonstration for rapid demobilization posed a risk, and to more than simply the Armed Forces. Mutinies had occurred in modern democratic militaries before. In April 1917, a large swath of the French Army refused to follow orders or attack German positions. Had the German high command known of the French Army's indiscipline, the allies might have been dealt a disastrous defeat, ending World War I with France defeated. Moreover, French communists had stoked this mutiny, although the inept French command, horrific conditions of life in the trenches, the austere and capricious French military disciplinary system, and thousands of dead and mutilated French soldiers certainly contributed to the size and scope of the mass refusal. In 1919, British soldiers publicly organized in Folkestone and Dover, demanding to be demobilized. While the war was already over, the so-called Folkestone mutiny made it difficult for the British government to maintain colonial and foreign policies, and adversaries such as the Turkish government under Mustafa Kemal were emboldened to sidestep armistice conditions. Moreover, British sailors mutinied in Invergordon, Scotland, in 1931, demanding higher pay, evidencing a weakness in Britain's premier armed service. In 1947, sailors in the Royal New Zealand Navy mutinied, demanding higher pay as well. Communism played a role in each of these mutinies, or so military commanders believed.[86]

The United States military was not in danger of a communist takeover in 1946, or at any time thereafter. Espionage was primarily the concern of the

---

85 Hoover to Truman, February 6, 1946 [HST R/21].

86 For the French Army mutinies of 1917, *see, e.g.*, Richard M. Watt, *Dare Call it Treason* (New York: Simon & Schuster, 1963); and Paul Marie de la Gorce, *The French Army; a Military-Political History*, Kenneth Douglas trans. (New York: G. Braziller, 1963). For the British Army riots in 1918–1919 *see* Ian F. Beckett, *A Nation in Arms: A Social Study of the British Army in the First World War* (Manchester: Manchester University Press, 1985), 213–41. On the Invergordon Mutiny *see*, Christopher M. Bell, "The Invergordon Mutiny, 1931," in Christoper M. Bell and Bruce A. Elleman, ed., *Naval Mutinies of the Twentieth Century: An International Perspective* (London: Frank Cass, 2003), 140–49.

military's leadership. Indeed, Patterson investigated the issue and concluded that thousands of men eligible for release were kept in the Army out of bureaucratic incompetence as well as a few who were kept in so that senior officers could continue to have chauffeurs and other soldiers to conduct personal tasks. But a few communists in the military represented a threat for another insidious reason. If American military forces appeared ill-disciplined, infiltrated with communists, and weak, communists in Europe and Asia would be emboldened to act against the west, and non-communists would be more likely to negotiate, rather than oppose communists. Moreover, Stalin would take notice of a weak American military and act more aggressively in Europe and Asia. After all, the smaller but better equipped American conventional forces relied on discipline along with technology to deter the larger Soviet numbers.[87]

In retrospect, it is debatable whether the small and ineffective demonstrations in Hawaii resulted in any gain for the communists. Certainly, Stalin's soldiers were making enemies in occupied Europe through their brutal treatment of civilians. Soviet soldiers raped and pillaged with little accountability, while American soldiers who did so were usually prosecuted in courts-martial. This undermined the communist position. But it is also true that by 1946, the Army's discipline had declined and this fact was certainly within Truman's and Attorney General Clark's knowledge, as well as that of the military's leadership. Dean Rusk, later Secretary of State under Kennedy and Johnson, believed that the lack of readiness of the military during the two years after Japan's surrender directly contributed to Stalin's increasing willingness to push American resolve and bully nations on the Soviet border. With varying degrees, the justices on the Court in the years immediately following World War II accepted the fact that the Soviet Union and CPUSA worked to undermine United States strength in a variety of hidden ways. A quarter century later, General J. Lawton Collins noted that he and other high-ranking officers believed that the 1946 demobilization problems emboldened communist leaders across the world.[88]

Fears of communist infiltration into the military would continue well beyond the Vietnam conflict, with some justification, but also with the rights of some individuals being trammeled as a result of such fears. In 1955, the Secretary of the Army issued a six page pamphlet titled, "How to Spot a Communist." In it, soldiers were informed that communists were predisposed to discuss civil rights, problems of racial and religious discrimination, and criticize anti-subversive legislation, as well as the need to unionize. Ultimately, the Army retracted the pamphlet on President Eisenhower's orders after prominent Democrats such as Lyndon Johnson protested its issuance. Nonetheless, the pamphlet evidenced the military establishment's mindset toward

87 Michael S. Sherry, *Preparing for the Next War: American Plans for Post-War Defense, 1941–1945* (New Haven: Yale, 1977), 192–3. *See also* generally, John Sparrow, *History of Demobilization in the United States Army* (DC: GPO, 1952).

88 Robert Ferrell, *Truman, A Life*, 227–8; John Lewis Gaddis, *We Now Know: Rethinking Cold War History* (New York: Oxford, 1997), 286–7; J. Lawton Collins, *War in Peacetime: The History and Lessons of Korea* (New York: Houghton-Mifflin, 1969), 39.

discipline within the ranks. The pamphlet's authors professed that the concerns over communism in the ranks dated to World War II.[89]

VI: Stone's Last Case: *Girouard v. United States,* and Black's Interim as "Acting Chief"

On April 22, 1946, Stone died as a result of a cerebral hemorrhage that occurred on the bench as he read his dissent in *Girouard v. United States*. Douglas had just articulated the majority's decision in which the Court concluded that the willingness to bear arms in the nation's defense was not a requisite to obtaining citizenship, because, "important as it is, it is not the only way in which our institutions may be supported and defended, even in times of great peril." Douglas went on to note that in a total war, the United States utilized nuclear physicists, engineers, construction battalion men, litter bearers, and medical personnel. Girouard, a Seventh Day Adventist from Canada had not refused to wear a uniform, but he claimed that his religious beliefs prevented him from killing a fellow human being. Stone argued that the majority had ignored the plain language of the naturalization statutes. But nowhere in the plain language was there a requirement to physically bear arms in the nation's defense.[90]

Stone, with Frankfurter's prodding, was convinced that Congress intended, in a 1942 statute, to deny citizenship from applicants who refused to physically bear arms or serve in the armed forces. Girouard had been willing to serve as a non-combatant but had never been called to do so. Stone, Frankfurter, and ultimately Reed dissented, and for Frankfurter the dissent proved a window into his linkage of honorable military service and the privileges of citizenship in a later, far more contentious case decided in 1958 titled as *Trop v. Dulles*.[91]

Between Stone's death and the appointment of a new chief justice, the Court's senior justice, Black, served as acting chief. Two petitions for *certiorari* involving war crimes trials stemming from Japanese conduct in the Philippine Islands were brought to his attention. Following the military commissions trials of Yamashita and Homma, the Army prosecuted Mariano Uyeki, a person of Japanese ancestry living in the Philippines prior to the Japanese invasion, working as a farmer. He assisted the Japanese military track American service members and participated in the murder of Philippine citizens. His defense counsel appealed to the Court, arguing that Uyeki was not a member of an invading force and should have been subject only to trial in the Philippine courts. This was an important point. Shortly after the appeal was filed, the Philippines attained full independence. The second petition was filed after the Philippines had achieved independence. The petitioner,

89 Anon., *How to Spot a Communist* (1955).

90 328 U.S. 61 (1946). On Stone's death, *see* Bruce Murphy, *Wild Bill: The Legend and Life of William O. Douglas* (New York: Random House, 2003), 243.

91 Frankfurter to Stone, March 30, 1946 [HFS/72].

Teodoro Cantos, likewise, was a Philippine national of Japanese ancestry who sometimes used the last name Tatishi, aided the Japanese occupation forces in committing atrocities against the local population. Both Uyeki and Cantos were sentenced to death.

In what became captioned as *Uyeki v. Styer* and *Cantos v. Styer*, the Court would have been confronted with a jurisdictional question of whether the Philippine Courts had sole jurisdiction since both petitioners were Philippine nationals and their conduct occurred in the Philippines. Moreover, the Philippine government had wanted jurisdiction to prosecute, but MacArthur insisted on military trials. Wiener acted as a go-between the War and Justice Departments in formulating how to approach both cases. But he also corresponded with Frankfurter, who advised him that in Stone's absence, Black might prevail on the issue of determining whether both trials met due process. "Some months later, when I privately spoke with Mr. Justice Frankfurter, who had been my teacher in law school, he remarked that if any member of the majority had undertaken to question any part of the C.J.s majority opinion, the Court would have become fractionalized, rendering impossible any decision on which a majority of the justices could agree," Wiener recorded, before concluding that Black would likely overturn *Uyeki* and *Cantos* on jurisdiction, but also comment on the lack of fairness in both trials.[92]

When Wiener approached Black with the government's brief, Black expressed to him that he had doubts about the "correctness of the Yamashita case." As a result, Secretary of War Robert Patterson and Attorney General McGrath concluded that it was in the best interests in the event of a future conflict, to make *Uyeki* and *Cantos* moot. But to do so, they had to confront MacArthur. To this end, Patterson employed Dean Rusk, who at the time was working as a special assistant to Patterson. MacArthur remained insistent that the Army execute both Uyeki and Cantos, and only after Patterson's order to transfer both men to the Philippine Government did MacArthur relinquish his authority. Although this event is not especially well-remembered, Frankfurter's advice to Wiener, and Black's influence over the process, maintained a construct of limited judicial intervention in war crimes trials. In 1977, Wiener summarized, "What I do know … is that by overruling MacArthur in those two cases, Judge Patterson prevented an impending erosion in the power of the United States in any future dealings with offenders against the laws of war." Had Stone remained on the Court, the outcome might very well have been different.[93]

---

92 *Uyeki v. Styer*, 329 U.S. 689 (1946); *Cantos v. Styer*, 329 U.S. 682 (1942).

93 Wiener to Robert Patterson, August 14, 1947 [Patterson/48]. In this letter Wiener is approaching Patterson about forming a private practice, but recalls the interaction with Frankfurter on the issue of Uyeki and Cantos; *see also*, Wiener to the Army Judge Advocate General, September 19, 1977 [FBWP].

Chapter 5
The Vinson Court: Communism, National Security, and Deference to the Military Establishment, 1946–1952

The "Vinson Court" saw the appointment not only of Vinson as the new Chief Justice, but two other justices who would impact the Supreme Court's military jurisprudence, Thomas Clark and Sherman Minton.

Vinson

After Stone's death, Truman could have turned to the Court to find a successor as chief, much as Roosevelt had with Stone. But the Court was already wracked by dissension. The two justices most likely to replace Stone were Jackson and Black. To Truman, Jackson's public accusation of Black's unethical conduct in not recusing himself in *Jewell Ridge* was proof enough that Jackson could not lead the Court. Although Truman favored Black over Jackson, he realized that if he appointed either of these men, the other would probably resign. Frankfurter had no desire to become chief justice and Douglas' political ambitions were sufficiently well known that Truman avoided him. Truman believed an unstable Court weakened the United States. On the advice of former Chief Justice Charles Evans Hughes, Truman turned to Frederick Vinson, a personal confidant who had served as a Kentucky Congressman, a judge on the United States Court of Appeals for the District of Columbia (where he served alongside Rutledge), and as Secretary of the Treasury.[1]

According to political scientist and later Pulitzer Prize-winning author Herbert Feis, himself a Frankfurter confidant, "Truman had a glowing admiration and trust for Vinson even though Vinson was conservative and short-sighted." Truman regarded Vinson, who always remained a staunch Truman ally, as a "straight shooter … a man to trust." Truman expected Vinson to be more than a justice, and Vinson continued to be an informal advisor and personal friend, the two frequently sailing the Potomac together on the *Williamsburg* and playing poker. In 1946, Vinson advised Truman against sharing atomic energy technology

1 On Vinson's nomination, *see* James St. Clair and Linda Gugin, *Chief Justice Vinson of Kentucky: A Political Biography* (Lexington: University Press of Kentucky, 2002), 160–61.

with the Soviet Union, when Stimson and Patterson believed this would diffuse tensions. In October, 1948, Truman wanted to send Vinson as a special envoy to the Soviet Union during the Berlin blockade and airlift crisis, believing Vinson's strong national security credentials would show the Soviet Union's leadership the United States would not give up West Berlin.[2]

Vinson had been a New Deal congressman and loyal Democrat who had supported organized labor. His fear of a spreading monolithic communism directed from Moscow heightened his willingness to blur the separation of powers in favor of the president and remain politically active. When, in 1952, Truman ordered the nation's private large steel mills seized, Vinson was one of only three justices to support him. Indeed, Vinson had previously advised Truman on the legality of the act, extrajudicial legal advice that would today be highly suspect. Vinson's short time as chief justice was disproportionate to the impact the Court had shaping military law during his tenure. Between 1946 and 1953, the Court not only decided military justice challenges, it also insulated the Department of Defense against tort suits from service members, and upheld selective service decisions on broad grounds.[3]

In 1938, Roosevelt had appointed Vinson to the Court of Appeals for the District of Columbia. Already that court consisted of several influential jurists including Duncan Groener, Harold Stephens, and Henry Edgerton. Wiley Rutledge joined him the following year as well. In *Davis v. Woodring*, decided in 1940, Vinson convinced Groener and Wilbur Miller to hold that the court did not have jurisdiction to force the Secretary of the Army to issue an honorable discharge where a soldier had been medically discharged after a few weeks of service for being underweight. In terms of veterans' rights, in another decision, he scolded the Treasury Department's general counsel for not permitting an officer receiving retired pay to practice law before the department.[4]

Few military law issues came before Vinson during his tenure on the D.C. Circuit, but as biographers James St. Clair and Linda Gugin point out, he regularly sided with the Executive Branch. For instance, in *Viereck v. United States*, Vinson, along with Groener and Miller, upheld the conviction of a pro-German citizen who failed to register with the Secretary of State as an agent acting

2 Herbert Feis, *From Trust to Terror: The Onset of the Cold War, 1945–1950* (New York: W.W. Norton, 1970), 132; *see also* Feis to Arlene V. Pratt, June 24, 1970 [HFP/GMU]. Arlene Pratt was Feis' researcher and proofreader from 1954 to 1972. On Vinson's relationship with Truman, *see* Robert J. Donovan, *Tumultuous Years: The Presidency of Harry S. Truman, 1949–1953* (Columbia, MO: University of Missouri Press, 1996), 386.

3 Herbert Feis, *From Trust to Terror*, 132; Frankfurter to Feis, November 24, 1953 [HFP/16]. On Vinson's extrajudicial advice to Truman, *see* Robert J. Donovan, *Tumultuous Years: The Presidency of Harry S. Truman, 1949–1953* (Columbia, MO: University of Missouri Press, 1996), 386.

4 *Davis v. Woodring*, 111 F.2d. 523 (CA DC 1940).

at the behest of a foreign government, only to see the Supreme Court overturn the decision.[5]

When Truman nominated Vinson to the Court, the other justices did not react negatively to the nomination. Sherman Minton, a future associate justice then serving on the Court of Appeals for the Seventh Circuit wrote to Black that while he was disappointed Truman did not appoint Black as chief, he believed Vinson would "make a good chief." Black conceded that Truman "faced a hard choice" in selecting a chief justice to succeed Stone, but he could "think of no reason why Vinson would not make a good chief justice." Douglas and Frankfurter initially welcomed him as well, though within a year, a consensus emerged on the Court that Vinson was neither a great intellect, nor an effective leader. Moreover, his appointment did little to stem the personal acrimony amongst the justices.[6]

Clark

In early 1949, Frank Murphy died and Truman nominated Thomas Campbell Clark in his place. Clark's nomination was another example of Truman placing personal knowledge of an individual over legal reputation or ability. As Attorney General, Clark lobbied for the position on the Court, recommending himself over other candidates. Harold L. Ickes, who had been Roosevelt's Secretary of the Interior, called Clark "a second rate political hack." Born in Texas and educated at the University of Texas Law School, Clark had been a district attorney, and then worked in the Justice Department during the New Deal. Unlike Stanley Reed, the Court's other southerner, Clark did not oppose desegregation in the Armed Forces or Chief Justice Warren's later drive for unanimity in *Brown v. Board of Education*. But he was staunchly anti-communist and often deferred to governmental claims of necessity in national security appeals. During World War II, Clark advised Attorney General Biddle on the internment of Japanese Americans, and he headed both the antitrust and criminal law divisions of the Justice Department where he advised that military jurisdiction could extend to civilians in United States territories such as Hawaii. He was also involved in the prosecution of several "turncoat citizens" who broadcast enemy propaganda to United States forces during World War II, including Iva Toguri D'Aquino, who was known as "Tokyo Rose."[7]

---

5 St. Clair and Gugin, *Chief Justice Vinson of Kentucky*, 114–15. *See also Viereck v. United States*,130 F.2d 945 (CA DC, 1943).

6 Minton to Black, June 7, 1946; Black to Minton June 14, 1946 [HLB/66]. On Vinson's reputation *see*, Jan Palmer, *The Vinson Court Era*, 7; and Michal R. Belknap, *The Vinson Court: Justices, Rulings, and Legacy* (Santa Barbara, CA: ABC-CLIO, 2004), 40.

7 There is no full length academic biography of Clark. Though even Sherman Minton now has a biography, Clark has not been the subject of scholarly law review articles. His daughter recently published a biography, however, which provides information on Clark's

Clark's military service included a stint in the Texas National Guard in 1918. At war's end, Clark replaced Biddle as attorney general, bypassing supposed frontrunner Charles Fahy for the position. Clark was committed to having the Federal Bureau of Investigation put an end to lynching and he supported Truman's civil rights legislation. Yet, he did not advocate reforms in the federal or state criminal justice systems and in fact helped develop Truman's loyalty programs. Truman believed Clark's anti-communism shielded him from charges that he was "soft" on communism. In July 1945, Clark analyzed Secretary of War Patterson and Judge Advocate General Myron Cramer's study group's conclusions on the administration of courts-martial, informing Congressmen John McCormack, the House majority leader, of his satisfaction that courts-martial were fair. For most of his judicial tenure he would defer to arguments of military necessity and vigorously champion the concept of a military "separate society."[8]

One of the more important aspects of Truman's selection of Clark is that while serving as Attorney General and in his early years on the Court, Clark did not believe that the Constitution "followed the flag." In the appeals of Robert Chandler and Robert Henry Best, two American citizens who broadcast propaganda for Nazi Germany during WWII, Clark asserted that the Court should not take jurisdiction over Best's appeal. The Army had conducted a warrantless search of Best's apartment in Vienna, but Best had already been imprisoned for four weeks and his apartment was cordoned off so there were no exigent circumstances. Clark's clerk advised him to vote for a grant of *certiorari*, but Clark demurred. Chandler likewise challenged the evidence in his trial as being illegally taken. Clark not only opposed a grant of certiorari based off Best's and Chandler's appeals, he also had an extra-legal reason. He claimed the Army was likely to arrest other turncoats in Korea, including Anna Wallis. Known as "Seoul City Sue," Wallis broadcast anti-American propaganda from North Korea, including the names of dead American soldiers. Clark concluded that the Court should not give Wallis and other "erstwhile traitors guidance or comfort that convictions would be overturned or sentences commuted " and that the armed forces should have "a free hand to deal with them."

Truman expected Clark to be a reliable conservative vote in the Court, while still supporting organized labor, but this was not always the case. In lacking a consistent jurisprudential philosophy, Clark could be swayed by Black, Douglas,

youth and government service. *See* Mimi Park Gronlund, *Tom C. Clark: A Life of Service* (Austin, TX: University of Texas, 2010), 1–37. On Clark's conduct in the nomination process *see* Bernard Schwartz, *Super Chief, Earl Warren and His Supreme Court* (New York: Oxford, 1983), 57. On Ickes' opposition to Clark, *see* Henry Julian Abraham, *Justices, Presidents, and Senators: A History of the Supreme Court Appointments from Washington to Bush II* (Lanham, MD: Rowman and Littlefield, 2008), 193.

8 Cramer to Patterson, July 24, 1945 [Patterson/132]; Jan Palmer, *The Vinson Court*, 12–13; and David Alistair Yalof, *Pursuit of Justices: Presidential Politics and the Selection of Supreme Court Nominees* (Chicago: University of Chicago Press, 1999), 34–5.

Jackson, Frankfurter, and later by Warren. It simply depended on the issue before the Court. Thus, while Clark generally found in favor of national security interests and military policies, there were exceptions. This was particularly the case in narrowing the military's jurisdiction over civilians after 1955, and his role in a number of selective service decisions.

Minton

A native Indianan, Sherman Minton was born into a poor rural family. His intellect and athletic prowess enabled him to attend Indiana University (IU), but he did not graduate because he entered into the IU law school on a full scholarship. After graduating first in his class in 1915, he attended Yale Law School to earn a master in laws while studying under former president and future chief justice William Howard Taft. During World War I, he served as a staff officer in General John J. Pershing's headquarters, and after the war attended the Sorbonne University in Paris. Involved in local Democrat politics, in 1934, Minton was elected United States Senator from Indiana. However, he supported Roosevelt's "Court-Packing" bill, and Indiana proved too conservative for his politics. In 1940, Minton lost a reelection bid, and the following year Roosevelt appointed him to the Court of Appeals for the Seventh Circuit.[9]

On Frankfurter's suggestion to Stimson in 1945, the War Department appointed Minton as the chairman of the War Department Clemency Board. In this capacity, he reviewed courts-martial records before recommending early release from confinement or restoration to duty. Secretary of War Patterson lauded Minton's service.[10]

Minton perplexed his fellow justices. In late 1944, he wrote to Black lambasting Thomas Dewey for running an unethical campaign while complimenting Wendell Wilkie as a true liberal. In late 1946, he told Black that he sympathized with Henry Wallace, who had been accused of communist leanings. A reliable ally to Frankfurter in terms of judicial restraint, Minton was steadily conservative and believed judicial activism was wrong, with narrow exceptions. His pre-Court views of national defense are found in his correspondences to Black, to whom he wrote to in 1946 criticizing *Estep*. "We ought to get plenty of business from the uncertainty of that decision," he challenged Black. In 1953 he sided with Truman on the seizure of steel mills, and he voted repeatedly to uphold government loyalty programs. On the other hand, even more than Clark, Minton found racism abhorrent

---

9 Belknap, *The Vinson Court: Justices, Rulings, and Legacy*, 83–5; Linda C. Gugin and James E. St. Clair, *Sherman Minton: New Deal Senator, Cold War Justice* (Indianapolis: Indiana Historical Society, 1997), 3.

10 Patterson to Lucas, July 6, 1945 [Patterson/132]; David Yalof, *Pursuit of Justices*, 34–9.

and supported Warren's drive for unanimity in *Brown v. Board of Education* as well as striking down restrictive covenants based on race.

Minton believed the United States could not ideologically defeat communism if it failed to live up to the full promise of the Bill of Rights at home, but he also was certain that internal communism posed a threat to the nation. He had experienced prejudice early in his political career. In 1920 when he unsuccessfully ran for Congress as a Democrat, the Ku Klux Klan opposed him for being in league with Catholics, even though Minton was a Protestant.[11]

On September 15, 1949, Truman nominated Sherman Minton to replace Wiley Rutledge who had died a week earlier. Minton and Truman had served in the Senate together, and after Roberts retired from the Court in 1945, Truman had considered nominating him before choosing Burton. Moreover, Black had lobbied for Minton, believing his nomination would add a New Deal liberal to the Court.

From 1946 to 1953, the Court's national security and military law decisions were deferential to the Executive Branch to a degree not seen since. However, when analyzed against the fears of communist subversion in the early Cold War, the Court's heightened deference is unsurprising. Additionally, when compared to the Court's criminal law jurisprudence, courts-martial do not stand out as an exception to the majority's notion of fair trial standards. Prior to Vinson's tenure, the Court had permitted a state to prosecute a civilian for an offense already adjudicated in federal court as not violating double jeopardy. The Court also found that a state prosecutor's argument to a jury that a defendant's assertion of the right against self incrimination was proof of guilt was not unconstitutional, even when the conviction resulted in a death sentence. The majority of the Vinson Court found no reason to alter these decisions.

During Vinson's tenure, a dispute arose between Black and Frankfurter as to whether the Fourteenth Amendment bound the states to the Bill of Rights, just as it did the federal government. Although the dispute did not directly apply to courts-martial, it cannot be ignored that Frankfurter, who believed that the states should be able to develop their own notions of due process, was reluctant to "straight-jacket" the states, and believed that Black's jurisprudential approach would increase federal judicial supervision over the states. Since the military was often equated to a separate sovereign rather than part of the federal law, the dispute had some implications for the military. Frankfurter did not believe in judicial abandonment over persons tried in state courts, but he felt that federalism was important to preserve. In reviewing courts-martial, the Court remained focused on the question of when the federal judiciary's *habeas* jurisdiction extended to courts-martial. Clearly, in light of its 1938 decision, *Johnson v. Zerbst*, the Court had abandoned the traditional narrow test

11 Belknap, *The Vinson Court, Justices Rulings, and Legacy*, 83–5; *See Barrows v. Jackson*, 346 U.S. 249 (1953); Minton to Black, October 10, 1944 [HLB/66]; Minton to Black, December 30, 1946 [HLB/66]; Minton to Black, March 28, 1946 [HLB/66]; Linda C. Gugin and James E. St. Clair, *Sherman Minton*, 60.

of jurisdiction over other sovereigns, but through Vinson's tenure, the Court decided appeals on the basis of what *did not* constitute a grounds for reversal of a conviction through a collateral attack, rather than what *did*.

In spite of *Duncan v. Kahanomoku*, in the collective mind of the Truman administration, an open question remained as to whether the military's jurisdiction could be extended to United States citizens. In *Duncan*, the Court had ruled that the military had no jurisdiction over citizens in the United States or its territories where the civil courts functioned. In this sense, *Duncan* was a reaffirmation of *Milligan*. Nonetheless, the Defense establishment's leadership believed that military jurisdiction should extend to citizens accompanying the United States military overseas, where the only other choice of jurisdiction at the time was the foreign court. In Germany, Italy, and Japan, national courts had yet to function by 1948. The majority of justices believed that *Milligan* did not apply to citizens in overseas bases and that military jurisdiction over civilians on overseas installations was essential to the discipline of military forces most likely to confront the Soviet military.[12]

As early as 1946, the justices believed Stalin was contemplating declaring war on the United States. Even the Court's liberals protested communist aggression and supported Truman's foreign policies. Douglas publicly lauded American aid to Greece in that nation's efforts to suppress a communist insurgency. In early 1946, he called Stalin's actions in Eastern Europe a declaration of World War III against the United States. In a public address in Los Angeles, Black articulated similar sentiments. Frankfurter was torn as to how far the government should go in prosecuting the Cold War. He was appalled at the government's treatment of Robert Oppenheimer, but the scientist was also Frankfurter's personal friend. Frankfurter also aligned himself Herbert Feis on where the blame for the Cold War rested and the unlimited extent to which the Soviet Union would commit espionage in the United States. To both men, the Soviet Union's leaders *wanted* the Cold War and intentionally heightened tensions because the Soviet military could not yet openly confront the United States. Frankfurter, then, often straddled a fence between individual rights and due process, and the claimed needs of national survival. No justice openly disagreed with Ambassador to the Soviet Union George Kennan's "Long Telegram," of February 22, 1946, which warned of "a tightly coordinated campaign" to spread communism. The differences between the justices had to do with how the government could constitutionally fight communism at home.[13]

---

12 *Duncan v. Kahanomoku*, 327 U.S. 304 (1946); *Ex Parte Milligan*, 71 U.S. (4 Wall.) 2 (1866). Whether the United States military had criminal jurisdiction over civilians overseas would be addressed by the Court later in cases discussed below.

13 On Douglas' commentary, *see* David C. Engerman, "Ideology and the Origins of the Cold War, 1917–1962," in *The Cambridge History of the Cold War*, Vol. I, Melvyn P. Leffler and Odd Arne Westad, eds. (Cambridge: Cambridge Univ. Press, 2010), 34. On

In 1960, Charles Fahy, in an answer to John Frank over whether the President deferred to the Attorney General on judicial nominations, wrote "ordinarily, I believe the views of the A.G. are given considerable weight, though there is some indication Pres. Truman's choices were personal, rather than the result of recommendations by the A.G." It was, perhaps, a matter of reciprocity that Truman's appointees were usually willing to give considerable deference to the Executive and Legislative branches in limiting the Bill of Rights. To be sure, Truman's appointees believed their votes were essential to ensure the nation's survival.[14]

I: The Political and Military Situation: 1946–1952

When the Japanese Government surrendered on September 2, 1945, the United States Army numbered over eight million soldiers. When combined with the Navy and Marine Corps, over 12 million men were in uniform. There were no plans to maintain a fielded military force of that size; by the end of 1946, there were less than one million soldiers on active service in the Army. In 1947, the size of the Soviet Union's military forces dwarfed that of the United States and Great Britain together. At the end of 1948, the United States Army was reduced to 554,030. By contrast, the Soviet Union still had over four million soldiers on active service, and with the communist takeover of China, a potential for the United States to confront over 10 million communist soldiers was not imaginary.[15]

Although in retrospect the use of atomic weapons on Hiroshima and Nagasaki ended the dominance of mass armies that began in the late sixteenth century, both the Republican-led Congress and Truman believed that the United States should at least preserve the nation's ability to call on a mass military. Instead of maintaining an expensive large standing army, Truman appealed for universal military training for all male citizens who reached age 18, and a large ready reserve. Under a universal military training program, all males between the age of 18 and 22 years would be subject to a six month training, followed

---

Feis, *see* Feis, *From Trust to Terror*, 25. Earlier, when Feis published a book on the Japanese decision to attack the United States, Feis acknowledged that Frankfurter's assistance was instrumental in the book being published. *See* Herbert Feis, *The Road to Pearl Harbor: The Coming of the War Between the United States and Japan* (New Jersey: Princeton, 1950), vii. *James Forrestal Diaries*, entry for February 17, 1946, Walter Millis, ed. (London: Cassel and Co., 1952), 140; *see also*, George Frost Kennan and John Lukacks, *George F. Kennan and the Origins of Containment* (Columbia, MO: University of Missouri Press, 1996), 9–10; Denise Botsdorf, *Proclaiming the Truman Doctrine: The Cold War Call to Arms* (Arlington: Texas A&M, 2008), 9–21.

14 Fahy to John Frank, November 15, 1960 [Fahy/6].

15 Russell Weigley, *History of the United States Army* (New York: MacMillan, 1967), 569.

by six months of military service. By contrast, selective service would draft a percentage of males into the military for a term of service ranging from two to four years, with an inactive status for another four. Thus, in an emergency, a citizen drafted under selective service could be forced into the military for an eight year period, while his undrafted peers were free to live their civilian lives. Under universal military training every male citizen shared an equal burden and risk.

There was a judicial component to the universal military training program. In 1946, Truman convened a universal military training study group. The group, co-chaired by Nobel physicist Arthur Compton, who had been instrumental in the Manhattan Project, and John Edward Davies, who had served as an ambassador to the Soviet Union and later advised Truman at the Potsdam Conference, included multiple judges. Samuel I. Rosenmann, a New York state judge who had advised Roosevelt alongside Frankfurter throughout his four terms, and William Hastie, a future judge on the Court of Appeals for the Third Circuit, and federal judge for the Virgin Island territories both served on the study group. Additionally, retired justice Owen Roberts, who had become the chairman of the Citizens Emergency Committee for Universal Military Training, lent Truman support for this program as well. Roberts and Army Chief of Staff George C. Marshall promoted universal military training to Congress. In 1947, Roberts urged Congress to postpone other legislative debates and schedule hearings on universal military training ahead of other matters.[16]

Universal military training represented a compromise between the expense and distrust of a large standing military and the national security needs of the American superpower to strengthen allies and dissuade the Soviet Union from invading a western European nation or encroaching into the Pacific. Peacetime universal service could certainly have posed constitutional questions. However, Vinson, Jackson, Frankfurter and Burton quietly endorsed this program. There is no record that Black opposed universal training on constitutional grounds. Douglas, Murphy, and Rutledge feared the encroachment of the military in both the executive and legislative branches, but they did not oppose an equal sharing of the nation's defense burdens.[17]

Opposition to universal military training was widespread. Conservative groups such as the Young Men's Christian Association, church leaders, and southern segregationists opposed it. Senator Richard Russell, an adherent of segregation, went so far as to demand that men brought into the service had to be able to

16 Report of the First Meeting of the President's Advisory Commission on Universal Military Training: January 24–25, 1947, pp. 1–13 [Joseph Edward Davies Papers]; Statement of Owen Roberts to Congress, June 26, 1947 [HST]; Clarence K. Streit, "Owen Roberts and the Atlantic Union," 104 *University of Pennsylvania Law Review* (1955) 354–67; Russell F. Weigley, *The American Way of War: A History of United States Military Strategy and Policy* (Bloomington, IN: Indiana University Press, 1973), 369.

17 Newman, *Hugo Black*, 379.

choose which unit they would be assigned, otherwise he would vote against it. The leadership of National Association for the Advancement of Colored People, the American Federation of Labor, and the Congress of International Organizations also opposed universal military training because they believed that the program would be unfairly administered.[18]

Universal military training failed in Congress, but selective service did not. In February, 1948, the communist party in Czechoslovakia, with Soviet assistance, overthrew the elected government. The communist party of that country was already strongly represented in its government, but the coup ended any hope for future free elections or forcing a Soviet retreat from Central Europe. The events in Czechoslovakia strengthened the fear that the European nations could not, on their own, protect themselves from communism. Events in Czechoslovakia were a catalyst for Congress legislating the Selective Service Act of 1948. Within this law, in a section known as the Elston Act, Congress also legislated a new, albeit short-lived, Articles of War. The act applied only to the Army and newly formed Air Force, but not the Navy, or Marine Corps.[19]

The 1948 Articles of War enabled an accused enlisted soldier to request a court-martial panel consisting of at least one-third enlisted men of his rank or higher. Clearly a democratic concept, the service of enlisted personnel on an enlisted man's court-martial was antithetical to the previous 300 years of military trials, which had been the sole province of commissioned officers. The Elston Act also required that both the prosecutor and defense counsel be licensed attorneys, and it reformed the appeal process. While not establishing an independent, civilian-led appellate court such as exists today, Congress required the Judge Advocate General of each service branch to establish independent review panels, and mandated that only the president could approve death sentences.[20]

The War Department's legal leadership endorsed the Elston Act. But for several congressmen and the legal academy, the Elston Act did not go far enough in mirroring civilian criminal trials, particularly in the appeals process. Courts-martial still lacked the direct equivalent of an independent judge. However, senior Defense Department and judge advocate leadership were entrenched and not persuaded by external criticism. Major Louis F. Alyea, a former Frankfurter student at Harvard, and the staff judge advocate for all reserve affairs, summed up the opposition against the act as unfounded:

---

18 Michael J. Hogan, *A Cross of Iron: Harry S. Truman and the Origins of the Modern Security State, 1945–1950* (London: Cambridge University Press, 1998), 120–29.

19 Hogan, *A Cross of Iron*, 129; also Frederick B. Wiener, "American Military Law in the Light of the First Mutiny Act's Tricentennial," 126 *Military Law Review* (1989), 1–89, 33; William E. Leuchtenberg, *A Troubled Feast: American Society Since 1945* (Boston: Little Brown and Co., 1983), 28.

20 Wiener, "American Military Law in the Light of the First Mutiny Act's Tricentennial," 35.

> Much unwarranted criticism of our military courts-martial system has resulted from conflicting, argumentative, and inaccurate views of some writers who have used phrases such as 'Prussianized court-martial system' and 'star-chamber justice' ... These arguments are misleading and certainly cannot be used truthfully when referring to the 1948 Articles of War.

Despite his support for the 1948 Articles of War, shortly after authoring this statement, Alyea worked under Professor Edmund Morgan, himself a World War I judge advocate and Frankfurter contemporary, in developing the new Uniform Code of Military Justice. Alyea looked to Frankfurter for advice during the UCMJ's drafting.[21]

The Berlin Crisis occurred almost in tandem with the Elston Act. On June 18, 1948, the West German government, with the support of the United States, British, and French governments announced the establishment of the "Deutsch Mark" currency. In response, the Soviet military blockaded American shipments traversing Soviet-occupied Germany into Berlin. This action limited supply to American, British, and French forces in Berlin to airlift. Berlin was not a strategic city for industrial reasons, but the blockade became symbolic of the Soviet effort to weaken the United States. Soviet actions also threatened to starve Berlin's civilian population. Shortly after the blockade, a massive airlift of supplies to the free population of Berlin began, but the Soviet Government's actions in harassing the airlift and bullying the population actions stoked war fears. Misjudging the anger of the German population toward them as well as Truman's resolve, the Soviets ended their blockade on May 18, 1949.[22]

Most distressing to the United States Government was the overthrow of China by communist forces under Mao Zedong. Allied with the United States against Japan during World War II, Mao split from his Nationalist coequal Chiang Kai-shek and defeated the nationalists in 1949. The fall of China to communism influenced domestic security and stoked fears of communism within the United States government. Joseph McCarthy and Richard Nixon accused the Truman administration of laxity in ferreting out traitors in the government. In July, 1947, Congressman George Dondero, a Michigan Republican, accused Secretary of War Robert Patterson of "turning a blind eye to communists" in the War Department. While much of the accusations were baseless and opportunistic, there was evidence of a few individual cases of allegiance to communism. Fortunately, military policy was influenced by more sophisticated analysis of how communism operated during Truman's presidency.[23]

---

21 Louis F. Alyea, *Military Justice Under the 1948 Amended Articles of War* (New York: Oceana Press, 1949), 95.

22 C.N. Barclay, *The New Warfare*, 18.

23 David Caute, *The Great Fear: Anti-Communist Purges* (New York: Simon and Schuster, 1978), 294–5.

In 1950, future Secretary of State John Foster Dulles published *War or Peace*, in which he warned that the Soviet Union was a unique enemy, because their leaders did not intend to enter into a full scale war with the west. "They control the world's greatest pool of dependable manpower and they have atomic weapons," he acknowledged. But, he conceded that unlike the Nazis and Fascists, the Soviet Government only viewed their military as a defensive force, to prevent an invasion, stating "communist doctrine does not give primary emphasis to conquest by military aggression." To Dulles, soon to become Secretary of State, and a generation of conservative leaders that he influenced, the real menace from communism was its commitment to class warfare through its military organization trained in propaganda, espionage, sabotage, and subversive warfare. Dulles believed that the "Cold War" was a Soviet invention of an intermediate stage between war and peace, and he feared that without a strong show of force by the United States, China would be but the first of many nations to fall under communist influence. In 1953, British General C.N. Barclay argued to the Army War College that the Soviet strategy centered on creating conflicts by proxy, and that the Korean conflict was a not an aberration.[24]

In 1951, Truman issued National Security Council Report number 68 (generally referred to as NSC-68). By its numbering, this obviously was not the first policy document that addressed the national security of the United States. In 1948, Truman issued NSC 20/4 which concluded that the Soviet Union possessed a large enough conventional force to overrun Western Europe and would possess an air force that would be capable of striking the United States by 1954. After the Soviet Union succeeded in testing an atomic weapon in 1949, the Truman administration's national security advisors, including future Secretary of Defense Clark Clifford, concluded that the Soviet military was capable of offensive action. NSC-68 called for a large increase in conventional and nuclear forces. The administration determined that an enlarged military would not only deter the Soviet Union and the expansion of communism, but strengthen Western Europe, the rebuilt governments in Japan and South Korea, and the former European colonies who aligned with the west. NSC-68 was classified until 1975, and it was not universally accepted within the administration, in part because of its stress on military deterrence over diplomacy.[25]

The Defense establishment's leadership was not immune from philosophical divisions on how to confront and contain communism. Douglas MacArthur, for instance, insisted that the stationing of forces in Europe was misguided

24 John Foster Dulles, *War or Peace* (New York: MacMillan, 1950), 112. In this work, Dulles also labeled Ho Chi Minh a threat to the free world; Barclay, *The New Warfare*, 18.

25 NSC 68, 33–5; Melvin Leffler, *A Preponderance of Power: National Security, the Truman Administration, and the Cold War* (Stanford, CA: Stanford University Press, 1992), 355–60; Robert J. Donovan, Tumultuous Years: The Presidency of Harry S. Truman (Columbia, MO: University of Missouri, 1982), 28; *See also*, Paul H. Nitze, *From Hiroshima to Glasnost: At the Center of Decision* (New York: Grove Weidenfeld, 1989).

and that the true fight against communism was in Asia. But Omar Bradley, the Chairman of the Joint Chiefs of Staff, believed this was too narrow a position, and if Western Europe fell, then the United States would find itself completely isolated. Such policy differences were not likely to weaken military discipline. More disturbing to military cohesiveness was the incessant bickering between the service branches over funding.[26]

After World War I, a small group of military aviation pioneers led by Italian General Giulio Douhet, British Air Marshal Sir Hugh Trenchard, and American General William "Billy" Mitchell, argued that the surest means to defeat an industrialized nation was to destroy its industrial centers. Air Force leaders after World War II were convinced that any future war with the Soviet Union would be won in the air and not at sea. Senior naval officers, and to a lesser extent the Army's leadership, opposed the Air Force. When the Truman Administration appeared to side with the Air Force and cancelled the production of several large naval vessels, a coterie of admirals revolted and took their arguments to the public. The conduct of one admiral, Daniel Gallery, was so egregious that Secretary of Defense Louis Johnson initially sought a court-martial. Eventually the Chief of Naval Operations was forced to retire, and the Secretary of the Navy forced to resign. Clearly, the conduct of senior military leaders, who openly accused their inter-service opponents and members of the administration of undermining the nation's security, had the possibility to undermine military discipline at all ranks. Later, Douglas would point to this in-fighting as evidence that the Court had to broaden its jurisdiction over military affairs.[27]

Korean War

On June 25, 1950, Communist North Korean forces invaded South Korea, and it appeared that the Army of the Republic of South Korea had disintegrated. The degree to which Stalin or Mao Zedong encouraged the invasion is questionable, but clearly the two leaders believed the invasion was another step in the advancement of communism across the world. In response, the United Nations Security Council condemned North Korea, and with Yugoslavia abstaining and the Soviet Union absent, the international body approved the use of military force to repel the invasion.

The Korean War was, in fact, a watershed event that shaped United States military policy for the following 40 years. Since that conflict, the older belief that the nation required only a small standing army disappeared. Truman did not ask Congress for a declaration of war prior to committing military forces

---

26 Omar Bradley, *A General's Life* (New York: Simon and Schuster, 1983), 523.

27 Robert J. Donovan, *Tumultuous Years*, 104–10; also Russell Weigley, *The American Way of War*, 376–8.

to combat, nor did he or Congress question the use of conscripted forces in a conflict without a formal declaration of war. Truman consulted with Congress to explain his actions one week after authorizing the deployment of soldiers on the peninsula, and for the most part, Congress approved the actions. Although Truman and the military establishment expected a quick victory, the Korean War was a conflict the United States was surprisingly unprepared to fight in light of the fact that World War II had ended only five years earlier. In a three year period, 36,000 American soldiers were killed, and another 80,000 injured. But, unlike in World War II, neither the nation nor the military was wholly focused on that conflict. Called a limited conflict or a "police action," the conflict had all the vestiges and dangers of a modern war, but not the number of soldiers employed. Chief Justice Rehnquist later described the Korean War as a conflict in which no more than a half million Americans participated at any one time, and which was not directly felt at home, but the public tired of the conflict nonetheless.[28]

Initially, American military forces performed poorly and were overwhelmed by the North Koreans. Then, despite being pushed into a small area in the south of the country, under MacArthur's command, American forces launched a successful amphibious assault at Inchon which ultimately pushed the North Korean military to the Chinese Border. In October 1950, the Chinese Army crossed into North Korea and pushed allied forces into South Korea once more.

Following the Chinese entry into the war, MacArthur openly stated his consideration of using nuclear weapons to end the conflict, even though he had not briefed or consulted Truman, and command and control of all nuclear weapons rested solely with the president. MacArthur had also wanted to carry the war into China, but the United Nations mandate prohibited expanding the war beyond the Korean Peninsula. Truman's relations with MacArthur were already contentious before the war and MacArthur's penchant for political activity including aligning with conservative Republicans added to Truman's distrust of the general. While Black and Douglas were already disposed to distrust MacArthur, the general's conduct during the war resulted in their fears of the military establishment's growth of power. Ultimately, in April 1951, Truman relieved MacArthur of his duties. Several congressmen, particularly the staunch anti-communists, opted to hold hearings on the removal, politicizing the military in the process.[29]

Although the Joint Chiefs of Staff sided with Truman, to several jurists, MacArthur's conduct eroded trust in the military's leadership. Douglas, Black,

---

28 James Coates and Michael Kilian, *Heavy Losses: The Dangerous Decline of American Defense* (New York: Viking Press, 1985), 2; Maeva Marcus, *Truman and the Steel Seizure Case: The Limits of Presidential Power* (Durham, NC: Duke University Press, 1994), 2; and, William Rehnquist, *The Supreme Court: How It Was, How it Is* (New York: William Morrow and Co., 1987), 42–4.

29 Dennis D. Wainstock, *Truman, MacArthur, and the Korean War* (Denver CO: Greenwood, 1999), 122–34.

and Frankfurter worried that civilian control over the military was in question. To Vinson and the judicial conservatives, the answer to these fears was simple: allow the military to retain a vigorous disciplinary system overseen by the Secretary of Defense and the service secretaries.[30]

Truman's dismissal of MacArthur and the Congressional hearings were not as damaging to civilian control of the military or military discipline as Douglas worried they might be. Military leadership openly backed Truman's policies in the Congressional hearings. In 1974, former Army Chief of Staff Maxwell Taylor wrote of the incident that "Truman showed that a President limited in popularity but long on courage could deal with a national military hero who had stepped out of line." Likewise, Omar Bradley, the Chairman of the Joints Chief of Staff, backed Truman's relief of MacArthur in testimony to Congress. However, that Congress had held hearings about MacArthur's dismissal was without historic precedent. Lincoln's removal of the ineffectual George McClellan from command of the Army of the Potomac in November, 1862 was controversial, but even then Congress did not formally second-guess the president's decision.[31]

By the time the governments of the United States and its allies, North Korea, and China agreed to an armistice on July 27, 1953, both Truman and the war had become unpopular in the United States, with Truman's popularity nearly as low as Richard Nixon's at the height of the "Watergate" hearings. This is an important point, because while there were no large protests against the conflict, many Americans were concerned that the nation would remain on an endless war footing. Importantly, the Korean War was the first war in which courts-martial were conducted under the UCMJ. In all, over 8,000 special and general courts-martial were adjudicated in theatre.

Labor Upheaval, War Industries, and National Security

Almost as soon as World War II ended, the Court's approach to national security and military readiness was evident in its non-military decisions. On May 21, 1946, the federal government seized coal mines after a prolonged strike in an effort to force both labor and management to agree on wages. Almost two months earlier, the United Mine Workers went on a nation-wide strike, but it was not the first post-war strike. Shortly after Japan's surrender, the nation saw strikes in the manufacturing, mining, and milling industries. The coal strike, however, was potentially the most upsetting to national security. After the government seizure, John L. Lewis, the president of the United Mine Workers, signed a contract with the Secretary of the Interior establishing wage

30 Bernard Brodie, *War and Politics* (New York: MacMillan, 1973), 84–8; Roger K. Newman, *Hugo Black*, 385.

31 Maxwell D. Taylor, *Swords and Plowshares: A Memoir* (New York: Norton, 1972), 174.

rates while the mines were under the government's control. Within six months, Lewis notified the secretary that the union would terminate the contract. To prevent a walkout and subsequent strike, the government obtained a judicial injunction against the union, but Lewis ignored the injunction claiming that other federal laws, particularly the Norris-La Guardia Act, provided the right to strike, even against the government. A district court found Lewis and the union guilty of contempt and fined him $10,000 and the union $3.5 million, with the potential of additional daily fines for non-compliance. Out a fear of a prolonged appellate process, the Solicitor General directly petitioned the Court to grant *certiorari*, claiming that a national emergency existed requiring bypassing the appeals court. Authoring for a bare majority, Vinson upheld the injunction on the basis that the government was not an employer and therefore possessed the authority to bar strikes in industries the government had essentially run.[32]

The decision, captioned as *United States v. United Mine Workers of America*, was convoluted. While Black and Douglas sided with Vinson on the LaGuardia Act's inapplicability to unions when the government acted as an employer, they disagreed with the criminal contempt finding. Both justices believed the union had acted in good faith under the mistaken belief that their acts were lawful. Douglas saw the case as an example of the Court "disregarding high principles and standards of justice and equality" and thought it strange the Court would set a fine in a criminal case it had never heard. On the other hand, Frankfurter, who convinced Jackson, Murphy, and Rutledge that the Act prohibited the government from preventing a strike, also convinced Jackson, Reed, and Burton that even if the union had disregarded the judicial injunction in good faith, it still constituted criminal contempt. Rutledge and Murphy dissented from Frankfurter's second position. Rutledge and Black feared that that this type of ruling could undermine the First Amendment. Vinson, for his part, saw the ruling as critical to national security, because, after all, the steel and manufacturing industries relied on coal, and if the economy weakened, American power weakened as well. Coal, steel, and manufacturing employed tens of millions workers and constituted the heart of the economy. Moreover, the nation remained on a war footing of sorts and Soviet bellicosity had increased. *United Mine Workers* was not intended to be an anti-union decision, but rather pro-national security. Except Burton, all the justices were generally pro-labor. The majority's decision helped to clarify the Court's military law decisions, demonstrating that national security and military readiness were the paramount focus of several justices.[33]

One year after deciding *United Mine Workers*, the Court determined that the government possessed the constitutional authority to recover excess profits

---

32 *United States v. United Mine Workers of America*, 330 U.S. 258 (1947); Ferren, *Salt of the Earth, Conscience of the Court*, 333–5.

33 William O. Douglas, *The Court Years* (New York: Random House, 1980), 102, 139.

from corporations engaged in defense contracting during World War II. In 1942, Congress had legislated the Renegotiation Act that permitted the Executive Branch to determine when a corporation engaged in war profiteering. The Undersecretary of War at the time, Robert Patterson, and the War Contracts Price Adjustment Board were empowered to make such determinations. Three companies sued the government, but in *Lichter v. United States*, a lengthy decision authored by Burton, the Court upheld the Renegotiation Act. *Lichter* is an important decision on the periphery of military law in the sense that it upheld a broad grant of Executive Branch authority from Congress, but it also provides some insight into Douglas' later criticism of the broad grant. Absent from Douglas' published dissent was a lengthier draft criticism that the law precluded judicial review of the Undersecretary's determinations that were made before 1943.[34]

The Uniform Code of Military Justice

Beginning in 1946 there was considerable public pressure to reform the military justice system. *Millions* of soldiers, sailors, and Marines were court-martialed during the war, many in circumstances that offended due process. The American Bar Association (ABA) lobbied Congress to reform the military justice system and continued its efforts, even after the Elston Act. The ABA was, at the time, politically conservative and supported government loyalty programs. Yet Frederick P. Bryan, the chairman of the ABA's special committee on military law, testified to Congress that the Articles of War undermined the morale of the military, precisely because it was perceived as unfair. "Morale and discipline will never be so high as when the individual soldier, sailor, or airman is convinced he is going to get a fully square deal if he is accused of a crime," Bryan testified to the House of Representatives in support of the UCMJ. Seven years after his testimony, Eisenhower appointed Bryan to the United States District Court for the Southern District of New York.[35]

Internally, the Air Force and Army Chiefs of Staff, and the Chief of Naval Operations pushed for thousands of clemency reviews of courts-martial, but opposed sweeping reforms. Despite opposition from the armed forces leadership, various legislative and executive committees were created to push for reform, the most important of which was the "Vanderbilt Committee," named for its president Arthur Vanderbilt, the Chief Justice of the New Jersey Supreme

34 *Lichter v. United States*, 334 U.S. 472 (1948); Douglas, original pencil draft, undated [WOD/169].

35 Hearings Before a Subcommittee of the Committee on the Armed Forces, House of Representatives, 81st Congress, 1st Sess, "A Bill to Unify, Consolidate, Revise, and Codify the Articles of War and Establish a Uniform Code of Military Justice (Washington, DC: GPO, 1949), 630–33.

Court. Federal judges such as Morris Ames Soper and Alexander Holtzoff, as well as Floyd Thompson, a former Illinois Supreme Court justice, served on Vanderbilt's committee, which was instrumental in the passage of UCMJ in 1950. Former justice Owen Roberts also advised their military reform efforts, and Holtzoff routinely reached to Frankfurter for advice on bringing civilian due process safeguards into courts-martial. Vanderbilt, Soper, and Holtzoff intentionally excluded senior military officers from their committees because of their desire for full independence from the War Department's pressures. That the basis for the UCMJ was formulated by distinguished jurists gave judicial conservatives confidence in the fairness of courts-martial under the UCMJ as well as the military establishment's administrative decisions.[36]

Many of the Vanderbilt Committee's proposals were incorporated into the Elston Act, and then the UCMJ. However, one reform the War Department opposed was the removal of commanders' authority to charge offenders and convene general courts-martial, a proposal that regained some Congressional support 60 years later in response to a perceived problem with command discretion in sexual assault cases. Both Holtzoff and Soper believed removal of this authority and re-vesting the decision in the service Judge Advocate Generals was an important reform to remove command influence over courts-martial. However, the War Department's leadership and Frankfurter believed that this particular reform would undermine the discipline necessary to follow the chain of command. Holtzoff, on Frankfurter's prodding, minimized this issue in the Vanderbilt Committee's final report. Again, Frankfurter had directly impacted law formation from his chambers.[37]

While none of the Court's decisions prior to 1953 arose from a court-martial prosecuted under the UCMJ, its passage had an almost immediate influence on the Court in boosting the justices' confidence in the fairness and efficacy of courts-martial. The UCMJ was singularly the greatest legal reform in the nation's military history. A significant departure from the Articles of War, the UCMJ brought courts-martial more in line with federal criminal trials. All service members would be tried under the same set of laws. A defined appeals system, the appointment of law officers, and adoption of rules of evidence similar to the federal rules, were part of the UCMJ, though military judges with powers similar to civilian trial judges did not exist until 1968. Congress showed a concern for reducing command influence over courts-martial as well, and provided greater oversight by the judge advocates general of the four military services. Finally, the establishment of a civilian Court of Military Appeals enabled a civilian court, independent of any

36 *See, e.g.*, Arthur Vanderbilt to Holtzoff, April 15, 1946 [AH-AHC/6]; Owen Roberts to Vanderbilt, June 19, 1946 [AH-AHC/6]; Holtzoff to Colonel Royal Irwin, August 26, 1946.

37 Holtzoff to Vanderbilt, November 12, 1946 [AH-AHC/6]; Alexander Holtzoff, Administration of Justice in the United States Military, *New York University Law Quarterly*, January 1947, 1–18.

command influence, to apply federal criminal and constitutional law principles to courts-martial during appeals. Frankfurter favored a civilian court to oversee appeals, though Wiener, his former student, opposed it.[38]

What did not change with the UCMJ was the continuation of Article 133 and Article 134, the general articles that permitted the military to charge a service member with a generalized descriptive offense such as "disorders to the prejudice of good order and discipline," and "conduct unbecoming an officer and gentleman." Additionally, the new code did not facially extend the federal judiciary's jurisdiction over courts-martial beyond what it had been prior to World War II. The extent of this jurisdiction continued to be defined by the federal courts themselves. The UCMJ indicated that the federal judiciary would not review court-martial convictions until the military judicial system fully considered all alleged errors in the process. Nonetheless, in the end, there were enough important guarantees of a fair trial to satisfy the ABA and a large part of the legal academy.

II: Military Justice: The "Vinson Court" and the Second World War

The first of the World War II cases involving courts-martial that percolated to the Court arrived in its 1946 term. In what Jackson labeled "a sordid three-sided case," the Department of Justice prosecuted an officer named Walter V. Radovich along with two civilians for fraud in a federal court, but the officer had also been court-martialed for conduct unbecoming an officer and gentleman for the same fraud. Samuel Ansell defended Radovich at his federal trial, court-martial, and on appeal. Ansell had been the deputy judge advocate general acting in the capacity as judge advocate general in World War I. Judge Advocate General Enoch Crowder took charge of the Army's conscription program during the war and left to Ansell the duty of overseeing courts-martial. After the war, Ansell clashed with Crowder, Secretary of War Newton Baker, most of the Judge Advocate General's Department, and a young Major Felix Frankfurter.

At the time, it was legally permissible for the Army to court-martial an officer for conduct unbecoming an officer and gentleman, even if the officer had been convicted in a federal or state court for the same offense. None of this was considered to violate the constitutional prohibition against double jeopardy. In 1907, the Court, in *Grafton v. United States*, had held that double jeopardy prohibited a federal prosecutor from prosecuting a soldier for murder acquitted

38 *See* generally, Marion T. Bennett, *The United States Court of Claims: A History*, Vol. II (Washington, DC: GPO, 1976), 119; also, Jonathan Lurie, *Arming Military Justice: The Origins of the United States Court of Military Appeals, 1775–1950*, 197–214. For Wiener's opposition to the establishment of a civilian appellate court, *see* Wiener to Robert Patterson, April 29, 1949 [Patterson/48].

in a court-martial for the identical offense. *Grafton*, was a narrow restraint on the Executive Branch from prosecuting a soldier already tried by a court-martial, but it did not appear to apply in the inverse. And in *Palko v. Connecticut*, the Court determined that a state could prosecute a person in a capital case even though the individual had been acquitted in a federal court. Notably, judicial liberals such as Brandeis, Stone, Cardozo, and Black had endorsed this doctrine.[39]

In 1855, Attorney General Caleb Cushing had specifically informed the Army's Judge Advocate General that a court-martial could proceed against a commissioned surgeon where the officer had already been convicted in a Texas state court for negligent murder. The surgeon had operated on a patient while drunk and the patient died. The question in that case was whether double jeopardy prevented such a prosecution since the statute of conduct unbecoming an officer and gentleman was not a specific prohibition against murder or drunkenness. To this end, Cushing wrote:

> an officer of the Army is bound by law to be a good citizen and therefore liable under such qualifications as the law prescribes to the same punishment with any other citizen for a given act. But he is also bound by law to be a gentleman and an officer whether in, or under command; and if he fails, is punishable or punished of not by the civil authorities, it is to be punished by military law according to the sanction of his fellow officers in subordination.

Thus two separate trials, where one was a court-martial, were held not to be double jeopardy when a unique military offense was tried in the one, but not the other.[40]

The two civilians who conspired with Radovich—Samuel and Elias Bayer—provided gifts and the sale of uniforms at wholesale prices to senior officers at Mitchell Field in New York to ensure that Samuel Bayer's son and nephew, both enlisted men, would not be sent to an overseas combat area. In early 1943, Federal Bureau of Investigation agents observed Elias Bayer giving a Colonel Jacobson, an officer who effectuated the transfer of Bayer's two enlisted relatives from a unit scheduled for deployment to a combat theatre to a safe domestic command at Mitchell Field, four tires as a birthday present shortly after the transfer. While at Mitchell Field, the two enlisted men came under the command of Major Radovich who, in turn, became "a frequent caller at the Bayers and the most

---

39 *Grafton v. United States*, 206 U.S. 333 (1907). Authored by Associate Justice John Marshal Harlan, a Civil War veteran, the Court conceded, "it may be difficult at times to determine whether the offense for which an officer or soldier is being tried is, in every substantial respect, the same offense for which he had been previously tried." As a result, Harlan determined that the decision would not "formulate any rule by which every conceivable case must be solved." *Palko v. Connecticut*, 302 U.S. 319 (1937).

40 Joshua Kastenberg, *Law in War, Law as War*, 66, quoting Caleb Cushing to John F. Lee, 1856, NA RG 153.1 Vol. 1.

constant recipient of their gratuities." The agents observed the Bayers giving Radovich golf clubs, theatre tickets, and suitcases. Nonetheless, in late 1943, Radovich transferred the two enlisted men to another airfield. Then, the Army transferred Radovich to a commando unit assigned to Burma. In late November, the Bayers gave Radovich $5,000. His attempts to deposit this much money, and the circulation of rumors about the Bayers' lavish gift-giving at Mitchell Field, resulted in the arrest and indictment of the Bayers and Radovich. The three men were jointly prosecuted and convicted in federal court, and sentenced to imprisonment.[41]

The Bayers and Radovich appealed to the Court of Appeals for the Second Circuit and that court, in a decision authored by Learned Hand, with Augustus Hand and Charles Clark in agreement, concerned itself primarily with evidentiary infirmities in the criminal trial. The three judges determined that the trial judge had improperly excluded exculpatory evidence from the jury. However, the three judges also noted that shortly after the Federal Bureau of Investigation's observation of Radovich, the Army transferred him to Burma, where he participated in difficult fighting against the Japanese Army. Indeed, before his court-martial, *Time Magazine* published a column on Radovich's success in shooting down four Japanese fighter aircraft. Army psychiatrists determined that Radovich suffered from mental strain caused by significant combat experience and confined him to a "ward for the insane," where he could only eat his meals with a spoon. The Bureau's agents extracted a confession from him while in this condition. Shortly after, the agents obtained another confession and this second confession was introduced both at Radovich's court-martial and at his federal trial.[42]

In 1940 in *Chambers v. Florida*, and again in 1943 in *McNabb v. United States*, the Supreme Court determined that a confession obtained in onerous, violent, or coercive conditions could be inadmissible. Likewise, a second confession taken under less austere conditions could be considered as tainted by the first and also inadmissible. This rule exists because otherwise, government law enforcement agents would be able to use an inadmissible coerced confession as a basis for setting up a second confession, under the principle that the confessor would feel compelled to speak.[43]

The appellate court determined that Radovich's second confession was inadmissible because of the conditions under which it was taken, making it an open question as to whether the court-martial had to be voided by the Secretary of War. On the advice of the Judge Advocate General, the Secretary of War

41 *United States v. Bayer*, 156 U.S. 964 (CA 2, 1946).

42 "Army and Navy: The Major and God," *Time Magazine*, November 13, 1944.

43 *Chambers v. Florida*, 309 U.S. 227 (1940); *McNabb v. United States*, 318 U.S. 332 (1943). The rule governing otherwise admissible later confessions taken by law enforcement agents after a confession obtained in violation of the Fifth Amendment was modified in *Oregon v. Elstad*, 470 U.S. 298 (1985).

ultimately voided the court-martial, thereby directly incorporating *McNabb* into courts-martial jurisprudence, a significant development. However, the Army eventually retried Radovich in a court-martial. Equally striking, the appellate court also determined that double jeopardy should have prohibited the Department of Justice from prosecuting Radovich, based on *Grafton*.

The War Department's leadership and the Attorney General alike were concerned enough with the appellate court's ruling to seek a grant of *certiorari* from the Court. The solicitor general appointed Frederick Wiener to argue on behalf of the War Department and he focused much of his argument on maintaining the traditional view of the relationship of double jeopardy and military law. Writing for the majority, Jackson conceded that Radovich was an officer with a heroic combat record, but there was substantial evidence that even from Burma he continued to manipulate the assignments of the two enlisted personnel. Radovich went so far as to have the two men transferred to his combat unit and then retransferred them to a non-combat unit in the United States. The Bayers' tried to raise the defense that they were victims of extortion, rather than willing participants in Radovich's actions, and the proof of this rested in evidence the trial judge suppressed. The judicially suppressed evidence might have helped the Bayers, but Jackson believed the trial judge acted properly in excluding it based on timeliness and the idea that it had the potential to harm, as much as hurt, the defense. As to Radovich's confession, Jackson pointed out that the initial confession was not offered into evidence, and the second confession, taken six months later, was admissible, presumably, because enough time had passed since the first confession. Finally, Jackson determined that double jeopardy did not bar the court-martial and federal court in this instance, concluding that the court-martial charge of conduct unbecoming an officer and gentleman, though for fraud, did not involve a conspiracy element, as had the federal civilian charges, and thus the two trials were for separate offenses.

Frankfurter and Rutledge disagreed with the majority. It was significant to Frankfurter that Radovich had bravely distinguished himself fighting against the Japanese in Burma, and while awaiting court-martial, the Army had him confined in psychopathic ward. It took the Army nine months to court-martial Radovich, and in Frankfurter's personal correspondence to Jackson, he pointed out that the judge advocate did not follow the strictures of the Articles of War at the court-martial. Although Frankfurter merely adopted the lower court's reasoning in his published dissent, he was far more impassioned in conference. Calling both Learned and Augustus Hand, "hard boiled," he pointed out that if these two judges—one of whom had created the doctrine of harmless error that enabled an appellate court to find error in a trial but declare that it would not have impacted the result and therefore a conviction would not be overturned—would overturn this case, the Court should honor the lower court's decision. "I have no bowels of compassion for these defendants, particularly the Bayers," he noted. "But I have strong views, as you know, about the laxity in the trials of federal criminals." This was not quite true. Frankfurter had a large well of sympathy for

Radovich, and in conference he urged his fellow justices to be liberally cautious before permitting a conviction of a war hero.[44]

Frankfurter did not, however, join Rutledge, who concluded that double jeopardy prevented the trial of the officer. In this instance, Rutledge stood alone in arguing that the court-martial charge of conduct unbecoming an officer and gentleman was substantially similar to the federal conspiracy charge. Over time, Rutledge's views have prevailed insofar as the Department of Defense has issued regulations almost prohibiting courts-martial where a state or federal sovereign has already prosecuted a service member, but in 1946, this was not the case.[45]

Not until 1949 did the Court review challenges to the fairness of courts-martial arising from World War II. There had certainly been ample opportunity to do so, but in the preceding four years, *Bayer* was the only court-martial-related case to come before the Court, and it was only tangentially related to courts-martial. The Court had been concerned with selective service and conscientious objection, the status of enemy combatants prosecuted under the codified law of war, and the limits of martial law, but not the fundamental core of military discipline. Beginning in 1949, however, the Court determined it could no longer ignore direct challenges to courts-martial. Petitioners contesting jurisdiction based on double jeopardy, questionable government conduct in the courts-martial, and even traditional claims against jurisdiction had percolated through the lower courts with conflicting results. Although not from the chief justice's direction, Black and Frankfurter, believed if the Court failed to provide overarching guidance to the lower courts, confusion and inconsistency in courts-martial practice would undermine the military's discipline and readiness. *How* the justices attempted to guide the practice of military law, however, was fractured with concurrences and dissents, and philosophical differences regarding the judiciary's role in influencing military law were evident in published decisions.

Although the majority of the justices readily sided with the executive branch on military matters, prior to the UCMJ's enactment, there were instances in which the Court forced the War and Naval Departments to adhere to the strict letter of the law, particularly in regards to its jurisdiction. Both the Articles for the Government of the Navy and the Articles of War had long confined court-martial jurisdiction over offenses to specific terms of enlistment. For example, a soldier who went absent without leave during one term of enlistment, but after

44 Frankfurter to Jackson, May 29, 1947 [RHJ/138]. On Learned Hand and the rule of harmless error, *see* Roger J. Traynor, *The Riddle of Harmless Error* 13 (Columbus, OH: Ohio State University Press, 1970), 94 and Hershel Shanks, *The Art and Craft of Judging: The Decisions of Judge Learned Hand* (New York: MacMillan, 1968), 254. Roosevelt considered Roger T. Traynor, a justice on the California Supreme Court, when he nominated Rutledge. However, Traynor's youth and the lack of a powerful sponsor pushed him down Roosevelt's list. Had Roosevelt been given another appointment, he might have selected Traynor. *See* Ferren, *Salt of the Earth, Conscience of the Court*, 214–15.

45 Frankfurter to Jackson, May 29, 1947 [RHJ/138].

an honorable discharge was allowed to reenlist, could not be prosecuted for the original absence because the Army knowingly permitted him to reenlist having excused the offense. Rooted in British military law, this bar was a *de facto* statute of limitation against reaching into past terms of enlistment to punish servicemen for known crimes, though there was no constitutional impediment to such trials.

As an example, in 1844 the army's adjutant general took Colonel David Twiggs to task over prosecuting a Private Pogue for desertion. Private Pogue had deserted, but then voluntarily returned to his unit and was subsequently reenlisted. Pogue's voluntary reenlistment voided the Army's jurisdiction to try the original offense, yet Twiggs had Pogue court-martialed anyway. "It is clearly my conviction that the case came under the 88th Article of War and that the court-martial had no jurisdiction after that fact," the adjutant general argued. "This issue was long since settled in Britain." The Court solidified this rule in 1872 in a brief decision where it ordered the War Department to pay a Civil War bounty to a soldier who deserted, but was restored to duty without trial. Although both the Navy and Army Articles of War had been congressionally altered, this basic jurisdictional premise was unchanged.[46]

In 1947, the Navy court-martialed an enlisted sailor named Harold E. Hirshberg for criminal misconduct during his confinement as a prisoner of war. Hirshberg had originally enlisted in 1936, and was captured by Japanese soldiers in early 1942 in the Philippine Islands. In 1946, the Navy awarded Hirshberg an honorable discharge, and the same day, he re-enlisted. Shortly after his reenlistment naval authorities charged him with abusing other prisoners of war at the behest of his Japanese captors. At his court-martial he argued that he was protected by the Hague Conventions of 1899 and 1907 as well as the Geneva Convention against a court-martial held under the Naval Articles because he acted at the behest of the Japanese Government, and was no longer a United States sailor. Both the court-martial and the subsequent United States District Court rejected his argument as meritless. However, on his appeal to Judge Clarence Galston of the Southern District of New York, Hirshberg argued that the misconduct occurred during a prior enlistment, broken by an honorable discharge, and therefore he was shielded from court-martial jurisdiction. Galston agreed, "reluctantly in light of [Hirshberg's] particularly reprehensible conduct," with Hirshberg and found that the naval court-martial did not possess jurisdiction.[47]

---

46 Adj. Gen. to Colonel Twiggs, June 24, 1844, NA RG 153.1 Vol. 1; also, *United States v. Kelly*, 82 U.S. 34 (1872). Interestingly, Norton P. Chipman, who had prosecuted Henry Wirz, the notorious commandant of the Confederate Andersonville Prison, represented the soldier, Private Kelly.

47 *United States ex rel. Hirshberg v. Malanaphy*, 73 F.Supp. 990 (D.N.Y. 1947). Judge Clarence Galston, a Herbert Hoover appointee, ruled in this case. He distinguished Hirshberg's case from *Ex parte Joly*, 290 F. 858 (D.N.Y. 1922), where a district court ruled

The Court of Appeals for the Second Circuit, in a decision authored by Learned Hand and Thomas Swan, reversed the lower court. Hand and Swan determined that the Naval Articles did not directly preclude jurisdiction in this case, and naval regulations in effect at the time of Hirshberg's reenlistment specifically authorized a court-martial from offenses occurring prior to an honorable discharge. Relying on *In re Grimley*, a nineteenth-century decision that stated that an enlistment is a contract, the appellate court found that Hirshberg had accepted the very jurisdictional conditions that enabled his court-martial. However, Judge Jerome Frank harshly criticized Hand and Swan in a dissent, pointing out that for 86 years the Army and Navy adhered to the rule that an honorable discharge precluded a court-martial for a known offense that occurred prior to the discharge's issuance. Frank conceded that nothing in the Constitution would have precluded Congress from extending jurisdiction to cover such instances, but the Legislative Branch had not done so, and what Congress failed to do, the Navy could not, by regulation, fix.[48]

In a brief decision the Supreme Court overturned the Second Circuit. Vinson assigned Black to author the Court's opinion and the conference notes indicate no dissent from Black's first draft. In conference Black argued that only Congress could legislate jurisdiction and it logically had done so on a British historic model. Like Frank and Galston, Black believed that Congress had not intended court-martial jurisdiction to extend past an honorable discharge even for a known offense committed during a prior enlistment. He noted that the Navy's extension of its jurisdiction occurred through the issuance of an internal regulation and this was an unlawful expansion of Executive Branch authority, because only Congress could determine the limits of court-martial jurisdiction. However, Black was silent as to Frank's contention that Congress could extend jurisdiction to crimes that occurred in prior enlistments. This won the justices over. Although Reed had initially expressed doubts about the wisdom of narrowing the military's jurisdiction, Black swayed him with his argument that Congress could always expand the ability to court-martial service-members such as Hirshberg. "You sound convincing and I shall be with you until some[thing] persuades me to my first position," Reed wrote on February 25, 1949. Within

---

that the Army could prosecute an officer whose offenses occurred prior to receiving an honorable discharge and then being re-commissioned. In that case, the judge held:

> Suppose it was discovered that an officer, before he entered the service, had committed a murder or was guilty of treason, can it be said that the Congress, in the interest of effective administration and regulation of the military forces, has not power to authorize a military tribunal to try such person, with the ultimate result of dismissal upon conviction? Picture the spectacle of a faithless and treasonable officer serving side by side with loyal men in combat with the enemy, because there was no power to dismiss such a man for previous disloyalty, discovered only after his entry into the service. The same view applies to lesser offenses, and I think is so obvious that extended discussion of this point is unnecessary.

48 *United States ex rel. Hirshberg v. Malanaphy*, 168 F.2d 503 (CA 2d 1948).

the week, the other seven justices indicated their agreement with Black. In 1950, when Congress enacted the UCMJ, it ensured that court-martial jurisdiction did, in fact, extend to known offenses that occurred in a prior enlistment, despite the issuance of an honorable discharge.[49]

After *Hirshberg* came *Wade v. Hunter*, which originated in a court-martial prosecuted in the closing days of the war in Europe. After the presentation of evidence and closing arguments, but before a verdict was issued, the court-martial panel sought further testimony from German witnesses. Because of the Army's rapid advance through Germany and the large numbers of refugees, the sought-after witnesses could not timely be found, and commanding general ordered the trial held in abeyance until such time as the witnesses could be located. This action was consistent with the Articles of War, because its unique rules governing courts-martial permitted the panel of officers sitting in judgment to call additional witnesses beyond what the prosecution or defense presented. Once the witnesses were located, a new court-martial with a different panel of officers convened over Wade's objection on double jeopardy grounds. The new court-martial convicted Wade of rape and sentenced him to lengthy imprisonment. Authored by Black, the Court held that in the absence of prosecutorial malfeasance, and despite the fact that under similar circumstances in a civilian trial the Army's action would have constituted double jeopardy, the second court-martial comported with due process.[50]

Black sarcastically argued military necessity as a valid consideration to the dissenters, penning, "in the absence of bad faith on the part of the commanding general, courts should not attempt to review his actions in a fighting theatre to determine whether he should have rearranged his invasion plans in order to have a court-martial continue its trial of a simple case." Black's argument evolved into a more subdued statement in the published opinion, which read: "This case presents extraordinary reasons why the judgment of the Commanding General should be accepted by the courts. At least in the absence of charges of bad faith on the part of the Commanding General, courts should not attempt to review his on-the-spot decision that the tactical situation required transfer of the charges." Perhaps Black had not yet come to fully regret his role in *Palko*, which enabled a state to prosecute a defendant after the defendant was acquitted in federal court for essentially the same offense. Black ultimately did regret *Palko*, and over time, sought to reverse its holding. It is likely if that if *Wade* had been decided two decades later, Black would have dissented from his original position. Murphy, Rutledge, and Douglas,

49 Stanley Reed to Black February 25, 1949 [HLB/301]; Vinson to Black, February 26, 1949; Jackson to Black, February 26, 1949 [HLB/301]; *United States ex rel. Hirshberg v. Cooke*, 336 U.S. 210 (1950).

50 *Wade v. Hunter*, 336 U.S. 684 (1949).

dissented arguing that the right against double jeopardy was fundamental, and trumped military exigency.[51]

Decided almost contemporaneously with *Wade*, *Humphrey v. Smith* presented a wholly different issue on the fairness of courts-martial. The decision arose from a claim of a flawed pretrial investigation of charges that later resulted in a court-martial conviction. The Bill of Rights specifically exempts courts-martial from its grand jury requirement, but both the Articles of War and UCMJ statutorily provide for a rough equivalent. Since 1806, the Articles of War codified investigation procedures akin to a grand jury, but which significantly differed in operation. Instead of a grand jury, the Articles of War mandated that pretrial investigations were conducted by a single officer, rather than by a large panel of grand jurors. An investigating officer was required to be a neutral advisor to the commanding officer in recommending whether an accused be brought to trial or charges dismissed, but the commander decided whether to convene a court-martial.[52]

Humphrey traversed to the Court through the Court of Appeals for the Third Circuit in a case with a different name, *Smith v. Hiatt.* That court reversed a district court's determination that an investigating officer's misconduct, though egregious, did not create such unfairness in the subsequent court-martial to the degree that the court-martial had to be divested of jurisdiction.[53] The appeal arose from an airman's rape conviction during the Second World War. The investigating officer, a "Lieutenant Todd," had also served as a provost marshal, charged with the duty of maintaining order on the installation to which Smith was assigned. Moreover, Todd commanded the military police who investigated the case. To two judges on the Third Circuit, Todd clearly abandoned his role as an impartial investigator. After Todd performed his duties as an investigator and recommended Smith be prosecuted in a general court-martial, the base commander appointed him as an assistant judge advocate to prosecute Smith. Additionally, while the judges conceded that the performance of defense counsel was not a matter for *habeas*, they expressed dissatisfaction with the fact that while an officer untrained in the law defended Smith, the prosecutors, including Todd, were lawyers.

The appellate court recognized that it did not possess the authority to review the "alleged errors," within the court-martial, but found the court-martial lacked jurisdiction based on the defective pretrial investigation. The court also found the Army's skirting of the requirement for the investigating officer to remain impartial noxious to fairness. And, the judges reasonably surmised Lt. Todd lied under oath in the district court that first addressed Smith's *habeas* appeal. In reversing

51 Hugo Black, pencil draft, circulated, undated [HLB/302]. Douglas did not articulate in any correspondence his reasons for dissenting. What remains is a cryptic note: "Justice Douglas asked me to tell you that if the above case goes down Monday, please note his dissent. If someone else writes a dissent, he may wish to join. But do not hold the case for him. Edith Allen to Hugo Black, April 15, 1949 [HLB/302].

52 *Humphrey v. Smith*, 336 U.S. 695 (1949).

53 *Smith v. Hiatt*, 170 F.2d 61 (CA 3, 1948).

the district court, and in effect overruling the court-martial, the appellate court concluded its decision with a statement reflecting a growing consensus on the practice of courts-martial during the war: "We recognize the enormous exigencies of the then general conditions, but we cannot permit them to serve as an excuse for the failure to give the soldier involved the express safeguards with which Congress provided him."

After granting *certiorari*, the Supreme Court's majority recognized procedural shortcomings in the pretrial investigation, but declined to overturn the court-martial conviction that they believed was conducted fully and fairly. One undated Black memorandum to the Court is insightful as to the majority's views. In it, he stated that the authority to determine whether a pretrial investigation was defective rested solely in the Army's Judge Advocate General, an instrument of the Executive Branch. However, Black posited that the federal judiciary could grant review of cases in which no pretrial investigation occurred.[54]

Led by Murphy, the three-justice dissent argued that the majority's decision frustrated congressionally mandated procedural safeguards in pretrial investigations, regardless of whether the resulting court-martial was conducted fully and fairly. In a civilian trial, a defective grand jury could divest a later trial of jurisdiction on due process grounds, and certainly prosecutorial misconduct in a grand jury would divest a subsequent court of jurisdiction. Murphy did not prevail in this instance, though after the establishment of the Court of Military Appeals in 1950, defective pretrial investigations would become a basis for overturning courts-martial convictions.[55]

Perhaps the most troubling aspect of *Humphrey v. Smith* was the majority's reliance on *Yamashita*. Though Black would eventually ensure that *Yamashita* was limited to the doctrine of command responsibility, and its holdings did not cripple due process in courts-martial, the Court repeated this reliance on *Yamashita* in *Hiatt v. Brown* in 1950. In *Hiatt v. Brown*, an appeal originating from a 1947 court-martial in Germany, the Court continued to give wide latitude to military discretion and reaffirmed the narrow traditional jurisdiction test for when federal courts could overturn a court-martial. The court-martial itself was unremarkable for the time. An African-American soldier named Eugene P. Brown was accused of premeditated murder, prosecuted, found guilty, and sentenced to life in prison. Brown was on sentry duty when two unarmed Polish Free Army sergeants accosted

---

54 Hugo Black, pencil draft, *Hiatt v. Smith*, undated [HLB/300]. Douglas was recovering from an accident and did not participate in this decision.

55 On the issue of divesting a grand jury of jurisdiction *see Hill* v. *Texas*, 316 U.S. 400 (1942) and *Crowley v. United States*, 194 U.S. 451 (1904). *See also*, *United States v. Claiborne*, 77 F.2d 682 (CA 8 1935). In Claiborne, the appellate court articulated, "The purpose of an indictment is to apprise the accused of the crime charged against him with such reasonable certainty that he can make his defense and not be taken by surprise by the evidence offered at the trial, and can be protected, after judgment, against another prosecution for the same offense." *Ibid.* at 689.

a German woman, and forced her into a guard post. Brown ordered the Polish sergeants out of the guard post and an altercation between the three men occurred. The altercation ended with Brown shooting and killing one of the sergeants. Two judge advocates defended Brown, and two judge advocates prosecuted the case against him. A 12-officer panel sat in judgment, and was guided, consistent with the Articles of War, by a "law officer" acting in a quasi-judicial role. But the law officer was not a judge advocate, which Article 8 of the Articles of War required, and this became the basis for the United States District Court of Georgia to grant *habeas* review and the determine that the court-martial was devoid of jurisdiction. Though conducted in Germany, the court-martial was conducted during a time of peace, and the commanding officer gave no explanation as to why a judge advocate was not appointed to be the law officer. Brown also argued that there was no evidence of premeditation, that as a sentry he had a duty to defend the woman, that there was no pretrial investigation of the murder charge, and that he received only a "token defense."[56]

To this end, the district court took up Brown's *habeas* appeal and held that:

> Congress evidently felt, especially in serious cases like the present one, that it was necessary for the protection of the accused and also of the public interest, that a lawyer, with the experience derived from service in the Judge Advocate General's Department, should sit in every court-martial case and expressly made this a condition precedent to the validity of such court-martial, except in the single instance where such officer was not available.

In upholding the district court, the Court of Appeals for the Fifth Circuit also derided the law member's performance and qualifications, concluding, "the arbitrary action of organizing this court-martial in complete disregard of the plain requirements of the 8th Article of War is manifestly reviewable, both as an abuse of discretion, and as a fatal organizational defect which effectually divests the court-martial of jurisdiction." The Fifth Circuit went further than the lower court noting that the court-martial "was replete with manifestly prejudicial errors and irregularities" that eviscerated Brown's due process rights.[57]

In conference, a majority of justices voted to overturn the circuit and district courts. Vinson assigned Clark to write the decision. Clark did not believe that the errors Brown alleged provided the district court with the basis to find the court-martial devoid of jurisdiction. Brown had argued that the law officer's incompetence resulted in several significant departures from the rules of evidence. Brown's commander, with the advice of an investigating officer, initially charged him with manslaughter, and without investigating further, the commander removed this charge and instead charged Brown with premeditated murder. This deprived Brown of the opportunity to cross examine the surviving Polish sergeant on the

56 *Hiatt v. Brown*, 339 U.S. 103 (1950).
57 *Hiatt v. Brown*, 175 F.2.d 276 (CA 5, 1949).

issue of premeditation at the pretrial investigation. And, moreover, the law officer permitted the exclusion of evidence that the two Poles were intoxicated at the time of the incident.[58]

Instead, Clark focused on whether the appointment of a judge advocate as a neutral law officer under the Eighth Article of War was discretionary or mandatory. Instead of answering the question of whether the law officer had to be a trained judge advocate such as the Fifth Circuit had done, Clark noted that the federal courts only had to determine whether the commanding officer "abused his discretion," in appointing a regular officer instead of a judge advocate. To the majority, the appointment of a line officer instead of a judge advocate was not deemed jurisdictional.

Burton concurred, believing the federal courts should not be permitted to inquire into the appointment of law officers, "even if it is alleged that the appointing authority's discretion in this regard was grossly abused." To Burton, the majority decision did not go far enough in protecting military discipline from judicial oversight.[59] Burton's concurrence had its roots in his clerk's advice. On February 2, 1950, his clerk urged "this is the sort of issue which, especially in wartime is not appropriate for judicial review." At the end of the month Burton informed Clark that while he supported the majority, he did not believe the draft decision stressed strongly enough that the absence of a judge advocate was not a jurisdictional defect as long as a competent officer was available to serve as a legal advisor. Because the Eighth Article of War did not, in its express language, require the law officer actually be a judge advocate, or for that matter a licensed attorney, Burton reasoned the Court should interpret that Congress could "hardly have meant that the propriety of such discretion is jurisdictional."[60]

Clark disagreed with Burton's suggestion and he made it clear that he was not wedded to the *Dynes v. Hoover* doctrine, which precluded the judiciary's authority to review courts-martial under limited fairness challenges. "I do believe that we should retain some language in the opinion that would give us the right to look into a gross abuse of discretion," Clark responded. "For example, if the record showed that the appointing authority had selected members of the court-martial with a view of securing a guilty verdict, or if he selected a law member that was so instructed we might wish to review the case." Burton did not prevail in convincing the majority. But neither did Black's arguments that Brown's court-martial was so fundamentally flawed that it was devoid of jurisdiction. Here Black appears to

---

58 *Ibid. See also*, *Hiatt v. Brown*, 1950 WL 78523 (Appellate Brief) (U.S. Jan. 1950) Brief for the Petitioner (NO. 359) *Hiatt v. Brown*, 1950 WL 78524 (Appellate Brief) (U.S. Jan. 30, 1950) Brief for the Respondent (NO. 359).

59 Burton, Conference notes [HLB/182].

60 H.L. to Burton, February 2, 1950 [HHB/182]; Burton to Clark, February 28, 1950 [HHB/193]. Burton wrote, "It seems to me, therefore, that we should decide this case on the ground that this availability is not jurisdictional rather than decide it on the ground that the commanding officer acted in this instance without actually abusing his discretion."

have transited away from his view a year earlier that the federal judiciary should largely remain outside of courts-martial.[61]

On November 10, 1950, the Court heard argument in two military law cases, *Whelchel v. MacDonald* and *Gusik v. Schilder*. In *Whelchel*, the Court unanimously upheld a court-martial conviction in which Douglas noted his approval of the 1948 modifications to the Articles of War. Although Whelchel's primary attack on his court-martial was centered on the military's interpretation of the insanity defense under pre-1948 Articles of War, he secondarily argued that his court-martial, which consisted of all officers, violated the Constitution's guarantee of a trial by one's peers. Regarding the insanity issue, courts-martial relied upon a nineteenth-century standard originating from British courts called the M'Naghten test, which essentially asked the court to determine whether the accused was overcome by an irresistible impulse or could comprehend right from wrong. This reliance did not necessarily make courts-martial unique, because several states also utilized the same test. This part of Whelchel's contention, however, was odd because at trial he had not raised a defense of insanity at all. After the court-martial, he appealed to the Army to reopen the trial to permit him to present the defense. Douglas wrote that the refusal to reopen the trial was not a proper *habeas* matter, though he caveated that had the insanity defense been denied to the accused at trial, the Court would have had an obligation to grant review.[62]

Prior to 1948, the Articles of War required courts-martial to be composed of officers, but under the 1948 Articles of War, Congress permitted an enlisted soldier or airman to request trial by a court-martial panel consisting of at least one third enlisted members. Whelchel sought a new court-martial with enlisted members. Surprisingly, in light of his later decisions that courts-martial were inherently bereft of due process because they could be unduly influenced to convict, Douglas dismissed this argument entirely, commenting that while the inclusion of enlisted members in courts-martial was laudable, "the fact that [Whelchel] was tried by a court-martial composed wholly of officers does not raise a question which goes to jurisdiction. Petitioner can gain no support from the analogy of trial by jury in the civil courts." Douglas then concluded with the statement "the right to trial by jury guaranteed by the Sixth Amendment is not applicable to trials by courts-martial or military commissions."

Gusik arose from a court-martial conviction for capital murder. Gusik had been convicted of luring two Italian "black-marketeers," onto a military base and then murdering both. In accordance with the Articles of War, the staff judge advocate at the military base and the Judge Advocate General of the Army

---

61 Clark to Burton, March 1, 1950 [HHB/193].

62 The Court, in providing an exposition of the insanity defense, upheld a state statute requiring a defendant to prove insanity beyond a reasonable doubt. *See, e.g.*, *Leland v. Oregon*, 343 U.S. 790 (1952). In the federal and military practice, the burden remained on the government. *See Davis v. Untied States*, 160 U.S. 469 (1895).

reviewed the case after its conclusion and determined there were no legal errors within the record of trial. Gusik sued for a release from confinement through a *habeas* writ challenging the court-martial's jurisdiction on the basis of a defective pretrial investigation.[63]

The central issue raised by Gusik was whether the *lack of retroactivity* of the review process in the new Articles of War denied him due process. A new provision in the Articles of War, codified as Article 53, provided a fuller appellate review procedure by the Army and Air Force Judge Advocates General before finding courts-martial conclusive. This would have been the point at which Gusik could have claimed a defective pretrial investigation, and after which he could have claimed an exhaustion of remedies appeal to a federal court. A district court subsequently ruled that the Army denied Gusik due process in failing to conduct a full and impartial pretrial investigation in compliance with Article 70 of the Articles of War.

The Court of Appeals for the Sixth Circuit reversed the district court, holding that Gusik was entitled to a review procedure based on the law at the time of his court-martial, and not a retroactive application of the new law, and that he had received such a review. Neither the district court nor the appellate court provided any detailed analysis on the nature of military law or the fairness of the Articles of War. Nor did Douglas, in authoring the unanimous opinion, criticize the military's legal construct. Instead, the Court upheld the appellate court's decision to deny *habeas*. Notably, Douglas' approach to courts-martial incorporated language that at the time evidenced a continuing trust in the military's separate judicial system, though he did so cautiously. Douglas was also angry with the lower court. In conference, Douglas noted "If this holding of the Sixth Circuit means that the decisions of the [judge advocate general] cannot be collaterally attacked, there is serious constitutional difficulty and courts-martial convictions will escape judicial scrutiny completely." However, he criticized the Executive Branch's argument to the Court that the new provision actually diminished the ability of aggrieved convicted servicemen to petition federal courts through *habeas* for redress. Douglas noted, "It is argued that this clause deprives the courts of jurisdiction to review these military judgments and therefore amounts to a suspension of the writ, but disagreed with this argument."[64]

In response to the argument of reducing *habeas* appeals, Douglas determined:

---

63 The facts of the case are found in the intermediate appellate decision. *See Gusik v. Schilder*, 180 F.2d 662 (CA 6, 1950). Gusik was initially sentenced to life, but the sentence was reduced to 16 years. After review, Gusik was transferred to a federal penitentiary in Ohio. The Articles of War that were in effect at the time of Gusik's court-martial were essentially the 1916 Articles of War. Gusik alleged he was denied effective assistance of counsel in his pretrial investigation because his trial counsel failed to call witnesses that might have cast doubt on the charges in the case. *Ibid.*

64 Douglas, Memorandum to the Court, undated, 1949, [WOD/205].

> These tribunals have operated in a self-sufficient system, save only as *habeas corpus* was available to test their jurisdiction in specific cases … If Congress had intended to deprive the civil courts of their *habeas corpus* jurisdiction, which has been exercised from the beginning, the break with history would have been so marked that we believe the purpose would have been made plain and unmistakable. The finality language so adequately serves the more restricted purpose that we would have to give a strained construction in order to stir the constitutional issue that is tendered.[65]

In light of his later opinions and correspondence, Douglas may have intended this language as a warning to the Executive Branch that he opposed the diminution of the rights of servicemen.[66]

This period of the Court's military justice jurisprudence was characterized by significant deference to the military establishment. The Court demonstrated deference to convening authorities in *Wade v. Hunter* and *Hiatt v. Brown*, deference to the military's assessment of the adequacy of pretrial investigations in *Humphrey v. Smith* and *Gusik*, the military's interpretation of double jeopardy in *Bayer*, and the constitutionality of the Articles of War's requirement that court-martial panels be comprised of officers in *Welchel*. Only *Hirshberg* swam against the current of the Court's repeated rulings in favor of the government, and even in that case, the Court was essentially enforcing the military's own rules regarding jurisdiction across enlistments.

III: The Lower Courts and Courts-Martial

Lower court decisions that the Court chooses not to consider can be a significant indicator as to the justices' jurisprudence. This is not to say that a denial of *certiorari* is dispositive on any issue. Throughout the twentieth century the Court has emphatically assured the nation that the denial of *certiorari* has no legal significance. Nonetheless, whether, in light of *Whelchel* and *Gusik*, the Court *intended* to signal the federal appellate and trial courts that they were able to expand their jurisdiction over courts-martial beyond the traditional test for *habeas*, the post World War II decisions of the lower courts resulted in some expansion. For instance, in 1948 the Court of Appeals for the Tenth Circuit determined that it had jurisdiction to determine whether a court-martial sentence to lengthy confinement violated the Eighth Amendment's prohibition against cruel and unusual punishment.

---

65 Douglas also detailed in a lengthy memorandum to the Court that the appellate courts in *Whelchel* and in *Gusik* were at odds, and that the Court had to make clear that *Whelchel* governed. "This view, while not the holding of the case, is in conflict with the opposite view in *Whelchel*. This point buttresses my feeling that cert should be granted." Douglas, second memorandum to the Court, 1949 [WOD/205].

66 *See, e.g.*, Douglas, Memorandum to the Court, undated, 1949, [WOD/205].

A court-martial sentenced a Marine to life imprisonment after finding him guilty of two charges of rape and one charge of obscene language. While the appellate court affirmed the conviction and sentence, the judges noted their offense at the government's argument that the court was without authority to review the sentence.[67]

The same year, the Court of Appeals for the Second Circuit held in *United States ex rel. Weintraub v. Swenson* that the federal judiciary would not grant *habeas* relief where the government complied with the statutory requirements of providing discoverable evidence to an accused, even where the statute itself might be open to challenge. This case arose from a court-martial of a judge advocate accused of accepting a bribe to throw a case. An audio recording of the acceptance of the bribe was poorly made, but the convening and reviewing authorities received an unauthenticated transcription of the bribery transfer, and the court-martial considered the transcript as evidence over Weintraub's objection. The district court cited *Yamashita*, in holding that it did not have jurisdiction to decide Weintraub's appeal. In a decision authored by Learned Hand, the appellate court ignored this point and determined that Weintraub's contention itself did not merit judicial review. Likewise the Court of Appeals for the Fourth Circuit in *Hironimus v. Durant*, an appeal related to *Weintraub*, determined that the military possessed jurisdiction over an officer placed on terminal leave, or, in other words, over an officer sent home awaiting her honorable discharge. The accused officer in this instance, Captain Kathleen Nash Durant, was ordered to return to active duty after being placed on leave in Chicago, only to be transported to Germany and court-martialed for stealing valuable historic Hohenzollern jewelry. Durant received a five-year sentence. The Court denied *certiorari* in both instances.[68]

Perhaps the most important lower court decision not appealed by the government was the Court of Claims' ruling in *Shapiro v. United States*. The Court of Claims was unique in that its jurisdiction extended only so far as the ability to reward an appellant payments against the government. The claims court could not overturn a court-martial by determining the court-martial possessed no jurisdiction as a result of procedural flaws or due process failures, but it could order the government to continue to pay a court-martialed service member that it determined had not been fairly treated by a court-martial. In September 1943, Lieutenant Sidney Shapiro defended a soldier of Mexican descent accused of rape in a court-martial where the evidence hinged on a woman's identification of her assailant. Convinced that the woman was motivated by racism and in his client's innocence, Shapiro violated a basic ethical cannon. Unbeknownst to the prosecution, he substituted another soldier for his client at the court-martial. The

---

67 *Powers v. Hunter*, 178 F.2d 141 (CA 10, 1949).

68 *United States ex rel. Weintraub v. Swenson*, 75 F. Supp. 600 (D.N.Y. 1947); *United States ex rel. Weintraub v. Swenson* 165 F.2d 756 (CA 2, 1948); *Hironimus v. Durant*, 168 F.2d 288 (CA 4, 1948).

woman identified the soldier posing as the accused as her assailant, but even after being made aware of the ruse, the court-martial convicted the accused soldier.[69]

On September 3, 1943, the Army charged Shapiro with violating the ninety-sixth article of war for "delaying the orderly process of the court-martial." Two hours after being charged, Shapiro was brought to trial and shortly after convicted and dismissed from the Army, with the equivalent of a dishonorable discharge. Shapiro's commanders refused to grant a delay so that he could be represented by a judge advocate or at least an officer with legal training. Instead, two of his friends with no legal qualifications defended him. The Secretary of the Army and President Roosevelt approved the court-martial as one among many. Shapiro appealed to the Court of Claims, which commented "a more flagrant case of military despotism would be hard to imagine." Shapiro had, after all, only shown through his ruse that the command might have been mistaken in charging his client in the first place, and to take him to trial for this, the claims court believed, was a "discredit to the administration of military justice." The Court of Claims restored Shapiro's lost wages, but it was unable, despite its forceful language, to order the Army to restore him to duty or void the court-martial. Frankfurter had hoped that the government would appeal this ruling and he intended to side with the claims court, but the War Department chose not to do so. Frankfurter would, within five years, repeatedly cite *Shapiro* in addressing what he believed should be a more liberal standard for court-martial review. The handling of Shapiro's court-martial achieved notoriety in the military legal community and has since been held up as an example of an unfair trial.[70]

IV: Jurisdiction over Civilians and Citizens

Jurisdiction Over Foreign Nationals

Between 1947 and 1950 the Supreme Court decided several significant issues regarding jurisdictional issues over foreign nationals, though the justices also passed on granting several dozen *habeas* petitions from Germans in United States and Allied custody. Not all captured Germans suspected of war crimes were prosecuted in international tribunals, and indeed the majority of trials

69 *Shapiro v. United States*, 107 Ct. Cl. 650 (Ct Cl 1947). In 1976, the Court of Claims judges, in writing a history of their court concluded that *Shapiro* was one of the four most important decisions in the court's history. *See* Marion T. Bennett, *The United States Court of Claims*, Vol. II, 119.

70 *See* e.g., John T. Willis, "The United States Court of Military Appeals: Its Origin, Operation, and Future," 55 *Military Law Review* 39 (1972): 39–52; and Jack L. Rives and Bradley P. Grant, "Explaining the UCMJ," *The Reporter*, (2000) 16–21. Lieutenant General Rives became the Judge Advocate General of the United States Air Force in 2004 and retired in 2010.

were not international. Some of the German petitioners were prosecuted by the United States military. The British, French, Canadian, Dutch, Belgian, and Soviet forces likewise held their own trials for persons they deemed to be lesser war criminals, even though the charges against such persons might include the murder of thousands of innocent persons. In the aftermath of *Yamashita*, the majority of the Court, and for that matter the federal judiciary, concluded that the judiciary did not possess jurisdiction to rule on military tribunals.

After the war, a United States military commission sentenced German Field Marshal Erhard Milch to life imprisonment after finding him guilty of overseeing slave labor and fatal medical experiments. In 1947, in *Milch v. United States*, Black, Douglas, Murphy and Rutledge, favored granting *habeas* review. Unlike on direct appeal cases which result in a grant of *certiorari* where only four votes are required, a *habeas* appeal requires five votes, and Milch was one vote short of getting the Court to review his appeal. The Court's denial of review angered Rutledge who chastised the justices voting against granting review as "a departure from the established and invariable practice."[71]

The following year in *Brandt et al. v. United States*, only Black, Murphy and Rutledge voted for *certiorari.* Karl Brandt had headed the Nazi euthanasia program and served as Hitler's personal physician. In what was billed as "the doctors' trial," 22 Nazi doctors were prosecuted, 16 convicted, and seven sentenced to death for war crimes.[72]

Almost contemporaneously, American military officer Willis M. Everett filed a *habeas* motion on behalf of Valentin Bersin, who was involved in the Malmedy Massacre. Again, Black, Douglas, Murphy, and Rutledge voted for review, but fell one vote short. Black drafted a memorandum for the conference, highlighting that the named petitioner was not a defendant, but rather a United States officer who "filed this petition out of a sense of public duty." The Germans sentenced to death had taken part in the massacre of American prisoners of war, but their confessions had been extracted through torture, and Black urged that the trials "were conducted in such way as to deprive the prisoners and their counsel of any possible chance to adequately set up their defense." *Everett* presents an interesting study, in one sense, because it placed Black and Senator Joseph McCarthy on the same side of an issue, with both seemingly favoring enhanced protections for accused war criminals. Prior to McCarthy's anti-communist notoriety, he held a hearing in the Senate to investigate the conduct of the war crimes trials. Ample evidence shows McCarthy was more interested in Wisconsin's German-American vote than ensuring due process.[73]

71 *Milch v. United States*, 332 U.S. 789 (1948).

72 *Brandt v. United States*, 333 U.S. 836 (1947).

73 *Everett v. Truman*, 334 U.S. 824 (1948); Rutledge, Memorandum to the Conference, October 29, 1947 [WR/159]. Black, Conference Memorandum, May 17, 1948 [HLB/292]. On McCarthy, *see* Frederic L. Borch, "The Malmedy Massacre Trial, the Military Court Proceedings and the Controversial Legal Aftermath," *Army Lawyer*, January 2011. On the

At the end of World War II, General MacArthur created military tribunals to prosecute Japanese government officers who were accused of committing atrocities, in a manner similar to the Yamashita and Homma tribunals. The World War II allies sanctioned the tribunals, but MacArthur's influence on the Japanese proceedings made them suspect. As the only five-star Army general in the Pacific, MacArthur had built a "cult of personality" around himself and there existed a concern that if he charged an individual, a finding of guilt was a foregone conclusion. One scholar of the war crimes trials has observed that MacArthur's influence even over the international military tribunals had no counterpart in the trials of Nazi war criminals.[74]

Several of the Japanese defendants, including two who had been sentenced to death, appealed their convictions directly to the Court. Although the defendants were in American custody, they had been sentenced by tribunals that included American allied judges and officers. Another issue of importance had to do with the named petitioner, Koki Hirota. While he was the Prime Minister of Japan between 1936 and 1937, Hirota had never served in the Japanese military. He was a career diplomat who had served as Japanese ambassador to the Soviet Union, and was instrumental in forming a diplomatic understanding with Germany and Italy. Hirota had also served as foreign minister during the Japanese destruction of Nanking. In 1946, the international tribunal convicted him of failing to prevent gross breaches of the laws of war, waging unprovoked war, and waging wars of aggression, and sentenced him to death. This was a controversial result because Hirota was the only Japanese *civilian* sentenced to death, and his control over the Japanese military's conduct in China was questionable.[75]

As in the cases of the two dozen German petitions, Frankfurter, Burton, Reed, and Vinson believed that the Court simply should deny *certiorari*. Douglas, who sometimes agreed with the four justices on this point, had begun to shift from his insistence in *Yamashita* that the Court not grant *certiorari*, to Black's, Rutledge's, and Murphy's position that the Court had an obligation to decide the issue of jurisdiction in a published decision. Ostensibly, Black, Rutledge, and Murphy would decide the Court had jurisdiction over the international tribunals, but would apply the deferential standard of review found in the judiciary's approach to courts-martial. Black's conference notes indicate that he and Rutledge were convinced that if Reed, Frankfurter, Burton, and Vinson prevailed, that would empower the Executive Branch. Perhaps because Rutledge

entire episode *see*, James J. Weingartner, *A Peculiar Crusade, Willis M. Everett and the Malmedy Massacre* (New York: New York University Press, 2000).

74 Yumi Totani, *The Tokyo War Crimes Trials: The Pursuit of Justice in the Wake of World War II* (Boston: Harvard, 2008), 28–30.

75 Michael Ferren, *Salt of the Earth, Conscience of the Court*, 412; Timothy P. Maga, *Judgment at Tokyo: The Japanese War Crimes Trials* (Lexington, KY: University of Kentucky, 2001), 134; Yumi Totani, *The Tokyo War Crimes Trials: The Pursuit of Justice in the Wake of World War II*, 231.

and Murphy insisted on expanding the test for federal courts' jurisdiction over military trials to include inquiries into claims of constitutional deficiencies as well as statutory non-compliance, the four conservative justices did not want to entertain the international tribunals at all. Additionally, if the Court were to overturn a military tribunal, they would be renouncing the decision of allied judges, not just Americans.[76]

To break the four to four split, on December 6, 1948, Jackson, who had abstained from the foreign cases because of his Nuremburg service decided to join with Black, Murphy, Douglas, and Rutledge. Jackson did not undertake this course because he favored their position. He understood that if he abstained from voting or sided with the conservatives, the Japanese defendants would still be executed, but the world would know that four justices had dissented, causing doubt as to the nation's Democratic institutions. "This stain, whether deserved or not, would be impressed upon the record of the United States in Oriental memory," Jackson cautioned. "If, however, I vote with those who would grant temporary relief, it may be that fuller argument and hearing will convert one or more of the Justices on one side or the other from the views that have equally divided them in the German cases."[77]

Fourteen days after Jackson authored an explanation of his decision to vote for *certiorari*, the Court, in a *per curiam* decision, determined that the federal judiciary did not possess jurisdiction to review an international tribunal, and that the Court's authority was limited to determining whether a tribunal was international or controlled solely by the authority of the United States. This opened the possibility to the federal judiciary possessing jurisdiction over future American military trials of foreign nationals, but not foreign nationals tried in international tribunals who were held in United States custody. Douglas concurred in the result, but added he believed the judiciary possessed the jurisdiction to inquire into how an alien prisoner came into the control of the executive branch, as well as the lawfulness of the imprisonment, and later contended that he had always felt the Court had jurisdiction over the American member of the tribunal. Although neither Murphy nor Rutledge survived to write their dissents, Rutledge's draft dissent showed he and Murphy feared that if MacArthur, a military commander that neither he, nor Murphy, Black, or Douglas trusted, could deny to Japanese civilians the constitutional protections afforded to citizens, then the Executive Branch would one day be able to deny the same to Americans it accused of aiding an enemy force. "If the *Yamashita* and *Homma* cases determined, as I thought, that enemy belligerents have none of our constitutional protections, it does not follow that they held enemy civilians to occupy the same denuded status," Rutledge began. Murphy, for his part, had argued that although the Executive Branch had argued that the tribunals that sentenced Hirota to death were "international," in fact, "MacArthur appears for

76 Rutledge, notes, undated [WR/161].

77 *Hirota v. MacArthur*, 335 U.S. 876 (1948).

all practical purposes to be an agent of American policy and commanded by American directives." In his concurrence, Douglas shared Rutledge's worries over the Executive Branch. He pointed out that the Court had denied *certiorari* in two instances involving American citizens arrested by the military overseas. In light of later arguments by George W. Bush Administration attorneys regarding Executive Branch supremacy, Rutledge and Douglas were prescient.[78]

In *Eisentrager v. Forrestal*, later to be captioned *Johnson v. Eisentrager*, German nationals who were captured in China, deported to Germany, detained at the Landsberg prison, and prosecuted in Germany by a United States military commission. The Germans appealed via *habeas* to the District Court for the District of Columbia. The specific basis for the prosecution in a military tribunal was that the German citizens, who were radio operators, continued to militarily aid Japan after Germany surrendered. This made them, in the opinion of the War Department and by the definition of international law at the time, war criminals. But they were not war criminals in the same category as concentration camp guards. Instead, they were much akin to Confederate soldiers who continued to fight after the major southern generals surrendered, or *Francs Tireurs*, who fought against Prussian soldiers after the collapse of Napoleon III's France in 1871.[79]

The Germans retained both Adolf Frank Reel and Milton Sandberg to represent them in what was almost a replay of *Yamashita*. The Germans' argument to the federal judiciary was that the commission which tried them was bereft of due process guarantees even compared to courts-martial held under the Articles of War, and violated the 1928 Geneva Conventions. The District Court summarily dismissed the Germans' petitions on the basis of jurisdiction, and without inquiring into the other claims. Reel, a 1929 graduate of Harvard Law School, had been one of Frankfurter's students, and a contemporary of Frederick Wiener. But by 1950, Reel was not likely to be warmly received by Frankfurter's allies in the federal judiciary or the War Department.[80]

Unlike in *Yamashita*, in *Eisentrager*, Reel first appealed to the lower courts. The Court of Appeals for the District of Columbia's decision, authored by Judge Elijah Barrett Prettyman, with Henry White Edgerton and James McPherson Proctor joining, determined that "any person who is deprived of his liberty by officials of the United States, acting under the purported authority [of the U.S. government],

---

78 William O. Douglas, *The Court Years*, 279; Hirota, draft dissent, December 6, 1948 [WR/168]; LHP to Rutledge, November 30, 1948 [WR/168].

79 *Eisentrager v. Forrestal*, 174 F.2d 691 (CA DC 1949). On Confederate guerillas, *see* Kastenberg, *Law in War, Law as War*, 303; on Francs-tireurs, *see* Geoffrey Wawro, *The Franco-Prussian War: The German Conquest of France, 1870–1871* (New York: Cambridge, 2003), 237–8.

80 *Eisentrager v. Forrestal*, 174 F.2d 691 (CA DC 1949); *Johnson v. Eisentrager*, 339 U.S. 763 (1950). "Obituary, Reel, 92, Defended Japanese General in 45 Trial," New York Times, April 10, 1990.

and who can show that his confinement is in violation of a prohibition of the Constitution, has a right to the writ [of *habeas corpus*]." The Court of Appeals concluded that the Fifth Amendment and Geneva Convention of 1929 entitled the foreign nationals to some access to the federal courts, and to be prosecuted in the same tribunals as service members.

In conference, Prettyman urged Proctor and Edgerton to accept that the writ of *habeas* "is the weapon of a single individual against all the forces of the majority," and that the writ should not be "destroyed by the majority of the people." He further argued that because the petitioners were not in the United States, it did not matter which federal court they filed in. Prettyman also worried about the effect that a denial of the writ would have on servicemen, and not only those challenging courts-martial, but also captured American servicemen seeking relief through foreign courts. Thus, though it is not apparent in the published decision, while *Eisentrager v. Forrestal* involved foreign petitioners, the court also kept in mind the rights of United States servicemen.[81]

The Court of Appeals' decision had an immediate effect on other trials. In *In re Bush*, a citizen employed by the War Department was arrested and prosecuted in Japan on suspicion of trafficking goods in the black market. In determining whether the judiciary possessed jurisdiction to review the military's actions, Judge Alexander Holtzoff determined that the trial court was "American" in nature, even though it was set up by an international agreement, and therefore *Eisentrager v. Forrestal* meant the district court had to review the merits of the appeal. In *Bush*, the government argued otherwise, and while it failed to convince Holtzoff, it would succeed in convincing the Court to deny *certiorari*. Holtzoff did not order the War Department to return the citizen to the United States while the appeals were pending, and due to the timing of the Court's grant of *certiorari* in *Eisentrager*, the luckless American citizen remained in custody in Japan. When the Court, in *Eisentrager*, reversed the appellate court and found the Eisentrager plaintiffs did not have the right of *habeas corpus*, it also, by implication, reversed Holtzoff. Holtzoff's failure to order the War Department to return the civilian would not be repeated in the critical *Toth v. Quarles* appeals in 1953.[82]

In hindsight, it was inevitable that the Executive Branch would petition the Court to grant *certiorari*. In conference, it became clear that Black and Douglas had picked up where Rutledge and Murphy had left off, and Jackson and Frankfurter remained steadfastly in the War Department's corner on the issue of non-interference with military tribunals over aliens. Vinson turned to Jackson to write for the majority, and Jackson's analysis rested on a sliding scale of rights in which citizens enjoyed the fullest array of individual rights, followed in a downward trajectory of aliens seeking citizenship, aliens residing

81 Memorandum, undated, No. 1053 *Eisentrager et al. v. Forrestal* [EBPP/48].

82 *In re Bush*, 84 F.Supp. 873 (D.D.C. 1949); *In re Bush*, 336 U.S. 971 (1949). A similar event occurred in occupied Germany. *See Bird v. Johnson*, 336 U.S. 970 (1949).

in the nation, aliens of unfriendly states, and captured belligerents at the bottom. None of Jackson's analysis in this area was meritless, and there was ample precedent to support his position, at least until his conclusion. There, he posited that if the Court of Appeals was correct, captured aliens would have greater rights than United States service members facing courts-martial. This was simply wrong; the federal judiciary's limited jurisdiction to inquire into the fairness of military commissions would be the same as for courts-martial. In a draft dissent, Black called Jackson's comparison "baseless rhetoric" adding to the Court's acrimony. On the other hand, Jackson rightly worried, as did Frankfurter, about the federal courts interfering with the military's ability to accomplish its various missions.[83]

Black dissented, joined by Douglas, and surprisingly, Burton. The majority had avoided the question of whether a war crime had been committed at all. Black pointed out that if the Germans had committed a war crime, then so too had thousands of Free French, Norwegian, and Dutch soldiers who fought alongside the British after the surrender of their respective countries. Black disclaimed that extending *habeas* to the Germans would hamper the military's ability to wage war. To the contrary, he argued that not extending "equal justice under the law"—the etched statement at the Court's entry—to all would erode the military's ability to successfully conduct military operations. Granting *habeas* would have forced the Court to answer the question Black found most important: whether there was a cognizable war crime and if so, what was the proper tribunal. Those questions would go unanswered for another 54 years. In fact, the Bush administration's post-9/11 establishment of the Guantanamo Bay detention facility for suspected terrorists would be based in large part on *Eisentrager*'s holding that foreign nationals detained by the United States outside the United States did not enjoy the right of *habeas corpus* and federal courts had no jurisdiction over such detainees. In *Rasul v. Bush*, the Court decided this reliance on *Eisentrager* was misplaced, finding the *Eisentrager* facts inapposite.[84]

Despite *Eisentrager*, and the Court's refusal to review over a dozen other appeals, Black and Douglas, continued to press for the federal judiciary's jurisdiction over military trials of foreign nationals. Partly this was because their allies in the lower courts believed that *Eisentrage*r could be reversed. For instance, Judge Jerome Frank congratulated Black for "a noble dissent," and looked forward to another opportunity to challenge the majority. When, in 1951, Oswald Pohl, a former Nazi protégé of Heinrich Himmler who administered the concentration camp program, appealed his death sentence issued by a United States military tribunal, Black sought to grant a stay of execution. The Army's leadership in Europe pressed for a quick execution before Pohl's appeals were

83 *Johnson v. Eisentrager*, 339 U.S. 763 (1950); Black, draft dissent, undated [RHJ/164].

84 *Rasul v. Bush*, 542 U.S. 466 (2004).

even considered, a fact that Black and Douglas found arrogant and without any regard to the judiciary's authority. Black did not intend to overturn the tribunal's jurisdiction, sentence or finding, but he found it abhorrent that the Court itself appeared to feed into the military establishment's diminished view of the federal judiciary, and that his fellow justices would not even consider a stay against the execution while a petition of *certiorari* was pending. "The papers on which we are asked to permit execution are wholly inadequate to enable me to dispose of the cases in such a summary manner," he urged. "Particularly shocking to me is the contention that we should deny these petitions any kind of hearing on the ground that the High Commissioner feels since appeals to the American courts have absolutely no merit, immediate execution is essential."

Although not directly regarding military law, another opinion during this period bears on the Court's deference to the political branches in matters of national security. On January 18, 1946, a German national named Ludecke was ordered removed from the country under the Alien Enemy Act, which empowers the President to order "enemy aliens" removed from the country during periods of "declared war." Prior to his removal, Ludecke was detained and filed a *habeas* action challenging his detention and pending removal based on the argument that the war had concluded. In *Ludecke v. Watkins*, the Court determined that the power conferred on the president by the Alien Enemy Act was plenary and could not be reviewed by the judiciary. Further, the Court noted that though the "shooting war" had concluded, the decision of when the declared war terminated was a political act to be determined by "treaty, legislation, or Presidential proclamation," not the courts. The Court's deference to the Executive in *Ludecke* affected not only the status of potentially deported enemy aliens, but the precedent that the political branches determine the termination of a war today affects when detained combatants must be returned to a host nation following war.[85]

Jurisdiction over Citizens Accompanying the Armed Forces

Although neither the federal judiciary nor the military establishment's leadership equated United States citizens with foreign nationals, questions arose as to the status of citizens under military jurisdiction once more. Civilian employees of the service branches constituted a large population of what had became referred to as "Americans accompanying the force." Additionally, for the first time in the nation's history large numbers of service members were stationed overseas for tours of long duration in non-combat settings. The military permitted commissioned and non-commissioned officers to move their families to

85 *Ludecke v. Watkins*, 335 U.S. 160 (1948). Frankfurter recalled *Ludecke* in his *Baker v. Carr* dissent, noting that it was not within the purview of the judiciary to determine the legal end of a conflict. 369 U.S. 186, 281–2 (1962). For discussion of *Ludecke*'s application to the end of legal authority to detain suspected terrorists, *see* Deborah N. Pearlstein, *Law at the End of War*, 99 *Minnesota Law Review* 143 (2014).

installations in the United Kingdom and its colonial holdings, as well as France, Italy, Japan, Germany, and Korea, as well as an array of other nations. By 1950, American military families and civil servants employed by the military, resided in 63 nations.

The Truman administration and much of the Legislative Branch assumed that military jurisdiction extended over citizens in the conquered countries such as Germany, Japan, and Italy, because the civil courts in those countries had ceased to function independently and the tribunals that did exist were supervised by the allies. This was based in significant part on earlier precedent. During the Civil War and in early reconstruction in the south, military commissions and provost courts exercised jurisdiction in cases involving southern citizens and northern traders. *Milligan* did not overturn those judicial activities, though later decisions modified the military's authority. Moreover, in the nineteenth century, United States citizens accused of crimes in foreign lands had been tried in consular courts. Such courts, which were established by treaties and other foreign agreements, were administered by the State Department, and fell far short of due process, but were often better for the defendant than the alternative of being tried in a late nineteenth-century court of China, the Ottoman Empire, or Japan, for instance. Importantly, in nineteenth-century decisions such as *In re Ross*, the Court had held that the Bill of Rights did not extend overseas, or in post-war terms, "the Constitution did not follow the flag."[86]

On the other hand, much had changed since *Milligan* and *Ross*, and the Truman administration narrowly focused their decision to establish military-administered courts against the alternative of reestablishing German, Italian, and Japanese courts with full jurisdiction. Yet, two other viable possibilities existed. The first was to extend a district court's jurisdiction through legislation into Germany, Italy, Japan, and the second would have been to create new federal districts in Europe and Japan. The former possibility exists today through the Military Extraterritorial Jurisdiction Act, under which civilians accompanying United States forces overseas can be tried prosecuted in United States District Courts by United States Attorneys, but it did not exist before 1995.[87]

86 *In re Ross*, 140 U.S. 453 (1891). In *Ross*, Justice Stephen J. Field articulated that "the Constitution can have no operation in a foreign country." Ross involved a merchant sailor accused of murdering one of his shipmates while anchored off Japan.

87 The specific delineation of the authorities of the occupation courts is found in Allied High Commission Documents, 15 Fed. Reg. 2086 (Apr. 13, 1950). For a general history and discussion of the functions and purposes of the commission, *see, e.g.*, Elmer Plischke, *History of the Allied High Commission for Germany: Its Establishment, Structure and Procedures* (Bonn: Historical Division, Office of the Executive Secretary, Office of the U.S. High Commissioner for Germany, 1951), 1; also, Eli E. Nobleman, *Military Government Courts: Law and Justice in the American Zone of Germany*, 33 *American Bar Association Journal*, 777, 778–9 (1947).

In 1949, Yvette Madsen, the wife of an Air Force officer, murdered her husband while the two were stationed in Germany. The military prosecuted her in the United States Military Government Court for Germany. Civilian judges, but no jury, served on this court, and it was administered by the military. The court lacked several of the safeguards enumerated in the Bill of Rights, to include a grand jury and trial by jury. After the court found her guilty and sentenced her to 15 years in prison, the Army transferred her to a West Virginia federal prison.

She appealed via *habeas* to the United States District Court for the Southern District of West Virginia, arguing not only that the military lacked jurisdiction to prosecute her in a court not explicitly created by Congress, but even if the military had jurisdiction, it was only for trial in a court-martial. The district court determined that since Germany lacked any judicial system and the president's war powers extended to ensuring a civil government, *Ross* coupled with *Quirin* clearly meant that the military's jurisdiction was constitutionally sound. As to Madsen's second contention, the district court ignored that fact that a court-martial has a quasi-jury, and had been established by Congress. Instead the district court focused on the military's authority to create commissions, such as what had occurred in the Civil War. Relying on Colonel Winthrop's treatise, the district court upheld the military's discretion to establish unique courts. The district court omitted an obvious fundamental tenet of constitutional law, perhaps intentionally. A citizen may always waive his or her rights, and perhaps the act of residing on a military base overseas constituted such a waiver. The Court of Appeals for the Fourth Circuit upheld the lower court, and also did not address this voluntary waiver question, even though the government raised it in their arguments.

The Supreme Court also ignored the question of voluntary waiver. In a decision authored by Burton, with only Black dissenting, the Court essentially held that when assessed against the history of military commissions, the Executive Branch had the authority to create tribunals. However, much like *Yamashita*, no discussion of procedural safeguards was evident in the majority's decision. Black dissented much for the same reasons that Chief Justice Salmon Chase concurred in *Milligan*. To Black, the establishment of military courts with jurisdiction over citizens in Germany, Italy, and Japan was done without congressional sanction. As a result, he believed that these courts were unlawful. *Madsen v. Kinsella* would be overturned within a half decade of its issuance, so its primary importance today is in tracing the Court's evolving military law and national security jurisprudence.[88]

As Attorney General, Clark had earlier advised Truman on the legality of prosecuting American civilians in military courts. On February 9, 1949, Clark informed Truman that the judicial scheme in Germany was sound, and that military courts afforded citizens most of the protections found in the Bill of Rights. However, he conceded that absent from those rights was the grand

88 *Madsen v. Kinsella*, 343 U.S. 341 (1952).

jury requirement as well as trial by a jury of one's peers. "Notable among the differences between the system of criminal justice established [by the President] and criminal justice as administered in the United States is the absence of a right to trial by jury in the Military Government Courts," Clark noted. "This difference, however, is not entirely surprising since the Military Government Courts in many respects bear resemblance to courts-martial, from which they are an outgrowth and of course do not provide for trial by jury."[89] Since Clark had advised the president on this very issue, he might have thought it wise to recuse himself, especially as his absence would not have made a difference in the outcome. But he did not, and his fellow justices—either unaware of his prior activity or not considering the ethical implications—did not object.

V: Selective Service and Conscientious Objection

Congress created a scheme in which a person could request conscientious objector status based on religious beliefs in the Universal Military Service and Training Act of 1948. The operative language "by reason of religious training and belief, is conscientiously opposed to war in any form," became a frequently contested issue. Conscientious objection, codified under section 6(j) of the act, required a conscientious objector applicant to fill out a form. If, after reviewing the form and providing an applicant with an interview, a local board denied conscientious objector status, the person had the right to appeal to a state appeals board. While the appeal was pending, the Federal Bureau of Investigation investigated the applicant's claims. A state appeals board was not bound by the Bureau's report, but it was required to give the report deference. The law also did not require the government to provide the Bureau's report to the applicant. The selective service law did not provide for a direct judicial review of the appeals board's final decision, though a denied applicant could seek *habeas* review. Also, the law did not specify at what point in the process an individual could seek judicial review, nor did the law apply to service members already serving who might have adopted a religious belief during their service. Until the advent of the all-volunteer force during the Nixon Presidency, this law remained basically intact with only minor modifications. Most importantly, the law was drafted in a manner so as to continue the relevancy of the Court's prior selective service and conscientious objector decisions and as a result, the new law did not affect earlier challenges to selective service. By 1949 there were 3,775 local draft boards and nine million men were registered for conscription. However, because of volunteer enlistments, only 35,000 new soldiers were drafted.[90]

Although the War Department's leadership might well have assumed that the issues surrounding selective service and conscientious objection were settled by

89 Clark to Truman, February 9, 1949 [HST R/21].

90 *See, e.g.*, *United States v. Geary*, 368 U.S. 144 (CA 2, 1966).

1946, this was not so. In 1947, in *Sunal v. Large*, the Court once more addressed the role of religious exemption from compulsory military service. The Court's *certiorari* grant combined two Jehovah's Witnesses petitioners who claimed they were ordained ministers, and therefore exempted from military duty. The two petitioners, Theodore Sunal and John Kulick, had exhausted their appeals through their local and state draft boards. In 1944, both men reported to a military processing center but refused to submit to induction and were convicted in federal court. The trial courts refused to let Sunal and Kulick present a defense that the local and state board denials were in error, and therefore they were entitled to an exemption. The two petitioners received different results on appeal. The Court of Appeals for the Fourth Circuit determined that the local and state board did not err in Sunal's case and therefore denied his *habeas* writ. By contrast, the Court of Appeals for the Second Circuit, in a decision authored by Learned Hand, held that because the trial court denied Kulick the right to present a defense to which he was entitled, his conviction had to be overturned.[91]

Both men petitioned for a *habeas* writ rather than "the normal and customary method of correcting errors" of appeal. In conference, Douglas surprisingly argued that *habeas* writs in military cases had been extended too far for his comfort. He particularly criticized the Second Circuit's decision, urging that if it were adopted, "we would be giving *habeas* the broadest scope, opening military law decisions to collateral attack." As a result of Douglas' stridency, Vinson assigned him to write for the majority. In reversing the Second Circuit and affirming the Fourth, the Court did not contest the claims of a Sixth Amendment right to present a defense raised by both Sunal and Kulick, but rather the means by which both petitioners brought their claims before the federal appeals courts.[92]

Frankfurter dissented, as did Murphy and Rutledge. Frankfurter conceded that writs of *habeas* usually reached the federal appellate courts in a faster manner because the nature of *habeas* is the claim that a wrongful imprisonment has occurred as a result of a glaring constitutional defect such as a lack of jurisdiction. He conceded that the two petitioners had not appealed through the conventional route of claiming error, yet found this factor irrelevant. He recognized there was a sound reason for their failure to take this path. *Estep*, in which the Court would determine that a petitioner could contest a local draft board's determination before a trial judge, had yet to be decided when their case was ripe for appeal. More importantly, Frankfurter pointed out that while traditionally *habeas* applied to claims that a court lacked jurisdiction altogether, by World War II, *habeas* extended to extradition decisions as well as claims of double jeopardy, contempt cases, and defects in jury panel selection.

91 George O. Flynn, *Louis B. Hershey, Mr. Selective Service* (Chapel Hill: University of North Carolina Press, 1985), 172; *Sunal v. Large*, 332 US 174 (1947); *Sunal v. Large*, 152 F.2d 165 (CA 4, 1945); *Kennedy v. United States ex rel. Kulick*, 157 F2.d 811 (CA 2, 1945).

92 *See* Douglas, Certiorari and Conference Notes [WOD/157]; WOD Conference Memorandum, May 1, 1947 [WOD/157].

In hindsight, it might appear ironic that Frankfurter allied with Murphy and Rutledge and championed greater access to the federal courts in military cases than Douglas or Black. Yet, for all of Frankfurter's conservatism, he would repeatedly put himself in the position of advocating access to the judiciary and fairness in military trials of American citizens.

Prior to the Court issuing *Sunal*, it decided *Cox v. United States*. Although in *Estep* the Court determined a petitioner could contest the local board's determination before a trial judge, it had not decided whether that right extended to presenting the issue to a jury. Reed, Jackson, Vinson, Burton, and Frankfurter agreed that Congress could foreclose defendants from asserting in criminal jury trials a defense based on draft board error. In *Cox*, two petitioners were ordained as ministers by the Jehovah's Witnesses' hierarchal leadership, but the petitioners also worked in regular lay occupations. In writing the majority opinion, Reed stressed this point. Douglas and Black dissented, believing that unorthodox faiths might consider a preponderance of their members to be ministers and Congress had not distinguished between people who work in regular employment versus those whose primary employment was in a church. Moreover, Douglas noted that the faith in question could no longer be considered anything but a religion, with a status equal to any other recognized faith. Murphy and Rutledge also dissented but their dissent rested on due process rather than statutory grounds. Both justices believed that the Sixth Amendment required the courts to permit a defendant to challenge a board's findings before a jury.[93]

VI: Administrative Governance of the Military

While much of the Court's attention focused on courts-martial, jurisdiction over civilians and foreign combatants, and conscientious objection, important administrative law issues arose within the context of military governance as well. For the first time in American history, large numbers of service-members married foreign spouses, and challenges from veterans who were denied benefits arose through the judiciary. Moreover, the Court reviewed the doctrine of sovereign immunity, because Congress granted several exceptions to the general rule that the federal government was immune from suit, but apparently foreclosed service-members from much of these exceptions.

Service Members and Foreign Spouses

In 1950, the Court, in *United States ex rel. Knauff v. Shaughnessy*, upheld an Immigration and Naturalization Service determination not to permit the wife of a service member entry into the United States. While some commentators have recognized the decision as significant because it distinguished between the rights

93 *Cox v. United States*, 332 US 442 (1947).

of citizens and aliens, the case is also important because of the symbolism of the decision in the anti-communist Cold War context as well as the Court's view of the intersection of the governance of the military and individual rights.[94]

At the conclusion of hostilities with Germany, Congress exempted "war brides" from a restrictive immigration quota system that had been statutorily mandated after World War I. Under the quota system, the number of immigration visas for persons of each nationality was limited to two percent of the total number of people of each nationality in the United States as of the 1890 national census. The quota system, much to Frankfurter's consternation, had effectively prevented thousands of European Jews fleeing Nazi persecution from entry into the United States. Ellen Knauff, a German native married Kurt Knauff, a naturalized American who served honorably in World War II, fighting against Germany, the country of his birth. Ellen Knauff, herself a Jew, had fled Germany for Czechoslovakia in 1938, and then travelled to Great Britain in 1939. She served in the Royal Air Force in World War II. Following the war, the United States Army employed her in Germany as a translator. When she attempted to enter into the United States, the Immigration and Naturalization Service director, with the concurrence of Attorney General Howard McGrath, detained her at Ellis Island, and then decided to deport her to Germany. She was not permitted a hearing to challenge the decision or defend against any derogatory information that the director relied on. The district and appellate courts determined that the War Brides Act did not provide any rights that would negate the authority of the Executive Branch to exclude war brides such as Knauff.[95]

In a decision authored by Minton, the Supreme Court concurred with the lower courts, and determined that there was no procedural right to challenge the Executive Branch's decision, even when the decision was undertaken in secrecy. Minton apparently believed rumors that Knauff was in the employ of the communist Czechoslovakian spy agency. The majority's decision offended Frankfurter, Jackson, Black, and Douglas, though Douglas was injured and took no part in the conference or the decision. Frankfurter was appalled that a citizen who honorably served in the military could be denied his spouse on the "mere say-so of an official," particularly because Congress had not constructed the statute in this manner. Likewise, Jackson disagreed with Minton's suggestion that the Attorney General had acted diligently in this case. After arguing "security is like liberty in that many are the crimes committed in its name," Jackson ended his dissent by admonishing the majority's confidence in the Immigration

94 James St. Clair and Linda Gugin, *Chief Justice Fred M. Vinson*, 262. St. Clair and Gugin state that the Cox decision was controversial, but do not explore why, other than to state the Court drew a significant distinction between the rights of citizens and those of aliens.

95 The quota system was established by the Immigration Act of 1924. In addition to severely limiting European immigrants to the United States, it completely barred immigrants from Asia. *United States ex rel. Knauff v. Shaughnessy* 338 U.S. 537 (1950).

and Naturalization Service and Department of Justice, concluding "this does not excuse a judge for sanctioning a procedure that is dangerously wrong in principle." In private, Jackson accused the Justice Department of leaking false information about Knauff to columnist Drew Pearson, an act that reminded Jackson of a "Nazi tactic."[96]

Knauff v. Shaughnessy was argued on December 5, 1949 and decided on January 16, 1950. The press expressed a good deal of outrage against the Court's decision. Four months later, Jackson, at Frankfurter's behest, did an unusual act he and other judicial conservatives would repeatedly criticize Douglas for. He issued a stay against Ellen Knauff's impending deportation, ordering McGrath to have her remain at Ellis Island while she petitioned Congress directly. The House of Representatives had, in fact, convened a hearing in Knauff's case. In his order, Jackson admonished the Justice Department, critically noting that it had months to produce some evidence of Knauff's disloyalty, but did not do so, and therefore the only logical conclusion was that McGrath quickened her deportation because the Justice Department had embarrassingly rested on unreliable information in making its determination. The source of the information against her turned out to be a jealous rival for her husband's affections in Germany. The House of Representatives Subcommittee on the Judiciary agreed with Jackson that the deportation would be a travesty and ultimately Knauff was permitted to remain the United States where she became a citizen. Knauff later authored a book and asked Frankfurter and Jackson for their permission to honor them with a dedication. Frankfurter responded that as a judge, he acted on the basis of "no other consideration than his conscience," which meant "honoring the nation's soldiers," and therefore would rather be omitted from the book altogether. Jackson had no objections to his name being listed, but stated "a judge deserves no credit for merely doing his duty."[97]

Coupled with *Madsen*, the Court in *Knauff* enabled a vast expansion of authority of the Executive Branch, including over the personal lives of service-members' civilian spouses and family members in a manner the Constitution's framers never intended. Additionally, fears of communism in the military, whether founded or not, led to the Court giving more importance to the Executive Branch's articulated needs of security than to the impact of that branch's actions on the statutory rights of citizens and service members. On January 17, 1949, Captain John M. Johns, an Army officer, wrote to Jackson, thanking him for his dissent. Like many soldiers, Johns married a German national. The government detained his spouse on Ellis Island for three months, and when Johns inquired

96 William Franklin Radcliff, *Sherman Minton, Indiana's Supreme Court Justice* (Indianapolis: Guild Press, 1996), 141; Jackson, personal note, "Knauff case" undated [RHJ/161].

97 Testimony Before the House of Representatives Subcommittee on the Judiciary, Monday, April 3, 1950; Knauff to Frankfurter, December 16, 1951; Frankfurter to Knauff, December 19, 1951 [FF-Harv/43]; Jackson to Knauff, December 19, 1951 [RHJ/164].

why, the Justice Department threatened him that if he continued to ask questions, his spouse would be indefinitely held. After three months, she was freed, and ultimately would become a citizen. It is likely that the majority of the nation's service-members would have echoed Captain Johns' approval of Jackson's dissent.[98]

Discharges: Deference to the Department of Defense

In the five years following Vinson's appointment, the Court considered how the service secretaries and state governments would have to adjudicate the disability claims of veterans of both world wars. They first did so in the context of a seemingly frivolous case, but one which could have considerably increased the numbers of veterans' claims as well as the liability for state and federal agencies. James J. Lamb, an Iowa veteran of World War I who had not served overseas, and indeed had only performed four days of military service from November 11, 1918 to November 14, 1918, filed a suit against Secretary of War Patterson to issue an honorable discharge. Lamb's purpose for doing so was a desire for state tax exemption that Iowa enacted to help families of active duty servicemen in World War II and honorably discharged soldiers. In 1918, the Army issued Lamb a document cancelling his military obligation and a certificate titled "discharge from the draft." The Iowa Department of Revenue and the state courts concluded that they had no authority to equate Lamb's discharge with an honorable discharge or force the federal government to upgrade Lamb's discharge. Technically he served honorably for four days, but no statute or Army regulations in 1918 required the Army to issue an honorable discharge certificate, and thousands of men similarly situated with Lamb were simply given a final pay amount and a discharge certificate.

The United States District Court for the District of Columbia dismissed Lamb's suit for "failing to state a cause of action." The United States Attorney argued that certificates of discharge for veterans of such short duration were solely an action for the Secretary of War, and not reviewable by the federal courts. Additionally, as over 20 years had passed, the U.S. Attorney argued that laches—that is, the argument that "if one party has slept on his or her rights for so long it is unfair to bring the other party to trial"—barred Lamb's claim against the Army. The Court of Appeals for the District of Columbia reversed the lower court, based partly on what the appellate court considered to be a matter of equity, and also because the three judges, Wilbur Miller, Elijah Barrett Prettyman, and Henry Edgerton, believed that the Secretary of War had a duty to strictly adhere to regulations, and in this instance, had failed to do so.[99]

Although Miller authored the opinion, Prettyman, who shaped military law cases in the important Court of Appeals for the District of Columbia throughout

98 Captain John M. Johns to Jackson, January 17, 1949 [RHJ/161].
99 *Lamb v. Patterson*, 154 F.2d 319 (CA DC 1947).

the ensuing 20 years, influenced the outcome of this decision. He insisted that laches did not bar Lamb from obtaining relief because he reasonably assumed that his discharge amounted to an honorable discharge until Iowa disabused him of this belief. Perhaps most stunning, in light of how Prettyman would later decide cases, was his view that the Secretary of War had a ministerial duty—that is an absolute requirement—to follow departmental regulations, and to err on the side of an individual rather than the War Department in close cases.[100]

Nominated to the appellate court by Truman in 1945, Prettyman was a World War I veteran, leaving the Army in 1919 with the rank of captain. He was a New Deal supporter, served as general counsel to the Bureau of Internal Revenue from 1933 to 1934, and then the city attorney for Washington, DC until 1936. He had also been assigned as a judge advocate for extended periods during his military service. In between his departure from federal service and appointment to the bench, he worked in private practice. Unlike William O. Douglas, who later claimed to lament his military service, Prettyman did not. In his diary entry of April 17, 1918, he penned, "I wonder if Kaiser Wilhelm Hohenzollern would be quite easy in his mind if he could see 2,000,000 Americans between 21 and 31 years old in perfect health, clothed, and fed and all at play. I imagined he would be more disturbed than he would be at the reserve army of the allies on his front!"[101]

As a judge advocate, Prettyman once advised his divisional commander to overturn a court-martial. The soldier was charged with refusing to obey a lawful order and disrespect to a superior officer. A company commander, Lieutenant Louis E. Lanborn had ordered a diminutive Private George E. Naylor to box a much "larger and healthier" soldier in an unauthorized boxing tournament. Naylor had responded to Lieutenant Lanborn, "can't you get someone else to box, I am sick." Lanborn mockingly responded, "it seems to me that the thing that is the matter with you instead of being sick is that there is something wrong with your backbone." To this, Naylor retorted, "Go ahead, God damn you! Smile all you damn please if [you] seem to get such a hell of fun out of it." Although Prettyman advised the brigade commander that the order to box was unlawful, since a surgeon had, in fact, placed Naylor on "the sick list," he conceded that Naylor's later statement was contemptuous. However, he urged that the three-year sentence was severe and should be reduced to a reprimand because Lanborn had goaded a sick and diminutive Naylor to fight for his personal entertainment. Prettyman's additional argument to the brigade commander was that if officers could freely violate the limits of their authority, as Lanborn had, then the authority of general officers would be diminished in the trenches.[102]

On April 3, 1941, eight months before Pearl Harbor, Attorney General Robert Jackson appointed Prettyman to the Selective Service Commission. "I feel that respected and outstanding men in the several states should be drafted

100 Prettyman, Conference Memorandum for Lamb v. Patterson, undated [EJBP/33].

101 Prettyman, diary entry, April 17, 1918 [EBPP/1].

102 Prettyman, Naylor file [EBPP/10].

to assist in the performance of this highly important task at this crucial period in our nation's history. Accordingly, I am respectfully requesting that you accept designation and appointment as a Special Assistant to the Attorney General to act as Hearing Officer for the Department of Justice in the District of Columbia," Jackson lobbied Prettyman. In 1943 Francis Biddle, who replaced Jackson as Attorney General, praised Prettyman's "efficiency and diligence in disposing of conscientious objector cases in the District of Columbia."[103]

Prettyman's jurisprudence, like Frankfurter's, could be exacting. In the post-war environment, he had no doubt that subversives posed a threat to the national security. Yet, in spite of the dangers from espionage and spying, he, like Frankfurter, would often demand the strictest adherence to due process. In 1950, he influenced the Court of Appeals to overturn a conviction against Judith Coplon, a communist spy who gave Soviet agents classified national intelligence. To Prettyman, the conduct of Federal Bureau of Investigations agents including wiretapping conversations between Coplon and her attorney was so egregious that the case had to be overturned. Prettyman also argued in a conference memorandum, "comments should be made upon some startling features of the case—perjury or lack of candor on witness stand by Bureau agents and destruction of wire-tap records."[104]

In the Lamb case, the Attorney General disagreed with the appellate court and petitioned the Supreme Court to grant *certiorari*. The Solicitor General appointed Frederick Bernays Wiener to argue for the War Department. In conference, Black criticized the appellate court claiming it "not only decided important questions concerning the power of the War Department, but also upset 25 years of the important War Department rulings and practices which have affected, and will hereafter affect, the status and claims of thousands of draftees of the First World War." After Vinson assigned Black to the case, Black included this phrase in the text of his opinion.[105]

Black wrote for a unanimous Court, all of the justices agreeing that the appellate decision required reversal. Black chose to resolve the case on the authority of the service secretary and the traditional role of a non-interfering judiciary. He urged his fellow justices to conclude that where a military branch follows its own regulations, so long as the regulations do not contravene law, the federal courts should not intervene. In this case, the Secretary of the Army had interpreted a statute as well as the War Department's regulations, and each provided a degree of flexibility. Therefore, Black argued, the Court should side with the Army. Not all of the justices agreed to this approach, but in the end all adopted it. In particular, Jackson was uncomfortable with extending deference

103 Jackson to Prettyman, April 3, 1941 [EBPP/3]; Biddle to Prettyman, January 12, 1943 [EBPP/3].

104 Prettyman to Proctor and Miller, undated, Coplon file 1950 [EJBP/54]. The case is *Coplon v. United States*, 191 F.2d 749 (CA DC 1951).

105 Black, conference memorandum [HLB /233].

into civil matters, though even in his own office, this view was singly his. His clerk advised him that the courts ought not interfere with the administrative decisions of the Army and as such, the Secretary of the Army should not be subjected to *mandamus*, a means for obtaining court jurisdiction over civil matters. Jackson noted to Black that while he agreed with the opinion's conclusion, he "would have preferred to go on laches alone," and not bothered at all with the more important question. At the same time, however, he did not want to spend time on a concurring opinion and concluded that if no other justice viewed the opinion similarly, he would simply sign Black's opinion.[106]

Torts: The Limits of the Military's Liability

In 1949, the Court in *Brooks v. United States* first addressed the question as to whether service members could sue the Department of Defense in tort cases. As the military's numbers increased, hundreds of thousands of military members and their families resided on installations, attended Department of Defense educational institutions, and were cared for by uniformed doctors and nurses. The Department of Defense's leadership assumed that the service branches were civilly liable for some tortuous conduct because of the Federal Tort Claims Act (FTCA). That act was designed to provide civilians a means for suing the government, instead of clogging up Congress with thousands of bills. In *Brooks*, two brothers who were both in the Army and their father, a civilian, were struck by an Army truck. The soldiers were off duty and driving in their own vehicle. The government unsuccessfully claimed that because the two brothers were soldiers, they were barred from suing the government. The FTCA stated in its clear language that District Courts possessed "jurisdiction over any claim founded on negligence brought against the United States." The Court, in an opinion authored by Murphy, found that an earlier version of the FTCA specifically exempted service members, but since that time, the exemption had been omitted from the statute and held that "any claim" included claims by service members. The Department of Defense argued that the Court's decision would open the door to soldiers suing commanders for making bad decisions in combat, but in this instance, Murphy called the government's arguments "sleeveless" and pointed out that the suit arose from a non-military event. Douglas and Frankfurter dissented in the case without writing an opinion. Instead, both justices adopted the lower court's determination that Congress failed to make an express provision for servicemen under the FTCA, and this omission had to be construed against the serviceman.[107]

---

106 MG to Jackson, undated [RHJ/138]; Jackson to Black, January 16, 1947 [RHJ/138].

107 *United States v. Brooks*, 840, 842 (CA 4, 1948). The appellate court noted, "This problem of statutory interpretation is close and difficult, due primarily to the inept draftsmanship on the part of Congress in failing to make clear and express provision as to

In 1950, the Court readdressed the issue of whether the military could be liable for injuries to servicemen that occurred as a result of their duties while in uniformed service in *Feres v. United States.* The Court combined three cases which had percolated through the federal trial and appellate courts. In the case arising from the named claimant, the issue arose in the Court of Appeals for the Second Circuit from a claim of wrongful death when a boiler exploded next to a barracks. There, the appellate court determined that *Brooks* notwithstanding, the officer's widow was precluded from suit. The second case, which arose through the Court of Appeals for the Fourth Circuit, involved a claim of medical malpractice. A surgeon had left a towel inside of an active duty patient after an operation, but the appellate court held that lawsuit was precluded. The third case originated in the Court of Appeals for the Tenth Circuit, which determined, similarly to the Fourth Circuit, that the government could not be liable for a wrongful death to an officer caused by a military doctor's negligence during a surgery. In a comprehensive decision, the Supreme Court upheld Congress' authority to bar active duty members from suing the United States Government in tort on the basis of negligence.[108]

Vinson assigned Jackson to write the opinion for an almost unanimous Court, which essentially determined that service members could not sue the military for injuries suffered as part of their duties. *Feres* limited *Brooks* to non-service-related injuries, such as when a military aircraft crashes into private property, killing the occupants of a house. The decision, which is to this day criticized by service members and in Congress, elicited little discussion between the justices. In late 1949 Clark informed his clerk that protecting the armed forces from tort suits was essential to the national defense. On November 25, Frankfurter informed Jackson, with unusual brevity, "I've read this and I am all for it." Burton agreed to join with Jackson the following day and by the end of the month, the other justices fell into line with the exception of Black and Minton. Black wanted to ensure that the door to non-service connected injuries, as enunciated in *Brooks*, was clearly left open, and Minton agreed. But by the end of the month, both justices tabled their concerns and joined Jackson's opinion. On December 1, 1950, Douglas wrote "please note that I concur in the result," but gave no indication as to his reasons.[109]

Feres would, over time, be criticized in the lower courts and the academic community. In large measure, this has occurred because the Court has ascribed

---

soldiers in the United States Army." But the judges also noted that they could infer that Congress intended to exempt service personnel from the FTCA.

108 *See Feres v. United States*, 177 F.2d 535 (CA 2, 1949); *Jefferson v. United States*, 178 F.2d 518 (CA 4, 1950); and *Griggs v. United States*, 178 F.2d 1 (CA 10, 1950).

109 Memo, OT 1949 [TCC-UT/B145]; Frankfurter to Jackson, November 25, 1950; Burton to Jackson, November 26, 1950; Vinson to Jackson, November 29, 1950; Tom Clark to Jackson, November 25, 1950, Sherman Minton, November 29, 1950, Black to Jackson, November 30, 1950 [all in/166]; *see also*, Jackson's tabulated notes in [RHJ/166].

exclusions to the FTCA that are absent from the plain language of either the statute or *Feres* itself. There have been many well-publicized instances where aggrieved service members or their families have been left without the full recourse in tort law against the cause of their injury. Examples of egregious Defense Department malfeasance for which tort actions by service members have been barred include: a male prisoner sexually assaulted at Fort Leavenworth when the prison authorities knew he was targeted by other inmates; the family of a soldier murdered by another soldier who Army officers knew posed a significant danger; the testing of lysergic acid diethylamide (LSD) on unknowing service-members; the murdered active duty spouse of a naval officer who had scored dangerously close to sociopathic levels on a submarine fitness psychological test; a marine sergeant who died of skin cancer after military doctors noted for eight years cancerous growths but did not inform him; and an airman whose botched gallbladder removal surgery required partial amputation of both legs. Each case has resulted in no government tort liability. On top of these extreme thousands of otherwise meritorious medical malpractice claims provide no relief to the aggrieved service-members.

In 1952, in *United States v. Caltex*, the Court determined that the Fifth Amendment's prohibition against uncompensated takings did not apply to the military's intentional destruction of private property when the purpose of the destruction was to prevent the property from becoming an enemy instrument of war. Following the Japanese invasion of the Philippine Islands in 1941, General MacArthur ordered the destruction of petroleum fields and transfer terminals as well as oil equipment. The private corporations did not dispute the necessity for the order, but sued for compensation. The Court, in a decision authored by Vinson, in looking to Civil War precedent, held that the government was immune from compensation. Black and Douglas dissented, but they did not question MacArthur's motives. *Caltex* was not a tort in the sense of a *Feres* type case, because it arose from a battlefield decision and the issue was whether the Constitution's "Takings Clause" required the government to reimburse Caltex. The Court decided that the wartime destruction of private property was not compensable under the "Takings Clause."[110]

VII: Conclusion

Between 1946 and 1952, the Court was often fractured into camps in which the majority deferred to the Executive Branch's stated requirements of national security, over the claims of infringement on individual and statutory rights. A minority of justices—Murphy and Rutledge until their deaths, and Black and Douglas—focused more on individual and statutory rights than on national security. During this period, particularly after the deaths of Murphy and Rutledge,

110 *United States v. Caltex*, 344 U.S. 149 (1952).

Black and Douglas were more willing to defer to actions directly sanctioned by Congress, but not when the Executive Branch acted unilaterally. Frankfurter often straddled the majority and minority, but he too would transition from deference to the Executive Branch. With the end of military tribunals over foreign soldiers and government officials, and the creation of the UCMJ, a majority of the justices would eventually shift away from deference to the Executive Branch, but that occurred in response to President Truman's order to seize private corporate property with the claim of enhanced powers during a national emergency, and then, shortly after, the arrival of a new Chief Justice.

Chapter 6
The Last Term of the Vinson Court: The Height of Deference to the Military Establishment, 1953

In the last year of Vinson's tenure as chief justice, the Court sorted through appeals addressing espionage, state secrets, communism, membership in subversive organizations, and racial inequality. Moreover, there were lingering disagreements on the extent of Executive power and a significant case regarding the limits of that power, *Youngstown Sheet & Tube*, was decided in the 1953 term. All of these cases were applicable in some way to military law and had influenced the Court's jurisprudence regarding the military establishment. Black and Douglas had, by 1953, come to believe, as constitutional law scholar Clinton Rossiter pointed out in 1951, that because "the president is the fountainhead of military justice," courts-martial were central to Executive Branch primacy. Since the extension of executive authority in all areas impacted on individual rights and had the potential to cripple democracy, Black's and Douglas' actions in shaping the nation's military law were focused on the broader view of ensuring freedom in the arena of individual rights and through emphasizing the separation of powers. As of 1953, Black and Douglas remained in the minority, though certainly Frankfurter, and to a lesser extent Jackson and Burton, might agree on nuanced points on the need to constrain the Executive Branch.[1]

If the Court's conservatives did not share Black's and Douglas' concerns and compartmentalized their decisions without considering a broader impact, it was not because they embraced pure deference to the military establishment, but rather because there existed a very real threat to the long-term survival of the United States and its allies. With a continued Soviet military buildup originating prior to Stalin's death, fears of Soviet espionage, and the ongoing Korean War, the Court could not ignore military law issues brought before it as had occurred in World War II. The Court would address appeals from selective service decisions as well as tort liability and internal security in the military. It also granted *certiorari* to an appeal arising from a court-martial for the first time in American history during an ongoing war. This appeal was accompanied by an implicit claim of racial disparity in the treatment of service-members facing courts-martial. However, with its focus on national security, claims of racial

1 Clinton Rossiter, *The Supreme Court and the Commander in Chief* (Ithaca, NY: Cornell University, 1951), 102.

inequality in the Armed Forces affecting courts-martial and the existence of other inequalities in the military were shunted aside. Throughout the Vinson Court, the Soviet military grew in both conventional force numbers and nuclear capability. Nonetheless, the Soviet government avoided open confrontation with the United States after the failed Berlin blockade. The Soviet Union's military structure and its capability worried the Court's conservatives. The Soviet forces were politically indoctrinated in manner with no counterpart in the west, and after the failed Berlin blockade, their military increased the numbers of political officers. The Soviet military disciplinary system became more focused on political offenses and desertion than on actual crime, leading one high ranking officer to state "the judicial organs of the Soviet Army are thus mere tools of the political imperatives of the regime." What this resulted in, however, was a Soviet military that western analysts believed was increasingly well disciplined and unlikely to weaken in the near future. A Soviet military command structure in lock-step with the Soviet central government was, from a distance, a potential fearsome instrument of war. From the Battle of Stalingrad in 1942, until the end of the Korean War, the Soviet military appeared to possess unswerving loyalty to Stalin and his successor Nikita Khrushchev. And Soviet forces were not directly involved in Korea, but rather poised against the west in Europe.[2]

I: Executive Authority and the Seizure of Private Property

Despite its fanciful "police action" label, the conflict in Korea was a war, though one unique in American history. Just as in the two preceding world wars, Americans were conscripted into military service and the armed conflict on the Korean peninsula required a modern industrial output. One unique feature of the war was its sanction by the United Nations, an aspect of the international armed conflict only occurring as a result of the Soviet Union's temporary self-imposed absence from the decision making process. There was also the unusual occurrence of the federal government seizing private property without a declared war. Federal government seizure of private property in wartime was not new to the Korean Conflict. During the Civil War and in World War II, the executive branch quarantined industrial and agricultural properties, and for the most part, did so with the federal judiciary's approval. But in those instances, there was a legislative or law of war mechanism underlying the seizure.

Judicial deference to Executive Branch claims of authority has an uneven history. In the opening days of the Civil War, Lincoln ignored Chief Justice Taney's *habeas* order in *Ex parte Merryman*. But, Taney acted in his capacity as a circuit judge and did not speak for the Court. In *Vallandigham* the Court allowed

2 Zbigniew Brzezinski, *Political Controls in the Soviet Army* (New York: Harvard Russian Research Center, 1954), 83. Frankfurter had discussed Soviet strengths with Brzezinski, as well as Herbert Feis, *see* Feis to Pratt, June 13, 1962 [HFP/GMU].

the military's seizure and trial of a former congressman who clearly sought to undermine the Union's war effort. In *Milligan*, the Court reversed course, though it did not expressly overrule *Vallandigham*. In World War II, the Court upheld the internment of citizens of Japanese descent, but following the war reaffirmed *Milligan* and found the expanse of martial law in Hawaii unconstitutional. Truman, who had upset liberals over the imposition of federal loyalty programs, now began to exert the Executive Branch's power in a manner similar to Roosevelt's but without Congressional sanction or a declaration of war. In 1950, Senator Robert Taft, an isolationist but powerful Republican who many considered likely to become the party's presidential nominee, called the war illegal. By 1952, although few congressmen joined with Taft, clearly the nation had tired of the conflict. The Court appeared to follow suit.[3]

Youngstown Sheet and Tube Company v. Sawyer

On April 8, 1952, in the midst of a labor dispute between unions and steel mill owners, Truman ordered the Secretary of Commerce Charles Sawyer, and notably *not* the Secretary of Defense, to seize commercial steel foundries, arguing that the continued production of steel was vital to the war effort in Korea, and the broader national defense and a stable economy. Immediately following this order, Truman invited Congress to develop legislation to address the issue, or to "reject the course of action I have followed in this matter."[4]

A brief note on the steel industries and organized labor is necessary to put the Court's decision in context. Except Jackson, all the justices were pro-labor, but Republicans had successfully linked communism to organized labor. Efforts to unionize steel workers dating to the late-nineteenth century were often bloodily suppressed with the assistance of state government police and militia forces. It was not until the New Deal where union negotiations with federal government mediation resulted in improved labor conditions and wages. But with unions gaining strength, strike threats became commonplace.

The leaders of steel industries, perhaps as a result of their anti-union animus, were never truly competitive with each other. In 1907, the corporate steel executives agreed to cooperate on wages and prices. In 1950, steel industries employed 600,000 workers, and a strike could bring the economy to a standstill. If steel production ceased, coal, railway, automobile manufacturing, and shipbuilding industries would suffer. Between 1950 and 1952, the steel corporations reaped record profits, without a commensurate raise in worker wages. As one scholar of the Court observed, a strike was inevitable, and with a pro-labor president, the end result would be detrimental to the steel owners.[5]

3 Maeva Marcus, *Truman and the Steel Seizure*, 3.

4 H.R. Doc. No. 82–422 (1952); Cong. Rec., Apr. 21, 1952, p. 4192.

5 Maeva Marcus, *Truman and the Steel Seizure*, 39–57.

A majority of the justices might have sided with the steel workers had the case arisen in a different time and as a purely labor matter. Truman's public comments on the seizure, echoed by Justice Department lawyers in oral arguments before various courts, however, troubled the justices. At a news conference on May 22, 1952, Truman not only claimed the authority to seize property without Congressional approval, he also hinted that he believed the judiciary did not have the jurisdiction to intervene. In one of his "give and take" moments with the press, he asserted in response to a question about the Court "nobody can take it away from the President because it is inherent in the Constitution."

If Truman's response appears to be a blind belief in the presidential authority to seize private property, his belief was partly shaped by the justices and recent seizures. In what was clearly a departure from the separation of powers doctrine, Vinson had previously advised Truman that the steel seizure was lawful. Vinson had not bothered to inform his fellow justices of his advice to the president. Clark also admitted that while serving as Attorney General, he informed Truman that such a seizure was permissible.[6] Moreover, Jackson had advised President Roosevelt of the legality of similar seizures before and during World War II.

Vinson's closeness to Truman was not without parallel, but it served neither leader well. Douglas continued to play poker with Roosevelt after joining the Court, and Frankfurter advised Roosevelt throughout the war. Justices Brandeis and John H. Clarke advised President Woodrow Wilson and Secretary of War Newton Baker on matters ranging from conscription to the government's role in labor-management relations during World War I. In 1948, Truman sought Vinson's advice on how to run his reelection campaign, and the president attempted to send the chief justice as an emissary to Joseph Stalin. Vinson had already advised Truman on unifying the military services, leading to the creation of the Department of Defense's and Joint Chiefs of Staff. In 1950, Truman lobbied Vinson to run for the presidency, but Vinson concluded his health could not withstand the rigors of campaigning.[7]

Two presidentially-directed factory seizures before and during World War II likely impacted Truman's decision to seize the steel mills, and directly influenced the government's legal strategy in defending Truman's steel seizures. Six months before the Pearl Harbor attack, a labor dispute closed the North American Aviation plant, which had been producing 20 percent of the United States' military airplanes. President Roosevelt issued an Executive Order to the Secretary of War to take over the plant, and 2,500 federal troops did so. Then Attorney General Robert Jackson opined that the President had the civil, military, and moral authority "to keep the Defense effort of the United States a

6 Truman's press conference is found in *Public Papers of the Presidents*, January 1, 1952–January 20, 1953 (Washington, DC: GPO, 1966), 136. For Vinson's and Clark's advice before the seizure *see* Michal Belknap, *The Vinson Court*, 25; Urofsky, *Division and Discord*, 209; and James E. St. Clair and Linda C. Gugin, *Chief Justice Vinson*, 190.

7 James St. Clair and Linda C. Gugin, *Chief Justice Vinson*, 190–96.

going concern."[8] Congress responded to this seizure by passing several laws, including the War Labor Disputes Act, which authorized the President to seize plants when labor disputes threatened war production.[9]

In one of several later seizures, Roosevelt ordered the United States Army to seize the Chicago offices of Montgomery Ward & Co. in April 1944, four months into a strike by 12,000 of the company's workers.[10] In this instance, the applicability of the War Labor Disputes Act was questionable, and the question of the President's constitutional authority was the key feature of the government's legal argument when it sought a declaratory judgment that the seizure was proper from a federal district court.[11]

After the conclusion of World War II, not only had the factual landscape of the United States' war footing changed, but so had the legal landscape. The seizure provisions of the War Labor Disputes Act expired in June 1947, and the new Taft-Hartley Act addressed labor disputes that threatened defense industries in a different way, by allowing the President to order a board of inquiry and the Attorney General to petition a federal court to enjoin a strike. Taft-Hartley did not authorize seizures.[12]

In light of this legal landscape, the steel companies filed for an injunction against the seizure in federal court. On April 9, 1952, Judge Alexander Holtzoff refused to issue a preliminary injunction against the president. A Truman appointee and World War I veteran, Holtzoff, weighed the corporations' arguments that the steel companies could suffer irreparable harm because the government would learn of their trade secrets and could enact a wage increase. The government argued that Truman possessed the authority to avert a national emergency in compliance with the Taft-Hartley Act, and an immediate injunction against the government was unnecessary. Holtzoff ruled against the steel companies, siding with the presidential authority to avert a national emergency. However, this was not the end of the appeals process because it only took into account the question of an injunction, and Holtzoff set April 24 as the date to determine the legality of Truman's actions.[13]

On April 24, Judge David A. Pine of the United States District Court for the District of Columbia, heard the steel mills' arguments for granting an

---

8 Letter of Jan. 12, 1945, from Hugh B. Cox, Assistant Solicitor General, to Al Woll, United States Attorney, in *United States v. Montgomery Ward & Co.*, No. 44 C 1611, Box No. 899, Civil Action Files, U.S. Dist. Ct. for the Northern Dist. Of Illinois, Record Group 21, National Archives and Records Administration—Chicago (NARA—Chicago).

9 War Labor Disputes Act, Section 3, Pub. L. No. 89, 57 Stat. 163, 164 (1943).

10 Executive Order 9438, 9 Fed. Reg. 4459 (1944).

11 Brief for the United States in Support of its Motion for a Temporary Injunction at 48, *United States v. Montgomery Ward & Co.*, No. 44 C 1611, Box No. 899, Civil Action Files, N.D. Ill., Records Group 21, NARA-Chicago.

12 Labor Management Relations Act, ch. 120, Section 206, 61 Stat. 136, 155 (1947).

13 Marcus, *Truman and the Steel Seizure*, 106.

injunction against raising wages. The government's brief and oral argument were a massive strategic blunder. In both, the government focused on the President's constitutional authority and the legality of the seizure, rather than on the impropriety of granting the injunction. In fact, during oral argument, the government's attorney argued that the Executive has unlimited power in time of an emergency.[14]

A World War I veteran, Pine had been employed in the Department of Justice prior to the nation's entry into that war, and on completion of his service, he rejoined the Department. In 1940, Roosevelt nominated him to the bench. As a result of the government's assertion of Presidential authority, Pine did not merely consider granting an injunction based on the economic injury the steel mill owners might suffer as a result of the seizure, but rather whether the president's actions were constitutional. On April 29, Pine issued a scathing opinion, concluding that the Constitution did not grant the President authority to "take such action as he may deem to be necessary … whenever in his opinion an emergency exists requiring him to do so in the public interest" and that there was an "utter and complete lack of authoritative support for [the government's] position."[15] The government's blunder, and Judge Pine's reaction to it, would set the stage for a showdown regarding Presidential authority at the Supreme Court.

In response to Pine's ruling, the government secured a stay from the Court of Appeals for the D.C. Circuit while it sought a writ of *certiorari* from the Supreme Court. While the Court considered granting *certiorari*, the government also appealed to the court of appeals to temporarily lift Pine's order. In a divided five to four vote, the appellate court voided Pine's order for two days, until the Court's grant of *certiorari*. Judge Elijah Prettyman recorded that the conference decision was contentious, and that all of the judges retreated to their chambers for personal prayers before voting. The judges on the appellate court did not directly review the executive's action, but rather whether to temporarily lift Pine's ruling while the Court decided the ultimate issue. Nonetheless, the appellate court's decision was symbolic of a fractured judiciary.[16]

By a seven to two vote, the justices voted in favor of *certiorari*, with only Burton and Frankfurter voting against. Frankfurter wanted to delay issuing any decision at all, hoping that Congress would either curtail the President or back him, thus avoiding a constitutional issue altogether. Moreover, Frankfurter had recently spearheaded a study on the increase of *habeas* claims from state and military prisoners and worried about the Court's expanded role in that arena. Based on a lunchtime meeting with Vinson, Reed, Clark, and Minton, Burton was certain that Vinson believed he had at least five votes in the president's

---

14 *See, e.g.*, Patricia Bellia, "Story of the Steel Seizure Case," in *Presidential Power Stories*, Christopher H. Schroeder and Curtis A. Bradley, eds (New York: Foundation Press 2009), 248–9.

15 *Youngstown Sheet & Tube Co. v. Sawyer*, 103 F. Supp. 569, 573, 576 (D.D.C. 1952).

16 Prettyman, diary entry [EBPP/1].

favor. On May 12 and 13, the Court heard arguments. Solicitor General Perlman pressed for a ruling that upheld the presidential authority to seize property, even when in conflict with Congress. For the most part, the justices directed few questions to John W. Davis, a former presidential candidate and the collective steel companies' counsel. Philip Perlman, who seemed unable to respond to a barrage of questions, did not impress the justices.[17]

Mindful that the Court's deliberations had been uncovered by the press in the past on May 16, 1952, Vinson encouraged his brethren to "take extra precaution to prevent any leak in respect to our deliberations." In conference he argued that the conflict in Korea and the potential for full-scale war in Europe made it imperative that presidential authority not be narrowed. Reed agreed with Vinson on this point, as did Minton, who became agitated, pounding the table claiming "there is an emergency. Truman seized the plants because the defense of the country required it!"[18]

Black disagreed, accusing Vinson of engaging in "irrelevancies." If, Black argued, the president possessed the quantum of authority the Chief Justice claimed then a president could routinely bypass Congress in sending the military into foreign conflicts or even using the Army at home. This was an important point to Black, as Truman had routinely flouted Congress, and had continually argued that the judiciary did not possess jurisdiction over military affairs. Black wanted a constitutional decision, not simply because, like Douglas, he believed Truman a poor replacement for Roosevelt, but because Truman refused to acknowledge restraints inherent in the separation of powers. Douglas wholeheartedly agreed with Black on this point. Although Frankfurter stressed unanimity, he encouraged every justice to write. Thus, in the middle ground opposing Truman, but not for all of the reasons that Black and Douglas articulated, were Frankfurter, Jackson, Burton, and, surprisingly, Clark.[19]

Black's insistence on a constitutional ruling took form in the first sentence of the decision: "We are asked to decide whether the President was acting within his constitutional power when he issued an order directing the Secretary of Commerce to take possession of and operate most of the Nation's steel mills." Although Black was interested in legal history and he frequently made use of it in his opinions, he emphatically dismissed the notion that because seizures had occurred in the past, such seizures were lawful. Importantly, Black stated there were two means by which Truman could have lawfully seized the mills: if the Constitution permitted it; or, if Congress expressly authorized it. Black answered both conditions in the negative, but the important focus of the decision was a rare Court articulation that the separation of powers, like the Bill of Rights, was instrumental in preventing

---

17 Frankfurter to the Conference, June 3, 1952 [HLB/314].

18 Linda C. Gugin and James E. St. Clair, *Sherman Minton*, 211.

19 Jackson, Conference notes [RHJ/176]; Vinson to the conference, May 16, 1952 [HHB/220].

tyranny, and that the Constitution's two features of separation of powers and individual rights were at once both exclusive and interrelated.

Frankfurter reluctantly entered the debate and joined with Black, but in a separate concurrence distinguished his reasons for doing so. Frankfurter was unwilling to ascribe to Black's strict textualist constitutional approach generally, but he agreed that it applied in the steel seizure case. Douglas wholeheartedly endorsed Black's decision, but he used more strident language in his concurrence. Citing a Brandeis dissent in the 1923 decision, *Myers v. United States*, Douglas made clear that the separation of powers did not permit the president, as commander in chief of the Armed Forces, to seize property absent a grant of Congress. "Our history and tradition rebel at the thought that the grant of military power carries with it authority over civilian affairs," he concluded.

Jackson authored a concurrence that has, more than Black's decision, become a rubric for judging whether the Executive Branch has overstepped its authority. The concurrence created a three lens analysis of presidential action. However, before articulating his analysis he first had to address inconsistencies in his tenure in the Executive Branch where he advised similar seizures were constitutional. There was, after all, a war looming in 1940 during the North American Aviation seizure, but the United States had not yet entered into it. (The Montgomery Ward seizure occurred at the height of the war.) In 1952, the nation was fighting a war, but the political branches of the government did not call it such. Jackson was able to differentiate between the 1940 North American Aviation seizure and the steel seizure on two factual grounds. The first, and strongest argument, was that the government had defense contracts with the aviation company that were vital to the nation. The second argument, perhaps written for public consumption, was that the aviation company was being threatened by a subversive communist movement. Mindful of his earlier advice, Jackson identified the factual differences between the earlier seizure and the current one from the bench and in his concurrence.[20] Some have suggested the purpose of the three-part analysis approach of Jackson's concurrence was really an attempt to create a paradigm that allowed his earlier advice to President Roosevelt to stand, while disallowing the steel seizure then before the Court.[21]

Perhaps as a result of his experience prosecuting Nazi War Criminals at Nuremberg, Jackson prefaced his analysis with a statement regarding the demise of the Weimar Republic in which the law permitted the Executive Branch of the German government to suspend individual rights in times of emergency and without regard to the elected Reichstag. Hitler had, as Jackson acknowledged, made full use of this power. Jackson's three-part analysis divided such extraordinary presidential action into instances where the president acts

20 Transcript of Oral Argument, *reprinted in* 48 Landmark Briefs and Arguments of the Supreme Court of the United States: Constitutional Law 920 (1975); Clinton Rossiter, *The Supreme Court and the Commander in Chief*, 60

21 Patricia Bellia, "Story of the Steel Seizure Case," 279.

according to a legislative grant, where the president acts in absence of either a congressional grant or denial of authority, and, when the president's acts are "incompatible with the express or implied will of Congress." Jackson clearly would have found the seizure lawful had Congress acted. The middle area—he called it a "zone of twilight"—might have enabled Truman's authority if either the president "enjoyed concurrent authority with Congress, or a combination of congressional inertia, indifference, or quiescence," coupled with the magnitude of events required the seizure. Jackson's concurrence has, some scholars argue, taken precedence over Black's decision.[22]

Burton's concurrence was a short addition to the published decision, and basically it reiterated that Truman had usurped Congress, and violated the separation of powers doctrine. In conference, he lauded both Black and Jackson, but to the later, he stated that he found the concurring opinion more persuasive. Indeed, Burton's focus was that Congress had created an avenue for the president to act in the Taft-Hartley Act, and the president had disregarded that avenue. Most surprisingly to Truman, Clark concurred with Black. Like Jackson, Clark as a former Attorney General had advised a president, in this case Truman, the man he now ruled against. Clark appeared to agree most with Burton that Congress had legislated an avenue for settling labor disputes, yet Truman had failed to follow the legislation.[23]

Not surprisingly Vinson, Minton, and Reed dissented. In some measure they likened Truman's seizure to an act of claiming eminent domain for the public good. They believed the decision would be a disaster for the nation's security, because it rendered the president powerless to defend against communism. The dissenters not only harkened to the Civil War experiences, but also in President Rutherford Hayes and President Grover Cleveland's use of federal troops to ensure commerce transit during violent railroad strikes. Although no statutes specifically empowered Hayes or Cleveland to use soldiers to the detriment of the nascent labor unionization efforts at the time, the federal judiciary appeared to support their acts. Finally, Vinson found it important that in World War II, Roosevelt's order to send forces to Iceland without congressional sanction was not challenged.

Although *Youngstown* was not an appeal arising from the use of the military to enforce the president's policies, it does serve as an important point of comparison to the Court's military law jurisprudence. The decision, when juxtaposed against

---

22 *See*, *e.g.*, R. Shep Melnik, "The Courts, Jurisprudence, and the Executive Branch," in Joel Aberbach and Mark A. Peterson, *The Executive Branch* (New York: Oxford, 2005), 460; Michal Belknap, *The Vinson Court*, 97; and Amanda DiPaolo, *Zones of Twilight: Wartime Presidential Powers and Federal Court Decision Making* (Lanham MD: Lexington, 2010), 29–31. Interestingly, Jackson cited to Clinton Rossiter's work on the rise of the Nazi Regime, *Constitutional Government: Crisis Government in the Modern Democracies* (Princeton: Princeton University Press, 1948).

23 Burton to Jackson, May 31, 1952 [HHB/220].

the Vinson Court's deference to the military establishment in 1953, is remarkable in two respects. First, the justices were no longer willing to accept blindly an assertion of wartime necessity by the Executive Branch. Second, the justices involved in the appeal did not initially consider the ramifications of their decision on the nation's military legal construct.

Though *Youngstown* would later affect arguments regarding the boundaries of the President's authority to address emergencies, including using the military, a majority of the justices clearly did not view the case itself as being about the military at all. First, it was significant that Truman ordered the Secretary of Commerce to effect the seizures, not the Secretary of Defense as had been done during World War II. Military action (seizure) was not at issue. Further, despite some of the government's alarmist rhetoric about national security in defending the seizures, there was seemingly scant evidence the military effort would be hampered by the labor dispute and anticipated steel shortage, which at the time of the seizures was only hypothetical, and by some estimates was six months away from affecting military production. Indeed, several justices indicated they perceived there was no real "emergency" at all, signaling that the case might have turned out differently if the Court had agreed with Truman's assessment of the facts. Justice Frankfurter even suggested at conference that the steel might soon be released for civilian rather than military use.[24] Further demonstrating that the non-military nature of the action was significant, Chief Justice William Rehnquist, a clerk of Justice Jackson's when *Youngstown* was before the Court, would later opine that the case would have been decided differently during World War II—in other words, had the case actually been about military necessity.[25]

Though *Youngstown* itself was not directly about the President's constitutional authority to use the military, the case is relevant to the President's use of the Executive Branch, including the military, and remains so today. To be sure, had *Youngstown* been decided in Truman's favor, it might have had a more immediate impact on the military. If, as Truman argued, the President possessed the authority to seize private property without Congressional approval, then the President was truly all powerful to do as he saw fit with the military in the face of emergency, subject only to *Milligan*. Ultimately, the government overplayed its hand in suggesting unlimited Presidential authority in the face of emergency, resulting in erosion of judicial deference to the Executive, including the military, though those effects would largely be felt after Vinson's death.

Douglas Becomes Outspoken on Military Policy

After World War II, William O. Douglas developed a relationship with *Look Magazine* and authored a series of articles for the monthly publication, analyzing military and political policies. On March 11, 1952, the magazine published his

24 Marcus, *Truman and the Steel Seizure*, 225–6; [WOD/221].

25 William Rehnquist, *The Supreme Court* (Vintage, 2001), 96–7.

article, "We Have Become Victims of the Military Mind," in which he criticized Truman for staffing the executive branch with individuals "who look at domestic affairs in terms of giving orders and expecting obedience." Douglas cautioned that as a result of the inundation of retired career officers in government agencies, the government would become monolithically orthodox in its views. He worried that the government's response to political demonstrations would be a police style crackdown, rather than a thoughtful investigation as to why the protest began in the first place. Drawing a parallel to foreign affairs, he claimed that the military did not know how to "win the affections of a people."

Douglas claimed that he did not question Omar Bradley, Dwight Eisenhower, George Marshall, or even Douglas MacArthur's integrity, but rather he criticized the desire to look strong militarily against the Soviet military threat, without emphasizing that the Soviet Union would have to be defeated at the political level "through emissaries who teach freedom and justice and show there is an alternative to war." Missing from the published article, however, was a visceral criticism of military education, which, in an early draft, Douglas lamented had not produced "a Shakespeare, Voltaire, Tolstoy, Gibbon, Toynbee, Aristotle, Plato, or Jesus, Mohammad, or Buddha." Equally important was that by 1952, Douglas despised MacArthur, and fretted over whether the Republican Party would nominate him. His earliest drafts omitted MacArthur's name from the list of exceptional military leaders and included inflammatory statements like "the military in American history has been justifiably suspect." Douglas did not fear that the military would topple the government, but he predicted that military solutions would increasingly take the place of diplomatic efforts, and in doing so, undermined one of democracy's most distinctive characteristics, tolerating a diversity of opinions.[26]

On December 16, 1952, Douglas predicted, in another *Look Magazine* article, that the French regime in Indo-China would fall. The article was the fourth in a series about Asia. In it, he commented that the French use of American weapons and their mastery of modern warfare were futile against the Viet Minh, and that the only force that could prevent a communist takeover was from within the Vietnamese population. Related to his earlier article, he worried that the military would push for increased involvement in Vietnam, alienating the local population in the process. Douglas did not write this article from an "ivory tower;" he had recently toured Vietnam and witnessed the Bao Dai government's conduct.[27]

In his fifth article on Asia, Douglas analyzed the state of the Korean War. He defended Truman's decision to send forces into Korea, considering it a necessity. "Had the North Koreans been victorious, there would have been a series of violent eruptions which by now might have extended the Communist power over vital

26 William O. Douglas, "We Have Become Victims of the Military Mind," March 11, 1952 [WOD/855].

27 William O. Douglas, "Indo-China Near Disaster," *Look Magazine*, December 16, 1952 [WOD/856].

areas," he cautioned. Douglas doubted that an all-out war with China would bring the struggle to an end, but barring a political settlement with China, he believed it might become necessary. Yet again, in Douglas' drafts, but absent from the published articles, was a criticism of MacArthur's conduct for baiting China into entering the conflict.[28]

Douglas' purpose in authoring the articles provides insight into his early efforts to narrow the military's court-martial jurisdiction and his increasing criticisms of the military establishment. From 1952 onward, he sought to weaken the executive Branch, even when Congress had sanctioned its authority. He was mostly alone in his efforts, though Black, Warren, Brennan, and even Frankfurter might occasionally join him in a decision. Their reasons for doing so were hardly to support his motivations, although by Lyndon Johnson's presidency, Black and Brennan were more willing to favorably consider his motives.

National Security and the Rosenberg Case

The Court's approach to military law was, by necessity, intertwined with real national security considerations, but differences of opinion between Black and Douglas on one side and Vinson, Jackson, and Truman's other appointees on the other, were visibly broadened in the last year of Vinson's tenure. Frankfurter, who often sided in principle with Black and Douglas, rarely joined in their dissents. The fracture between the three justices in 1953 weakened the dissents in the two important military governance decisions that year. But, the fracture was also apparent in the decisions involving communism and espionage.

During World War II, the Soviet Union's spy agencies penetrated the Manhattan Project as well as British scientific programs. The Soviet Union was thought to be far behind the west in the development of nuclear energy and weapons. However, on August 29, 1949, the Soviet Union detonated its first atomic weapon, and it became clear the United States' atomic program had been severely compromised. German-born British citizen Klaus Fuchs, along with some Manhattan Project engineers and scientists, provided Soviet scientists with enough information to produce the bomb. However, in the United States, the Federal Bureau of Investigation focused on couriers of information and technical engineers, rather than on turncoat scientists. Ethel and Julius Rosenberg, David Greenglass, and Martin Sobell were implicated in spying for the Soviet Union.

On April 5, 1951, the Rosenbergs and Morton Sobell were convicted for espionage under the 1917 Espionage Act, and the federal district judge (rather than a jury), Irving Kaufman, sentenced the Rosenbergs to death. Kaufman's governance of the trial was open to criticism. On June 19, 1953 the Rosenbergs were put to death in the electric chair. The case was highly publicized across the world in a manner reminiscent of the Sacco and Vanzetti trial. In the two years

28 William O. Douglas, "The Choice in Korea: Recognize or Crush Red China," *Look Magazine*, December 30, 1962 pp. 12–14; draft, undated, [WOD/856].

between the announcement of sentence and the execution, multiple appeals were filed on their behalf. The Court denied seven petitions for *certiorari*. Vinson, Reed, Minton, and Clark steadfastly voted against each petition. Frankfurter and Black voted to grant each petition for differing reasons. The Court's behavior was a microcosm of its approach to national security, and it provides further insight as to its military law jurisprudence.

During the trial, Irving Saypol, the federal prosecutor, clearly acted unethically, and along with his assistant, Roy Cohn, created a conundrum for the federal judiciary. Saypol provided information to the press that the prosecution would call a witness named William Perl who would corroborate the Rosenbergs' guilt. Saypol's extrajudicial statements to the media were designed to secure a conviction by prejudicing an un-sequestered jury. To be sure, the Rosenbergs were guilty of espionage, and moreover, they were ideologically motivated to commit espionage, but Saypol's statements to the press were beyond what the American Bar Association's model code of professional responsibility allowed, if this code had been binding on federal courts. On sentencing the Rosenbergs to death, Judge Kaufman attributed their actions to emboldening the communist invasion of South Korea and other belligerent acts, as well as being responsible for the deaths of tens of thousands of soldiers. Kaufman grossly exaggerated the extent of the damage the Rosenbergs committed, which appalled both Frankfurter and Black.[29]

On February 25, 1952, the Court of Appeals for the Second Circuit upheld the conviction, despite concerns over Saypol's conduct. On appeal, the Rosenbergs, through their attorneys, argued that their death sentence violated the Eighth Amendment's prohibition against cruel and unusual punishment, the prosecutors had not provided the names of all of their witnesses in a timely manner, and Saypol had bullied William Perl into not testifying by indicting him for perjury, knowing that his testimony would have undermined the prosecution's case. The three judges—Jerome Frank, Harrie Chase, and Thomas Swan—were by no means conservative, but it appeared to them that although the trial had been conducted in a less than stellar manner, the errors were not of a quantum to overturn the conviction.

As noted above, the Court refused to grant *certiorari* seven times, the first denial occurring on June 7, 1952. Initially, Black urged that the Court grant review, arguing that the death penalty for espionage should not be considered constitutional in peacetime. Five months later, the Court refused reconsideration, though this time Frankfurter joined Black. Unlike Black, however, Frankfurter published his argument for granting review. Douglas did not join with Black or Frankfurter in either vote, and Burton recorded that he was surprised by Douglas'

29 Melvin Urofsky, *Division and Discord*, 178–83; St. Clair, *Vinson*, 248–51; James Haynes and Harvey Klehr, *Early Cold War Spies*, 143; *see* Joseph Sharlitt, *Fatal Error: The Miscarriage of Justice that Sealed the Rosenbergs' Fate* (New York: Scribner, 1989), 15.

vehemence in voting against review, in what was almost a reprise of his actions in *Yamashita*.[30]

After the Court's refusal, the Rosenbergs' attorneys raised the issue of Saypol's conduct for the first time on appeal. Although that court was unmoved by their arguments, the Court of Appeals for the Second Circuit criticized Saypol, but concluded that since the defense counsel did not raise the issue at the trial, the issue was not appealable. This ruling was consistent with a basic premise of American appellate law. Issues known to the defense, but not objected to at trial are usually waived for appeal. On April 11, 1953, the Court again refused to grant *certiorari*, with only Black and Frankfurter voting in favor. Shortly after, Douglas informed the Court that he had changed his mind and believed that *certiorari* should be granted, but with only three votes in favor of *certiorari*, the appeal remained one vote shy.[31]

Douglas' change of heart caused a stir in the Court, in large part because he drafted a vigorous dissent denouncing the prosecutors. Jackson called Douglas' dissent the most shameful act he had ever seen, though he agreed with Frankfurter that Saypol's conduct was reprehensible and would vote to grant *certiorari* if for no other reason than to water down Douglas' dissent. Minton too, who was normally not given to accusing other justices of misconduct, thought Douglas was acting bizarrely, if not unethically. In response, Douglas withdrew his dissent for publication, but not his vote.[32]

On June 6, 1953, the Rosenbergs' attorneys appealed once more to Judge Kaufman, alleging that Saypol had relied on perjured testimony from the Rosenbergs' coconspirator, David Greenglass. Again, the Court did not grant *certiorari*. In conjunction with seeking a grant of *certiorari*, the attorneys also unsuccessfully petitioned Jackson for a stay against the execution. By June 15, 1953, two things appeared certain: the Court was going to take its recess and the Rosenbergs would be put to death within the week. However, a new team of attorneys joined with the Rosenbergs' attorneys and brought in a new argument that challenged that the Atomic Energy Act of 1946 superseded the Espionage Act of 1917, and because the newer act required a jury to sentence the accused, the death penalty could not be lawfully carried out. Although the Rosenbergs might have been sentenced to death by a jury at any rate, this new appeal created a significant constitutional question. But the appeal was before its time. Only since

30 Harold Burton, Diary entry, June 18 and 19 [HHB]; Frankfurter, Memorandum, June 4, 1953 [FF/56].

31 Frankfurter to Vinson, May 6, 1953 [FF/65-Harv]; Douglas, Memorandum to the Conference, May 22, 1953 [HHB/248].

32 *See* William Cohen, "Justice Douglas and the Rosenberg Case: Setting the Record Straight," 70 *Cornell Law Review* 211, 234 (1985); Linda C. Gugin and James E. St. Clair, *Sherman Minton*, 227.

2002 must all death penalty sentences be the product of a jury's decision rather than a judge's.[33]

Prior to the Court's summer recess, Douglas reviewed the new *certiorari* petition and considered the Rosenbergs' request for a stay of execution. Jackson was the appropriate circuit justice to decide the matter, but when Douglas referred the Rosenbergs' request to him, Jackson demurred, suggesting Douglas should decide the matter. Douglas heard the case in his chambers and left the Supreme Court building at one o'clock in the morning to avoid the waiting press. Remarkably, he drove to Chief Justice Vinson's home to tell him he was considering issuing the stay. In an hour-long conversation, Vinson tried to dissuade Douglas, but the next day, June 17, 1953, Douglas granted a stay of execution and immediately left Washington by car, headed to the west coast. In a highly unusual, and perhaps unethical, *ex parte* communication, Attorney General Herbert Brownell lobbied Vinson to reverse the stay and Vinson called the Court into a special session. Douglas learned only accidentally about the special session on the radio, while unloading luggage from his car into a motel outside Pittsburgh. Douglas immediately phoned his secretary, who advised him Vinson had not tried to reach him to participate in the rehearing, despite the fact Douglas had left the chief justice with a detailed itinerary of his travels.

Whether Vinson had the authority to call the special session, which appears to have been designed to exclude Douglas, caused intense arguments among the justices. In any event, Douglas made it back to Washington in time to participate in oral arguments and conference. After lengthy oral arguments on June 18, by a six to three vote, the Court, with Black, Frankfurter, and Douglas dissenting, vacated Douglas' stay of execution. The federal government executed the Rosenbergs the next day.[34]

Douglas was convinced that Vinson acted unethically in the name of national security, and Vinson's opinion clearly shows that national security trumped the technical protections of due process such as whether the government could choose one law over another, more relevant law. The central issue to the Court in overturning Douglas' stay was whether the Court even had the authority to do so on short notice, and without a full review of the merits underlying the stay, a reality Vinson acknowledged had no precedent. Vinson's opinion, however correct it might arguably have been in its result, also evidences a slovenliness that characterized his approach to military law. Vinson believed that the security of the nation required a disciplined force, and therefore the federal judiciary

33 Douglas, Memorandum to the Conference, May 22, 1953 [WOD/230]; *see Ring v. Arizona*, 536 U.S. 584 (2002).

34 James F. Simon, *Independent Journey: The Life of William O. Douglas* (New York: Harper & Row, 1980), 185; Linda Gugin and James E. St. Clair, *Chief Justice Fred M. Vinson*, 251–2; William O. Douglas, *The Court Years: An Autobiography* (New York: Random House, 1980), 80–82.

had to stay out of the military's criminal and administrative judgments, or those judgments that arose from espionage trials.

Trial of General Grow

The Rosenberg episode was merely one instance of Soviet attempts to gain scientific ground on the United States. In 1951, the Army court-martialed Major General Robert W. Grow for failing to safeguard classified information. Grow, a decorated senior officer who commanded a division in George Patton's Third Army in World War II, had kept a personal diary since the 1930s. After the war, he headed the U.S. military advisory mission in Iran, and in 1950, was appointed military attaché to Moscow. While on leave in Frankfurt, West Germany, a Soviet agent broke into Grow's hotel room and photographed the diary. Grow was not a communist and, like Patton, believed war with the Soviet Union was inevitable and should occur sooner than later. Nonetheless, the Soviets learned important intelligence from an unwitting Grow.

Grow's diary contained entries on bombing targets inside the communist bloc as well as statements that the traditional rules of warfare should not apply in the event of war. But it also referenced material which had been classified as top-secret. A pro-communist East German newspaper printed excerpts and photostats of the diary, with accompanying commentary from a British military defector, who later published a book on the diary. In response, General Maxwell Taylor and other senior military leaders, as well as members of Congress, demanded a court-martial, which ultimately occurred. Taylor charged Grow with failing to safeguard classified information, but Grow was given the opportunity to retire in lieu of court-martial. He refused to do so, and was convicted by a court-martial that sentenced him to be reprimanded and suspended from duties for six months. In 1957, Eisenhower remitted the sentence, which maintained the record of a conviction, but without punishment.[35]

In 1952, Grow unsuccessfully appealed to the federal judiciary. Given that he received no prison sentence or punitive discharge, as well as the Vinson Court's general deference to the military, this is not surprising. No justice voted to grant *certiorari*. The Department of Defense's leadership's action in Grow's case showed that they not only feared communists in their ranks, they also were willing to set an example in prosecuting the highest levels of military leadership for unintentionally but negligently jeopardizing national security.

35 *See United States v. Grow*, 11 C.M.R. 77 (1953). This episode is well documented in George Hoffman, *Cold War Casualty: The Court Martial of Major General Robert W. Grow* (Kent, OH: Kent State, 1993), 1–39.

II: Selective Service and Conscientious Objection

The Selective Service Act directed the Federal Bureau of Investigation to investigate the veracity of conscientious objector applicants' claims. In *United States v. Nugent*, the Court consolidated two petitions that argued the Fifth Amendment required full access to the Bureau's reports relied on by the appeals boards on their conscientious objector claims. The Act did not require providing a claimant access to the report, and *Nugent* did not involve a criminal trial in which the rules for providing a defendant discovery of evidence were applicable. Moreover, *Jencks v. United States*, in which the Court determined the Constitution required disclosure of confidential evidence in criminal trials, had yet to be decided. Neither of the petitioners in *Nugent* were communists or members of another listed subversive organization, but rather were Jehovah's Witnesses. The Court of Appeals for the Second Circuit had, however, in both cases, ruled that the investigative report had to be disclosed to a claimant challenging a denial before the appeal board.[36]

In writing for the majority, Vinson focused on the fact that the Bureau's investigation was advisory rather than binding on an appeal board. Although Vinson recognized that classes of citizens had sincere religious convictions against military service, the Court observed that these classes were not constitutionally entitled to full disclosure of evidence. "The Selective Service Act is a comprehensive statute designed to provide and marshal the available manpower of the country, to impose a common obligation of military service on all physically fit young men. It is a valid exercise of the war power. It is calculated to function-it functions today-in times of peril," Vinson concluded. In an era of heightened state secrecy, the majority's decision was not surprising.[37]

Frankfurter, Black, and Douglas dissented. Frankfurter admonished the majority for disregarding Learned Hand, Jerome Frank, and Thomas Swan, who had determined Congress intended to have the full report provided to a denied claimant. Frankfurter was unwilling to go so far as to find a constitutional right of access, but he believed that in the absence of a clear statutory statement, the right to access had to be considered as outweighing any governmental interest in secrecy. Although Douglas and Black joined Frankfurter, they separately dissented, admonishing the government for the use of secret information, and came closer to claiming a constitutional impediment to the government's conduct. As a sign of Douglas' growing distrust of the Defense and Justice Departments, he concluded "the use of statements by informers who need not confront the person under investigation or accusation has such an infamous history that it should be rooted out from our procedure."

36 *United States v. Nugent*, 200 F.2d 46 (CA 2, 1953); and *United States v. Packer*, 200 F.2d 540 (CA 2, 1953)

37 *United States v. Nugent*, 346 U.S. 1 (1953).

In *Dickinson v. United States*, decided at the same time as *Nugent*, the Court addressed the continuing issue of how far to extend the ministerial exemption to selective service. The difference between a ministerial exemption and religious exemption is that persons in the latter category might still be assigned to defense or public work. The Selective Service Act did not enable the government to conscript ordained ministers, because to do so could result in depriving congregations of their leaders. However, large numbers of Jehovah's Witnesses considered themselves as ministers in addition to their moral opposition to war. Henry Dickinson was an ordained minister, but he also worked a layman's job as a radio repairman. The local and appeals boards found that his lack of full time clergy work eviscerated the exemption and the Court of Appeals for the Ninth Circuit agreed, sustaining Dickinson's conviction in the process. Writing for the majority, Clark did not approach the issue as a constitutional matter, but rather concluded that the local and appeals boards relied on guesswork. "When the uncontroverted evidence supporting a registrant's claim places him *prima facie* within the statutory exemption, dismissal of the claim solely on the basis of suspicion and speculation is both contrary to the spirit of the Act and foreign to our concepts of justice," Clark concluded. Jackson, Burton, and Minton dissented. Vinson had recently died and was not involved in the decision, though according to Jackson's conference notes, and in light of his prior positions on selective service, he would have likely joined with the dissent. Initially, Minton authored a dissent, but Burton believed that Jackson, who had worked to reverse *Gobitis* in *Barnette*, was in a better position to show that what was at stake was not institutionalized bigotry against a religion, but rather the nation's security, and convinced Minton not to criticize forcefully the majority.[38]

III: State Secrets and National Security in the Torts Context

On March 9, 1953, Vinson led the Court into narrowing the government's tort liability under the FTCA. On October 6, 1948, a B-29 Bomber exploded in mid-air over Waycross, Georgia. In addition to the active duty aircrew, five civilian scientific researchers employed by the Radio Corporation of America (RCA) were on board, three of whom were killed. Not all of the crew perished, and the Air Force's internal safety investigation concluded the crash occurred as a result of negligence. Like many aircraft in the military's arsenal, the B-29 had already aged and several bombers had crashed because of poor maintenance. In one month alone in 1948, the Air Force lost 28 aircraft due to maintenance failures. Although the Air Force's investigation was kept secret, the widows of the three dead civilians

38 *Dickinson v. United States*, 346 U.S. 389 (1953); Jackson, conference vote tabulation [RHJ/186]; Burton to Jackson, November 21, 1953 [RHJ/186].

sued the government in the United States District Court for the Eastern District of Pennsylvania.[39]

Chief Judge William H. Kirkpatrick assigned himself to decide the case. A World War I veteran who had served in the Army Judge Advocate General's Corps, and one term in the House of Representatives, Kirkpatrick was appointed to the bench by President Coolidge in 1927. The government asserted a privilege against disclosing the Air Force investigation on the basis that it would hamper future investigations, and secondarily, the government claimed that the mission's experiments were so important that disclosing the investigative report would jeopardize national security. Both the Secretary of the Air Force and the Air Force Judge Advocate General appeared before Kirkpatrick to argue this point, but Kirkpatrick ordered the report produced for his *in camera* review to determine which sections could be released to the plaintiff widows. When the Air Force failed to comply, Kirkpatrick ruled that the failure constituted proof of the Air Force's negligence. The Air Force, in turn, appealed to the Court of Appeals for the Third Circuit. That court, in a decision authored by Albert Branson Maris, upheld Kirkpatrick's ruling as well. In essence, both the district and appellate courts found the Executive Branch's claim of a "state secrets" privilege did not trump the FTCA. The appellate court drew an analogy to criminal cases where the government either had to disclose evidence or drop charges against a defendant. This should have been no surprise, as the FTCA places the government in same position as a private party being sued. On the other hand, the analogy is imperfect; government has discretion over prosecutorial decisions, but not over whether it will be sued.[40]

Vinson authored the majority decision, reversing the lower courts and upholding the "state secrets privilege." His constitutional scholarship was, on the whole, paltry. Black, Frankfurter, and Douglas dissented, but did not author a dissent, other than to state that they agreed wholly with Judge Maris' opinion. On the other hand, Vinson clearly articulated his view of the importance of state secrets and airpower. "We cannot escape judicial notice that this is a time of vigorous preparation for national defense," he wrote. "Experience in the past has made it common knowledge that air power is one of the most potent weapons in our scheme of defense, and that newly developing electronic devices have greatly enhanced the effective use of air power. It is equally apparent that these electronic devices must be kept secret if their full military advantage is to be exploited in the national interests."[41]

In a superb study on *Reynolds*, legal scholar Louis Fisher points out that the Court's decisional processes overlapped with *Youngstown*, as well as in the vicinity

39 For a recitation of the facts arising in the decision, *see*, *Reynolds v. United States*, 192 F.2d 987 (CA 3, 1951)

40 Louis Fisher, *In the Name of National Security: Unchecked Presidential Power and the Reynolds Case* (Lawrence, KS: Kansas University, 2006), 29.

41 *United States v. Reynolds*, 345 U.S. 1 (1953).

of the Rosenberg case. Fisher concluded that Vinson produced an incoherent decision "tilted away from the rights of private citizens and fair procedures, and supportive of arbitrary executive power." Fisher also discovered that the claim of the necessity for secrecy made in 1949 and in 1953, was not truly based on the need for secrecy, but rather to cover up the Air Force's discovery of its own negligence. *Reynolds* was not only incoherent, it was also pragmatic, and Fisher is right that the decision undermined the concept of an open government.

Reynolds also occurred during the Court's conferences in *Orloff v. Willoughby* and *Burns v. Wilson*, a point that Fisher's otherwise impressive study omits. When *Rosenberg*, *Sawyer*, and *Reynolds* are coupled with *Orloff* and *Burns*, it becomes clear that a majority of the justices were willing to defer to claims of military necessity more than at any time since 1865. This would ultimately change the following year, after Vinson's death and replacement by Earl Warren. Nonetheless, no analysis of judicial intent in *Orloff* or *Burns* would be complete without considering *Reynolds*, and no conclusive analysis of the judicial role in shaping the nation's military laws would be possible, not only for assessing the lasting impact of the Vinson Court's decisions, but also how far the Court under Warren was to move from where it had been under Vinson.[42]

Although the focus on state secrets (or the abuse of the claim of state secrets), is proper in analyzing *Reynolds*, the decision's relation to *Feres* and the related *Johansen v. United States*, cannot go unnoticed. *Johansen* did not originate from a military tort exempted from the FTCA, but rather in the context of an admiralty decision. Under the Federal Public Vessels Act, a civil servant is not entitled to bring suit against the government for injuries caused by the negligent handling of a public vessel. In 1944, a civilian was killed when an Army transport ship struck a harbor defense mine. Another petitioner was injured in 1949, while the ship he worked on was docked. Neither vessel was a merchant ship—the government owned both—but the legal definition of merchant and public vessel was blurry. The Court's majority, led by Reed, determined that the Employee's Compensation Act provided the lawful remedy of disability payments. Such payments were invariably less than what could be won under other avenues of redress. Black dissented, and oddly was joined by Vinson, Minton, and by Douglas as well. The difference between the dissent and majority was Black's insistence that unless Congress expressly defined exemptions, then individual claimants were entitled to the greater benefit, consistent with the Seventh Amendment. In this respect, Black continued with his *Galloway* jurisprudence from World War II. Vinson's and Minton's participation in the dissent is more perplexing, although in joining Black they were able to convince him to remove any language about the individual's

42 Fisher, *In the Name of National Security*, 253.

relation to the federal government, or for that matter, regarding the growth of the military's influence in law.[43]

One other decision issued in 1953 regarding government liability for negligence is instructive on the Court's heightened deference to national security and the military establishment. In *Dalehite v. United States*, the Court determined that the government could not be held liable if it exercised its discretionary oversight in areas of vital national interest. *Dalehite* arose from two almost simultaneous commercial cargo vessel explosions outside of the Port of Texas City, Texas. Both vessels carried ammonium nitrate, an important ingredient in both explosives and fertilizer. None of the government agencies involved in the overseeing of maritime or transportation safety were statutorily directed to inspect each and every cargo vessel or determine whether the cargoes had been safely loaded for transport. However, the government had a significant oversight role from the production of the nitrate through the loading on the vessels.

The statutory creation of the various agencies enabled inspectors, including military personnel, to exercise their discretion in inspecting cargo vessels and chemical manufacturing plants. Thus, when the survivors of decedents sued the government for negligence, the Court of Appeals for the Fifth Circuit, in overturning a district court, determined that the government could not be held liable under the FTCA for failing to exercise its fullest discretion. Had the vessels been under the government's direct control, the appellate court would have likely reached a different result, and the decision did not preclude suit against the commercial operators of the vessels.[44]

In a four to three vote, the Court upheld the appellate court. Douglas and Clark did not participate, though it is likely that Clark would have sided with the majority and Douglas with the dissent. The majority, in a decision authored by Reed, concluded that the government could not be held liable under the FTCA for merely exercising its discretion, because Congress had not expressly created an avenue for suit in such instances. The issues were whether Congress had enabled suit against the government and whether the government's oversight of the activity by commercial entities rise to the level of negligence for liability purposes. In conference, as well as in their dissent, Frankfurter, Jackson, and Black worried that the majority had enabled the government to freely jeopardize public safety under the aegis of national security.[45]

Jackson's draft dissent began with the statement, "one of the unfortunate results not anticipated by the advocates of the Federal Tort Claims Act has been to throw the powerful influence of the Government on the side of lax standards

43 *Johansen v. United States*, 343 U.S. 427 (1942); Vinson to Black, May 23, 1952 [HLB/312].

44 *Dalehite v. United States*, 346 U.S. 1953 (1953).

45 Frankfurter to Jackson, undated, June 1953 [RHJ/181]; Jackson, conference notes, April 6–8, 1953 [RHJ/181].

of care in the class of cases it defends." By the time the dissent was published the statement was modified and placed toward the end of the dissent. Black wanted to keep Jackson's draft phrases in the published decision, but Frankfurter claimed them to be a distraction. Most importantly, Black worried that government negligence in the name of national security would be shielded by both *Reynolds* and *Dalehite*, and the two decisions would encourage government misconduct. When Vietnam veterans discovered in the 1980s that their exposure to a chemical defoliant known as Agent Orange was directly linked to life-ending cancers, the Department of Defense and the defoliant producers would attempt to shield their liability based on *Dalehite*, confirming Black's earlier fears.[46]

IV: *Orloff v. Willoughby and Burns v. Wilson:* Decisions of Lasting Influence

Although *Youngstown, Reynolds, Rosenberg,* and *Dalehite* have shaped jurisprudence on Executive Branch authority and liability, two other critical decisions issued in 1953 arose from different aspects of military governance over its service members. The first of these decisions involved the military's prerogative to assign individual service members to particular military duties. The second decision presented an ambiguous and unintended liberalization of the traditional jurisdictional test governing when, and under what circumstances, the federal judiciary could review courts-martial. This decision would prove vexing for the federal courts from its issuance through to the present.

Orloff v. Willoughby: Communism in the Military

In 1953, the Court in *Orloff v. Willoughby*, issued a decision that not only reflected increasing concerns about the military's need to defend against communists in the ranks, but also a reaffirmation of the Court's traditional reluctance to overturn the military's administrative decisions. The "doctors draft law" enabled the military to conscript doctors, dentists, and psychiatrists who were over the age of 26, an age that ordinarily would have precluded conscription. Psychiatrist Stanley Orloff applied for a commission as an officer in the Air Force. The President commissioned Orloff into the Air Force, but on July 24, 1951, two days before his induction, the commission was revoked, and on June 26, 1951, the Army inducted him with the rank of private, the lowest enlisted rank. In considering the applicable draft laws and case precedent, neither the Army's action in conscripting Orloff, nor the revocation of his commission, violated his constitutional rights. The Secretary of the Air Force revoked Orloff's commission based on his refusal to complete a background investigation, designed to

46 Jackson, rough draft, May 1, 1953 [RHJ/181]; Black to Jackson, April 17, 1953 [RHJ/181]' Jackson to Black, April 23, 1953 [RHJ/181]; Frankfurter to Jackson, undated, May, 1953 [RHJ/181].

discover whether individuals seeking a commission had ever participated in anti-government activities or joined one of the subversive organizations on the Attorney General's List. The Army induction was lawful in the sense that Orloff's educational deferment had ended. From 1942 onward, Orloff had been deferred from military service because of his student status, as an undergraduate and later as a medical student.

Orloff did not refuse to go into the Army and therefore he violated no law, nor did he claim conscientious objection to military service. However, once in uniform and receiving pay, he reapplied for a commission and challenged his status to the District Court for the District of Columbia, claiming his enlisted status in the Army violated the conscription laws because he was 27 years of age when inducted into the Army to serve in a non-medical-professional capacity. That court dismissed Orloff's petition based on what it considered his voluntary status in the nation's capital. Orloff was assigned to a military installation in the western states, and the Army had simply permitted him to take leave in the District of Columbia. Once Orloff conceded that his presence in the District was voluntary, the district court concluded that it did not have jurisdiction to determine the issue.[47]

One month later, the District Court for Washington state, where Orloff was stationed, determined it had jurisdiction to adjudicate his claims. Nonetheless, the judge, William Lindberg, ruled adversely to Orloff, specifically finding that the Army's action was not unconstitutional. Lindberg conceded that Orloff's status as an enlisted man was contrary to the expectations of the "doctor's draft law," but concluded he did not have the authority to order the Army to commission Orloff or discharge him. Moreover, Lindberg correctly interpreted that the draft law conferred no rights to Orloff. In its plain language, the "doctor's draft law," did not prohibit the Army from using medical professionals in other duties, including as enlisted men. Following the standard approach of non-interference in military matters, Lindberg determined, "It is not for the court to say whether such action was proper or not, and the court must assume that the Armed Forces acted properly in that matter."[48]

Orloff next appealed to the Court of Appeals for the Ninth Circuit. His attorneys, John Caughlan and Siegfried Hesse had previously represented suspected communists, which could not have helped his case. In 1940, the King

---

47 *Orloff v. Lovett*, 101 F.Supp. 750 (D.D.C. 1951). On December 17, 1951 Judge James Robert Kirkland, a Roosevelt appointee, determined the court did not possess jurisdiction.

48 *United States ex rel. Orloff v. Willoughby* (D. Wash. 1952). Judge William James Lindberg, a Truman appointee, heard argument on January 4, 1952 and issued his decision five days later. Lindberg noted that during the time of Orloff's appeal, the Army was evaluating whether to commission Orloff or maintain him in his enlisted status, but he evidenced distrust in the Army decision process concluding that Orloff would likely be kept in enlisted status.

County prosecutor removed Caughlan from his position as a deputy prosecutor for refusing to sign a loyalty oath. In 1948 the United States Attorney convinced a grand jury to indict Caughlan for perjury for denying under oath that he had never been a CPUSA member, but a jury later acquitted him of the charge. As with some other military law cases, Caughlan's retention as Orloff's attorney was a factor. The fact that the counsel of record had ties—real or alleged—to communism fed the military establishment's belief that the CPUSA and the Soviet Union continually attempted to undermine the nation's military.

Although Caughlan argued Orloff's conscription was an unconstitutional retribution for Orloff's exercise of freedom of association, the appellate court framed the issue as statutory and non-constitutional in nature. The court conceded that the Army had assigned Orloff to a medical support role, although he clearly was not employed as a doctor. Yet, even had the Army assigned Orloff to another duty, wholly unrelated to medicine, the appeals judges opined that it would not find the assignment unconstitutional, because unlike conscientious objectors, who Congress mandated to be used in specific employment in non-combatant roles, the "doctors draft law" contained no such mandate. "There is nothing to indicate that men inducted under this new section of the draft law are to be treated, after entrance into the armed forces, differently from men inducted under other provisions," the court held.

Both the American Medical Association and its dental counterpart had protested the "doctors draft law" in 1948, because the law enabled the very fate that befell Orloff, though their protests had more to do with a national shortage of doctors and dentists than protecting the rights of inductees. In its hearings, the Senate Armed Services Committee assured the American Medical Association that no doctor would be drafted into the enlisted ranks, but Congress never statutorily prohibited what occurred in Orloff's case. In its conclusion, the appellate court placed the blame for Orloff's enlistment solely on Orloff. "It was appellant's refusal to comply with regulations that resulted in his commission being revoked," the court held. "[He] cannot be said to be without fault in causing the situation in which he now finds himself."[49]

The Court granted review in early 1953. This time David Rein and Stanley Faulkner were Orloff's counsel of record. Rein had defended Caughlan in an earlier trial for perjury, and both he and Faulkner had ties to CPUSA similar to

49 *Orloff v. Willoughby*, 195 F.2d 209 (CA 9 1952). Judge Louis Earl Goodman concurred and dissented from the majority opinion. He agreed that Orloff's refusal to divulge his prior affiliations resulted in his enlisted status. However, in other instances in which an individual found themselves, through no contribution of their own, in Orloff's predicament, the military would have to release the inductee to civilian status. "In my opinion, Congress intended that a drafted doctor should be a doctor in the military service, unless his own refusal prevents. Otherwise, he should be discharged and returned to civilian medical status," Goodman urged. Goodman also dissented from the court's refusal to grant Orloff a rehearing.

Caughlan's. In 1952, Rein had unsuccessfully represented non-citizens in the Court who were faced with deportation as a result of ties to foreign communist groups. In Congress, Rein was accused of being a CPUSA member and, in one instance, in assisting the party's subversion operations in the Army. Likewise, Faulkner represented citizens forced to testify before the House Un-American Activities Committee ("HUAC"), as well as conscientious objectors. There is no mention in the justices' correspondence that Rein and Faulkner were communists, but their presence as counsel surely convinced the Executive Branch that Orloff's refusal to answer standard background questions proved he was another CPUSA subversive who would weaken national security if given the opportunity to do so.[50]

Vinson assigned the opinion to Jackson, who, like the lower court, framed the appeal as statutory rather than constitutional in nature. In conference, Jackson initially pushed for a remand to the district court, even though he believed Orloff's arguments were specious. Nor did he spare the Army his cutting disdain for their position. In conference and in his published opinion, Jackson equally criticized the Army and Orloff as "parties [who] changed positions as nimbly as if dancing a quadrille." The government initially argued to the lower courts that the Army had the authority to place Orloff where it saw fit, but before the Supreme Court, the assistant solicitor general backtracked and conceded that the Army had to assign Orloff to a medical field. In making this concession, the assistant solicitor general urged that the lower courts had erred, but even so, the Army had correctly assigned Orloff to a medical position. Orloff initially argued that he was entitled to a medical position regardless of rank, but to the Court he argued he was entitled to a commission or to be discharged.[51]

The justices in the majority agreed that Congress obligated the military in the "doctors draft law" to assign conscripted persons to medical positions. A failure to comply with the statute would, Jackson pointed out, raise issues of bad faith and discrimination. However, he disagreed with Orloff's contention that he either had to be commissioned or discharged. Jackson noted that in 1950, Congress redefined the Army's medical corps to include not only commissioned officers but also "such other members of the Army as may be assigned thereto by the Secretary of the Army." In essence, Jackson concluded that the Army had not acted arbitrarily, but instead, its placement of Orloff, even as an enlisted man, reasonably comported with the law.

Jackson also elaborated beyond the district court and Ninth Circuit as to the causes of Orloff's enlistment. He pointed out that Orloff avoided military

---

50 The case in which Rein represented non-citizens was *Harisiades v. Shaughnessy*, 343 U.S. 946 (1952). For accusations of his ties to communism, *see*, *e.g.*, "Communist Infiltration in the Army, Hearing before the Permanent Subcommittee on Investigation of the Committee on Government Operations, 83d Cong, S. Res. 40, V I (1953); Faulkner, Obituary, New York Times, August 23, 2005.

51 *Orloff v. Willoughby*, 345 U.S. 82 (1953).

service in World War II because of his college and medical school deferments. To Jackson, it was important that Orloff refused initially to sign a loyalty certificate and to provide information on his past associations designated by the Attorney General as subversive. (This included a refusal to state whether he had been a member or supporter of the CPUSA.) As to Orloff's demand for a commission or discharge, Jackson penned into the decision that Orloff "appears to be under the misconception that a commission is not only a matter of right, but is to be had upon his own terms." In that vein, Jackson recognized that the Army historically commissioned medical personnel, and that Orloff might be the first serviceman who did not obtain a commission. But Jackson also countered that Orloff was also perhaps the first doctor to "haggle" about his loyalty. And so, to Jackson and the majority, it was Orloff who "was out of step," not the military.

Jackson conceded that while loyalty oaths and their accompanying questions asked of prospective officer applicants might be meritless, the Court could not second-guess the President and order him to commission an individual. Nor would the Court see fit for the judiciary to oversee the military's assignment of duties, because this simply was not a matter for *habeas*.[52] In his concluding paragraph, Jackson reiterated that Orloff's lengthy appeals had enabled him to avoid service in wartime Korea, because the Army had kept him in the United States. But it was the majority's second paragraph from the end of the published decision, essentially a modern iteration of *Dynes v. Hoover*, that would leave a lasting imprint in the judiciary's approach to myriad issues ranging from whether an officer had the authority to order a soldier to have a haircut, to determining free speech infringement claims:

> We know that from top to bottom of the Army the complaint is often made, and sometimes with justification, that there is discrimination, favoritism or other objectionable handling of men. But judges are not given the task of running the Army. … The military constitutes a specialized community governed by a separate discipline from that of the civilian. Orderly government requires that the judiciary be as scrupulous not to interfere with legitimate Army matters as the Army must be scrupulous not to intervene in judicial matters. While the courts have found occasion to determine whether one has been lawfully inducted and is therefore within the jurisdiction of the Army and subject to its orders, we have found no case where this Court has assumed to revise duty orders as to one lawfully in the service.

52 On his second attempt to obtain a commission, Orloff admitted: "I have attended public meetings of the Civil Rights Congress and the National Council of American-Soviet Friendship. In 1943, I co-authored a radio play for the latter organization. Over a period of 7 1/2 months I attended classes at the Jefferson School of Social Sciences (ending in the Spring of 1950). With respect to any other organizations contained on the annexed list I am compelled to claim my Federal Constitutional Privilege."

This statement on the relationship between the judiciary and Army originated in a challenge from Justice Clark to Jackson. On February 2, 1953 Clark asked Jackson whether his original position could be interpreted as granting to Orloff a legal right, but then characterizing that right as unenforceable in the federal courts. Clark's challenge was merited because it would be unique in American history for a court to find the existence of a citizen's right, but then to consider the right outside of the federal judiciary's jurisdiction. Taken to an extreme, Clark appeared to be asking whether communists or other persons deemed as subversive would be shut off from redress against the government in the federal courts. The next day, Jackson defended his opposition to remand the case to the district court, admitting that he initially favored a remand. "Further study of the matter convinces me that I was completely wrong in the idea," he began. "We cannot direct trial of the issue unless we define some issue to be tried, and how to do that without taking on the job of running the Army is more than I am able to figure out." This answer satisfied Clark.[53]

Vinson commended Jackson for his draft *Orloff* decision, which differed little from the final published version, and he supported Jackson's new opposition to remand. The Chief Justice admitted that he too initially favored remand, but Jackson's arguments persuaded him that it "might bring about a result completely at variance with my views relative to affirmance." Minton also, readily complimented Jackson, and in so doing articulated his views on the judiciary's relationship to the military. "I agree the government can keep him and assign him to duty as 'medical and allied specialist categories' and it would be unseemly for the courts to run the Army as you point out," Minton began. "I think we have done too much running of the Army already and I join you in affirming."[54]

Two separate dissents accompanied the majority opinion. Frankfurter authored one, in which Black and Douglas joined, and Black authored a second, in which Frankfurter and Douglas joined.[55]

Black chastised the majority for refusing to remand Orloff's case to a district court to determine whether he was, in fact, employed in a medical field. "I cannot understand why [the majority] feels called on to affirm this admittedly erroneous judgment by deciding disputed facts on mere unsworn statements of parties here," Black commented. This was only one of many criticisms. Black argued that the Army treated Orloff as a pariah for asserting a privilege and then committed a statutory violation when it did not commission him, but then asserted he was a doctor nonetheless. Moreover, he pointed out that the Army had to concede that Orloff was the only enlisted doctor in American history. As a final criticism, Black concluded "This whole episode appears to me to be one of

53 Clark to Jackson, February 2, 1953 [TCC-UT/A25]; Jackson, Conference Memo, February 3, 1943 [FF/R69].

54 Vinson to Jackson, February 3, 1953 [RHJ/183] Minton to Jackson, February 4, 1953 [RHJ/183].

55 Frankfurter to Black, March 7, 1953 [FF/R69].

a too-rapidly increasing number to which Americans in a calmer future are not likely to point with much pride."

Before drafting his dissent, Frankfurter authored a memorandum he circulated to all of the justices. He agreed that the commissioning of officers was solely vested in the Executive Branch and not subject to judicial control. "No doubt about that," he emphasized. Nonetheless, he urged the Court to consider that a commission might legislatively become a condition of retaining a person in the military, and Congress enacted the doctors draft law with this implicit condition.

Consistent with his applying non-constitutional grounds to decide most military law issues, Frankfurter stayed away from the First and Fifth Amendment, and did not touch on Orloff's suspected ties to communism. Rather, he focused on the fact that Orloff was too old to be drafted under the conventional conscription laws at the time of his induction as an enlisted man. It was, however, the government's conduct that frustrated Frankfurter, and he accused Jackson of indifference in not holding the government accountable to its own regulations. "This seems to me the more inadmissible in view of the change of position, which seems to me shabby, by the Government as it is driven from position to position to keep this fellow, at all hazards, in the Army, though he could not be drafted under 'the doctor's draft law,' he concluded. Frankfurter's jurisprudence in holding the Executive Branch accountable to the statutes would prevail by the end of the decade. In *Harmon v. Brucker*, the Court later instructed the Department of Defense that though service-members could be discharged from the military for pre-service ties to organizations deemed by the Attorney General as subversive, the military could not issue any type of discharge other than "honorable," unless Congress specifically authorized other discharges.[56]

In his dissent, Frankfurter conceded that the authority to commission officers vested solely with the President, and the judiciary could not control presidential determinations on fitness for government service, at least where national security was the determining factor. In Orloff's case, however, Frankfurter argued that the doctors draft law required that a failure to commission had to result in a discharge from military obligation. Frankfurter reminded the majority that Congress had promised the American Medical Association that the military would only use inducted doctors as commissioned officers performing medical duties. Importantly, he did not find that Orloff had a right to a commission regardless of his prior ideological affiliations—Frankfurter called these "quirky notions"—but rather, either the Army had to commission Orloff or discharge him from the military.

Senate Select Investigation Committee's Army Hearings

At the same time Orloff's case transited through the federal judiciary, another doctor who obtained a commission in the Army, Irving Peress, was at the center

56 Frankfurter, Memo to the Conference, February 4, 1953 [FF/R69].

of the nation's attention. Peress earned a degree in dentistry from New York University in 1940, and in late 1941, he attempted to obtain an Army commission. After the Army deemed him underweight, he established a private practice. During the Korean War, the Department of Defense inducted him into the military, but he applied for a commission under the doctor's draft law and came into the Army as a captain. Prior to his commissioning he claimed under oath that he had never been a member of a subversive organization. However, in late 1952 he indicated that he had, in fact, taken part in organizations deemed by the Attorney General as subversive. As a result of inefficacious Army bureaucracy, Peress was promoted to major despite being placed under surveillance.[57]

Senator Joseph McCarthy became aware of Peress shortly after the promotion and publicly demanded the Army convene a court-martial. This was not the first time McCarthy criticized the Department of Defense for laxity in its internal security, or for other reasons. As a junior senator, and prior to his anti-communist campaign, he took part in an investigation over the Army's prosecution of German soldiers involved in the Malmedy Massacre. In December 1944, German soldiers murdered American prisoners of war outside the Belgian town of Malmedy and were later interrogated and prosecuted in a questionable manner in a United States military trial. McCarthy claimed that the Army tortured the captured Germans into confessing, and the war crimes trials which followed failed due process. He also foolishly accused no less an icon than George C. Marshall of coddling communists within the State Department as well as in the Department of Defense.[58]

In late 1953, an empowered McCarthy demanded that Secretary of the Army Robert T. Stevens provide complete access to his subcommittee investigation all documents and individuals involved in the Army's Loyalty and Security Appeals Board. Stevens resisted McCarthy's demands and in early 1954, Peress was discharged with an honorable discharge. McCarthy then responded by subpoenaing Peress, General Ralph W. Zwicker and Secretary Stevens to testify. McCarthy's focus during the Army hearings involved far more than Peress. He attempted to expose laxity in the Army's security program at its science and engineering laboratory at Fort Monmouth, New Jersey. Julius Rosenberg had worked at the laboratory in 1943, and two scientists assigned there fled to the

57 A good background to Peress is found in Robert Griffith, *The Politics of Fear: Joseph R. McCarthy and the Senate* (Amherst: University of Massachusetts, 1987), 256–7; also, David M. Oshinsky, *A Conspiracy So Immense: The World of Joe McCarthy* (London: Oxford, 2005), 365–72; and Stephen Ambrose, *Nixon: The Education of a Politician, 1913–1962* (New York: Simon and Schuster, 1988), 330–33.

58 Griffith, *The Politics of Fear*, 20–23; Oshinsky, *A Conspiracy So Immense*, 75–6. McCarthy's attack on the treatment of German prisoners of War was likely motivated by his need to gain German-American votes in his reelection bid in 1952. McCarthy was also closely allied with Milwaukee businessman, Walter Harnischfeger, an American reputed to have had ties to pro-Nazi groups prior to World War II. However, McCarthy himself was not necessarily anti-Semitic.

Soviet Union shortly after the Rosenbergs were arrested in 1950. The presence of communists at Fort Monmouth was not new news when McCarthy began his investigation, but the fact that Peress was also stationed in New Jersey gave rise to allegations of a continuing problem at the post.[59]

Although Peress' case never came before the judiciary, the justices were aware of it, and they labored under the Cold War environment, not only regarding the right of public employment, but also in the realm of labor and criminal laws. In 1947, the Republican-led Congress passed the Taft-Hartley Act over Truman's veto. This law imposed limitations on the right to strike, particularly prohibiting secondary strikes and boycotts. Although the law was primarily a rollback against pro-labor New Deal legislation, Section 9 of the law prohibited CPUSA members from serving in union leadership positions.[60] Almost contemporaneously, Truman issued Executive Order 9835, which set up a comprehensive loyalty program for vetting federal employees. The Executive Order also enabled the Attorney General to list subversive organizations. Attorney General Thomas Clark listed 82 organizations as subversive. Later, the list was successfully challenged in the Court, and Clark recused himself from several decisions because of his role in creating the list.[61]

During World War II, Frankfurter attempted to define the dangers that internal communism presented in *Schneiderman*, but he was only able to author a dissenting opinion with no precedential value. Later, Frankfurter would be torn as to how far the government could go in prosecuting the Cold War. He was appalled at the government's treatment of Robert Oppenheimer, but the scientist was Frankfurter's personal friend.[62]

Douglas and Black believed fears over communism were overblown, and the "Red Scare" a danger to civil liberties. In 1950 when journalist Westbrook Pegler attempted to link Frankfurter to communism and Alger Hiss, and congressmen considered subpoenaing the justice, Black took notice. "There are ominous signs that Justice Frankfurter is about to be made the target of powerful forces gathering strength from the present national hysteria," Black warned his former clerk and now Yale professor John Frank. Frankfurter, for his part, distanced personal attacks on his loyalty from his jurisprudence, but even Vinson feared the Court would become a political target of anti-communists in Congress.[63]

---

59 Griffith, *The Politics of Fear*, 244–7.

60 Melvin Urofsky, *Division and Discord*, 197.

61 William Wiecek, *The Birth of the Modern Constitution*, 431.

62 *See* Feis, *From Trust to Terror*, 25. Earlier, when Feis published a book on the Japanese decision to attack the United States, Feis acknowledged that Frankfurter's assistance was instrumental in the book being published. *See* Feis, *The Road to Pearl Harbor: The Coming of the War Between the United States and Japa*n (New Jersey: Princeton, 1950), vii.

63 Black to Frank, April 17, 1951 [JPFP/1]; Vinson to Black, June 15, 1951 [HLB/306].

The justices' reaction to public fears of internal communism played out in three decisions in 1950 and 1951. In *American Communications Association, C.I.O v. Douds*, *Joint Anti-Fascist Committee v. McGrath* and *Dennis et al. v. United States*, the Court determined the extent to which the government could reach into limiting the First Amendment in the face of communism. Neither decision arose from a military act, but each possessed national security aspects important to the nation's defense.[64]

In *Douds*, the Court, with only six justices participating in the decision, determined that section nine of the Taft-Hartley Act, which required organized labor union leaders to take an anti-communist oath or have their union divested of the National Labor Relations Act's protections, did not violate the First Amendment. Douglas, Clark, and Minton took no part in the decision. Section nine was designed to prevent politically motivated strikes that could weaken national security. The CPUSA and other Communist organizations had attempted to strike at war industry factories prior to World War II, and in one case, during the war. Labor organizations protested the law on the basis that it contravened the First Amendment right to freedom of association by limiting who was entitled to run for an essentially private office. Authored by Vinson, the Court's majority looked to Congressional authority to regulate commerce, and then adopted a statement that would later prove influential in several free speech challenges to courts-martial: "Although the First Amendment provides that Congress shall make no law abridging the freedom of speech, press or assembly, it has long been established that those freedoms themselves are dependent upon the power of constitutional government to survive."[65]

Frankfurter concurred in the majority's decision with the caveat that certain provisions of the act would run afoul of the Constitution if used in the criminal courts under a charge of perjury. That is, he worried that an individual who disavowed CPUSA membership or sympathy for communism, might still share in some of the goals of the party and then be prosecuted for perjury. Jackson also concurred, but with a significant exception. He recognized the CPUSA's unique features which set it apart from other movements. Almost reiterating Frankfurter's dissent in *Schneiderman*, he stated "the Communist Party alone among American parties past or present is dominated and controlled by a foreign government. It is a satrap party which, to the threat of civil disorder, adds to the threat of betrayal into alien hands." Jackson clarified that section 9 did not outlaw the CPUSA or prohibit its members from electioneering for

64 *American Communications Association, C.I.O v. Douds*, 339 U.S. 282 (1950); *Joint Anti-Fascist Committee v. McGrath*, 341 U.S. 123 (1951); and *Dennis et al. v. United States*, 341 U.S. 494 (1951).

65 Douglas was recovering from an injury resulting in a fall from a horse. Minton had been nominated but not yet confirmed by the Senate. And, Clark recused himself from the decision since, as Attorney General, he had advised President Truman on the matter. *See* William Cohen, *Constitutional Law: Civil Liberties and Civil Rights*, 49

public office, but rather was a legitimate congressional limitation of union activities. However, he believed the requirement that union officers take an oath disavowing a belief in the overthrow of the government by violence or other unlawful means unconstitutional. Jackson urged that without an overt act, the requirement to disavow a belief violated the First Amendment. "While the Governments, State and Federal, have expansive powers to curtail action, and some small powers to curtail speech or writing, I think neither has any power, on any pretext, directly or indirectly to attempt foreclosure of any line of thought," he concluded. Unsurprisingly, Black dissented, arguing that the act was passed to exclude certain beliefs from the economic arena. He compared the act to the prosecutions of Protestants in sixteenth- and seventeenth-century France, as well as the then contemporaneous English prosecutions of Catholics, Quakers, and Baptists.

In *Joint Anti-Fascist Committee v. McGrath*, the Court rejected the Attorney General's placement of three specific organizations on the subversive list. The organization named in the decision had supported anti-Franco forces during the Spanish Revolution. A second organization named the National Council of American-Soviet Friendship sought to lessen friction between the two nations by distributing Soviet educational materials in the United States, much of which were materials about the United States. The third organization was a fraternal benefit society incorporated under New York insurance law. Each of the organizations was able to prove that they did not fall into the definition of "subversive" and that the Attorney General had ignored the full facts before issuing his ruling. Rather than find Executive Order 9835 or the Loyalty Board unconstitutional, the Court determined the Attorney General's act of placing the organizations on the subversive list arbitrary and outside of the authority conferred by the executive order, and required the executive branch to provide an avenue for groups to challenge their placement on the list.

If the public believed that *Joint Anti-Fascist Committee* signaled that the Court was curtailing the loyalty program, this was mistaken, because in *Dennis v. United States*, the Court broadened the "clear and present danger" test to include to "whether the gravity of the 'evil,' discounted by its improbability, justifies such invasion of free speech as is necessary to avoid the danger." Learned Hand authored this language in the Court of Appeals for the Second Circuit decision, but the Court, at Frankfurter's urging, adopted it wholesale.

Dennis arose in 1948, from the prosecution of 12 CPUSA leaders, including Eugene Dennis, of organizing and assembling "persons who teach and advocate the overthrow of the United States Government by force or violence," and "knowingly and willfully" advocating the same. Dennis was instrumental in trying to foster demobilization protests and mutinies in the Army in 1946, and Paul Crouch had warned of Dennis' other attempts to infiltrate the military. The trial lasted nine months, and by contemporary standards failed due process. The Federal Bureau of Investigations eavesdropped on the defendants' lawyers, who in turn contributed to eroding the efficacy of the trial by badgering the judge and defending communist ideology. But the defense counsel were not alone in causing the collapse of an orderly trial. Judge Harold Medina's conduct during the trial included publicly berating defense counsel, and he abandoned his duty of impartiality. At the end of the trial, Medina found the defense attorneys in contempt, ordering them to prison. This finding, in turn, led to the disbarment of several attorneys. In 1953, Truman elevated Medina to the Court of Appeals for the Second Circuit, where he would decide several military law appeals, including conscientious objector cases.[66]

Ironically, in World War II, Medina, then serving as a defense counsel, had represented Anthony Cramer who was convicted of treason after assisting the German saboteurs who were ultimately prosecuted and sentenced to death. This point is instructive for both assessing Medina's conduct in the trial as well as the Court's approach to *Dennis*. The attorneys unsuccessfully challenged Medina's contempt and disbarment rulings to the Court of Appeals for the Second Circuit as well as the Court. In *Sacher v. United States* and *In re Isserman*, a majority of the Court determined that Medina's disbarment of attorneys was not merely a matter of judicial governance of attorney conduct, but also a national security matter. Ultimately, after Vinson's death, the attorneys were readmitted to the Court to practice law.[67]

The contemptuous conduct of the attorneys in the Dennis trial became a national security concern in the sense that the federal and state bars used it as anecdotal proof against the CPUSA. Licensed attorneys affiliated with the CPUSA or other organizations began to take on Department of Defense clients, including service-members, in a wide variety of cases, including security clearances and allegations of misconduct. Since an accused has a right to counsel and access to evidence, the government faced the problem of providing evidence to an attorney it distrusted. The greater concern was the appearance that these attorneys would undermine military discipline in their approach to filing suits against the military in federal court. The historic record shows that both concerns were not unreasonable.

There is another aspect to analyzing *Orloff* that is partly related to *Douds*. Although the military's requirements of secrecy and trustworthiness set it apart from public employment, the Court's national security and military law decisions can, and should, be analyzed in light of the judiciary's historical approach to communism, particularly in the labor and employment law arena. Beginning in the late-nineteenth century, state legislatures codified offenses designed to criminalize advocacy for communism, anarchism, and in some respects,

66 Melvin Urofsky and Paul Finkleman, *March of Liberty*, 75859; Noah Feldman, *Scorpions: The Battles and Triumphs of FDR's Great Supreme Court Justices*, 340–41; also, Melvin Urofsky, *Division and Discord*, 175; "Communist Trial Ends With 11 Guilty," Life Magazine, October 24, 1949, 31–5.

67 *Sacher v. United States*, 343 U.S. 1 (1952); and *In re Isserman*, 345 U.S. 280 (1952).

socialism. Conservatives feared that communists would open a second front through organized labor, even though the majority of union members fought for wages and safety, and not to import communism. In World War II the federal government created offenses designed as anti-communist measures, but that were broad enough to apply to many organizations. In the aftermath of World War I, the Court had addressed subversion in the context of both free speech rights and the impact of subversive actions on the military. But at no time prior to 1945 was the CPUSA itself outlawed.

During World War I, Congress legislated the Espionage Act and the Sedition Act. In 1919, the Court, in *Schenk v. United States*, upheld the conviction of the Socialist Party of America's secretary for sending leaflets to 15,000 citizens, encouraging them to exercise their rights against being conscripted. Justice Oliver Wendell Holmes, a Civil War veteran, authored a unanimous decision in which the Court adopted the "clear and present danger" test to determine whether speech could become criminal. In order for speech to be criminal, the individual would have to have intended for a nefarious result to occur and the result would have to be likely as well. This is where the analogy to "shouting fire in a movie theatre" first found judicial approval. In 1927, the Court upheld state penal restrictions on free speech in *Whitney v. California*. Ironically, the petitioner in *Whitney* was former Secretary of War Edwin Stanton's niece, and Stanton had labored to maximize military jurisdiction during the Civil War to prosecute dissent. In this decision, the Court upheld a state anti-syndicalism statute that enabled the criminalization of speech having the tendency to "incite crime, disturb the public peace, or endanger the foundations of organized government and threaten its overthrow." Thus, the Court permitted a state to move beyond the intent of the speaker, and simply charge the speech itself. Both *Schenck* and *Whitney* would apply to the military's governance during the Cold War, particularly during the Vietnam conflict. In addressing challenges to the military's restrictions on political speech, both the military courts of appeal and the federal judiciary would rely on these two decisions to uphold the lawfulness of the restrictions.[68]

In 1922, the Court addressed the use of military forces against communism in a decision originating in a court-martial held in Vladivostok, Siberia. In July 1918, prior to the collapse of Germany, President Wilson authorized the deployment of military forces to guard weapons stockpiles in Vladivostok and Archangel in Russia. The Czarist Russian government had already collapsed and been replaced by a Soviet government under Vladimir Lenin, but pro-Czarist and pro-Kerensky—or "White Russian"—forces attempted to reassert control. The British and French governments advocated using allied forces in Russia to assist the White Russians, but Wilson decided against using United

68 *Schenck v. United States*, 249 U.S. 47(1919); *Whitney v. California*, 247 U.S. 357 (1927). On Whitney's influence, *see, e.g.*, *Culver v. Secretary of the Air Force*, 559 F.2d 622 (CA DC, 1977).

States forces in any offensive operations against the Soviets. In part Wilson's decision was akin to "walking a tightrope" because Congress had not authorized the use of these forces in their declaration of war against Germany, and a few congressmen alleged Wilson had exceeded his authority. Most troubling, after Germany's collapse, small scale mutinies amongst the allied soldiers occurred in both Archangel and Vladivostok.[69]

In 1920, the Army court-martialed Private Roy Marshall in Vladivostok for robbery and sentenced him to five years imprisonment. While awaiting transfer from Alcatraz to McNeil Island military prison, Marshall appealed to the federal courts under a *habeas* writ. Marshall claimed that his confession was obtained under duress, the specification he was charged under was faulty, and the stationing of forces in Russia without an express declaration of war or congressional authorization rendered the court-martial without jurisdiction. In other words, he argued that having sent soldiers to a conflict in Russia without congressional sanction, no court-martial possessed jurisdiction.

The Court, in *Collins v. McDonald*, relying on a half century of precedent, found that criminal charges did not have to be drafted with precision, and it determined that a claim of an unlawfully coerced confession was not a proper *habeas* matter. Most importantly, the Court held that the question of court martial jurisdiction over soldiers serving in what came to be commonly referred to in the Vietnam era– though not in the language of 1920—as "an illegal war," was "trivial." Since the enactment of the UCMJ, neither the federal judiciary nor academia has cited to *Collins* with any regularity, though Professor Lichtman notes it as a "win" in his article on the Court's deference to the military for the obvious reason that the decision represents another decision limiting *habeas* challenge for military members. However, the Court's deference was not merely to the military but more importantly to the Executive Branch in not entering into the political thicket of foreign affairs and military policy. Even Brandeis did not believe that the Court should address the question of whether Wilson exceeded his authority.[70]

In 1938, Congressman Martin Dies was named chairman of the newly formed Special Committee to Investigate Un-American Activities. Shortly after its formation, Dies' committee claimed that the Executive Branch was "infested with communists, radicals, and other dangerous persons." The following year, Congress passed an amendment to the Hatch Act, barring Communists from federal employment. In 1940, Congress passed the Alien Registration Act, more commonly known as the Smith Act. During World War II, the Justice Department prosecuted only a few persons under these laws, but following the Japanese

69 John Whiteclay Chambers and Fred Anderson, *The Oxford Companion to American Military History* (New York: Oxford, 1999), 627–9.

70 *Collins v. McDonald*, 258 U.S. 416 (1922); *see* Steven B. Lichtman, "The Justices and the Generals: A Critical Examination of the U.S. Supreme Court's Tradition of Deference to the Military, 1918–2004," 65 *Maryland Law Review* 907 (2006), 950.

surrender, the political climate changed and national security, coupled with anti-Communism, became the leading political and social issue. In 1945, the House of Representatives made the Dies Committee permanent and from that point until its termination in 1975, it was known as the House Un-American Activities Committee (HUAC).[71]

In 1946, in *United States v. Lovett*, the Court determined that a federal law that prohibited paying salary to 39 specifically named government employees the Dies Committee had deemed "radical bureaucrats" and "affiliates of Communist Front organizations," was unconstitutional. The employees did not challenge the law on First Amendment grounds, but rather on the basis that the law constituted a bill of attainder (a legislative act declaring an act criminal and punishing a person or persons without judicial trial) Black authored the majority opinion to which two justices concurred, but none dissented. The majority determined that since Dies' committee had singled out the 39 employees and referred to its findings as indictments, the law constituted a bill of attainder, in violation of Article I, Section 9 of the United States Constitution. Black also noted that both the Senate and Roosevelt acquiesced to the law because Dies and the House of Representatives had threatened to cut off war funding if the Senate failed to approve the law.[72]

The loyalty programs and anti-communism statutes were problematic for several reasons, particularly because their overuse trammeled on individual rights. Moreover, opportunists such as Senators Joseph McCarthy and Richard Nixon were enabled to accrue power through accusations and inquests based on spurious information. The anti-communist ideologues not only targeted CPUSA members but also the larger group of so-called "Fellow Travelers." This latter group consisted of intellectual elites and others who believed in communism, but not through the suppression of freedoms as had happened in the Soviet Union and China. There was, in fact, little consensus as to what members in this category believed. Some espoused compatibility between Christianity and Communism, an idea antithetical to the teachings of Karl Marx. A "fellow traveler" could accept certain aspects of communism, but refuse to participate in the means to achieve the tenets. The statutes and executive order did not effectively distinguish between

71 Geoffrey R. Stone, *Perilous Times: Free Speech in Wartime from the Sedition Act of 1798 to the War on Terrorism*, (New York: W.W. Norton, 2004), 354; Melvin Urofsky and Paul Finkleman, *A March of Liberty: A Constitutional History of the United States, Vol. II*, (2002), 734; Melvin Urofsky, *Division and Discord*, 159–61; and Ted Morgan, *Reds: McCarthyism in Twentieth Century America* (New York: Random House, 2003), 187–9.

72 *United States v. Lovett*, 328 U.S. 303 (1946). Frankfurter concurred but argued that the law was not a bill of attainder, but rather an invalid withholding of pay. For his part, President Roosevelt denounced Dies' actions as an unconstitutional bill of attainder. *See* Melvin Urofsky and Paul Finkleman, *March of Liberty*, 731.

CPUSA members and "fellow travelers" or other persons who merely believed that some of the CPUSA's tenets were laudable.[73]

In 1951, in *Garner et al. v. Board of Public Works of Los Angeles et al.*, the Court upheld the termination of 17 city employees who refused to comply with California's loyalty oath requirements for public servants. The decision, authored by Clark, determined that the oath requirement did not constitute a bill of attainder, because the oath requirement was a general regulation which merely provided prospective and general standards of qualification and eligibility for employment, rather than a punishment, as had been the case in *Lovett*. The normally conservative Burton dissented because the law used to terminate the employment of the 17 petitioners enabled a similar fate for persons who had been members of the CPUSA when that party was transparently legal. Likewise, both Black and Douglas dissented.[74]

One year later, in *Adler v. Board of Education, City of New York*, the Court upheld New York's loyalty oath requirement for its teachers. No teacher had been fired, but a class of teachers sued, claiming that the requirement was unconstitutional. Writing for the majority, Minton conceded that individuals have the right to "assemble, speak, think, and believe as they will" but then he followed with "they have no right to work for the State in the school system on their own terms." Frankfurter dissented from the Court taking jurisdiction at all, claiming the teachers lacked standing to sue, because none of them had lost their employment. Douglas dissented, with Black joining, arguing that a public employee does not forfeit their civil rights, including those rights protected under the First and Fourteenth Amendments. Particularly troubling to both Black and Douglas was the element of guilt by association in which an organization is deemed subversive by the Justice Department without a chance to defend itself, and then an individual citizen is at risk for losing municipal employment by having been a member of the organization. The time honored standard proof of guilt by showing evidence of overt acts was abandoned under the majority's construct. Although he joined with Douglas, Black also separately dissented, adding that the state statute would mould people into a singular intellect.[75]

In 1953, the Court decided *Wieman v. Updegraff*, reversing the Oklahoma Supreme Court by finding unconstitutional a state law that prohibited public employment to anyone not swearing that they were not a member of a subversive organization on the Attorney General's list. Writing for the majority, Clark reasoned that membership in a subversive organization could be innocent, in the sense that a person could be a member of an organization but not know of the leadership's designs. Additionally, a person could join an organization at a time when the organization was lawful, only to terminate

73 David Caute, *The Fellow Travelers: Intellectual Friends of Communism* (New Haven: Yale University Press, 1981), 5.

74 *Garner et al. v. Board of Public Works of Los Angeles et al.*, 341 U.S. 716 (1951).

75 *Adler v. Board of Education, New York*, 342 U.S. 485 (1952).

the relationship when the organization ceased being so. Classifying innocent association with knowing association violated the Due Process Clause of the Fourteenth Amendment, Clark concluded. The majority sidestepped the First Amendment questions Black found critical to this line of cases. "We need not pause to consider whether an abstract right to public employment exists. It is sufficient to say that constitutional protection does extend to the public servant whose exclusion pursuant to a statute is patently arbitrary or discriminatory," the majority concluded. Black authored a concurrence, joined by Douglas in which he reminded the majority that the First Amendment was what was at stake in these decisions. Historian Melvin Urofsky points out that Clark intended to make clear that mere membership in a subversive organization was not enough to prove that a person was subversive. Black would not have, in all likelihood, shared Urofsky's belief in the majority's intention in *Wieman*. To Irving Dillard, a *Saint Louis Post-Dispatch* journalist, Black explained his concurrence as a continuation of Jefferson's intents underlying the First Amendment.[76]

None of the Court's employment and labor decisions were specifically designed with the military establishment in mind, but each would have an effect on the judiciary's approach to military law, particularly in the realm of security clearances as well as administrative discharge processes. And certainly the decisions established a common denominator and a basis to assess *Orloff* and related later internal security appeals.

Burns v. Wilson

A 1953 decision that highlighted the Court's disagreement on the parameters of civilian federal jurisdiction over courts-martial arose in the context of three Air Force courts-martial tried in 1949 on the island of Guam. Captioned as *Burns v. Wilson*, the Court issued a plurality opinion that Frankfurter attacked as historically flawed in his two dissents, and from which Black and Douglas also dissented. Vinson authored the plurality opinion, apparently with the intent of preserving the traditional narrow definition of jurisdiction. But as a result of a sloppily articulated decision, Vinson's intent has not survived, and *Burns* has come to stand for a proposition other than what he, and presumably the plurality, believed it would. The fault for the flawed opinion in this case, however, was not entirely Vinson's. Counsel for both the government and two of the airmen

76 *Wieman v. Updegraff*, 344 U.S. 183 (1952). Black wrote: "It may be significant that many of those who are supposed to be the strongest for First Amendment Liberties go no further than did these Federalists of the alien and sedition laws period. An opposite view then was that the United States was without power to pass laws that abridged discussion of public questions at all. That view prevailed when Jefferson was elected. No such group *see*ms to be advocating such a view today." Black to Irving Dillard, January 7, 1953 [HLB/317]; *see also*, Melvin Urofsky, *Division and Discord*, 163.

the court-martial sentenced to death also poorly argued the *habeas* aspects of the case.

On December 11, 1948, Air Force officials listed Ruth Farnsworth, a white civilian female defense employee, as missing. She was discovered unconscious three days later, badly beaten and raped, the island's local naval police (the Navy was responsible for manning the civil police force) and Air Force investigators believed that an airman named Calvin Dennis was responsible for the assault. Although none of the federal courts would inquire into the issue, the military investigators focused their case solely on African-American suspects, interrogating over two dozen airmen and administering lie detector tests. Farnsworth did not identify her attacker as an African American, and indeed, because she died shortly after being discovered, there was no identified assailant. On the night of Farnsworth's disappearance, Dennis drove an Air Force shuttle bus around the base, though he took a break to watch a movie.

On January 7, 1949, naval investigators discovered a smock under the seat of the shuttle vehicle Dennis drove. The investigators claimed the smock had pubic hair on it matching Dennis.' Four days later, civilian naval police took Dennis into custody, and the island's chief investigator, a Commander James P. Hackett who had been hired from the Chicago Police Department, obtained four disjointed confessions from Dennis. The confessions were taken under conditions reminiscent of those which had previously concerned the Court, including the use of sodium pentothal, at that time thought to be a truth serum. In his confessions, Dennis implicated two other airmen: Airman Herman Dennis and Staff Sergeant Robert Burns. Herman Dennis also implicated himself in a confession under similar conditions, but Burns did not confess. Burns, a veteran of World War II, had been awarded the Bronze Star and Purple Heart. Missing from the Air Force review determining the reasonableness of the death penalty was a complete recognition of his prior honorable service. Considering the rarity of African-American soldiers being awarded the Bronze Star, he was in a strong position to argue for leniency.[77]

Lieutenant Colonel Edward F. Daly, the staff judge advocate to the local airbase commander, became convinced that the naval police arrested the wrong men and had produced false confessions from Herman and Calvin Dennis.

---

77 *See* NAACP petition for writ of habeas to the United States District Court and Department of Justice Response. [NAACP, Part IX, B/57]. The Department of Justice did not contest the facts the NAACP presented as listed here. However, it introduced the Judge Advocate General's investigation into the court-martial, which determined the court-martial proceedings were proper. That investigation did not inquire into the interrogations and confessions. There is one book on this case, a self-published study. *See* Robert Leland Athey, *Please Don't Cry for Me: The Ruth Farnsworth Murder Story* (Philadelphia: Xlibris, 2000). This work is largely sympathetic to the government, concludes that the three airmen were guilty of the rape and murder, and does not provide much analysis to the decision. The Secretary of the Air Force merely wrote: "He served honorably in the Army from 16 November 1943 to 25 February 1946 prior to enlisting for three years in the United States Air Force on 30 January 1948." *See United States v. Burns*, ACM 1893 (1951).

According to Daly, in a later affidavit, Hackett, in the presence of one other witness, admitted that he promised Herman Dennis leniency and when asked about how he and a fellow detective were able to obtain confessions, he answered, "you know how we do that—roughed them up a bit." Daly would also claim in his affidavit that Air Force investigators and Hackett hid evidence of a Filipino soldier's dog tags discovered near Farnsworth, and a bloodied naval officer's uniform from the defense. Oddly, Daly would testify in the courts-martial and did not mention the dog tags.[78]

Hackett conducted "third degree interrogations" of Herman and Calvin Dennis, of the type Frankfurter and Douglas had earlier disparaged. It is also clear that today these confessions would be suppressed. By his own admission, Hackett employed an interrogation methodology developed by Fred E. Inbau, which, at the time, advised police to make full use of racial stereotypes and mental coercion by exaggerating the quantum of evidence against a suspect. A decade after *Burns*, the Court had become so concerned with this very interrogation technique that it determined in *Miranda v. Arizona* that the police had to inform a suspect of their right against self-incrimination.[79]

The other witness, a civilian assistant to Daly named Mary Louise Hill, later provided a sworn affidavit supporting Daly's version of the discussion. Daly took the unusual step of becoming Burns' and Dennis' defense counsel. But, Daly's command charged him with conduct unbecoming an officer for public intoxication, and "moral turpitude," and removed him from the case, threatening him with court-martial. Daly was forced into retirement shortly after. After Daly's removal, a commissioned chaplain attempted to raise money for a civilian defense counsel to take the case, but the Air Force commander of the installation thwarted him from doing so. The chaplain, E.E. Grimmett, contacted the NAACP, but then assured the organization that the airmen were competently represented. Military regulations against soliciting funds from enlisted personnel were stringently enforced. As a result, Burns' military counsel had one day to prepare for a death penalty offense; not surprisingly, the defense case lasted roughly an hour and a half. The Air Force court-martialed the three men separately and all three were convicted and sentenced to death, though Calvin Dennis' sentence was commuted to a term of years in exchange for testifying against Herman Dennis and Burns.[80]

The trials began on 28 May, 1949, before the UCMJ had been implemented, and therefore there was no court of appeal established with jurisdiction to review the three courts-martial. The appeals process consisted of an advisory board

78 Lt. Col Daly affidavit, January 21, 1952 [NAACP, Pt IX, B/57].

79 *See* Fred E. Inbau, *Lie Detection and Criminal Interrogation* (Baltimore: Williams and Wilkins, 1942), 1–142. Hackett's use of this technique is found in the record of trial.

80 Mary L. Hill affidavit, January 21, 1952, Calvin Dennis affidavit, September 6, 1951 [NAACP, Pt IX, B/57] Robert L. Carter, *A Matter of Law: A Memoir in the Struggle in the Cause of Civil Rights* (New York: New Press, 2005), 78.

of three officers convened by the Judge Advocate General. All three accused airmen were defended by military counsel. One of the counsel, Lieutenant Colonel Adrian Tolen, later advanced to become a brigadier general and the third ranking officer in the Air Force Judge Advocate General's Corps when he retired in 1969. Tolen believed in Burns' innocence and would later assist the NAACP in Burns' appeals.

After the military appeals process brought no relief to the three airmen, the NAACP's leadership decided to represent Herman Dennis and Robert Burns in challenging their convictions and sentences in federal court, with the claim that the court-martial was unfair to the point of depriving it of jurisdiction. The NAACP director assigned attorneys Franklin D. Reeves, Thurgood Marshall, and Robert L. Carter to this case, at the same time they worked on what became captioned as *Brown v. Board of Education*. Unlike the defense team in *Orloff*, these men could hardly be considered communists or subversive, though attempts were certainly made to present them in this light. During World War II, Carter had experienced racism in the Army. A Harvard graduate, he was commissioned into the 332d Fighter Wing, later known as the Tuskegee Airmen, but was prohibited from entering officers clubs and attending other "whites only" functions. While at Lockridge Air Base, Ohio, he successfully represented an African-American soldier accused of rape, but was removed from further law duties after the case. Along with several other officers, Carter was administratively discharged from the Army without a service characterization, so that he could be drafted back into the enlisted ranks. William Hastie, who later served as a judge on the Court of Appeals for the Third Circuit, successfully challenged the decision and Carter was awarded an honorable discharge. In 1961, President John F. Kennedy appointed Thurgood Marshall to the Court of Appeals for the Second Circuit, and in 1965, President Johnson appointed him to the Court.[81]

Surprisingly, the NAACP's legal strategy did not rest on allegations of racism or disproportionate treatment. Instead, the attorneys only argued that Air Force and Navy officials suppressed evidence favorable to the accused men. As evidence, the NAACP pointed out that a beer can, a bloodied naval officer's uniform, and a set of "Filipino dog tags," were found near the crime site, but information as to this potentially exculpatory evidence was never provided to the accused airmen or their defense counsel. Additionally, the NAACP argued that the denial of Lieutenant Colonel Daly as defense counsel, the obstruction of the chaplain's efforts to retain civilian counsel, the harsh interrogation measures, and the court-martial occurring in an atmosphere of public anger and

81 *See* generally, Carter, *A Matter of Law*, 45–78; and Robert L. Carter, biographical materials, [Robert Carter Papers/1]. For Marshall's biography and experience with the military, *see* Mark Tushnet, *Making Civil Rights Law: Thurgood Marshall and the Supreme Court* (New York: Oxford University Press, 1997) 20–48. Tushnet however, does not cover Marshall's role in *Burns v. Wilson*.

hysteria created a quantum of unfairness sufficient to divest the court-martial of jurisdiction.[82]

To the NAACP legal team, all of this meant that the court-martial failed the Fifth and Sixth Amendments. In a sense, the NAACP presented an argument similar to that in *Powell v. Alabama*, where a much more conservative set of justices overturned state convictions because of the mob hysteria invading the courtroom. But the differences between the facts in *Powell* and the sentiment on Guam were vastly different. In *Powell*, Alabama's solicitor general did not deny the conditions surrounding the trial, but before the federal judiciary the military did deny a prejudicial atmosphere existed. The veracity of the Air Force's claim of an orderly court-martial was questionable. Where the NAACP failed is that they did not cite the Court to *Shapiro*, nor did they argue that an all white male court-martial panel of officers was unconstitutional. In essence, the NAACP deferred to the military, even though their attorneys had previously argued that all white juries in civilian criminal trials were unconstitutional.[83]

Later, Frederick Wiener and Frankfurter would find the NAACP's strategy inexplicable. The affidavits attached to the NAACP's brief were more than enough to make the case that the three airmen had been treated more harshly because of their race. Daly, a judge advocate with field grade rank, believed this to be the case. Calvin Dennis alleged in an affidavit that Hackett, "threatened to pin the crime on me and said, every niggar he got hung he would get a promotion." Daly's assistant swore that investigators had rifled through Daly's case files and exculpatory evidence disappeared. Added to this was the experience of African-American servicemen stationed in Guam. From 1944 onward the NAACP had investigated clear instances of mistreatment of African-American sailors and airmen. Moreover, as the Guam police were Navy employees, they were not an independent law enforcement agency.

On April 10, 1952, Judge James W. Morris in District Court for the District of Columbia heard arguments on the *habeas* issue of whether to order the Air Force to release Herman Dennis and Robert Burns. Morris, a Roosevelt appointee, served in the Army in World War I, attended the University of North Carolina for his undergraduate and law studies, and had been employed in the Justice Department from 1933 until his appointment to the bench in 1939. He was a North Carolina contemporary of Kenneth Royall as well.

In refusing to order the Air Force to release Dennis and Burns, Morris determined that the court-martial was lawfully constituted, and therefore the civil courts were not empowered to "inquire into the regularity of the proceedings." He also noted that the Air Force Judge Advocate General had conducted an "extensive inquiry" into the court-martial record and the conduct of all parties at the trial, and President Truman approved the proceedings and sentences for the two airmen. Morris' decision was hardly surprising in light of *Hiatt*, a case he cited

82 Petition for Writ of Habeas Corpus Before the District Court, Part IX, B/57.

83 *Ibid.*

in concluding the federal court did not possess jurisdiction to overturn the court-martial through a collateral determination.[84]

Dennis and Burns next appealed to the Court of Appeals for the District of Columbia, which heard argument on June 18, 1952. Chief Judge Duncan Groener assigned Prettyman, James Proctor, and David L. Bazelon to the decision. All three judges accepted the concept of expanded jurisdiction in that a lawfully constituted court-martial could be so flawed and bereft of due process, that the federal judiciary could determine the court-martial's jurisdiction did not exist. The Court's decision in *Whelchel v. MacDonald* had already intimated acceptance of the expanded approach, and now in plain language the appellate court adopted this intimation into its decision. Had the NAACP pursued an appeal that included an accusation of racism, they might have had a receptive audience in Prettyman. While serving as a judge advocate in World War I, Prettyman was upset that his command had more kindly treated suspected Bolsheviks found guilty of the serious offense of urging a mutiny than toward African Americans convicted of minor offenses.[85]

However, in what became captioned as *Burns v. Lovett*, Prettyman and Proctor determined that the errors the NAACP alleged were insufficient to divest the court-martial of jurisdiction. Both judges agreed that the allegations made against the Air Force, if true, were substantial. They recognized that a denial of counsel, coerced confessions, a trial conducted in the shadow of mob hysteria, and prosecutorial misconduct could void a criminal conviction on appellate review. However, Air Force authorities through the Judge Advocate General's investigation and the military's appellate procedure found the court-martial was conducted fairly and within the strictures of the Articles of War. In conference, Prettyman noted that Daly did not bring up the issue of Filipino dog-tags or the bloodied naval officers uniform until a year after the courts-martial were over, and he did not testify at the courts-martial at all. To Prettyman, Daly's accusations against the government withholding evidence were "baseless." Other federal judges awaited the appellate court's decision. Notably among the appellate judges, Chief Judge John Biggs on the Third Circuit Court of Appeals sought information from Prettyman on their deliberations before *Burns v. Lovett* was decided.[86]

The majority's opinion was not a blind affirmance of the government's position. In the published opinion, Prettyman criticized the government's counsel, Lieutenant Colonel Walter Kiechel, Jr., for arguing that the Bill of Rights did not apply to the military. Kiechel did not make this argument from whole cloth, because the Supreme Court had, in the past, indicated this was

84 *Dennis v. Lovett*, 104 F.Supp. 350 (D.D.C. 1951).

85 Prettyman, diary entry for September 6, 1918 [EBPP/1].

86 Prettyman, conference memorandum and first draft, *Burns v. Lovett* [PEBP/Box 62]; On the interest of the outcome of the case, *see* Chief Judge John Biggs to Prettyman, August 16, 1952 [PEBP/Box 62].

the case in the trials of enemy combatants and foreign residents. The Court had never, however, articulated this position for service members in a court-martial review case. In response, Prettyman cited to several cases which all but mandated due process of law to military trials, and went so far as to state that due process standards were applicable in both civil and military trials. Significantly, he included *Shapiro v. United States*, the Court of Claims' decision which arose from the prosecution of a defense counsel. In doing so, he enunciated a new standard that, taken in its entirety, created a middle ground between the complete denial of federal court jurisdiction over courts-martial, and the expanded jurisdiction Dennis and Burns claimed.[87]

Ultimately, Prettyman, with Proctor's agreement, articulated that each allegation of impropriety was answerable in favor of the military. For instance, Prettyman accepted at face value that Lieutenant Colonel Daly, the counsel that Herman Dennis initially selected was unavailable because Daly was under investigation for criminal activity. The conditions under which the confessions were taken were, not surprisingly, disputed by the civil authorities on Guam, though there was ample evidence to sustain the NAACP's claims that the confessions were coerced. But the military authorities did not find the coercion unlawful and neither did Prettyman and Proctor. Finally, the evidentiary objections Burns and Dennis raised were already addressed through the military review process to Prettyman's satisfaction, as were other allegations of what amounted to prosecutorial misconduct. Prettyman also noted that even if the alleged errors were accurate, none of them rose to a level requiring reversal. In affirming the District Court, and with it the court-martial convictions and sentence, Prettyman concluded the "accused were vigorously defended at all points. Actions of the military authorities appear to have conformed meticulously to the rules of procedure, and the reviews were exhaustive."[88]

Bazelon dissented, though he agreed that an expanded definition of *habeas* jurisdiction meant only that federal courts could determine on a case by case basis, whether individual courts-martial were riddled with constitutional errors and therefore devoid of due process and jurisdictionally defective. In such instances, the federal courts could then collaterally overturn the court-martial conviction or sentence, which, to Bazelon, was required for the Burns and Dennis courts-martial. "I cannot agree, however, that we should narrow our scrutiny of courts-martial by singling out individual allegations to determine

87 *Burns v. Lovett*, 202 F.2d 335, 342 (CA DC 1952). The standard was:

(1) An accused before a court-martial is entitled to a fair trial within due process of law concepts. (2) The responsibility for insuring such fairness and for determining debatable points is upon the military authorities, and their determination are not reviewable by the courts, except (3) that, in the exceptional case when a denial of a constitutional right is so flagrant as to affect the 'jurisdiction' (i.e., the basic power) of the tribunal to render judgment, the courts will review upon petition for *habeas corpus*.

88 *Ibid.* at 347.

just how 'flagrant' the allegedly unconstitutional actions are," he urged. "Such an approach could whittle down the 'freedom writ' and virtually withdraw the military from its reach. The fairness of a trial must be determined by appraisal of the whole rather than by picking and choosing among its component parts."

Unlike Prettyman and Proctor, Bazelon was convinced that the sworn affidavits of the chaplain and Lieutenant Colonel Daly's civilian assistant proved that a concerted effort to deny the airmen a fair trial existed. To Bazelon, the prosecution's misconduct included destroying evidence, bullying witnesses, and preventing one of the accused airmen from raising funds to hire a civilian defense counsel. He acknowledged that these allegations were not matters which the court-martial panel heard or knew of, and which were investigated "by high military authorities." Nonetheless, he believed that the District Court had the obligation to investigate independently each allegation because if true, the jurisdictional efficacy of the courts-martial did not exist.

Bazelon's dissent was a driving factor in the Court granting *certiorari*, at least where Frankfurter, Black, and Douglas were concerned. The three justices lobbied Vinson to vote for *certiorari*, and with the chief justice's agreement, the requisite number was met. Vinson, though, had a different opinion on how the case should be decided and assigned himself to author the Court's opinion. He was unable to obtain a majority, and what resulted was a stumbling plurality opinion.

Vinson conceded that the three airmen had exhausted all available remedies. He also noted that the allegations against the government would, if true, have the cumulative effect of denying due process. However, because the Board of Military Review and the Air Force Judge Advocate General had investigated the allegations as well as the record of trial to a degree which exceeded the requirements of the 1948 Articles of War, Vinson maintained the rule that federal courts were not statutorily empowered to intervene when the court-martial was otherwise lawfully constituted. "These records make it plain that military courts have heard petitioners out on every significant allegation which they now urge," Vinson argued. Under this stricture, only if the military had refused to investigate the allegations, would the District Court have jurisdiction to overturn the court-martial. The specific language the plurality used, however, would not result in uniformity of practice in the lower courts: "when a military decision has dealt fully and fairly with an allegation raised in [a habeas corpus petition], it is not open to a federal civil court to grant the writ simply to reevaluate the evidence."[89]

The plurality sidestepped the issue of whether Calvin and Herman Dennis' confessions were involuntarily extracted by Hackett. The courts-martial occurred in a time when the federal judiciary had just begun to expand *habeas* over state criminal trials, and confessions and other police conduct were the issue in the majority of such appeals in the decade following *Chambers v. Florida.*

89 *Burns v. Wilson*, 346 U.S. 173 (1953). On June 5, 1953 Justice Clark penned to Chief Justice Vinson that he not only agreed with Vinson's draft, but also that habeas in military appeals also had to be restrictively applied, Clark to Vinson [TC-UT/A25].

Herman Dennis claimed that Hackett had failed to read him his rights against self-incrimination as required under the Articles of War. In reviewing Herman Dennis' court-martial, the Air Force Judge Advocate General concluded, "it should be pointed out that at the time these statements were made, such ritualistic reading was not then required by applicable military law." A decade after the Court decided *Burns*, it would find that the police failure to advise a suspect of the right against self-incrimination would deny the prosecution the authority to introduce the confession at trial. Ironically, the mode of interrogation employed by Hackett, a series of treatises on confessions by criminologist Fred E. Inbau, would also become part of the reason the Court would later create the rule requiring rights advisement.[90]

While the plurality permitted the execution of the airmen, it included an unnecessary statement on the fairness of military law that Vinson intended to serve as a cautionary message to lower courts reviewing courts-martial. He approvingly commented that, "Congress has taken great care both to define the rights of those subject to military law, and provide a complete system of review within the military system to secure those rights." To Vinson and the plurality, the new UCMJ was not "a patchwork effort to plug loopholes," but rather a "top to bottom" reform. (However, the airmen in *Burns* were prosecuted under the old Articles of War and not the UCMJ, a point either lost on Vinson, or at least rendering his commentary irrelevant.) In essence, when the military "fully and fairly" followed the UCMJ, the civil courts were not to reevaluate the evidence of the court-martial. The relatively undefined phrase "fully and fairly" would eventually cause a lack of uniformity in the federal judiciary's interpretation of their jurisdictional authority over courts-martial.

Believing that the plurality did not explicitly adhere to the old rule limiting judicial intervention in courts-martial, Minton concurred. "To extend jurisdiction over military courts required Congressional sanction," he argued. "We have but one function, namely, to see that the military court has jurisdiction, not whether it has committed error in the exercise of that jurisdiction." After all, two years earlier, in *Hiatt v. Brown*, the Court articulated the traditional narrow jurisdiction definition as the correct statement of law, and now, Minton argued, it had abandoned both *Hiatt* and *In re Grimley*, decided 63 years earlier. Jackson too concurred, but did not state his reasons for doing so. Vinson's opinion never explicitly answered Minton's charge, but in conference he insisted that he had not abandoned the traditional standard.

---

90 Fred E. Inbau, *Lie Detection and Criminal Interrogation* (Baltimore: Williams and Wilkins, 1942). Professor Inbau, and later his associate John E. Reid, after studying police practices advised police to rely on deception in some instances, and in the early editions of their works also advised police to interrogate African Americans in a manner different than Caucasians. The majority of the Court would be appalled at this practice, leading in part to *Miranda v. Arizona*.

Frankfurter, in his first dissent, did not hint that he believed racism affected the court-martial. However, he protested the rapidity with which Vinson and the Court's plurality pressed to have their opinion published before he and all of the justices were able to review the courts-martial and investigative records. Frankfurter disagreed with Vinson, and commensurately with Minton, on the limited jurisdiction of federal courts to review military cases, although he stated that greater deference had to be paid to military appellate processes, "than to those reached by the highest court of a State." Yet he did not advocate reversing the lower court or even ordering a remand, even though the lives of three airmen were at stake. Instead he urged the Court to order reargument for a later date, only after each justice was able to examine the entire record, beginning with the court-martial through the post-conviction investigation. Frankfurter also pressed for reargument in *Brown v. Board of Education*, and would later do so successfully in a case involving military jurisdiction over civilians. But where he succeeded in convincing his fellow justices on the merits of reargument in school segregation, he failed in *Burns*.

Douglas and Black dissented separately from Frankfurter. Both justices believed that enough evidence pointed to unlawful coercion in taking Herman Dennis' confession. In 1943, the Court had reversed federal convictions based on unlawful coercion in securing confessions. More significantly, in 1949 the same three lawyers for Burns and Dennis were successful in arguing for the Court to overturn the Indiana Supreme Court on the issue of whether a death sentence could be sustained despite an unlawfully coerced confession. Frankfurter had authored that opinion, noting that a deprivation of food and sleep, as well as time in solitary confinement could render a confession inadmissible on the basis of due process. "A confession by which life becomes forfeit must be the expression of free choice. A statement to be voluntary of course need not be volunteered. But if it is the product of sustained pressure by the police it does not issue from a free choice," Frankfurter had penned.[91]

Douglas and Black also believed that because Calvin Dennis' interrogation and commutation of a sentence to life imprisonment was promised in exchange for inculpating Herman Dennis and Robert Burns, it also deprived the two airmen of due process. In one of the stranger elements in the trial, the prosecution had claimed, based on both Dennises' confessions, that Calvin Dennis' and Herman Dennis were half-brothers. By the time the Court granted *certiorari*, the claim of a blood-relationship between the two Dennis brothers was disputed, and ultimately proved to be wrong. To Black and Douglas, this fact alone evidenced that the confessions were involuntary, and if known at the time of the trial it would have weakened the prosecution's case. Remembering Douglas' investigation into police practices of "third degree interrogations," during the 1929 Wickersham Commission, his dissent is not surprising. Neither he nor Black were convinced

91 *McNabb v. United States*, 318 U.S. 332 (1943); and *Watts v. Indiana*, 338 U.S. 419 (1949).

that the Air Force Judge Advocate General's review was "a considered appraisal." Indeed, to Douglas and Black, what neither the plurality, Prettyman and Proctor, nor the District Court considered was that the Judge Advocate General's review on the voluntariness of the confession only determined that since the court-martial believed the confessions voluntary and reliable, the trier of fact had determined the issue and little further inquiry on this matter was required. In light of the standard the Court earlier set in *Chambers v. Florida*, there was a reasonable question as to whether the confession should have been admissible in the first place.[92]

Black and Douglas did not advocate a revolutionary new expansive jurisdiction. Both justices conceded that federal courts were limited in reviewing courts-martial to matters of jurisdiction, but they did not subscribe that this limitation was defined "in the historic sense." Nor did the two justices believe that the Fifth and Sixth Amendments were inapplicable to military trials. Instead, Douglas pointed out that only the right to a grand jury was enumerated not to apply to military trials. To all the dissenters, including Frankfurter, the rest of the Bill of Rights wholly applied. After all, the prohibition against double jeopardy protected servicemen, even though the Court had determined six years earlier in *Bayer* that the military could prosecute servicemen charged with its unique common law offenses regardless of what the serviceman might have been charged with in federal court.

Missing from their dissent, as well as Frankfurter's, were their beliefs that the three accused airmen had been denied a fair trial because of their race. Douglas' hand-written draft cited to *Powell v. Alabama*, but the published dissent did not. There is no explanation for Douglas omitting a section on the conditions of the court-martial being tried in a carnival atmosphere, other than the counsel arguing the case did not make this point and Douglas confined himself to the specific claims of Burns' and Dennis' counsel.[93]

Three weeks after the Court published *Burns v. Wilson*, Frederick Wiener lobbied Frankfurter to redouble his efforts to push his fellow justices to reconsider the case and, as would happen in another military jurisdiction opinion which arose four years later during the Warren Court, grant a rehearing. "I agree unreservedly with your view that reargument was called for," Wiener wrote his former professor. "After all, the NAACP counsel for the petitioner had no special competence in the field of military law and Cummings, S.G. for the respondent—of whom I speak as a former colleague—has no special competence in any field of law." Wiener also pointed out several mistakes evident in Vinson's opinion. In the plurality opinion, the courts-martial were listed as Army courts, but in fact, the men were tried in Air Force courts-martial. Vinson's lauding of the UCMJ was also irrelevant since the men were prosecuted under the 1948 Articles of War. To Wiener, the Air Force failed to follow the Articles of War to the detriment of the three accused

92 For the "considered appraisal" of the confession *see United States v. Dennis*, ACM 1892, at 885–7.

93 Douglas, pen draft, undated [WOD/232].

airmen. He did not elaborate as to why he believed this to be the case, but given Wiener's often pro-military views, his frequent agreement with Frankfurter and other conservative justices on deferring to the military and Executive Branch in national security matters, and his meticulous scholarship, there likely was some action of the prosecution, military command, or Judge Advocate General that he saw as repugnant to due process.[94]

On October 12, 1953, Frankfurter published a second dissent after the Court voted to deny Burns and Dennis a rehearing. Neither Black nor Douglas joined with him, however. In his second dissent, Frankfurter took Vinson to task for a having published a poorly reasoned opinion. He acknowledged that for over a century, the federal judiciary was constrained on *habeas* writs to only determine whether courts-martial possessed jurisdiction in the narrow, traditional mode. But, in 1937, the Court in *Johnson v. Zerbst* already expanded *habeas* jurisdiction to include review over errors which "amounted to a deprivation of constitutional right." Authored by Black, *Zerbst* arose not from a court-martial, but from a federal criminal trial in which two defendants were prosecuted without defense counsel (the defendants were United States Marines who committed a criminal act while on leave). Frankfurter reminded the plurality that the Court of Claims had repeatedly incorporated *Zerbst* in determining jurisdiction over courts-martial, and that court had consistently accepted an expanded jurisdictional definition. Notably, he criticized both the government and the NAACP for not focusing their arguments to *Shapiro* or, more importantly, *Zerbst.*[95]

Frankfurter's criticism against Vinson was not only for his failure to consider *Zerbst* or *Shapiro*, it was also for the plurality's commentary found on page 140 that, "this Court has played no role in (the development of military law); we have exerted no supervisory power over the court which enforce it ...." Turning to Winthrop's seminal *Military Law and Precedents*, Frankfurter proved that courts-martial, though not a part of Article III of the Constitution, were bound to adhere to the judiciary's decisions. Also, Frankfurter reminded the Court that Article 38 of the 1920 Articles of War mandated that federal evidentiary rules applied to courts-martial, a mandate carried over to the UCMJ in 1950. To Frankfurter, this was an important point for two reasons. He urged that federal *habeas* jurisdiction had to extend beyond the traditional narrow definition because Congress intended through the UCMJ for the expanded definition to apply. More importantly, while he believed the system of military justice was structurally fair, an expanded jurisdiction would help ensure that courts-martial were conducted in accordance with due process, including through all appellate avenues, and that the failure to do so would be correctable in the federal courts.

Wiener, for his part, did not keep his criticism of the plurality a private matter between himself and Frankfurter. In 1957 he published a two-part article in the *Harvard Law Review* analyzing the intent of the Constitution's

94 Wiener to Frankfurter, July 5, 1953 [FF/R67].

95 *Burns v. Wilson*, 346 U.S. 844 (1953) [petition for rehearing].

framers regarding the Bill of Rights and military trials. This was, and remains, an important matter for the rights of servicemen, and the federal courts have relied on Wiener's work in this area since. In the second part of his article, Wiener argued that Vinson failed to consider the extent that *Zerbst* required civil courts to exercise *habeas* jurisdiction over courts-martial. "The question was not much discussed by counsel; and when it was raised by Mr. Justice Frankfurter in his opinion on the petition for rehearing, the Court was not interested," Wiener lamented.[96]

On January 28, 1954, Air Force authorities executed Herman Dennis and Robert Burns at the Northwest Military Airfield, Guam. The NAACP had petitioned President Eisenhower to commute the sentences, for the first time alleging that racism had so tainted the trial as to render the court-martial unfair. Eisenhower relied on Vinson's plurality and ordered the execution. The military legal community did not warmly embrace *Burns*. Judge Advocates General and the Department of Defense' legal counsel believed that the decision created murkiness for the federal courts. General Albert Kuhfeld, the Air Force's Deputy Judge Advocate General, articulated the military's tepid reaction to *Burns* in a speech to the American Bar Association in 1955, with both Frankfurter and the former solicitor general and federal judge Charles Fahy in attendance. Kuhfeld argued that Minton's concurrence was "the correct course of law," and that while *Burns* did not wholly expand *Zerbst*, it departed from *Hiatt v. Brown* and its predecessors. Fahy, who had fought to uphold the constitutionality of interning American citizens of Japanese descent in World War II, disagreed with Kuhfeld. He argued that racism had infected the court-martial, and that Kuhfeld's failure to acknowledge this fact would undermine judicial confidence in courts-martial. But, Kuhfeld steadfastly denied all allegations of disparate treatment.[97]

Truman appointed Fahy to the Court of Appeals for the District of Columbia in 1950. His military experience included service in World War I, where he flew naval aircraft with the British Air Force as a liaison, and was awarded the Navy Cross. His early government service included a stint as the National Labor Relations Board's first general counsel, and then the Justice Department, where he ultimately became the nation's Solicitor General. After his tenure as Solicitor General, he advised General Eisenhower on establishing control over

---

96 Frederick Wiener, "Courts Martial and the Bill of Rights: The Original Practice," 72 *Harvard Law Review* (1958), 266–304, 298. Wiener concluded his article that while the framers did not mandate that the Bill of Rights applied to courts-martial he believed Congress needed to move in this direction. "Consequently, I am still hopeful that, eventually, the military accused on collateral review will be accorded the same scope of inquiry as the civilian defendant, and that such review will be placed squarely on the proposition that military personnel, like civilians, are within constitutional protections."

97 Fahy, notes, undated 1955 [Fahy/8]; Gloster B. Current, Notice to All Branches, Oct 16, 1953 [NAACP, Pt II, Box 123].

German legal institutions, and then served on Truman's Committee on Equality of Treatment and Opportunities in the Armed Forces. While on this committee he clashed with Kenneth Royall, prompting the latter's retirement. Roosevelt, Truman and Kennedy had considered Fahy for the Court, but other candidates superseded him. After his death, it became apparent that he had been privy to intelligence reports significantly diminishing the likelihood of an internal threat within the Japanese-American population, yet argued to the Court in *Hirabayashi* and *Korematsu* that the threat existed. If Fahy had been willing to tolerate anti-Asian racism during World War II, he would prove unwilling to tolerate it afterward, particularly while he served on the appellate court.[98]

Writing his memoirs in 2006, Judge Robert Carter conceded that the school desegregation appeal in *Brown* diverted much of his time away from Dennis' and Burns' appeals. The appeals process, he claimed, haunted him more than any other issue he worked on. On the other hand, Carter lauded the Air Force Judge Advocate General's Corps' assistance during the appeals process which he characterized as "not exceeded by any court or agency personnel before whom [he] practiced in the entire twenty-seven years of his legal profession." Nonetheless, the majority's decision and eventual execution of Burns and Dennis evidenced to the African-American community that the law had replaced lynching but achieved the same result. Douglas would ultimately agree with Carter, in more vociferous words in his opinions than in Carter's memoirs.[99]

V: *Burns* and the Lower Courts

By the time *Burns* was argued, Minton and Burton had made clear that they believed the doctrine of "separate but equal" was unconstitutional, which raises the questions of whether and why the Court ignored the racial aspects of Burns' and the two Dennis' courts-martial. If the justices deliberately ignored the racial aspects of the courts-martial, the plurality's decision may be explainable in light of their views of the military justice system being a system akin to the state criminal justice systems. After all, in *Adamson v. California*, the Court found that a state prosecutor's comment equating the defendant's silence at trial was evidence of guilt did not violate due process because, much to Black's disgust, the Court concluded the rights guaranteed by the Fifth Amendment were not binding on the states through the Fourteenth Amendment. And, in *Louisiana ex rel. Francis v. Resweber*, even Black conceded that an unsuccessful electrocution did not preclude another attempt under the Eighth Amendment.

98 Peter Irons, *New Deal Lawyers* (Princeton, NJ: Princeton University Press, 1982), 234; Keith D. McFarland and David Roll, *Louis Johnson and the Arming of America* (Bloomington: Indiana University Press, 2005), 164

99 Robert L. Carter, *A Matter of Law*, 108–11.

There are a number of other examples of the Court finding that state criminal trials that did not meet federal standards of due process were nonetheless sound. But, there were exceptions. For instance, in *In re Oliver*, Frankfurter and Jackson dissented from a decision that determined that due process prohibited a judge serving as a one-person grand jury. If upheld, the Court would have allowed the states to have a judge become a participatory vote in a criminal court's ultimate decision. (Both justices conceded that such a system could not exist in the federal criminal courts.) On the other hand, the Court ignored the conditions under which the courts-martial had occurred, including sharing similar features to a mob pressured criminal trial in Alabama. This digression indicates Vinson and the conservative majority were willing to grant a great deal more deference to the military than to the states.[100]

The *Burns* plurality opinion has created confusion as to the judiciary's role in two respects. Vinson's commentary on the Court's absence in the development of military law continues to resonate in cases into the twenty-first century. Perhaps the clearest example of this confusion occurred four years after the decision was handed down, in the same appellate court that initially decided Burns had received a fair trial. In 1957, Judges Edgerton and Fahy on the Court of Appeals for the District of Columbia argued that *Burns* enabled the civil courts to determine claims that a court-martial lacked jurisdiction if the manner in which it was conducted denied the accused soldier "basic constitutional rights." Prettyman believed otherwise, and encouraged the court to return to the older, narrower position. The appellant, Private John E. Day had been court-martialed and sentenced to death in 1950 after being found guilty of murdering both a Korean man and his baby. One of Day's contentions against the court-martial was that the law officer failed to provide the court-martial an instruction on the lesser included offenses of unpremeditated murder and manslaughter. Neither of these offenses carried the death penalty. The Court of Military Appeals affirmed the sentence in 1953, though one of the three judges dissented, asserting the majority mistakenly placed a primary responsibility on defense counsel to ensure a fair trial.[101]

While in confinement in Japan, Day unsuccessfully appealed to the District Court for the District of Columbia. That court agreed with the government's argument that because Day remained in Japan, it possessed no *habeas* jurisdiction. After this failure, the Army transferred Day to Fort Leavenworth and he appealed to the District Court of Kansas on the similar grounds that he had been denied a fair trial. After failing on this *habeas* request, he appealed next to the Tenth Circuit Court of Appeals. That court, on the basis of *Burns*, determined that its jurisdiction only extended to determining whether Day was denied any "basic constitutional

100 *In re Oliver*, 333 U.S. 257 (1948); Rutledge, Conference Notes, n.d. 1948 [WR/159].

101 *United States v. Day*, 9 CMR 46 (CMA 1953). Day also was found guilty of sexually assaulting the deceased baby's mother.

rights." Having found jurisdiction, however, the Tenth Circuit ruled that no basic rights had been denied.[102]

Day next appealed to the Court of Appeals for the District of Columbia from the District of Columbia District Court's denial of jurisdiction. Edgerton and Fahy were initially determined to remand the case to the lower court, because that court's denial was based on a geographic distinction that had since been discarded. Prettyman was not willing to do so. The three judges all agreed that the scope of their jurisdiction was severely narrow, and Edgerton drafted a conference memorandum to this effect. "I am to write a short opinion remanding the case but Judge Prettyman thinks we should affirm," Edgerton began. "We all agree that the function of the District Court in such a case is very narrow under the *Burns* case and that the court had jurisdiction, in the territorial sense and otherwise." This, however, still went too far for Prettyman and he responded by defining jurisdiction "as the power to enter judgment" and then adding that since the Tenth Circuit had already determined Day's court-martial suffered from no denial of due process, the District Court for the District of Columbia could not now rehear the arguments. Prettyman worried that if such a precedent were set, a court-martial could be challenged contemporaneously in several circuits, a worry later proved valid in two important Vietnam-era cases.[103]

In conference, Fahy admitted that the failure to provide to a court-martial accurate instructions on lesser included offenses was problematic. "My inclination, though it is not yet a definite conclusion, is that in this capital case, the omission of an adequate instruction on the lesser offense of unpremeditated murder was a denial of due process," he claimed. Edgerton conveyed back to Fahy that he had little sympathy for Day, calling his offense "unsavory" and claiming that his impulse to prevent an execution was "greatly mitigated" by Day's brutality.[104]

Prettyman, however, dissented from these views. "The power of a civil court to issue a writ of habeas corpus in a military case is severely limited," he argued, before citing *Yamashita*, *Eisentrager*, and *Burns*. Prettyman reminded Edgerton and Fahy, "we went through all this in *Burns v. Lovett*, and the Court admonishing us against examining into the actual phases of these proceedings, affirmed our judgment."[105]

---

102 *Day v. Wilson*, 235 F. 2d 379 (CA 10 1956).

103 Edgerton to Prettyman and Fahy, April 2, 1957 [EBPP/73].

104 Fahy to Edgerton, February 28, 1958 [Fahy/32]; Edgerton to Fahy, March 7, 1958 [Fahy/32].

105 *Day v. Wilson*, 247 F.2d 60 (CA DC 1957). Ultimately the lower court upheld the court-martial and sentence. *See Day v. Wilson*, 155 F.Supp. 469 (D.D.C. 1957). Indeed, the lower court held, the record was:

> abundantly clear that the petitioner has been afforded every constitutional right. He was tried by a General Court-Martial under procedures established by Congress acting pursuant to the Constitution which puts the regulation of the armed forces in the Congress. His conviction was affirmed by the United States Court of Military Appeals

None of these discussions were evident when the circuit court issued its short *per curiam* decision. "We find nothing in the record that would have justified the District Court in issuing the writ," the court held. In a concurrence, Fahy acknowledged that the issue of lesser included offenses instructions still remained, but surprisingly added, "the inadequacy which existed was not so grave as to have deprived appellant of due process of law or of any other constitutional right, or to have deprived the court-martial of jurisdiction." As a result, he concluded that federal courts did not possess jurisdiction to disturb the court-martial "on a collateral attack." Although Day appealed to the Court, a grant of *certiorari* was not forthcoming.

Several circuit courts, and ultimately the Court itself, did not interpret Vinson's plurality as he intended, instead relying on the case for an opposite conclusion. As late as 2002, the Court of Appeals for the Third Circuit, in criticizing three decades of its prior decisions, observed that "the federal courts' interpretation of *Burns* has been anything but clear." The Third Circuit borrowed this language from a 1990 Court of Appeals for the Tenth Circuit decision which had also criticized itself for a lack of uniformity regarding what "full and fair consideration" meant. No court, however, including the Tenth Circuit, which briefly analyzed the intent of some of the justices in deciding *Burns*, found that the disparity in interpretation originated with Vinson's opinion. Retired Justice Reed, sitting in 1960 by special designation on the Court of Claims, while reviewing both *Burns* and the claims court's decision in *Shapiro*, articulated Vinson's intent more clearly than most of his judicial brethren ever would. "If the courts-martial have given fair consideration to petitioner's constitutional rights, it is unnecessary for this court to consider again whether or not the final judgment of the court-martial might be collaterally attacked by plaintiff in this court for loss of jurisdiction due to violation of defendant's constitutional rights," Reed authored. The retired justice did not stop there and instead articulated that Minton's "more traditional" concurrence was the correct view of federal court jurisdiction.[106]

which is the established tribunal to review proceedings of this character. Thereafter, his conviction and sentence were confirmed and ordered executed by the President of the United States."

106 *Brosius v. Warden, United States Penitentiary*, 278 U.S. 239 (CA 3 2002); *Dodson v. Zelez*, 917 U.S. 1250 (CA 10 1990); *Begalke v. United States*, 288 F.2d 606 (Ct Cl 1960).

Chapter 7
Conclusion

Judicial deference to the military establishment, at its zenith during the last year of the Vinson Court, declined within a half decade. The Uniform Code of Military Justice, which had been enacted in 1950, turned military justice from the swift, commander-centric system of the Articles of War to a more "civilian-like system" replete with due process protections. This "civilian-like" nature of the UCMJ likely encouraged the judiciary to craft rulings that molded the military system into a more recognizable form of criminal justice. More importantly, appeals under the new UCMJ arose during a time of increasing judicial mistrust of the executive branch's foreign policy escapades. Dwight Eisenhower's election in November 1952 was followed 10 months later by his appointment of Earl Warren as Chief Justice, and in later years by the respective appointments of John Marshall Harlan II, William Brennan, and Potter Stewart to the Court. Though the Court would decide far more military law appeals than it had during the pre-UCMJ period, three important cases—*United States ex rel. Toth v. Quarles*, *Reid v. Covert*, and *Trop v. Dulles*—illustrate the Supreme Court's shift away from deference to the military.[1]

The election of Eisenhower, a career military officer, to the White House might have suggested continued judicial deference to the military, especially in light of the Soviet Union's and Communist China's expanded influence in Asia, Europe, and South America. And yet, Eisenhower's first two appointments to the Supreme Court would each play a significant part in undoing the judiciary's deference to the military, beginning with the appointment of Chief Justice Earl Warren, which Eisenhower would later call his "worst mistake."

Tempting as it may be, it would be inaccurate to ascribe the shift toward increased individual rights and away from deference to the military solely to the appointment of the ultimately liberal Warren as the Chief Justice. Though Warren would eventually become known as a champion for civil rights, Eisenhower had little reason to suspect that Warren would become an activist justice or lead the Court to side with individual rights over claims of military necessity. In fact, while serving as California's attorney general during World

1 There were, to be sure, aspects of courts-martial that had no civilian counterpart. For instance, courts-martial lacked a trial judge until 1968 when a military judge became statutorily required. And, along with a small number of states, an accused's guilt could be established by a two-thirds majority of votes, rather than unanimity. On the lack of a requirement of unanimity in criminal trials, *see*, *Apodaca v. Oregon*, 406 U.S. 404 (1972) and *Johnson v. Louisiana*, 406 U.S. 356 (1972).

War II, he had lobbied *for* the internment of citizens of Japanese descent, was silent on civil rights, and never openly opposed discriminatory laws against Asians or Latinos in California. Shortly after arriving on the bench, Warren even balked at staying the executions of Burns and Dennis, two courts-martial he conceded were pervaded by racism, perhaps motivated by not wanting to be seen as weakening the military while awaiting Senate confirmation after his recess appointment.[2] Regarding deference to the military, the 1954 Warren would evolve into something quite different, ultimately joining numerous majority opinions limiting military jurisdiction and eventually warning of "attempts of our civilian Government to extend military authority into other areas," noting that wartime claims of military necessity that might be given judicial sanction are not necessarily constitutional.[3]

While hard to pinpoint precisely when distrust of the executive branch's foreign policy became acute among the justices, Truman's failed attempt to assert national security as the basis for a domestic industry seizure in *Youngstown* is certainly a marker. As discussed in the previous chapter, the administration's aggressive position that the executive could do nearly anything in the name of national security no doubt caused at least some of the justices to be wary of executive power. Specific justices were starting to voice their concerns.

Black was not convinced that large numbers of communists had infiltrated the military and was disgusted by Senator McCarthy's attack on the Army's leadership. In late 1952, McCarthy accused senior leaders in the Army of blindly permitting communists to gain access to critical national security secrets. Nor was Black blindly enamored of all military leadership. He had supported Truman's firing of Douglas MacArthur and believed MacArthur's supporters' claims of communist dangers overblown.[4]

Douglas warned of even greater implications. Recently returned from a world-wide trip, Douglas had learned first-hand that Egyptian President Gamal Nasser had prosecuted citizens in military courts contrary to Egypt's constitution. In Algeria the French military was empowered to enforce the local laws as well, which he believed undermined confidence in France's democracy. In 1954, Douglas concluded that the French were facing disaster in Morocco because of their heavy-handed use of the military, including the use of military

2 *Burns v. Wilson*, 346 U.S. 137 (1953). Victor R. Hansen to Warren, January 7, 1954 [UPA, Vol. III, Warren papers]; Warren to Hansen, January 8, 1954 [UPA, Vol. III, Warren papers].

3 Lucas Powe, Jr., *The Warren Court and American Politics* (Cambridge, MA: Belknap, Harvard University Press, 2002), 78–113, provides an excellent documentation of Warren's transition in security cases. Earl Warren, "The Bill of Rights and the Military," 37 *New York University Law Rev* (1962) 181.

4 Roger K. Newman, *Hugo Black*: A Biography 385; Arthur Herman, Joseph McCarthy: *Reexamining the Life and Legacy of America's Most Hated Senator* (New York: The Free Press 2001), 238–359.

courts to prosecute civilians. Douglas warned Black and Warren that although the lower court's decision and government's arguments only considered that former servicemen were amenable to military jurisdiction for offenses that occurred while on service, he feared that permitting this expanded jurisdiction would open the door for further jurisdictional expansion.[5]

The judiciary's distrust of the military came in part from the military's stinging criticism. In early 1954, MacArthur complained to J. Edgar Hoover "his best bet for the brains of subversive leadership in the country is Felix Frankfurter." MacArthur, ever the politically minded general, had already retired from the Army and his presidential ambitions were dashed when the Republican Party selected the far more humble Eisenhower instead. Nonetheless, MacArthur retained influence not only in the military establishment but also in Congress. At times, he claimed that communism came from foreign—and Jewish—sources. Frankfurter was, in light of this irrational prejudice, MacArthur's obvious target. If MacArthur intended to influence Frankfurter, his criticism had the opposite effect. As judicial deference to the military gave way to greater judicial supervision of the military, Frankfurter would be instrumental in this process, even in instances where he did not adopt Black's and Douglas' positions.[6]

Eisenhower's closest cabinet officer, Secretary of State John Foster Dulles, was a staunch anti-communist who believed that the United States had to be both anti-communist and anti-imperialist at the same time, even though for the first time in history United States forces were stationed across the globe. On the Court, Warren, Black, Frankfurter, and Douglas, disapproved of Dulles, in part, because, greater numbers of American service members were stationed in foreign lands with no plan as to how long this phenomenon would last. In 1954, Frankfurter wrote to political scientist Herbert Feis, "If we'll survive Dulles, I'm almost prepared to believe in a merciful god." As a result, while the judiciary generally deferred to the military establishment and Congress on Selective Service appeals, it did not do so in jurisdictional matters over civilians.[7]

5 William O. Douglas, *Strange Lands and Friendly People* (New York: Harper, 1951), 188; William O. Douglas, *The French are Facing Disaster in Morocco Again* (New York: Cowles, 1954); For information on Nasser's military courts, see Joel Gordon, *Nasser's Blessed Movement: Egypt's Free Officers and the July Revolution* (New York: Oxford University Press, 1992), 196.

6 On MacArthur, see Arthur Sabin, *In Calmer Times: The Supreme Court and Red Monday* (Philadelphia: University of Pennsylvania, 1999), 3.

7 John L. Gaddis, *We Now Know*, 168; also Douglas Kinnard, *The Secretary of Defense* (Lexington: University of Kentucky Press, 1980), 47–53; Frankfurter to Herbert Feis, 1953 [HFP-LOC/17].

United States ex rel. Toth v. Quarles

The first UCMJ appeal to come before the Supreme Court arose in the context of the new code's jurisdiction. Section 3(a) of the code permitted the prosecution of former servicemen who committed offenses while on active duty. This was not an entirely novel jurisdictional extension since retired officers were subject to courts-martial jurisdiction under the Articles of War. However, Section 3(a) extended jurisdiction to former enlisted men and officers who were not receiving retired pay, but who had committed offenses while on duty. This was the first time Congress expressly permitted this jurisdictional expansion, although during the Civil War, for other reasons, an extensive military jurisdiction over civilians had been asserted.[8]

In *United States ex rel. Toth v. Quarles*, the Air Force had discharged the defendant Toth before discovering his role in a murder of a Korean civilian while he was on active duty. Toth's sister filed a writ of *habeas corpus* in the District Court for the District of Columbia, which upheld Section 3(a). At the appellate court, all three judges agreed that there was no constitutional infirmity, and concluded that Section 3(a) was constitutional because it merely made Toth liable for an offense he was charged with committing, in a trial forum which possessed jurisdiction over the offense and the person. The appellate court accepted the government's argument that a case arises when an offense occurs, and not, as Toth argued, when a person is formally charged. In arriving at this decision, the appellate court relied on a negative inference from *Hirschberg* in which the Court had not found a constitutional jurisdictional error in a court-martial of a sailor who committed an offense during a prior enlistment, but rather had decided the issue on statutory grounds.[9]

The Court unanimously voted for *certiorari*, but after argument on February 8 and 9, 1955, the justices struggled to find common ground for a majority decision. Warren insisted on a majority rather than a plurality opinion and he did not want a repeat of *Burns*, which he believed was a slovenly plurality. This is not to suggest that Warren opposed the government, because originally he did not, but no opinion initially could garner more than three justices' votes. On June 6, 1955, the case was restored to the docket, and reargued on October 13, 1955. In conference it became clear that that there was no consensus amongst the justices. Douglas and Frankfurter were adamantly against permitting Section 3(a)'s expanded jurisdiction on constitutional grounds. Ultimately, disbelief of the "communist threat" and fears of ever-expanding military jurisdiction caused a slim majority to side with Toth over the Department of Defense, and Warren assigned Black to write the majority decision.[10]

8 Joshua Kastenberg, *Law in War, Law as War*, 5.

9 *United States ex rel. Toth v. Quarles*, 350 U.S. 11 (1955).

10 Simon Sobeloff, Notes, draft arguments, undated, 1955 [SSP/26]; Confirmation

Importantly, Black's opinion denigrated courts-martial as inferior courts with a lesser quantum of due process, observing that civilian juries were superior to courts-martial. Not surprisingly, as he had in *Kahanamoku* in 1946, Black based his reasoning on *Milligan*. Black recognized that the primary duty of the military was to prepare to fight wars, not hold trials and felt it necessary to concede that "most military personnel have a high degree of honesty and sense of justice." On the other hand, he cautioned that military trials had never matched civil trials in fairness, particularly in the selection of court-martial personnel in comparison to civil juries. At the time of Toth's court-martial, military tribunals did not have a truly independent judge and the Court of Military Appeals was in its infancy, so it was not yet known what contribution that court would make toward fairness. Black concluded the decision with a statement which would increasingly characterize the Warren court's winnowing of military jurisdiction. He resurrected the argument from *Milligan* that extended military jurisdiction was a menace to a free society. "There are dangers lurking in military trials which were sought to be avoided by the Bill of Rights and Article III of our Constitution," he concluded. "Free countries of the world have tried to restrict military tribunals to the narrowest jurisdiction deemed absolutely essential to maintaining discipline among troops in active service." This language was absent from *Kahanamoku*, but *Toth* can certainly be considered as an extension of the earlier opinion.

Toth demonstrated a continual growing divide between conservatives who believed that the military's fullest jurisdiction was essential to a disciplined force and therefore the preservation of democracy, and the liberals who were convinced that the very construct of laws the conservatives advocated would undermine the nation's democratic institutions and signal the world that the United States was no more confident in its democracy than were foreign governments on the precipice of communism.

Reid v. Covert ("*Reid II*")

For the first time in American history, in the aftermath of World War II and the onset of the Cold War, large numbers of American service-members were stationed overseas and thousands of family members accompanied them. Additionally, significant numbers of civilians employed by the military resided overseas. At overseas installations, Congress had legislated military jurisdiction over civilians working or residing on military installations through a UCMJ provision enumerated as Article 2(11).

In the last days of the Court's 1955 term, the Court decided *Reid v. Covert* and *Kinsella v. Krueger*, two decisions regarding military jurisdiction over civilians residing overseas. The cases were billed within Court's memorandum as "the

hearing notes, [Simon Sobeloff Papers [SSP/2]; Frankfurter to Black, October 26, 1955 [JMH-SGM/5].

murdering wives cases," as both petitioners were civilian women convicted of murdering their active duty husbands. Relying on *In Re Ross* and *Madsen v. Kinsella*, the case in which the Court had held a civilian defendant could be tried in a military-government tribunal established in the American-occupied portion of West Germany, Clark upheld Congress' jurisdictional grant to the military over civilians residing overseas. The initial *Reid* and *Krueger* cases would be overturned a year later after re-argument. Warren, Douglas, and Black, who dissented in the initial *Reid* case due to worries about the inherent dangers of expansive military jurisdiction, convinced the newly-appointed Brennan to join their opinion and convinced Harlan to switch to ruling in defendant Covert's favor in a concurrence.[11]

Warren assigned Black to write the plurality opinion, in which Black included a statement that even though the offenses committed by the two "murdering wives" were significant, the fact that over 95 percent of the crimes for which civilians were prosecuted in military trials overseas were petty in nature was irrelevant to the greater issue. As to the government's argument that jurisdiction was important to the military's effectiveness in deterring Soviet aggression, Black responded with the admonition that "illegitimate and unconstitutional practices get their first footing in that way, namely, by silent approaches and slight deviations from legal modes of procedure." Thus, to Black, the fact that the two women, or that thousands of minor offenders, might go free as a result of the government's lack of establishing a civilian court process was less evil than diminishing the Bill of Rights.

Frankfurter later noted that *Reid II* had four votes to deny the military all jurisdiction over civilians in peacetime, but two justices—Frankfurter himself and Harlan—concurred only to the extent that military jurisdiction could not extend to civilians charged with capital cases. Nonetheless *Reid II* was an influential decision for reasons other than limiting military jurisdiction. It incorporated an extensive use of British and American legal history, particularly the distrust of standing armies corresponding to the extension of jurisdiction over civilians. The majority also effectively cabined *Ross* as part of an imperialist legacy, the legal

11 *Reid v. Covert*, 351 U.S. 487 (1956); *Kinsella v. Krueger*, 351 U.S. 470 (1956). After the publication of *Reid* and *Krueger*, Warren circulated a memorandum to the Court expressing his reservations with Clark's decision. The memorandum began: "The opinions of the majority in these cases concern me because they gravely threaten one of the fundamental relationships upon which our government is built—the supremacy of the civil over the military branch, and because they violate a personal right guaranteed to every American citizen in unequivocal language by the Constitution—the right to a trial by a jury after indicted by a grand jury." Warren to the Court, September 22, 1956 [EW/575]. *Reid I* was argued on May 3, 1956, and decided on June 11, 1956. Reargument was heard on November 5, 1956, and the *Reid II* decision published on June 11, 1957. 351 U.S. 470 (1956). *Kruger* was argued and decided on the same dates as *Reid I*. The case was consolidated with *Reid I*, and reargued on the same dates. *In re Ross*, 140 U.S. 453 (1891); *Madsen v. Kinsella*, 343 U.S. 341 (1952).

value of which was at best a contextual artifact of an earlier era, and could no longer be considered precedent.

The military establishment's leaders were angrier with the Court over its decision in *Reid II* than in *Toth.* Fredrick Wiener, who represented the two wives in the initial argument as well as in the re-argument, later explained that the military's leadership believed that civilians could become fifth columnists in peacetime with impunity.[12] Legal scholars have attempted to place *Reid II* within the context of other criminal law decisions. Lucas Powe posited that the decision rested as a hybrid between criminal law and national security, and to an extent this view makes sense. *Reid II* may certainly be seen as part of a process of developing greater rights to persons accused of crimes. On the other hand, Alexander Bickel argued that although the majority did primarily look at *Reid II* as a matter of jurisdiction, there was a secondary question regarding capital punishment. To Bickel, *Reid II* can be "explained as groping efforts toward the shaping and reduction of the ultimate question of capital punishment itself." The problem with Bickel's thesis is that the issue of capital punishment is absent from the conference and justices' correspondences. *Reid II* should primarily be viewed as a matter of lessening the judiciary's deference to assertions of the national security needs and to the military establishment.[13]

Trop v. Dulles

Of significant lasting importance to military law was the Court's analysis of Congressional intent to enable the Executive Branch to brand permanently certain courts-martial offenders. In 1958, Warren led the Court to further curtail Executive Branch authority over individual rights in a decision that not only established parameters as to the extent of the military's ability to determine the lifetime worth of an individual through their disciplinary system, but in doing so also redefined the importance of citizenship. When a civilian is convicted in federal court, the civilian is then encumbered by a record of a federal conviction along with whatever jail sentence may be adjudged. When a service-member is convicted, one of the possible punishments is a punitive discharge, which adds an additional lifetime stigma to the conviction record and imprisonment length, if any.

In 1864, at the height of the Civil War, Congress coupled the loss of citizenship with desertion. Known in some instances as denaturalization and in other cases as expatriation, the loss of citizenship in 1864 usually meant exclusion from the nation's political processes, though state laws were mixed

12 Frederick B. Wiener, "Advocacy at Military Law: The Lawyer's Reason and the Soldier's Faith," 80 *Military Law Review* (1978) 1–28; 10; and Wiener papers [UVA].

13 Lucas Powe, *The Warren Court and American Politics*, 109–13; Alexander Bickel, *The Least Dangerous Branch: The Supreme Court at the Bar of Politics*, 2nd ed. (New Haven: Yale University Press, 1986), 241.

in the degree of exclusion that might occur. The law governing the loss of citizenship resulting from a conviction for desertion and a dishonorable discharge remained in effect through both world wars. By the end of World War II, the loss of citizenship had the potential to create "stateless persons" who had to seek the approval of foreign governments for safe harbor or refugee status. In World War II, roughly 7,000 service members who were court-martialed for desertion were also sentenced to a dishonorable discharge and thereby forfeited their citizenship; thousands of other soldiers were likewise court-martialed for desertion but did not receive a punitive discharge and therefore retained their citizenship.[14]

One of the men who lost his citizenship through this process, Private Albert Trop, had been confined to a military stockade resulting from a court-martial in 1944, but escaped and deserted. The Army court-martialed Trop once more, and this time he was convicted and sentenced to three years at hard labor and a dishonorable discharge. Trop did not desert for political reasons; he had not spread subversive literature or provided information to an adversary. In 1952, while applying for a passport, he discovered that he had forfeited his citizenship. *Trop* was contentious, because the Eighth Amendment prohibition against cruel and unusual punishment seemed to conflict with the military's ability to have a fully disciplined force in wartime. To the Court's conservatives, this requirement of military reliability and discipline permitted the coupling of citizenship to desertion.[15]

In his majority opinion, Warren derided the government's argument that expatriation was not penal in nature, but rather ancillary to the offense. In this respect Warren showed a better historic understanding for the reasons underlying the Civil War era statute than Frankfurter. He then turned to the issue of whether expatriation violated the Eighth Amendment. To answer this question he believed it necessary to state why capital punishment was not cruel and unusual, but rendering a person stateless was. To do so, he turned to the practice of "civilized nations," and found that only Turkey and the Philippines imposed denationalization as a penalty. Forcible divestiture of citizenship, "destroys for the individual the political existence that was centuries in the development," he concluded.

To understand Trop as merely an Eighth Amendment case, however, is to miss the real significance of the case for military law. It is true that Trop's appeal was decided alongside other non-military appeals against the stripping of citizenship, but *Trop* can be distinguished for a number of reasons. The stripping of citizenship in Trop's case did not occur as a result of any his affirmative acts. Another distinguishing feature exists in the justices' conference discussions. In conference Warren made it clear that he intended to oppose the government's contention that the military had the authority to strip a citizen of his citizenship simply because of a wartime desertion. In early 1958, he forwarded a

14 Joshua Kastenberg, *Law in War, Law as War*, 317–20.

15 *Trop v. Dulles*, 356 U.S. 86 (1958).

memorandum to the justices deriding the expansion of military authority. "Three times in the past three years we have been confronted with an exercise of military power far in excess of its rightful sphere of operation," he began, citing *Toth*, *Reid*, and *Harmon* (a case in which the Court had found the Secretary of the Army had exceeded his statutory authority when including pre-service activities in a discharge characterization). "I for one believe that had the military prevailed in these cases, there would have ensued a fundamental change in the civilian-military relationship in this country." Warren concluded his memorandum by reminding the justices that the duty to guard against the encroachment of military jurisdiction had to do with the preservation of democracy. Though Warren included some of this language in his published opinion, the decision did not contain the warning about a change in civil-military relations. Though the opinion largely focused on the question of the appropriateness of expatriation as punishment, the real significance of the case is the motivation of the majority to prevent military overreach, in so doing upending a century of deference to the military.[16]

By the time Frankfurter retired on August 22, 1962, the Court had abandoned its prior deference to the military establishment and the needs of national security. Perhaps neither President John F. Kennedy nor President Lyndon Johnson appreciated this transition, because in other matters such as civil rights and government authorities, the justices had issued decisions that comported with their national and international goals. The military establishment's leaders also do not appear to have understood that in the first eight years of Warren's tenure a dramatic shift away from deference to the military had occurred and that as a result, civil-military relations had changed. To be sure, the United States still possessed a massive conventional force with service-members, dependents, and family members stationed across the world. And Congress had not openly opposed the presidential use of the military as an arm of foreign policy. Moreover, perhaps because Black and Douglas had sided with the Executive Branch in *Korematsu* and *Yamashita*, apparently little thought was given to whether the judiciary would remain removed from taking a critical role in influencing military policy. But just as the Court and the lower judiciary had actively pursued civil and individual rights in overturning segregation laws and expanded the rights of persons in criminal trials, the judges and justices would also become active in shaping military affairs during the ensuing decade as the nation sent hundreds of thousands of service members, well over half drafted, into a war in Southeast Asia.

16 Warren, Memorandum to the Conference, March 1958 [Brennan I: 11/f 1].

Bibliography

Manuscript Papers and Personal Collections

American Heritage Center

Guy, George F.
Holtzoff, Alexander

Harvard University

Frankfurter, Felix

Hoover Institution Archives, Stanford University

Crouch, Paul
Fellers, Bonner

Library of Congress

Baker, Newton Diehl
Biddle, Francis
Black, Hugo L.
Bowen, Catherine Drinker
Brant, Irving
Burton, Harold Hitz
Davies, Joseph Edward
Douglas, William O.
Fahy, Charles
Feis, Herbert
Frank, John P.
Frankfurter, Felix
Jackson, Robert H.
Knox, Philander
LaFollette, Robert M.
Leventhal, Harold
Libby, Frederick
Palmer, John McCauley
Patterson, Robert P.
Philbrick, Herbert

Prettyman, E. Barrett
Rutledge, Wiley B.
Stimson, Henry L.
Stone, Harlan Fiske
Truman, Harry S.
Walsh, Thomas

Northwestern University

Wigmore, John Henry

Princeton University, Seeley G. Mudd Library

Fraenkel, Osmond
Harlan II, John Marshall
Sobeloff, Simon

United States Army Military History Institute

Miles, Nelson A.

University of Kentucky

Reed, Stanley Forman
Vinson, Frederick

University of Michigan

Murphy, Frank

University of Texas

Clark, Tom C.

University of Virginia

Wiener, Frederick B.

Yale University Library

Stimson, Henry Lewis

Government Documents

Allied High Commission Documents, 15 Fed. Reg. 2086, Apr. 13, 1950.
Army Reorganization Hearings Before the House Committee on Military Affairs, Sixty-Fifth Congress, 3d Sess, on H.R. 14560 "To Reorganize and Increase the Efficiency of the Regular Army," DC: GPO, 1919.
Hearings Before a Subcommittee of the Committee on the Armed Forces, House of Representatives, 81st Congress, 1st Sess, "A Bill to Unify, Consolidate, Revise, and Codify the Articles of War and Establish a Uniform Code of Military Justice," Washington, DC: GPO, 1949.
How to Spot a Communist, Department of the Army, 1955.
Military Installations in North Africa and the Middle East. Remarks of Senator James M. Tunnell in the Senate of the United States, February 15, 1945, and remarks of Senator Harold H. Burton, February 19, 1945, relative to their investigation of military installations in North Africa and the Middle East, Washington, DC: Government Printing Office, 1945.
National Security Council Report 68, National Security Council, 1950.
Public Papers of the Presidents, January 1, 1952–January 20, 1953, Washington, DC: GPO, 1966.
Statement Concerning the Treatment of Conscientious Objectors in the Army, Washington, DC: War Department, 1919.
The Case of General Yamashita: Memorandum, Courtney Whitney, US Army, 1949.
Second Report of the Provost Marshal of the United States to the Secretary of War On the Operation of the Selective Service System to December 20, 1918, General Enoch Crowder, DC: GPO, 1919.

Books

Abraham, Henry Julian, *Justices, Presidents, and Senators: A History of the Supreme Court Appointments from Washington to Bush II*, Lanham, MD: Rowman and Littlefield, 2008.
Altschuler, Glenn C. and Blumin, Stuart M., *The GI Bill: A New Deal for Veterans*, New York: Oxford, 2009.
Alyea, Louis F., *Military Justice Under the 1948 Amended Articles of War*, New York: Oceana Press, 1949.
Ambrose, Stephen, *Nixon: The Education of a Politician, 1913–1962*, New York: Simon and Schuster, 1988.
Athey, Robert Leland, *Please Don't Cry for Me: The Ruth Farnsworth Murder Story*, Philadelphia: Xlibris, 2000.
Ball, Howard, "Loyalty, Treason, and the State, An Examination of Justice William O. Douglas's Style, Substance, and Anguish" in *He Shall Not Pass This Way Again: The Legacy of William O. Douglas*, Steven Wasby, ed., Pittsburgh: University of Pittsburgh Press, 1997.

Ball, Howard, *Hugo L. Black: Cold Steel Warrior*, New York: Oxford, 1996.
Ball, Howard, *Of Power and Right: Hugo Black, William O. Douglas and America's Constitutional Revolution*, New York: Oxford, 1992.
Beaver, Daniel R., *Newton D. Baker and the American War Effort, 1917–1919*, Lincoln: University of Nebraska Press, 1966.
Beckett, Ian F., *A Nation in Arms: A Social Study of the British Army in the First World War*, Manchester: Manchester University Press, 1985.
Belknap, Michal, *The Vinson Court: Justices, Rulings, and Legacy*, Santa Barbara, CA: ABC-CLIO, 2004
Bell, Christopher M., "The Invergordon Mutiny, 1931," in Christoper M. Bell and Bruce A. Elleman, ed., *Naval Mutinies of the Twentieth Century: An International Perspective*, London: Frank Cass, 2003.
Bellia, Patricia, "Story of the Steel Seizure Case," in *Presidential Power Stories*, Christopher H. Schroeder and Curtis A. Bradley, eds, New York: Foundation Press, 2009.
Bennett, Marion T., *The United States Court of Claims: A History*, Vol. II, Washington, DC: GPO, 1976.
Berry, Mary Francis, *Stability, Security, and Continuity: Mr. Justice Burton and Decision Making on the Supreme Court*, Westport, CT: Greenwood, 1978.
Bickel, Alexander, *The Least Dangerous Branch: The Supreme Court at the Bar of Politics*, 2nd ed., New Haven: Yale University Press, 1986.
Blumenson, Martin, *The Duel for France, 1944: The Men and Battles that Changed the Fate of Europe*, New York: DaCapo reprint, 2000.
Botsdorf, Denise, *Proclaiming the Truman Doctrine: The Cold War Call to Arms*, Arlington: Texas A&M University Press, 2008.
Bradley, Omar, *A General's Life*, New York: Simon and Schuster, 1983.
Brodie, Bernard, *War and Politics*, New York: MacMillan, 1973.
Brzezinski, Zbigniew, *Political Controls in the Soviet Army*, New York: Harvard Russian Research Center, 1954.
Burton, Harold Hitz, *600 Days Service: A History of the 361st Infantry Regiment of the United States Army*, Portland, OR: James Kearns & Abbot Co., 1921.
Capozolla, Christopher, *Uncle Same Wants You: World War I and the Making of the Modern American Citizen*, New York: Oxford, 2008.
Carter, Robert L., *A Matter of Law: A Memoir in the Struggle in the Cause of Civil Rights*, New York: New Press, 2005.
Caute, David, *The Fellow Travelers: Intellectual Friends of Communism*, New Haven: Yale, 1981.
Caute, David, *The Great Fear: Anti-Communist Purges*, New York: Simon and Schuster, 1978.
Chambers II, John Whiteclay, "Conscientious Objectors and the American State from Colonial Times to the Present," in Charles C. Moskos, ed., *The New Conscientious Objection: From Sacred to Secular Resistance*, New York: Oxford, 1993.

Chambers II, John Whiteclay, *The Tyranny of Change*, New Brunswick, NJ: Rutgers University Press, 1992.

Chambers II, John Whiteclay and Fred Anderson, *The Oxford Companion to American Military History*, New York: Oxford, 1999.

Chang, Iris, *The Rape of Nanking: The Forgotten Holocaust of World War II*, New York: Basic Books, 1997.

Coates, James and Michael Kilian, *Heavy Losses: The Dangerous Decline of American Defense*, New York: Viking Press, 1985

Collins, J. Lawton, *War in Peacetime: The History and Lessons of Korea*, New York: Houghton-Mifflin, 1969.

Cooper, Jerry, *The Rise of the National Guard: The Evolution of the American Militia*, Lincoln: University of Nebraska Press, 1997.

Cooper, Philip J., "William O. Douglas: the Conscience of the Court," in *The Burger Court: Judicial and Political Profiles*, Charles M. Lamb, ed., 2000.

Current, Richard N., *Secretary Stimson: A Study in Statecraft*, New York: Archon, 1970.

Dallek, Robert, *Franklin D. Roosevelt and American Foreign Policy, 1932–1945*, New York: Oxford, 1995.

Dickson, Del, ed., *The Supreme Court in Conference (1940–1985), The Private Discussions Behind Nearly 300 Supreme Court Decisions*, New York: Oxford, 2001.

DiPaolo, Amanda, *Zones of Twilight: Wartime Presidential Powers and Federal Court Decision Making*, Lanham, MD: Lexington, 2010

Donovan, Robert J., *Tumultuous Years: The Presidency of Harry S. Truman, 1949–1953*, Columbia, MO: University of Missouri Press, 1996.

Douglas, William O., *An Almanac of Liberty*, New York: Doubleday, 1954.

Douglas, William O., *Being an American*, New York: John Day, 1948.

Douglas, William O., *Strange Lands and Friendly People*, New York: Harper, 1951.

Douglas, William O., *The Court Years: The Autobiography of William O. Douglas*, New York: Random House, 1980.

Douglas, William O., *The French are Facing Disaster in Morocco Again*, New York: Cowles, 1954.

Dulles, John Foster, *War or Peace*, New York: MacMillan, 1950.

Dunne, Gerald T., *Hugo Black and the Judicial Revolution*, New York: Simon & Schuster, 1977.

Duram, James C., *Justice William O. Douglas*, Boston, MA: Twayne, 1981.

Eiler, Keith E., *Mobilizing America: Robert P. Patterson and the War Effort, 1940–1945*, New York: Cornell, 1997.

Engerman, David C., "Ideology and the Origins of the Cold War, 1917–1962," in *The Cambridge History of the Cold War*, Vol. I, Melvyn P. Leffler and Odd Arne Westad, eds, Cambridge: Cambridge University Press 2010.

Fasset, John D., *New Deal Justice: The Life of Stanley Reed of Kentucky*, New York: Vantage, 1980.

Feis, Herbert, *From Trust to Terror: The Onset of the Cold War, 1945–1950*, New York: W.W. Norton, 1970.

Feis, Herbert, *The Road to Pearl Harbor: The Coming of the War Between the United States and Japan*, New Jersey: Princeton, 1950.

Feldman, Noah, *Scorpions: The Battles and Triumphs of FDR's Great Supreme Court Justices*, New York: Twelve, 2010.

Ferrell, Robert, *Harry S. Truman: A Life*, Columbia, MO: University of Missouri Press, 1994

Ferren, John M. *Salt of the Earth, Conscience of the Court: The Story of Justice Wiley Rutledge*, Chapel Hill: University of North Carolina Press, 2004.

Fine, Sidney A., *Frank Murphy in World War One*, Ann Arbor: Michigan Historical Collections, 1969.

Fine, Sidney A., *Frank Murphy, The Washington Years*, Ann Arbor: University of Michigan, 1984.

Fisher, Louis, *In the Name of National Security: Unchecked Presidential Power and the* Reynolds *Case*, Lawrence, KS: Kansas University, 2006.

Fisher, Louis, *Nazi Saboteurs on Trial*, Lawrence, KS: Kansas University Press, 2003.

Flynn, George O., *Louis B. Hershey, Mr. Selective Service*, Chapel Hill: University of North Carolina Press, 1985.

Fosdick, Raymond Blaine, and Smith, Reginald Heber, *Criminal Justice in Cleveland*, Cleveland: The Cleveland Foundation, 1922.

Freedman, Max, *Roosevelt and Franklin: Their Correspondence, 1928–1945*, Boston: Little Brown & Co., 1967.

Fuller, J.F.C., *The Second World War: A Strategical and Tactical History*, New York: DaCapo Reprint, 1992.

Gaddis, John Lewis, *We Now Know: Rethinking Cold War History*, New York: Oxford, 1997.

Garraty, John A. and Mark C. Carnes, eds, *American National Biography*, New York: Oxford University Press, 1999.

Gettleman, Marvin, *The Dorr Rebellion, A Study in American Radicalism: 1833–1849*, New York: Random House, 1973.

Glueck, Sheldon, *Roscoe Pound and Criminal Justice*, New York: Oceana Press for the National Council on Crime and Delinquency, 1965.

Gordon, Joel, *Nasser's Blessed Movement: Egypt's Free Officers and the July Revolution*, New York: Oxford University Press, 1992.

Green, Thomas H., *Martial Law in Hawaii, December 7, 1941—April 4, 1943*, Washington, DC: Judge Advocate General's Department, 1947.

Griffith, Robert, *The Politics of Fear: Joseph R. McCarthy and the Senate*, Amherst: University of Massachusetts, 1987.

Gronlund, Mimi Park, *Tom C. Clark: A Life of Service*, Austin, TX: University of Texas, 2010.

Gugin, Linda C. and James E. St. Clair, *Sherman Minton: New Deal Senator, Cold War Justice*, Indianapolis: Indiana Historical Society, 1997.

Hall, Kermit L., *The Oxford Guide to Supreme Court Decisions*, New York: Oxford, 2001.
Hall, Timothy, *Supreme Court Justices: A Biographical Directory*, New York: Facts on File, 2001.
Haynes, John E., and Harvey Klehr, *Early Cold War Spies*, New York: Cambridge, 2006.
Herspring, Dale R., *The Pentagon and the Presidency: Civil-Military Relations from FDR to George Bush*, Lawrence, KS: Kansas University Press, 2005.
Hickey, Donald R., *The War of 1812: A Forgotten Conflict*, Urbana: University of Illinois, 1995.
Hodgson, Godfrey, *The Colonel: The Life and Wars of Henry Stimson, 1867–1950*, New York: Knopf, 1990.
Hoffman, George, *Cold War Casualty: The Court Martial of Major General Robert W. Grow*, Kent, OH: Kent State, 1993.
Hogan, Michael J., *A Cross of Iron: Harry S. Truman and the Origins of the Modern Security State, 1945–1950*, London: Cambridge University Press, 1998.
Hoyt, Edwin, *Three Military Leaders: Heihachiro, Isoroku Yamamoto, Tomoyuki Yamashita*, Tokyo: Kadansha International, 1993.
Inbau, Fred E., *Lie Detection and Criminal Interrogation*, Baltimore: Williams and Wilkins, 1942
Irons, Peter, *New Deal Lawyers*, New Jersey: Princeton University Press, 1982
Jackson, Robert H., *Constitutional Government: Crisis Government in the Modern Democracies*, Princeton, NJ: Princeton University Press, 1948
Jose, Ricardo Trota, *The Philippine Army, 1935–1942*, Manila: Ateneo De Manila University Press, 1992.
Kalman, Lara, *The Strange Career of Legal Realism*, New Haven: Yale, 1996.
Kastenberg, Joshua, *Law in War, War as Law: Brigadier General Joseph Holt and the Judge Advocate General's Department in the Civil War and Early Reconstruction, 1861–1865*, Durham, NC: Carolina Academic Press, 2011.
Kennan, George Frost and John Lukacks, *George F. Kennan and the Origins of Containment*, Columbia, MO: University of Missouri Press, 1996.
Kinnard, Douglas, *The Secretary of Defense*, Lexington: University of Kentucky Press, 1980
Knell, Herman, *To Destroy a City: Strategic Bombing and its Consequences in World War II*, New York: Da Capo, 2003.
Knock, Thomas J., *To End All Wars*, Princeton, NJ: Princeton University Press, 1992.
Lael, Richard, *The Yamashita Precedent: War Crimes and Command Responsibility*, Wilmington, DE: Scholarly Resources, 1982.
Lash, Joseph P., From the Diaries of Felix Frankfurter, New York: Norton, 1974.
Lee, Richard T. and Richard F. Starr, *Soviet Military Policy Since World War II*, San Francisco: Stanford University Press, 1983.

Leffler, Melvin, *A Preponderance of Power: National Security, the Truman Administration, and the Cold War*, Stanford, CA: Stanford University Press, 1992

Leuchtenberg, William E., *A Troubled Feast: American Society Since 1945*, Boston: Little Brown and Co., 1983.

Leuchtenburg, William E., Foreword in Robert H. Jackson, *That Man: An Insider's Portrait of Franklin D. Roosevelt*, New York: Oxford University Press, 2004.

Leutchenberg, William E., *The FDR Years: On Roosevelt and His Legacy*, New York: Columbia University Press, 1995.

Lockmiller, David, *Enoch Crowder: Soldier, Lawyer, and Statesman*, Columbia, MO: University of Missouri Press, 1955.

Lurie, Jonathan, *Arming Military Justice: The Origins of the Court of Military Appeals, 1775–1950*, Vol. I, Princeton, NJ: Princeton University, 1992.

MacArthur, Douglas, *Reminiscences*, New York: McGraw, 1964.

MacDonnell, Francis, *Insidious Foes: The Axis Fifth Column and the American Home Front*, New York: Oxford University Press, 1995.

Maga, Timothy P., *Judgment at Tokyo: The Japanese War Crimes Trials*, Lexington, KY: University of Kentucky, 2001.

Mahon, John K., *The War of 1812*, New York: Da Capo Reprint 1972.

Mallory, Sean L., *Henry L. Stimson and the Decision to Use the Bomb Against Japan*, New York: Cornell University, 2008.

Manchester, William, *American Caesar: Douglas MacArthur, 1880–1964*, New York: Little Brown and Co., 1978.

Marcus, Maevas, *Truman and the Steel Seizure Case: The Limits of Presidential Power*, Durham, NC: Duke University Press, 1994.

Marie de la Gorce, Paul, *The French Army; a Military-Political History*, Kenneth Douglas, trans., New York: G. Braziller, 1963.

Marshall, Thomas R., *Recollections of Thomas Marshall: Vice President and Hoosier Philosopher*, Indianapolis: Bobbs-Merrill, 1925.

Mason, Alpheus Thomas, *Harlan F. Stone: Pillar of the Law*, New York: Viking, 1953.

McFarland, Keith D., and Roll, David, *Louis Johnson and the Arming of America: The Roosevelt and Truman Years*, Bloomington: Indiana University Press, 2005.

McGinty, Brian, *Lincoln and the Court*, Cambridge, MA: Harvard University Press, 2008.

Melnik, R. Shep, "The Courts, Jurisprudence, and the Executive Branch," in Joel Aberbach and Mark A. Peterson, eds, *The Executive Branch*, New York: Oxford, 2005

Millis, Walter, ed., *James Forrestal Diaries*, London: Cassel and Co., 1952.

Morgan, Ted, *Reds: McCarthyism in Twentieth Century America*, New York: Random House, 2003.

Moskos, Charles, and Chambers, John W., *The New Conscientious Objection: From Sacred to Secular Resistance*, New York: Oxford University Press, 1993.

Murphy, Bruce, *Wild Bill: The Legend and Life of William O. Douglas*, New York: Random House, 2003.
Newman, Roger K., *Hugo Black: A Biography*, New York: Fordham, 1994.
Newman, Roger K., ed., *The Yale Biographical Dictionary of American Law*, New Haven: Yale, 2009.
Nitze, Paul H., *From Hiroshima to Glasnost: At the Center of Decision*, New York: Grove Weidenfeld, 1989.
O'Donnell, Pierce, *In Time of War: Hitler's Terrorist Attack on America*, New York: The New Press, 2009.
Oshinsky, David M., *A Conspiracy So Immense: The World of Joe McCarthy*, London: Oxford, 2005.
Palmer, Jan, *The Vinson Court Era*, New York: AMS Press, 1990.
Piccigallo, Phillip, *The Japanese on Trial: Allied War Crimes in the East, 1945–1951*, Austin: University of Texas Press, 1979.
Plischke, Elmer, *History of the Allied High Commission for Germany: Its Establishment, Structure and Procedures*, Bonn: Historical Division, Office of the Executive Secretary, Office of the U.S. High Commissioner for Germany, 1951.
Powe, Jr., Lucas, *The Warren Court and American Politics*, Cambridge, MA: Belknap, Harvard University Press, 2002.
Powell, William S., *Dictionary of North Carolina Biography, Vol. V*, Chapel Hill: University of North Carolina Press, 1994.
Radcliff, William Franklin, *Sherman Minton, Indiana's Supreme Court Justice*, Indianapolis: Guild Press, 1996.
Reel, A. Frank, *The Case of General Yamashita*, Chicago: University of Chicago Press, 1949.
Rehnquist, William H., *All Laws But One*, New York: Knopf, 1998.
Rehnquist, William H., *The Supreme Court: How It Was, How it Is*, New York: William Morrow and Co., 1987.
Renstrom, Peter, *The Stone Court: Justices Rulings, and Legacy*, Santa Barbara, CA: ABC-CLIO, 2011.
Richardson, Susan R., "Reds, Race, and Research: Homer P. Rainey and the Grand Texas Tradition of Political Interference," in, Roger L. Geiger, *Perspectives on the History of Higher Education*, New Brunswick, NJ: Transaction Publishers, 2005.
Roalfe, William R., *John Henry Wigmore: Scholar and Reformer*, Evanston, IL: Northwestern University Press, 1977.
Rosen, Jeffrey, *The Supreme Court: The Personalities and Rivalries that Defined America*, New York: MacMillan, 2007.
Rossiter, Clinton, *The Supreme Court and the Commander in Chief*, Ithaca, NY: Cornell University, 1951.
Sabin, Arthur, *In Calmer Times: The Supreme Court and Red Monday*, Philadelphia: University of Pennsylvania, 1999.

Savage, Sean J., *Roosevelt: The Party Leader, 1932–1945*, Lexington, KY: University of Kentucky Press, 1991.
Schlegel, John Henry, *American Legal Realism and Empirical Social Science*, Chapel Hill: University of North Carolina Press, 1995.
Schlesinger, Arthur M., *The Coming of the New Deal, Vol. II, 1933–1935*, New York: First Mariner, 1958.
Schlesinger, Arthur, *Robert Kennedy and His Times*, New York: Houghton Mifflin, 1978.
Schmidt, Regin, *Red Scare: FBI and the Origins of Anticommunism in the United States, 1919–1943*, Copenhagen: Museum Tusculanum Press, 2000.
Schwartz, Bernard, *A History of the Supreme Court*, New York: Oxford University Press, 1993.
Schwartz, Bernard, *Super Chief, Earl Warren and His Supreme Court*, New York: Oxford, 1983.
Schwartz, Bernard, *The Ascent of Pragmatism*, Boston: Addison Wesley, 1989.
Shanks, Hershel, *The Art and Craft of Judging: The Decisions of Judge Learned Hand*, New York: MacMillan, 1968.
Sharlitt, Joseph, *Fatal Error: The Miscarriage of Justice that Sealed the Rosenbergs' Fate*, New York: Scribner, 1989
Sherry, Michael S., *Preparing for the Next War: American Plans for Post-War Defense*, 1941–1945, New Haven: Yale, 1977.
Simon, James F., *Independent Journey: The Life of William O. Douglas*, New York: Harper & Row, 1980.
Simon, James F., *The Antagonists: Hugo Black, Felix Frankfurter and Civil Liberties in Modern America*, New York: Simon and Schuster, 1990.
Simpson, Keith, "Lieutenant General Arthur Percival," in John Keegan ed., *Churchill's Generals*, New York: Quill, 1991.
Smith, Robert Ross, *Triumph in the Philippines*, Washington, DC: Office of the Chief of Military History, Department of the Army, 1963.
Sparrow, John, *History of Demobilization in the United States Army*, Washington, DC: GPO, 1952.
Spector, Ronald, *Eagle Against the Sun: The American War With Japan*, New York: Vintage Press, 1985, 167–78
St. Clair, James and Linda Gugin, *Chief Justice Vinson of Kentucky: A Political Biography*, Lexington: University Press of Kentucky, 2002.
Stamps, T. Dodson, ed., *A Military History of World War II, Vol. II: Operations in the Mediterranean and Pacific Theatres*, New York: United States Military Academy, 1953.
Stone, Geoffrey, *Perilous Times: Free Speech in Wartime*, New York: W.W. Norton, 2005.
Story, Joseph, *Commentaries on the Constitution of the United States, Vol. II*, ed. Thomas Cooley, Boston: Little Brown & Co, 1873.
Taylor, Maxwell D., *Swords and Plowshares: A Memoir*, New York: Norton, 1972.

Totani, Yumi, *The Tokyo War Crimes Trials: The Pursuit of Justice in the Wake of World War II*, Cambridge, MA: Harvard University Press, 2008.
Traynor, Roger J., *The Riddle of Harmless Error*, Columbus, OH: Ohio State University Press, 1970).
Tushnet, Mark, *Making Civil Rights Law: Thurgood Marshall and the Supreme Court*, New York: Oxford University Press, 1997.
Urofsky, Melvin I., "The Roosevelt Court," in William Henry Chafe, *The Achievement of American Liberalism: The New Deal and Its Legacies*, New York: Columbia University Press, 2003.
Urofsky, Melvin, *A March of Liberty: A Constitutional History of the United States, Vol. II, 1877–Present*, Oxford: Oxford University Press, 2002.
Urofsky, Melvin, *Division and Discord: The Supreme Court Under Stone and Vinson*, Columbia, SC: University of South Carolina, 1997.
Urofsky, Melvin, ed., *The Supreme Court Justices: A Biographical Directory*, New York: Routledge, 1994.
Urofsky, Melvin, *The Warren Court: Justices, Rulings, and Legacy*, Santa Barbara, CA: ABC-CLIO, 2001.
Urofsky, Melvin and Paul Finkleman, *A March of Liberty: A Constitutional History of the United States*, New York: Oxford University Press.
Vile, John R., *Great American Lawyers*, Santa Barbara, CA: ABC-CLIO, 2001.
Wainstock, Dennis D., *Truman, MacArthur, and the Korean War*, Denver, CO: Greenwood, 1999.
Walker, Samuel, *Popular Justice: A History of American Criminal Justice*, 2d ed., rev., New York: Oxford University Press, 1997,
Watt, Richard M., *Dare Call it Treason*, New York: Simon & Schuster, 1963.
Wawro, Geoffrey, *The Franco-Prussian War: The German Conquest of France, 1870–1871*, New York: Cambridge, 2003.
Weigley, Russell F., *The American Way of War: A History of United States Military Strategy and Policy*, Bloomington, IN: Indiana University Press, 1973
Weigley, Russell, *History of the United States Army*, New York: MacMillan, 1967.
Weingartner, James J., *A Peculiar Crusade, Willis M. Everett and the Malmedy Massacre*, New York: New York University Press, 2000.
Wiecek, William, *The Birth of the Modern Constitution: The United States Supreme Court, 1941–1953*, New York: Cambridge, 2006.
Wooster, Robert A., *Nelson A Miles and the Twilight of the Frontier Army*, Lincoln NE: University of Nebraska Press, 1992.
Yalof, David Alistair, *Pursuit of Justices: Presidential Politics and the Selection of Supreme Court Nominees*, Chicago: University of Chicago Press, 1999.

Articles

"Army and Navy: The Major and God," *Time Magazine*, November 13, 1944.
"Communist Trial Ends With 11 Guilty," *Life Magazine*, October 24, 1949.

Alsop, Joseph, "The Powerful Imaginer," *Washington Post*, April 19, 1954.
Anon., "Remembering the Fourth Circuit Judges: A History from 1941 to 1998," 55 *Washington and Lee Law Review* (1998), 471.
Anon., *The Judge Advocate General Journal*, Vol. II, No 1 (1945).
Anthony, J. Garner, "Hawaiian Martial Law in the Supreme Court," 57 *Yale Law Journal* (1947), 27.
Borch, Frederic L., "The Malmedy Massacre Trial, the Military Court Proceedings and the Controversial Legal Aftermath," *Army Lawyer*, January 2011
Cohen, William, "Justice Douglas and the Rosenberg Case: Setting the Record Straight," 70 *Cornell Law Review* (1985), 211.
Douglas, William O., "Indo-China Near Disaster," *Look Magazine*, December 16, 1952.
Douglas, William O., "The Choice in Korea: Recognize or Crush Red China," *Look Magazine*, December 30, 1962.
Fairman, Charles, "The Supreme Court on Military Jurisdiction: Martial Rule in Hawaii and the Yamashita Case," 59 *Harvard Law Review* (1946), 833.
Gershman, Bennet L., "Hard Strikes and Foul Blows: Berger v. United States 75 Years After," 42 *Loyola University of Chicago Law Journal* (2010), 177.
Glazier, David G., "The Laws of War: Past, Present, and Future: Article: Precedents Lost: The Neglected History of the Military Commission," 46 *Virginia Journal of International Law* (2005), 5.
Holtzoff, Alexander, "Administration of Justice in the United States Military," *New York University Law Quarterly*, January 1947.
Hutchison, "The Black-Jackson Feud," 1988 *Supreme Court Review* (1988), 203.
Kastenberg, Joshua E., "A Sesquicentennial Historic Analysis of Dynes v. Hoover and the Supreme Court's Bow to Military Necessity: From its Relationship to *Dred Scott v. Sandford* to its Contemporary Influence," 39 *University of Memphis Law Review* (2009), 595.
Kessler, Jeremy K., "The Administrative Origins of Modern Civil Liberties Law," 114 *Columbia Law Review* (2014), 1083
Lee, R. Alton, "The Army Mutiny of 1946," *The Journal of American History*, Vol. 53, No. 3 (Dec., 1966)
Lichtman, Steven B., "The Justices and the Generals: A Critical Examination of the U.S. Supreme Court's Tradition of Deference to the Military, 1918–2004," 65 *Maryland Law Review* (2006), 907.
Lusky, Louis, "Footnote Redux: A Carolene Product Reminiscence," 82 *Columbia Law Review* (1982), 1093.
Nobleman, Eli E., *Military Government Courts: Law and Justice in the American Zone of Germany*, 33 *American Bar Association Journal* (1947), 777.
Pearlstein, Deborah N., "Law at the End of War," 99 *Minnesota Law Review* (2014), 143.
Reel, A. Frank, "Playing Pontius Pilate: War Crimes Procedure Hypocritical," *Montreal Star*, April 1, 1971.

Rives, Jack L. and Bradley P. Grant, "Explaining the UCMJ," *The Reporter*, (2000) 16.

Savage, David G., *U.S. Official Cites Misconduct in Japanese American Internment Cases*, Los Angeles Times, May 24, 2011.

Schlobohm, Otto, "The Constitutionality of the Selective Draft Law," 6 *Georgetown Law Journal* (1917), 11.

Streit, Clarence K., "Owen Roberts and the Atlantic Union," 104 *University of Pennsylvania Law Review* (1955), 354.

Viereck, George S., "LaFollette Favors Repeal of Draft Law," *Viereck's American Weekly*, Vol. VII, No. 1, August 8, 1918, pp. 11.

Warren, Earl, "The Bill of Rights and the Military," 37 *New York University Law Review* (1962), 181

Whelan, Joan"Guy Sees Little Comparison in Yamashita, Calley Cases," *Casper Star Tribune*, June 3, 1971.

Wiener, Frederick B., "American Military Law in the Light of the First Mutiny Act's Tricentennial," 126 *Military Law Review* (1989), 1.

Wiener, Frederick B., "Advocacy at Military Law: The Lawyer's Reason and the Soldier's Faith," 80 *Military Law Review* (1978), 1.

Wiener, Frederick, "Courts Martial and the Bill of Rights: The Original Practice," 72 *Harvard Law Review* (1958), 266.

Willis, John T., "The United States Court of Military Appeals: Its Origin, Operation, and Future," 55 *Military Law Review* (1972), 39.

Case Index/Table of Cases

Index

For Product Safety Concerns and Information please contact our EU representative GPSR@taylorandfrancis.com
Taylor & Francis Verlag GmbH, Kaufingerstraße 24, 80331 München, Germany

www.ingramcontent.com/pod-product-compliance
Ingram Content Group UK Ltd.
Pitfield, Milton Keynes, MK11 3LW, UK
UKHW010957180926
475701UK00004B/416
* 9 7 8 1 0 3 2 0 9 8 0 1 2 *